Archibald Hamilton Bryce

First Greek Reader

For the Use of Schools

Archibald Hamilton Bryce

First Greek Reader
For the Use of Schools

ISBN/EAN: 9783743484054

Manufactured in Europe, USA, Canada, Australia, Japa

Cover: Foto ©Paul-Georg Meister /pixelio.de

Manufactured and distributed by brebook publishing software (www.brebook.com)

Archibald Hamilton Bryce

First Greek Reader

FIRST GREEK READER:

For the Use of Schools.

BY

ARCHD. H. BRYCE, LL.D., D.C.L., F.R.S.E.,

RECTOR OF THE EDINBURGH COLLEGIATE SCHOOL.

LONDON:
T. NELSON AND SONS, PATERNOSTER ROW;
EDINBURGH; AND NEW YORK.

1892

Preface.

THIS volume is at once a Grammar, a Reader, an Exercise-Book, and a Vocabulary. Its aim is twofold:—*First*, To give a complete view of the Inflexions of Nouns and Verbs, with a careful regard to simplicity and clearness; and, *Secondly*, To supply a series of interesting and easy lessons in continuous reading.

In the grammatical part of the work care has been taken not to overload the text with minutiæ and exceptions, which serve only to confuse and bewilder the beginner; but to afford merely the amount of information considered necessary in a First Course. The Nouns and Verbs are so arranged, that each class of Inflexions is kept separate and distinct; and numerous Exercises follow each paradigm, in order that the characteristics of one group may be fixed in the mind of the pupil before his attention is invited to another. The Nouns of the Third Declension have been classified on a plan which, it is hoped, will lead to a due appreciation of the peculiarities belonging to that multiform division. (See, especially, Appendix, p. 160.)

The Verb has been set forth in one tabular view, and has been introduced as little as possible in the earlier Exercises, from the conviction that the method of teaching it piecemeal, and in a desultory manner, without any regard to similarity of stem or of meaning, is certain to result in confusion to the pupil and disappointment to the master.

Adjectives should always be taught simultaneously with Substantives, and each gender-form by itself, as suggested in the text (Section II. 6, and III. 3); but to afford facilities for comparing form with form, and to gratify those Teachers who may prefer the old mode, paradigms have been printed in full declension at p. 43, *sqq*. In the section on the Comparison of Adjectives, a new arrangement has been proposed, which aims at giving simplicity as well as symmetry to a chapter of Greek grammar hitherto unnecessarily complicated, and devoid of unity of principle.

The Rules of Contraction will be found brief, simple, and comprehensive.* They have been borrowed, with the kind permission of the author, from

---

* It must be borne in mind, that in regard to the Rules of Contraction, of Euphony, of Accent, &c., as laid down in this first course of Greek lessons, all the minutiæ and exceptions are not given; the less common peculiarities belong to a second course, or to a systematic and complete Grammar. The principles set forth will, it is believed, be found to cover everything required in the use of this volume.

a forthcoming Greek Grammar by the Rev. Dr. Bryce of Belfast.

The Exercises of Part I. are intended mainly as a praxis on the Inflexions, and to this end the strict logical arrangement of the Syntax has been entirely subordinated.* The Rules of Construction have therefore been introduced in such order, and to such an extent, as has been deemed most consistent with the general plan, and most conducive to rapid progress.† The sentences, which by easy steps increase in difficulty, have been selected, as far as possible, from classical authors; but the choice of words and of appropriate phrases has been very much restricted by peculiar features in the design of the work. The names of familiar objects, and words of frequent occurrence in general reading, claim a primary place in the Vocabulary of elementary works dealing with a foreign language; and such have therefore been chosen in preference to more rare and more dignified terms. They have been largely taken from the Reading Lessons of Part II., in order that the principle of frequent repetition may have as much play as possible; and that, when students arrive at the more difficult task of unravelling complex sentences, the often recurring faces of old friends may, by diminishing their difficulties, encourage them onward

---

* A companion volume to the present is in preparation, which will assume the form of an Exercise-Book, and in which the Syntax will be the primary object of attention.
† A brief *resumé* of the Syntax of Simple Sentences will be found in the Appendix.

in their labours. Sentences of an abstruse or philosophical kind, such as too often form the staple of Introductory Readers, have been avoided, as tending rather to repel than to invite the young. The English portions of the Exercises are meant merely as examples for imitative practice, and are not intended to supersede the use of a methodically arranged Manual of Greek Composition. Vocabularies have not, for very obvious reasons, been attached to the Exercises, but have been supplied at a different part of the book, p. 164.

It is of the utmost consequence that, in studying a foreign language, pupils should daily, and from the very first, make practical use of the principles and facts which they learn from the Grammar. For such praxis short and easy clauses are, in the earlier stages, indispensable, but it is possible to continue their use to an unnecessary extent, inasmuch as the power of a boy to grapple with the difficulties of complex sentences is by no means in proportion to the time spent in analysing simple sentences. It has therefore been deemed prudent to introduce promiscuous reading lessons as soon as the learner has fairly got over the Parts of Speech and their companion Exercises. And thus the Extracts forming Part II. have been chosen with this view, that, while the pupil's ingenuity is exercised in the discrimination of mixed grammatical forms and the analysis of compound sentences, his mind may at the same time be interested in the subject-matter of his task, and his ambition not disheartened by any great syntactical difficulties. In some of the specimens, a little irregularity of construction is occasionally observable; but this is of less consequence than at a more advanced stage in a youth's progress. Poetry, and detached pieces of dry historical detail, have, for very evident reasons, been excluded. To Part II. a few brief Notes have been added.

The Greek Vocabulary has been constructed on the principle of giving the primary signification of each word, even though the word be not found in that sense in the Extracts; and of tracing the derived meanings so far as is necessary to illustrate the different instances in which it will be met with. Limited space, however, has greatly restricted the carrying out of this idea to an adequate length; which is the more to be regretted, since the value of the process as a mental exercise can scarcely be over-estimated.

The principal laws of Euphony and of Accentuation have been given in an Appendix rather than in their proper place, that the period and the mode of their introduction may the more distinctly be left to the Teacher's discretion. Those gentlemen, however, who have charge of large classes, will find it much more satisfactory to content themselves, in the first place, with thorough drill in the Inflexions; and, when these are once mastered, the doctrine of the Accent and the principles of Euphony will be acquired with comparative ease, and with infinitely less of confusion in the mind of the young. If the ear be accustomed from the beginning to the proper accent, the subsequent learning of the rules will be a very easy task indeed.

HIGH SCHOOL OF EDINBURGH,
June, 1862.

NOTE.

IN the first two editions of this work a slight deviation was made, in the arrangement of the Cases of Nouns, from the order usually followed. The change was determined on after mature deliberation, and after a highly satisfactory trial with a large class; but at the urgent request of many Teachers the Editor has been induced to revert in the present issue to the old established order. Those, however, who prefer the new arrangement will find the Nouns so printed at p. 223. This is not the place to enter into the more subtile arguments, logical and philological, which may be advanced in favour of the alteration; for a few of these the student of maturer years is referred to the preface of Professor Madvig's Latin Grammar, Wood's translation, second edition. The considerations which will weigh most with Teachers in adopting the change are those of convenience and mnemonic utility. It may therefore be laid down, generally, that the more the forms of Cases are reduced in number, or the more that like Cases are grouped together, even though not reduced in number, the simpler does the system of Declension become to the learner. Thus the forms of Neuter Nouns are acquired with much less difficulty, and retained with much more ease, than those of Masculines and Feminines, from the fact that they have really only three Cases,—μῆλ·ον, μήλου, μήλῳ: for it must be remembered that "a Case is not the word used in a certain construction, but the word used in a *certain form by virtue of the construction;*" and that, consequently, "there are no more Cases in a language than there are distinct forms of Cases." Again, in the Dual, in all Declensions, the advantage of this arrangement is so obvious that it has long since been adopted by common consent. But if we follow this grouping principle farther, we shall also find it of great service in the Declension of Masculines and Feminines. Thus, in the First Declension, it is an invariable rule that *the Vocative and Accusative follow the Nominative both in vowel and in quantity ;**—*i.e.*, η and ης in the Nom. have η in the Voc. and ην in the Accus. ; ᾱ has ᾱ and ᾱν ; ᾰ and ας have ᾰ and ᾰν ; and, accordingly, in such Nouns as γλῶττα and δόξα we shall find, by the new arrangement, all the Cases with α (δόξα, δόξα, δόξαν) by themselves, and those with η (δόξης, δόξῃ) by themselves. In Nouns of the Third Declension, like μάντις and πῆχυς, in which the last vowel of the stem is changed in the Nom., the three Cases (Nom., Voc., and Accus.) which take ι and υ respectively, are brought together, and those (Gen. and Dat.) which retain the last vowel of the stem are in like manner brought together ; as, μάντι-ς, μάντι, μάντι-ν; μάντε-ως, μάντε-ϊ: πῆχυ-ς, πῆχυ, πῆχυ-ν ; πήχε-ως, πήχε-ϊ. The large class of Adjectives in -υς (as γλυκύς) may be here noticed as adding strength to this argument, and the two Irregular Adjectives, πολύς and μέγας ; in which, so arranged, all the irregularities are set side by side, and are thus more easily remembered. And here it will be remarked, that in the Nouns just referred to, the beginner has only one change of vowel to recollect, since the stem (μαντε-, γλυκε-, πολλ-, μεγαλ-, &c.) which appears in the Gen. and Dat. continues throughout the Dual and Plural ; whereas his difficulties are much increased if he is required to chop and change from one to the other. Syncopated Nouns, as μήτηρ, ἀνήρ, κύων, and also words like βοῦς, γραῦς, and βασιλεύς, supply similar arguments, which will be readily appreciated.

Again, when the Teacher proceeds to inculcate the principles and rules of Accentuation, he will find that, by this arrangement of Cases, he will save much labour both to himself and his pupils. Thus, in words accented like αὐλή and σκιά, the *acuted* Cases (Nom., Voc., and Accus.) come together, and the circumflexed (Gen. and Dat.) together ; and in those like γλῶττα, δοῦλος, μῆλον, and ἄνθρωπος, the Cases similarly accented come together, (with, of course, the slight exception in the plural.) So in the large classes of Nouns represented by μήτηρ and θήρ (*i.e.*, syncopated Nouns and those with dissyllabic Genitives and Datives), the Cases (Nom., Voc., and Accus. of all Numbers) which retain the accent on the radical syllable follow each other ; and those, on the contrary, which agree in throwing forward the accent on the inflexion (*i.e.*, the Genitives and Datives of all Numbers) follow each other in immediate sequence.

---

* Except, of course, those three classes of Nouns in ης, Section II. 5, which have the Vocative in ᾰ.

Many other arguments, deduced from special cases, might be brought forward, but it is unnecessary. The observant student will note such for himself, and the Latin language will supply him with many similar reasons.

One practical objection may be urged against the proposed change, namely, that as Lexicons and Dictionaries give the Genitive Case, confusion will be caused to boys between it and the Accusative. But it will be at once acknowledged that this objection has force only in the case of those who have not thoroughly mastered the Inflexions,—and of such there should be none.

Suggestions to Teachers Using this Book.

1. The Masculine Nouns of the First Declension should not be learned till the inflexions of the Second Declension are well known.

2. The Attic Second Declension will be better omitted until the common forms of all the declensions are thoroughly mastered.

3. Let Adjectives be learned simultaneously with Substantives, and each gender-form by itself, the pupil being always required to name the substantive-paradigm whose inflexions are found in the adjective. If the three genders are learned all together, the pupil is confused in the multiplicity of forms, and the declension of an adjective becomes to him little more than the repetition of a rhyme, which must all be gone over before the required part is produced. The practice of declining an adjective along with a noun is very useful.

4. Since the Exercises on the Verbs are purposely less full than those on the other parts of speech, it will be advisable that, so soon as the Nouns of the Third Declension are learned, a small portion of the verb λύω be prescribed daily, till the whole Active Voice is familiar to the student. The Verb is the great puzzle to boys, and it is therefore of the utmost consequence that it be learned very gradually, and impressed very surely. The Teacher will find the best results follow, if, in declining verbs, the pupils are made to append an accusative or other appropriate case to each form; as, λύω τὸν ἵππον, *I unyoke the horse;* λύεις τὸν ἵππον: πιστεύω τῷ ἡγεμόνι, *I trust to the guide;* πιστεύομεν τῷ ἡγεμόνι, *we trust to the guide,* &c.

5. The List of Words belonging to each Exercise (see Appendix, p. 164, *seq.*) should be thoroughly learned and frequently repeated; and when the class has reached the connected readings of Part II. the Teacher should continue this vocabulary-practice, by giving to his pupils, with shut books, now the English, and now the Greek words of every lesson, requiring in reply the corresponding terms:

CONTENTS.

SECTION	PAGE
XI. Pure Verbs— Class I., with Exercises,	68
XII. Mute Verbs—Class II., with Exercises,	72
XIII. Liquid Verbs—Class III., with Exercises,	79
XIV. Passive Voice, Middle Voice, and Deponent Verbs, with Exercises,	85
Miscellaneous Exercises,	87
XV. Verbs in -μι, with Exercises,	89
XVI. Irregular Verbs in -μι,	100

PART II.

EXTRACTS FOR READING, &c.

I. The Witticisms (of Hierocles),	107
II. Anecdotes of Philosophers, Statesmen, and Kings,	110
III. Fables of Æsop,	115
IV. Dialogues of Lucian,	123

NOTES TO PART II.

I. To the Witticisms (of Hierocles),	141
II. To the Anecdotes,	143
III. To the Fables of Æsop,	144
IV. To the Dialogues of Lucian,	146

APPENDIX.

Euphony—Rules of,	153
Accents—Rules of,	154
Syntax of Simple Sentences—Synopsis of,	156
Third Declension in Latin and in Greek Compared,	160
Contracted Verbs, Table of,	161
Vocabularies to the Exercises,	164

GENERAL VOCABULARY—GREEK,	173
GENERAL VOCABULARY—ENGLISH,	215
THE DECLENSIONS, ETC., WITH THE CASES IN AN ALTERED ORDER,	223

FIRST GREEK READER.

PART I.
THE PARTS OF SPEECH.

SECTION I.
THE LETTERS.

1. The Greek Alphabet consists of twenty-four letters:—

Capitals.	Small letters.	Pronunciation.	Name.	Capitals.	Small letters.	Pronunciation.	Name.
Α	α	a	Alpha.	Ν	ν	n	Nu.
Β	β	b	Beta.	Ξ	ξ	x	Xi.
Γ	γ	g	Gamma.	Ο	ο	ŏ	O-mĭcron.
Δ	δ	d	Delta.	Π	π	p	Pi.
Ε	ε	ĕ	E-psīlon.	Ρ	ρ	r	Rho.
Ζ	ζ	z	Zeta.	Σ	σ or ς	s	Sigma.
Η	η	ē	Eta.	Τ	τ	t	Tau.
Θ	θ	th	Theta.	Υ	υ	u	U-psīlon.
Ι	ι	i	Iota.	Φ	φ	ph	Phi.
Κ	κ	k	Kappa.	Χ	χ	ch	Chi.
Λ	λ	l	Lambda.	Ψ	ψ	ps	Psi.
Μ	μ	m	Mu.	Ω	ω	ō	O-mega.

2. The letters are of two classes, *Vowels* and *Consonants*.

3. The Vowels are seven ; viz.—

ε ο always short ;
η ω always long ;
α ι υ variable,—*i.e.*, representing either short or long sounds.

4. Consonants are either—

(1.) Semivowels,* λ, μ, ν, ρ, ς ; or,
(2.) Mutes, π, β, φ ; κ, γ, χ ; τ, δ, θ.

5. The Mutes admit of a double classification ; (1.) According to the organ by which they are pronounced ; and (2.) According to the degree of breathing employed in their utterance ; thus,—

LABIALS.	PALATALS.	LINGUAL DENTALS.	
π	κ	τ	Light or sharp.
β	γ	δ	Intermediate.
φ	χ	θ	Rough or flat.

6. ψ, ξ, ζ are *double* consonants, being equal—

ψ to πς, βς, φς (pronounced as πς).
ξ to κς, γς, χς (pronounced as κς).
ζ to δς or σδ.

7. Diphthongs are composed of two vowels com-

---

* A vowel sound has two characteristics:—*First*, It *comes freely* in pronunciation ; and, *Secondly*, When it is once formed *it can be prolonged*. The Semivowels possess this second property, and hence their name of "*half vowels.*" The Semivowels λ, μ, ν, ρ are also called "*Liquids,*"—ὑγρά, *i.e.*, the *watery* letters,—from the facility with which they change their position in a word without essentially altering the word, or disguising the proper stem : thus, θ-άρ-σος is also written θ-ρά-σος ; θ-νή-σκω (Doric, θ-να-σκω), has its 2 Aorist ἔθ-αν-ον : from *t-re-s*, in Latin, we have *t er* and *t-er-,ius*; in Scotch, *b-ur.nt* and *b-ru-nt*. Compare in English *cent-re* and *cent-er*.

bined together in pronunciation. They are of two kinds, *Proper* and *Improper*, otherwise called *Genuine* and *Spurious*. The first vowel of a Diphthong is called the *Prepositive*, the second the *Subjunctive*.

Genuine : ει   ευ   οι   ου   αι   αυ
Spurious : η*   ηυ   ῳ   ωυ   ᾳ   (ηυ)   and υι

8. In the Genuine Diphthongs both vowels are short, and are therefore of *equal weight;* but in the Spurious the first is long, and therefore in pronunciation overbalances the succeeding short, which, in consequence, is not heard. When the *Subjunctive* of a Spurious Diphthong is ι, it is written *below* its companion vowel (ι subscript), except in the case of capital letters; as, ῃ, (not ηι),—but Ἡι.

9. A vowel at the beginning of a word is marked with a *breathing*. The rough breathing (*spiritus asper*), made thus ‘, denotes that the vowel sound is to be preceded by the sound of the English *h;* as, ὑπό = hupo. The smooth breathing (*spiritus lenis*), made thus ’, merely indicates the absence of the rough; as, ἀπό = apo.

10. The breathing is marked over the second vowel of a Diphthong ; as, αὐλή.

11. The letter υ at the beginning of a word has always the rough breathing; and ρ, though a consonant, is similarly marked, as, ῥήτωρ = rhetor.

---

* Observe that the *Spurious* Diphthongs are made from the *Genuine* by simply lengthening the short *Prepositive* into its corresponding long ; thus, ει becomes η, and οι, ῳ ; ευ, ηυ, and ου, ωυ.

12. There are three Genders—Masculine, Feminine, Neuter.

13. There are three Numbers—the Singular, used of one,—the Dual, of two and *no more*,—the Plural, of two *or more*.

14. There are five Cases—Nominative, Vocative, Accusative, Genitive, and Dative.

15. There are three Declensions. The declension to which a noun belongs is known by the inflexion of the genitive singular.

16. There are eight Parts of Speech :—

DECLINABLE.	INDECLINABLE.
Substantive (Noun) ;	Adverb ;
Adjective (Noun), including Article ;	Preposition ;
	Interjection ;
Pronoun ;	Conjunction.
Verb.	

SECTION II.

FIRST DECLENSION.

1. The nouns of this declension end, in the nominative singular, in one of the four terminations, η, α, ης, ας. Nouns in η and α are feminine; those in ης and ας are masculine.*

---

* Every declinable word may be divided into two parts, the *stem* and the *inflexion*. The stem is that part which remains *unaltered* throughout all the cases and numbers, as αὐλ- in αὐλ-ή : the *inflexion* is that part which suffers change, as, -η, -ης, -α, -αιν, -ων, &c. The stem of a noun may be ascertained by taking away the inflexion of the genitive singular,—*e g*, from -σκι-ᾶς take away -ας, and σκι- remains as the stem ; from αὐλ ῆς take away -ης, and αὐλ- remains.

	SINGULAR.	DUAL.	PLURAL.
(1.) N.	αὐλ-ή, a court.	αὐλ-ά, two courts.	αὐλ-αί, courts.
G.	αὐλ-ῆς, of a court.	αὐλ-αῖν, of two courts.	αὐλ-ῶν, of courts.
D.	αὐλ-ῇ, to or for a court.	αὐλ-αῖν, to or for two courts.	αὐλ-αῖς, to or for courts.
A.	αὐλ-ήν, a court.	αὐλ-ά, two courts.	αὐλ-άς, courts.
V.	αὐλ-ή, O court.	αὐλ-ά, O two courts.	αὐλ-αί, O courts.

2. Those nouns which end in α (Alpha) preceded by a vowel or ρ, retain α in all the inflexions; e.g.—

	SINGULAR.	DUAL.	PLURAL.
(2.) N. & V.	σκι-ά, a shadow.	σκι-ά, two shadows.	σκι-αί, shadows.
G.	σκι-ᾶς, of a shadow.	σκι-αῖν, of two shadows.	σκι-ῶν, of shadows.
D.	σκι-ᾷ, to or for a shadow.	σκι-αῖν, to or for two shadows.	σκι-αῖς, to or for shadows.
A.	σκι-άν, a shadow.	σκι-ά, two shadows.	σκι-άς, shadows.

In like manner is declined σφαῖρ-α, a ball.

3. But if final α of the nominative be preceded by a consonant, η appears instead of α in the inflexion of the genitive and dative singular; as,—

	SINGULAR.	DUAL.	PLURAL.
(3.) N. & V.*	γλῶττ-α (or γλῶσσ-α), a tongue.	γλώττ-α, two tongues.	γλῶττ-αι, tongues.
G.	γλώττ-ης, of a tongue.	γλώττ-αιν, of two tongues.	γλωττ-ῶν, tongues.
D.	γλώττ-ῃ, to or for a tongue.	γλώττ-αιν, to or for two tongues.	γλώττ-αις, to or for tongues.
A.	γλῶττ-αν, a tongue.	γλώττ-α, two tongues.	γλώττ-ας, tongues.

* The Attics preferred ττ to σσ in words like the above.

4. Masculine nouns in ης and ας make their genitive in -ου, but in all other cases are declined like feminines in η and α, the ς of the nominative being dropped in the vocative singular:—

	SINGULAR.	DUAL.	PLURAL.
(4.) N.	τελών-ης, a toll collector.	τελών-α, two toll collectors.	τελῶν-αι, toll collectors.
G.	τελών-ου	τελών-αιν	τελων-ῶν
D.	τελών-ῃ	τελών-αιν	τελών-αις
A.	τελών-ην	τελών-α	τελών-ας
V.	τελών-η	τελών-α	τελῶν-αι
N.	νεανί-ας, a young man.	νεανί-α, two young men.	νεανί-αι, young men.
G.	νεανί-ου	νεανί-αιν	νεανι-ῶν
D.	νεανί-ᾳ	νεανί-αιν	νεανί-αις
A.	νεανί-αν	νεανί-α	νεανί-ας
V.	νεανί-α	νεανί-α	νεανί-αι

5. But the following, though ending in -ης in the nominative, have the vocative singular in -ă:—

(1.) Nouns in -της, as ναύτ-ης, voc. ναῦτ-α.
(2.) National names, as Σκύθ-ης, voc. Σκύθ-α.
(3.) Verbal nouns (compounded of a substantive and verb) which are formed by adding -ης to the last consonant of the verb, as ἀρτοπώλ-ης, a dealer in bread: voc., ἀρτοπῶλ-α, from ἀρτοπωλ-έω.

6. The feminine forms of adjectives, in -η or -α, are declined like the substantives given above; as, κλεινή, famous, like No. 1; ἁγία, holy, like No. 2; πᾶσα, all, every, like No. 3.

7. (SYNTAX) RULE I.—*An adjective agrees with its own substantive in gender, number, and case ;* as, ἅγιος θεός : ἅγιαι θεαί.

8. (SYNTAX) RULE II.—*The prepositions,* ἐν, *in, among ; and* σύν, *together with* (*Latin,* cum), *govern the dative.*

EXERCISE I.

(1.) τὴν* μάχην. τῆς αὐλῆς. τῇ κόρῃ. ἡ θήκη. τὰς κόρας. τὼ (τὰ)† θήκα. τῶν κορῶν. τὴν σφενδόνην. αἱ πυλαί. τῆς σελήνης. ταῖν κόραιν. ἐν τῇ σκηνῇ. σὺν τῇ κόρῃ. σὺν ταῖς κόραις. ἐν ταῖς πύλαις. ἐν τῇ μάχῃ. ἐν ταῖς χηλαῖς. σὺν ταῖς νύμφαις. τὰς νύμφας. ἐν τῇ ὕλῃ. τῆς ἀδελφῆς. τὼ (τὰ) ἀδελφά. τῆς ἐμῆς ἀδελφῆς.

(2.) ἡ μυῖα. τὼ (τὰ) μυία. ὦ μυῖα. τὴν λαιάν. τὼ (τὰ) θεά. τῆς σκιᾶς. τὴν βασίλειαν. τὼ (τὰ) παρειά. τὴν πήραν. τῆς θύρας. τὰς θύρας. σὺν τῇ στρατιᾷ. ἐν ταῖς παρειαῖς. ἐν τῇ δεξιᾷ. ἐν δεξιᾷ. τῶν ἀγκυρῶν. τὰς σφαίρας. τῆς σφαίρας. ἐν τῇ πρώρᾳ. αἱ θύραι. ταῖν θύραιν.

Of the battle. The maidens. The (two) maidens. In the sling. With the fly. With the (two) flies. The moon (*accus.*) A ball. The ball. The (two) balls. With the balls. In the ball. Of the doors. The doors. The door's. The doors'. The two cottages. In the cottages. The two queens. For the queens. O queen! Of the army. In the armies.

---

* For the Inflexion of the Article, see under Second Declension ; and for its uses, consult Appendix, p. 156.

† The Attics generally make the nominative and accusative dual feminine of the article τώ, and not τά.

EXERCISE II.

(3.) ἡ ἄκανθα. ἄκανθαι. τράπεζα. ἡ τράπεζα. τῆς ἀκάνθης. τὴν γλῶτταν. τὴν ἄκανθαν. ἐν τῇ τραπέζῃ. τῆς γλώττης. αἱ ἄκανθαι. τὴν δόξαν. τὼ (τὰ) μάζα. τὴν μάζαν. σὺν τῇ Μούσῃ. σὺν ταῖς λεαίναις. τῶν μαζῶν. ἐν ταῖς τραπέζαις. ἐν τῇ γλώττῃ. τὼ (τὰ) τραπέζα. τῶν γλωττῶν.

(4.) ναύτης. ὁ ναύτης. τὸν ποιητήν. ὦ ποιητά. τῶν ναυτῶν. τῷ ναύτῃ. τὼ ποιητά. οἱ Σκύθαι. ἐν τοῖς Σκύθαις. σὺν τῷ Πέρσῃ. ὦ Πέρσα. ὦ Πέρσῃ.* τὼ Σκύθᾱ. οἱ ναῦται. τοὺς δεσπότας. Σκύθᾰ. Σκύθᾱ.† σὺν τοῖς πολίταις. ὦ ναῦτα. τὼ ναύτα. τοῦ ναύτου. τῶν πολιτῶν. τοῦ δεσπότου. τὼ πολίτα. ὦ πολῖτᾰ. ὦ πολῖτᾱ.

Of a thorn. Of the thorn. Of the two thorns. The two thorns. The thorns. The two Persians. For the sailors. Of the poets. Of the Scythian. Of (*king*) Perses. With (*king*) Perses. With the Persian. Of the citizen. The citizens (*accus.*) The sailors (*accus.*) The two citizens. For the two citizens. Along with the masters. O master! O masters! Ye sailors! O poets! Among the poets. The table (*accus.*) The thorns (*accus.*) Of glory. The Muses. O Muses! Ye Muses! For the lionesses. The cakes. In the cake. Of the lioness. The two lionesses.

---

* Observe that Πέρσα is the vocative of the national name, *a Persian;* and Πέρσῃ of the individual name, *Perses.*

† α in the vocative of masculines is short, but α in the nominative, accusative, and vocative dual is long.

the same inflexions as δοῦλος; and the neuter, the same as μῆλον. The feminine of such adjectives, in -η or -α, belongs to the First Declension, as already remarked in Art. 6 of preceding Section.

EXERCISE IV.

(1.) τοῦ ἀετοῦ. τῷ δακτύλῳ. τὼ δακτύλω. ὦ δοῦλε. τὸν δοῦλον. τὼ ἵππω. τῶν δούλων. τὸν ἵππον. οἱ δοῦλοι. τὸν λευκὸν ἵππον. τοῦ κήπου. οἱ κῆποι. οἱ καλοὶ κῆποι. καλὼ κήπω. τοὺς ἵππους. τοῖν δούλοιν. τοῖς ἀετοῖς. τοῖς λευκοῖς ἀετοῖς. τὼ θεώ. τῷ θεῷ. σὺν τῷ θεῷ. ὦ θεός.*

(2.) τὸ δῶρον. δῶρον. τῷ δείπνῳ. τὸ μῆλον. μῆλα. τὰ μῆλα. τὼ ξυρώ. τὰ ξυρά. τῶν ᾠῶν. τὰ φύλλα. τοῖς μήλοις. τοῖν ξυροῖν. τοῦ δώρου. ὦ πλοῖον. ὦ πλοῖα. ὦ πλοίω. τῷ πλοίῳ. τῶν δείπνων. σὺν τοῖς ξυροῖς. ἐν τῷ πλοίῳ. σὺν τοῖς μήλοις. σὺν τοῖν πλοίοιν.

The two eagles. With the two horses. Of the horse. Of the horses. For the eagles. In the gardens. The eggs. The two apples. The white horse. The small boat. The white eggs. The eagle's eggs. The eagles' white eggs. The gods (*accus.*) For the slave. In the apple. At (ἐν or ἐπί) dinner.

4. (SYNTAX) RULE V.—*The prepositions* ἀνά, up along ; *and* εἰς, *into, govern the accusative.*

5. (SYNTAX) RULE VI.—*The prepositions* ἄνευ, without ; ἀντί, in front of ; ἀπό, away from ; ἐκ (*or*

---

* Θεός (like *Deus* in Latin) has the vocative the same as the nominative; so also φίλος, often, but not always.

ἐξ) out of, *i.e.*, from the midst of; ἕνεκα, on account of; and πρό, before, *govern the genitive*.

6. (Syntax) Rule VII.—*The conjunction* καί, *and*, *connects words and clauses* co-ordinatively.

7. (Syntax) Rule VIII.—*Since two singulars are equal to a plural, two singular subjects connected by a co-ordinative conjunction* (καί, &c.) *have a verb or adjective in the plural;* as, ὁ ἵππος καὶ ὁ ὄνος χρήσιμοί εἰσι.

EXERCISE V.

ὁ δοῦλος τοῦ γεωργοῦ ἐστι πιστός. οἱ ὄνοι εἰσὶν ἐν τῷ τοῦ ἰατροῦ κήπῳ. οἱ δάκτυλοι τοῦ ἀνθρώπου μικροί εἰσι. ἡ γνάθος τῆς κόρης ἐστὶ μαλακή. οἱ ἵπποι τοῦ κυρίου εἰσὶν ἐν τῇ ὕλῃ. τὼ ὄνω ἐν τῷ κήπῳ ἐστόν. ὁ βωμὸς τοῦ θεοῦ ἐστιν ἱερός. αἱ γνάθοι τῆς ἵππου μακραί εἰσι. ὁ μόσχος ἐστὶν ἐν τῷ ναῷ. ἡ χαίτη τοῦ ἵππου ἐστὶ δασεῖα. ὁ κύριος σὺν τοῖς δούλοις ἐν τῷ ἀγρῷ ἐστι. τὰ τῆς δάφνης φύλλα ἐστὶ* ξηρά. ἐν τῷ τοῦ ἰατροῦ κήπῳ αἴγειρός ἐστι λευκή. τὼ τῆς κόρης ὀφθαλμώ ἐστον γλαυκώ. ἀνὰ τὴν ὁδόν. εἰς τὰς Ἀθήνας. ἐκ τῶν Ἀθηνῶν. ἀνὰ τὴν εἰς τὰς Ἀθήνας ὁδόν. σὺν τῷ ἵππῳ τοῦ ἀρότου. ἀνὰ τοὺς ἀγροὺς τῶν γεωργῶν. ἵππος καὶ ὄνος ἐν τῷ κήπῳ εἰσί. ἵππω καὶ ὄνω. ἵπποι καὶ ὄνοι. ἀνὰ τὰ τῆς αἰγείρου φύλλα. ἐκ τοῦ κήπου. ἀπὸ τοῦ κήπου. ἐκ τῶν φύλλων. ὄνος καὶ ἵππος ἐν τῇ αὐλῇ εἰσι. εἰς ὕλην καὶ εἰς σκηνήν. κατὰ τὴν ἀγυιάν.

---

* In Greek, *neuter plurals* usually take the verb in the *singular*.

The ass and the lioness are in the hut. The husbandman is foolish. The garden is small. The gods are venerable (*reverend*). The poplar tree is smooth. The eyes of the girl are small. The slave's wallet is empty. The husbandman's tables are smooth. The queen's palace (*court*) is empty. The girl's voice is sweet. The girls and their brothers are in the garden of the farmer. The doctor's horse is in the citizen's court-yard. The two doctors are in the house of the citizen. Into the citizen's court-yard. Out of the poet's hut. Away from the ploughman's hut.

8. The article ὁ, ἡ, τό, *the* or *this*, is an adjective, and differs but slightly from the regular inflexions. It has no vocative, and in the masculine and feminine of the nominative singular and plural omits the τ of the stem. It is declined as follows:—

	SINGULAR.			DUAL.			PLURAL.		
	Masc.	Fem.	Neut.	Masc.	Fem.	Neut.	Masc.	Fem.	Neut.
N.	ὁ	ἡ	τό	τώ	*τώ (τα)	τώ	οἱ	αἱ	τά
G.	τοῦ	τῆς	τοῦ	τοῖν	ταῖν	τοῖν	τῶν	τῶν	τῶν
D.	τῷ	τῇ	τῷ	τοῖν	ταῖν	τοῖν	τοῖς	ταῖς	τοῖς
A.	τόν	τήν	τό	τώ	τώ (τα)	τώ	τούς	τάς	τά

9. THE ATTIC SECOND DECLENSION.

This form of declension is merely a modification of the more common inflexion, as given in δοῦλος. The nouns in -ως are masculine or feminine; those in -ων, neuter.

---

* See note †, page 15.

	SINGULAR.	DUAL.	PLURAL.
N. & V.	λαγ-ώς, masc.,	λαγ-ώ,	λαγ-ῴ,*
	a hare.	two hares.	hares.
G.	λαγ-ώ	λαγ-ῴν	λαγ-ῶν
D.	λαγ-ῴ	λαγ-ῴν	λαγ-ῷς
A.	λαγ-ών†	λαγ-ώ	λαγ-ώς
N. A. & V.	ἀνώγε-ων, neut.	ἀνώγε-ω	ἀνώγε-ω
G.	ἀνώγε-ω	ἀνώγε-ων	ἀνώγε-ων
D.	ἀνώγε-ῳ	ἀνώγε-ῳν	ἀνώγε-ῳς

The masculine and feminine of adjectives in -ως are declined like λαγώς, and the neuter like ἀνώγεων; as ἵλεως, ἵλεων, *propitious*.

EXERCISE VI.

οἱ λαγῴ ἐν τῷ ἀγρῷ εἰσι. ὁ ταῶς σὺν τῷ λαγῴ ἐν τῷ τοῦ πολίτου ἀνώγεῴ ἐστι. ἀνὰ τὸν κάλων. εἰς τὸ ἀνώγεων. ἐκ τοῦ ἀνώγεω. ἐκ τοῖν ἀνώγεων. τὰ ἀνώγεῴ ἐστι μικρά. οἱ κάλῳ νέοι εἰσί. αἱ κεφαλαὶ τῶν λαγῶν μικραί εἰσι. ὁ λεώς ἐστιν ἐν τοῖς ἀνώγεῳς. τὼ ταῶ ἐν τῇ ἅλῳ ἐστόν. σὺν τοῖς ταῶς. οἱ πολῖται ἐν τῷ τοῦ θεοῦ νεῴ εἰσι. ἡ οὐρὰ τοῦ ταῶ λαμπρά ἐστι. ἡ τοῦ λαγὼ κέρκος βραχεῖά ἐστι.

The peacocks and the hares are in the garden. The sailor is in the upper room. The upper chambers of the house are empty. Hares are swift. The two cables are old. The cables are in the fore part (*of the ship*). The anchor and the cables are in the

---

* Observe that wherever there is an *iota* in the inflexion of the common form, like δοῦλος, there is an *iota* subscript in the Attic form; thus, nominative plural -οι, in Attic declension ῳ.

† The ν of the accusative is frequently dropped, especially in proper names.

prow. The peacocks are in the farmer's thrashing-floor. The citizen and the poet are in the upper chamber of the house. Hares' scuts (*i.e.*, tails) are short.

SECTION IV.
THIRD DECLENSION.

1. In the First and Second Declensions the stem of a noun may be easily distinguished even in the nominative; but in the Third Declension it is so disguised, by the omission of consonants or the modification of vowels, that it cannot be known without reference to one of the oblique* cases. The following classification groups the nouns of this declension *according to the change which takes place on the stem in the nominative.*†

(I.) 2. *The* FIRST CLASS *contains those nouns which have the pure stem in the nominative; as,—*

	SINGULAR.	DUAL.	PLURAL.
N. & V.	λειμών, masc., a meadow.	λειμών-ε, two meadows.	λειμῶν-ες, meadows.
G.	λειμῶν-ος	λειμών-οιν	λειμών-ων
D.	λειμῶν-ι	λειμών-οιν	λειμῶ-σι‡
A.	λειμῶν-α	λειμῶν-ε	λειμῶν-ας

---

* The accusative, genitive, and dative are called *oblique*, or *dependent* cases, because subject to the *government* of other words; the nominative and vocative are called *independent* cases, or *casus recti*, because they are not liable to such regimen.

† In reading a Greek author, the problem which a young student is most frequently called upon to solve, in regard to nouns, is, "To find the nominative from an oblique case," and not *vice versa;* and it is hoped that the arrangement of nouns adopted in the text will render this a comparatively easy task.

‡ The dative plural ought to be, in full, λειμών-σι; but the letters τ, δ, θ, ν were not allowed to stand before ς, and thus it becomes λειμῶσι. This principle must be carefully noted, as examples of it are constantly recurring.

	SINGULAR.	DUAL.	PLURAL.
N. & V.	θήρ, masc., *a wild beast.*	θῆρ-ε, *two wild beasts.*	θῆρ-ες, *wild beasts.*
G.	θηρ-ός	θηρ-οῖν	θηρ-ῶν
D.	θηρ-ί	θηρ-οῖν	θηρ-σί
A.	θῆρ-α	θῆρ-ε	θῆρ-ας

3. (SYNTAX) RULE IX.—*Transitive verbs govern the accusative;* as, ὁ παῖς τὴν σφαῖραν ῥίπτει.

4. The present indicative active of a Greek verb is declined as follows:—

Singular, λείπ-ω, λείπ-εις, λείπ-ει,
I leave. *thou leavest.* *he leaves.*

Dual, λείπ-ετον, λείπ-ετον,
you two leave. *they two leave.*

Plural, λείπ-ομεν, λείπ-ετε, λείπ-ουσι,
we leave. *you leave.* *they leave.*

In like manner decline ἔχω, *I have.*

EXERCISE VII.

θηρός. τοῦ θηρός. τῶν χηνῶν. τὼ θῆρε. τοῦ χηνός. τῆς χηνός. σὺν τῇ χηνί. τὼ χῆνε. τὰς χῆνας. διώκει τὰς χῆνας. ἡ κόρη διώκει τὰς χῆνας. τοὺς χῆνας. οἱ ναῦται τοὺς χῆνας διώκουσι. οἱ θῆρες διώκουσι τοὺς ἀνθρώπους ἐν τῇ ὕλῃ. οἱ θῆρες ἐν τῷ λειμῶνί εἰσι. οἱ δοῦλοι διώκουσι τὸν θῆρα ἐκ τοῦ λειμῶνος. μῆνες. οἱ μῆνες ἱεροί εἰσι. τῶν θηρῶν. ὁ χὴν σὺν τοῖς θηρσὶ ἐν τῷ λειμῶνί ἐστι.* ἀπὸ τοῦ

---

* A singular subject followed, as here, by σύν, with a noun, may have a plural verb, so that ἐστί may become εἰσί.

λειμῶνος. ἡ κόρη διώκει μυῖαν ἀνὰ τὸν λειμῶνα. ἐν τοῖς λειμῶσι πολλαί εἰσι μυῖαι. ὁ ἰατρὸς τὸν λαγὼν διώκει. λευκὸν ἔχω χῆνα.

The head of the goose. The wild beast's tail. The tails of the two wild beasts. The sailor hunts the wild beast into the hut. The lioness pursues the goose into the court. The Greeks pursue the Persians into the forest. The meadow is smooth. We are hunting the peacock up the garden of the Greek. We hunt lionesses in the forests of the Scythians. O Scythian! the wild beast is pursuing the girl. The bull pursues the farmer along the road.

(II.) 5. To the SECOND CLASS belong those nouns which in the nominative add ς to the pure stem, as ἥρω-ς, ἥρω-ος. In many nouns the final ς is combined with the preceding consonant into one of the double consonants, ξ or ψ, as κόραξ for κόρακς, γύψ for γύπς.

	SINGULAR.	DUAL.	PLURAL.
N. & V.	ἥρω-ς, a hero.	ἥρω-ε two heroes.	ἥρω-ες heroes.
G.	ἥρω-ος	ἡρώ-οιν	ἡρώ-ων
D.	ἥρω-ι	ἡρώ-οιν	ἥρω-σι
A.	ἥρω-α = ἥρω	ἥρω-ε	ἥρω-ας
N. & V.	γύψ	γῦπ-ε	γῦπ-ες
G.	γυπ-ός	γυπ-οῖν	γυπ-ῶν
D.	γυπ-ί	γυπ-οῖν	γυψ-ί
A.	γῦπ-α	γῦπ-ε	γῦπ-ας

6. The accusative singular of the Third Declension usually ends in α: but when the nominative ends in -ις, -υς, -αυς, or -ους, it takes ν instead of α; as, κίς, κίν; ἰχθύς, ἰχθύν; ναῦς, ναῦν; βοῦς, βοῦν. On this last example, see p. 37, No. 18.

	SINGULAR.	DUAL.	PLURAL.
(3.) N.	ἰχθύ-ς, masc., a fish.	ἰχθύ-ε, two fishes.	ἰχθύ-ες = ἰχθῦς, fishes.
G.	ἰχθύ-ος	ἰχθύ-οιν	ἰχθύ-ων
D.	ἰχθύ-ι	ἰχθύ-οιν	ἰχθύ-σι
A.	ἰχθύ-ν	ἰχθύ-ε	ἰχθύ-ας = ἰχθῦς
V.	ἰχθύ	ἰχθύ-ε	ἰχθύ-ες = ἰχθῦς
N.	μῦ-ς, masc., a mouse.	μύ-ε, two mice.	μύ-ες = μῦς, mice.
G.	μυ-ός	μυ-οῖν	μυ-ῶν
D.	μυ-ί	μυ-οῖν	μυ-σί
A.	μῦ-ν	μύ-ε	μύ-ας = μῦς
V.	μῦ	μύ-ε	μύ-ες = μῦς

EXERCISE VIII.

τοῦ ἥρωος. τὸν δμῶα. τὼ ἥρωε. τῶν θώων. οἱ μυκτῆρες τοῦ θωός. τοὺς σύας. οἱ χῆνες τοῦ γεωργοῦ ἐν τῷ λειμῶνί εἰσι. ὁ θὼς καὶ ὁ σῦς ἐν τῷ τοῦ ἰατροῦ κήπῳ εἰσί. οἱ ἥρωες σὺν τοῖς ναύταις ἐν τῇ αὐλῇ εἰσι. αἱ κόμαι τῶν ἡρώων ξανθαί εἰσι. ὁ ἰχθὺς ἐν τῇ θαλάττῃ ἐστί. σὺν τοῖς μυσί. ἀνὰ τοὺς μυκτῆρας τοῦ μυός. γῦπες σκληροί εἰσι. ἡ γλῶττα τοῦ γυπὸς τραχεῖά ἐστι. οἱ γῦπες καὶ οἱ κόρακες ἐν τῇ ὕλῃ εἰσί. εἰς κόρακας![*] οἱ μύρμηκές εἰσι σοφοί. αἱ πτέρυγες τοῦ

---

[*] This is a kind of imprecation, like our "Go, be hanged." Compare the Latin phrases, *Abi in malam partem; Abi in malam crucem; Pasce corvos.*

κόρακος καὶ αἱ τοῦ γυπὸς μακραί εἰσι. αἱ φλέβες τοῦ σκύλακός εἰσι κεναί. οἱ ναῦται μαχαίρας ἔχουσι. ὁ ἐμὸς ἀδελφὸς τὰς κόμας ξανθὰς ἔχει.

Jackals are fierce. The citizen hunts the jackal out of the garden. Two vultures are chasing the geese up the meadow. The girl is chasing a mouse through the court. We hunt wild beasts in the forests. He crops the vulture's wings. The girls are chasing the flies away from the bread. The two girls are cutting the flies' wings. (*King*) Perses is pursuing a jackal in the forest. The farmer's daughter leaves the bread in the hut. The mice are eating the loaves. The citizens are pursuing the thief.

(III.) 7. In the THIRD CLASS are included those nouns which have the final vowel of the stem lengthened in the nominative; as, ποιμήν, from stem ποιμεν- as found in the genitive, ποιμέν-ος.

	SINGULAR.	DUAL.	PLURAL.
N. & V.	ποιμήν, masc., *a shepherd.*	ποιμέν-ε, *two shepherds.*	ποιμέν-ες, *shepherds.*
G.	ποιμέν-ος	ποιμέν-οιν	ποιμέν-ων
D.	ποιμέν-ι	ποιμέν-οιν	ποιμέ-σι
A.	ποιμέν-α	ποιμέν-ε	ποιμέν-ας

Note.—But nouns that have *not* the accent on the last syllable of the nominative have the pure stem in the vocative; as, δαίμων, voc. δαῖμον; ῥήτωρ, voc. ῥῆτορ.

8. To this class belong syncopated nouns like πατήρ, which throw out ε in the genitive and dative singular. In the dative plural α is substituted for ε, but is placed after the ρ, and not before it:—

SINGULAR.	DUAL.	PLURAL.
N. μήτηρ, *a mother.*	μητέρ-ε *two mothers.*	μητέρ-ες *mothers.*
G. μητρ-ός (for μητέρ-ος)	μητέρ-οιν	μητέρ-ων
D. μητρ-ί (for μητέρ-ι)	μητέρ-οιν	μητρά-σι
A. μητέρ-α	μητέρ-ε	μητέρ-ας
V. μῆτερ	μητέρ-ε	μητέρ-ες
N. ἀνήρ,* masc., *a man = Latin, vir.*	ἄνδρε, *two men.*	ἄνδρ-ες, *men.*
G. ἀν-δ-ρός	ἀνδρ-οῖν	ἀνδρ-ῶν
D. ἀν-δ-ρί	ἀνδρ-οῖν	ἀνδρά-σι
A. ἄν-δ-ρα (for ἀνέρα)	ἄνδρ-ε	ἄνδρ-ας
V. ἄνερ	ἄνδρ-ε	ἄνδρ-ες

In κύων, masculine or feminine, *a dog*, the syncope occurs in all the cases except the nominative and vocative singular:—

SINGULAR.	DUAL.	PLURAL.
N. κύων, *a dog.*	κύν-ε *two dogs.*	κύν-ες *dogs.*
G. κυν-ός	κυν-οῖν	κυν-ῶν
D. κυν-ί	κυν-οῖν	κυ-σί
A. κύν-α	κύν-ε	κύν-ας
V. κύον	κύν-ε	κύν-ες

---

* It often happens that μ or ν is, by the omission or transposition of a vowel, brought into contact with another liquid. Such a combination of sounds was very disagreeable to a Greek ear, and to avoid it, a consonant *kindred* to the first of the two concurring liquids was inserted, for the sake of euphony. Thus, after the labial

9. Some nouns combine the peculiarities of classes II. and III.; thus, αἰδώς, *gen.* αἰδό-ος, stem αἰδο-, *sense of shame*, both adds -ς to the stem, like ἥρως, and also lengthens the last vowel in the nominative, like ποιμήν. So likewise ἀλώπηξ (*i.e.*, ἀλώπηκς), *gen.* ἀλώπεκ-ος, stem ἀλωπεκ-, *a fox;* and all adjectives in -ης, as σαφής, ἀληθής, &c.

EXERCISE IX.

ὁ τοῦ ἀνδρὸς αὐχὴν καλός ἐστι. ἡ φωνὴ τῆς ἀηδόνος ἡδεῖά ἐστι. ὁ γὺψ τὴν ἀηδόνα διώκει. τὸν τῆς κόρης αὐχένα θαυμάζω. τὰ μῆλα εἰς τὴν τοῦ ποιμένος πήραν ῥίπτει. οἱ ποιμένες σὺν τοῖς γειτόσι ἐν τῷ λειμῶνί εἰσι. ὁ τοῦ ποιμένος κύων σοφός ἐστι. τὼ ποιμένε σὺν τοῖς κυσὶ ἐν τῷ τοῦ δεσπότου κήπῳ εἰσί. ὁ κύων διώκει μῦν ἀνὰ τὴν χιόνα. ἡ καλὴ τριήρης τῆς βασιλείας ἐν τῷ λιμένι ἐστί. αἱ τοῦ ἀνδρὸς κόραι νήπιαί εἰσι. αἱ κόραι σὺν ταῖς μητράσι καὶ τοῖς πατράσι τὰς χελιδόνας θαυμάζουσι. ἡ κέρκος τῆς ἀλώπεκος δασεῖά ἐστι. τὼ ἀλώπεκε ἐν τῇ τοῦ ποιμένος σκηνῇ ἐστον (or εἰσι). ἐν τῷ Ἀθηνᾶς νεῷ κίονές εἰσι πολλοί. ὁ τοῦ πολίτου γείτων ἀληθής ἐστι φίλος.

The shepherds admire the pillars in the temple of the god. The shepherd's daughters persuade their (*i.e.*, the) father. The swallows leave the house. The queen admires the beautiful triremes. There

---

μ, β, another labial, was inserted; as, γαμ-ε-ρός, γαμ-ρός, γαμ-β-ρός, a *son-in-law:* while after the lingual ν, δ, another lingual, was used; as, ἀν-έ-ρος, ἀν-ρός, ἀν-δ-ρός. So from *num-e-r-us*, the French *nom-b-re* and our *num-b-er;* from *gen-e-r-is* (from *genus*) the French *gen-r-e* and our *gen-d-er*.

are two beautiful triremes in the harbour. In Athens there was a beautiful temple to Athena. The girl writes in the snow with a rod. The poet writes letters. The girl throws apples into the poet's cottage. The shepherd wonders at the bushy tail of the fox. The two shepherds are shearing the sheep. The dogs are hunting mice in the farmer's garden.

(IV.) 10. The FOURTH CLASS includes those nouns which drop the last letter of the stem in the nominative. Most members of this class end in α, and are neuter:—

	SINGULAR.	DUAL.	PLURAL.
N. & V.	Ξενοφῶν, masc., Xenophon.		
G.	Ξενοφῶντ-ος		
D.	Ξενοφῶντ-ι		
A.	Ξενοφῶντ-α		
N. A. & V.	σῶμα, neut., a body.	σώματ-ε, two bodies.	σώματ-α, bodies.
G.	σώματ-ος	σωμάτ-οιν	σωμάτ-ων
D.	σώματ-ι	σωμάτ-οιν	σώμα-σι

11. Some nouns combine the peculiarities of classes IV. and III.; thus, λέων, *gen.* λέοντος, both drops the final τ of the stem, like Ξενοφῶν, and also lengthens the last vowel, like ποιμήν: stem λεοντ-, with τ dropped, λεον-, and with ο lengthened to ω, λέων.

SINGULAR.	DUAL.	PLURAL.
N. λέων,	λέοντ-ε	λέοντ-ες
a lion.	two lions.	lions.
G. λέοντ-ος	λεόντ-οιν	λεόντ-ων
D. λέοντ-ι	λεόντ-οιν	λέου-σι*
A. λέοντ-α	λέοντ-ε	λέοντ-ας
V. λέον	λέοντ-ε	λέοντ-ες

So also adjectives and participles like τύπτων, except that τύπτων and other participles have the vocative in -ων, like the nominative.

EXERCISE X.

τὸ τοῦ κυνὸς σῶμα ἐν τῷ ποταμῷ ἐστι. ἐκ τοῦ ἅρματος. εἰς τὸ ἅρμα. τὰ τῆς θαλάττης κύματα μακρά ἐστι. ἐν τοῖς τῆς θαλάττης κύμασι. Ξενοφῶντος ἄγαλμα καλὸν ἐν τῷ οἴκῳ τοῦ ποιητοῦ ἐστι. γάλα πολὺ καὶ μέλι ἐν τῇ τοῦ Πέρσου σκηνῇ εἰσι. ἀνὰ τὰ βήματα τοῦ ναοῦ.

ἡ χαίτη τοῦ λέοντος δασεῖά ἐστι. γέροντές εἰσι ξηροί. τὸ τοῦ ἄρχοντος βῆμα ἐν τῷ ναῷ ἐστι. αἱ κόμαι τῶν γερόντων λευκαί εἰσι. τὼ τοῦ ἄρχοντος ὑπηρέτα ἐν τῷ ἅρματί εἰσι (or ἐστον). τὼ ὑπηρέτα ἐν τῷ τοῦ ἄρχοντος ἅρματί εἰσι.

---

* A syllable is called long, either when its *vowel* is naturally long (η, ω, ᾱ, &c.), or when *two consonants* (not being a *mute* and a *liquid*) follow a vowel naturally short. Thus, in the dative plural, λέοντ-σι, the second syllable, -οντσ-, is long, since ο (though short in itself) is followed by three consonants; but as neither τ nor ν can stand before ς, both of them are thrown out, and the word is reduced to λέοσι. In this form, however, the syllable (-οντσ-), formerly long, has been reduced to -οσ-, which is short; and, to compensate for this, the ο is changed into its kindred diphthong -ου, so that λέοσι becomes λέουσι. Similarly, nouns whose stem ends in -εντ make their dative plural in -εισι; and those in -αντ in -ᾱσι. The same change is seen in ὀδούς, *a tooth*, from stem ὀδοντ-; and κτείς, *a comb*, from stem κτεν-: and in participles in -εις, as τιθείς for τιθέντς. This principle of *compensation* is of very frequent occurrence in Greek, and the application of it explains many forms otherwise inexplicable.

The men leave the bodies of the lions in the woods. The queen admires the lion's mane. The mane of the lion is shaggy. The steps of the altar are steep. The boy eats much bread and honey. The tents of the Scythians are white. Xenophon leaves the land of the Persians. The master orders his (*i.e.*, the) servants. The girl eats bread without honey. The Scythians eat much honey. Because of the lion. We admire the eyes of the girl. You admire the nightingale's voice.

(V.) 12. To the FIFTH CLASS belong those nouns which drop one dental (τ, δ, θ, ν), or more, before ς in the nominative; as, παῖς (for παι-δ-ς), παιδός; γίγας (for γιγα-ντ-ς), γίγαντος:—

	SINGULAR.	DUAL.	PLURAL.
N. & V.	λαμπάς, fem., a torch.	λαμπάδ-ε, two torches.	λαμπάδ-ες torches.
G.	λαμπάδ-ος	λαμπάδ-οιν	λαμπάδ-ων
D.	λαμπάδ-ι	λαμπάδ-οιν	λαμπά-σι
A.	λαμπάδ-α	λαμπάδ-ε	λαμπάδ-ας
N. & V.	ὄρνις, m. or f., a bird or fowl.	ὄρνιθ-ε two birds.	ὄρνιθ-ες, birds.
G.	ὄρνιθ-ος	ὀρνίθ-οιν	ὀρνίθ-ων
D.	ὄρνιθ-ι	ὀρνίθ-οιν	ὄρνι-σι
A.	ὄρνιθ-α, or ὄρνιν*	ὄρνιθ-ε	ὄρνιθ-ας

13. Masculine adjectives, like μέλας, *black*, and participles in -ας and -εις, belong to this class:

---

* Words which end in a dental have two forms of the accusative if the accent is *not* on the last syllable; but if it be, as in ἀσπίς, *a shield*, the accusative has only one form, ἀσπίδα, *not* ἀσπίν.

also the indefinite pronoun τίς, *any one, a certain one;* and the interrogative τίς, *who, which, what.*

Indefinite pronoun, τίς, τίς, τί, *a certain one:—*

	SINGULAR.			DUAL.		
	Masc.	Fem.	Neut.	Masc.	Fem.	Neut.
N.	τὶς	τὶς	τὶ	τιν-έ	τιν-έ	τιν-έ
G.	τιν-ός	τιν-ός	τιν-ός	τιν-οῖν	τιν-οῖν	τιν-οῖν
D.	τιν-ί	τιν-ί	τιν-ί	τιν-οῖν	τιν-οῖν	τιν-οῖν
A.	τιν-ά	τιν-ά	τὶ	τιν-έ	τιν-έ	τιν-έ

	PLURAL.		
	Masc.	Fem.	Neut.
N.	τιν-ές	τιν-ές	τιν-ά
G.	τιν-ῶν	τιν-ῶν	τιν-ῶν
D.	τι-σί	τισ-ί	τισ-ί
A.	τιν-άς	τιν-άς	τιν-ά

Interrogative pronoun, τίς, *who, which, what :—*

	SINGULAR.			DUAL.		
	Masc.	Fem.	Neut.	Masc.	Fem.	Neut.
N.	τίς	τίς	τί	τίν-ε	τίν-ε	τίν-ε
G.	τίν-ος	τίν-ος	τίν-ος	τίν-οιν	τίν-οιν	τίν-οιν
D.	τίν-ι	τίν-ι	τίν-ι	τίν-οιν	τίν-οιν	τίν-οιν
A.	τίν-α	τίν-α	τί	τίν-ε	τίν-ε	τίν-ε

	PLURAL.		
	Masc.	Fem.	Neut.
N.	τίν-ες	τίν-ες	τίν-α
G.	τίν-ων	τίν-ων	τίν-ων
D.	τί-σι	τί-σι	τί-σι
A.	τίν-ας	τίν-ας	τίν-α

14. It may be stated, generally and loosely, that the accusative case is used to indicate *movement*

towards, or *movement along;* the genitive, to express the *source,* or *origin,* or *place whence;* and the dative, to denote *proximity,* or *nearness,* or *juxtaposition.* Hence the preposition παρά, *beside,* or *by the side of,*

(a) When governing the accusative, signifies *motion towards* (*to the side of,* or *by the side of,* i.e., *parallel to); as,* παρὰ τὸν κίονα, (moving) *towards* (the side of) *the pillar;* παρὰ τὸν ποταμόν, *along by* (the side of) *the river.*

(b) When governing the genitive, signifies *motion from beside;* as, παρὰ τοῦ κίονος, *from beside the pillar.*

(c) When governing the dative, signifies *rest at the side of, near,* or *with* (*apud); as,* παρὰ τῷ κίονι, (in a position) *beside the pillar.*

15. The preposition κατά, when governing the accusative, signifies *along,* or *down along;* when governing the genitive, *down from.*

16. ἦν means *I was;* or *he, she, it was.* ἦσαν means *they were.*

EXERCISE XI.

ἐν τῷ λέβητι μέλι ἦν γλυκύ.* οἱ λέβητες τοῦ νεὼ λαμπροὶ ἦσαν. ὁλκάδες πολλαὶ ἐν τῷ λιμένι ἦσαν. ἥ τε ἀσπὶς καὶ ἡ κόρυς τοῦ ἥρωος νέαι εἰσί. αἱ λαμπάδες σὺν τοῖς λέβησι ἐν τῷ τοῦ κριτοῦ δόμῳ ἦσαν. ὁ παῖς τοῦ ἄνακτος ἐν τῷ τοῦ γίγαντος ἄντρῳ ἦν. τὸ ᾠὸν τῆς ὄρνιθος ἐν τῇ ἀσπίδι ἦν. αἱ ῥῖνες τῶν παίδων

---

* On the declension of γλυκύς see next class, VI.

μικραί εἰσι. παῖδές τινες σφαῖραν ῥίπτουσι. αἱ χλαμύδες τῶν Περσῶν καλαὶ ἦσαν. οἱ τῶν δούλων τρίβωνες μέλανές εἰσι. δοῦλός τις μῦν διώκει. πάντες οἱ παῖδες, καὶ πᾶσαι αἱ κόραι, σὺν τοῖς πατράσι καὶ ταῖς ἀδελφαῖς, ἐν τῷ παραδείσῳ εἰσί. οἱ τοῦ ἄνακτος ὀδόντες λευκοὶ ἦσαν. κόρας τινὰς ἐν τῷ τοῦ ἄνακτος κήπῳ βλέπομεν. παρὰ τοῦ νεὼ βαίνει. παρὰ τὸν κίονα βαίνουσι ποιμένες τινές. ἡ σφαῖρα παρὰ τῷ κίονί ἐστι. δεσπότης τις δούλους ἔχει πολλούς. τίς ἐστιν ὁ ἀνήρ; τίνα τὸν κίονα βλέπεις; ποῦ ἐστιν ὁ παῖς; ποῦ εἰσιν οἱ ἄνακτες; ποῦ ἦσαν οἱ λέβητες; τίνας ποιμένας λέγεις;

From-beside the temple. To-the-side-of the temple. The slaves have black cloaks. A certain judge had (εἶχε) two faithful slaves. In the temple of a certain god there were beautiful caldrons. What poet do you speak of? Whose asses do you see? The girls are plaiting their hair. The master strikes his slave with* his shield. Two merchant-men of-some-kind (τις) are sailing into the harbour. He sees a (*certain*) torch in the court. Which key has the slave? What shield has the warrior? What ball are the boys throwing? Who is king of the Persians? From what port do the merchantmen sail for Greece? The king is hunting a hare along the sea (*shore*).

(VI.) 17. The SIXTH CLASS embraces those nouns

---

* *With* is not to be translated here by σύν, but by the dative (instrumental) of the noun.

in which the final vowel of the stem is changed in the nominative; as, τεῖχο-ς for τεῖχε-ς, *gen.* τείχε-ος; γλυκύ-ς for γλυκέ-ς, *gen.* γλυκέ-ος. The substantives in -ος of this class are neuter.

	SINGULAR.	DUAL.	PLURAL.
N.	μάντι-ς, masc., a prophet or seer.	μάντε-ε, two prophets.	μάντε-ες = μάντεις, prophets.
G.	μάντε-ως*	μαντέ-οιν	μάντε-ων
D.	μάντε-ϊ = μάντει	μαντέ-οιν	μάντε-σι
A.	μάντι-ν	μάντε-ε	μάντε-ας = μάντεις
V.	μάντι	μάντε-ε	μάντε-ες = μάντεις

	SINGULAR.	DUAL.
N. A. & V.	τεῖχο-ς, neut., a wall.	τείχε-ε = τείχη, two walls.
G.	τείχε-ος = τείχους	τειχέ-οιν = τειχοῖν
D.	τείχε-ϊ = τείχει	τειχέ-οιν = τειχοῖν

PLURAL.

N. A. & V. τείχε-α = τείχη
walls.

G. τειχέ-ων = τειχῶν

D. τείχε-σι

EXERCISE XII.

ὁ πέλεκυς ὀξύς ἐστι. τὸν βαρὺν πέλεκυν θαυμάζομεν. τῶν παλαιῶν μάντεων δεινὴ ἦν ἡ δύναμις. τὸν τοῦ μάντεως πώγωνα κείρουσι. τὸ αἷμα κατὰ τὸν λεῖον πέλεκυν ῥεῖ.

τὸ τῆς πόλεως τεῖχος μακρὸν ἦν. κατὰ τοῦ ὄρους βαίνει ποιμήν τις. τὸν τοῦ Ξενοφῶντος υἱὸν διδάσκει ὁ σοφιστής. ἀνὰ τὸ τοῦ ναοῦ τεῖχος κοχλίας τις

---

* Substantives of this kind usually take the Attic genitive in -ως, but adjectives retain the simple -ος, as ἡδέ-ος.

ἕρπει. εἰς τὸ ἄστυ φεύγει ὁ μάντις. ὄφιν τινὰ ἐκ τοῦ ἄστεος διώκουσιν οἱ παῖδες. μέρος τι τῆς πόλεως δῆλον ἦν. τὸ μακρὸν στῆθος τοῦ ἀνθρώπου θαυμάζει ὁ ὄχλος. ὁ ποιμὴν ὄφιν τινὰ ἀνὰ τὸ ὄρος ἕρποντα βλέπει. ναοῦ τινος τὸν ὄροφον ἐν τῇ τοῦ ὄρεος κορυφῇ βλέπει ὁ ποιμήν. τὸ ξίφος βαρύ ἐστι. παρὰ τοῦ κίονος φεύγει ὁ λαγώς. οἱ παῖδες τὰς σφαίρας παρὰ τῷ κίονι λείπουσι. ὁ κύων τὴν ὄρνιθα (or ὄρνιν) παρὰ τὸν κίονα διώκει, ἡ δὲ εἰς οἶκόν τινα φεύγει.

(VII.) 18. In the SEVENTH CLASS are ranged those nouns which have the diphthong αυ, ευ, or ου, before the final ς of the nominative. The υ of the diphthong represents the obsolete letter F (Digamma) vocalized, thus, βοῦς for βοϜς, like Latin *bōs* for *bovs*, *bŏv-is*. In declension the υ disappears before vowels, but is retained before consonants, and at the end of the word; thus:—

SINGULAR.	DUAL.	PLURAL.
N. βοῦς, m. or f., an ox or cow.	βό-ε, two oxen.	βό-ες = (βοῦς), oxen.
G. βο-ός (bŏ-v-is)	βο-οῖν	βο-ῶν
D. βο-ΐ (bŏ-v-i)	βο-οῖν	βου-σί
A. βοῦν	βό-ε	(βό-ας) βοῦς
V. βοῦ	βό-ε	βό-ες = (βοῦς)
N. βασιλ-εύς, masc., a king.	βασιλέ-ε, two kings.	βασιλέ-ες, -εῖς, kings.
G. βασιλέ-ως	βασιλέ-οιν	βασιλέ-ων
D. βασιλέ-ϊ, βασιλεῖ	βασιλέ-οιν	βασιλεῦσι
A. βασιλέ-ᾱ	βασιλέ-ε	βασιλέ-ᾱς, -εῖς
V. βασιλ-εῦ	βασιλέ-ε	βασιλέ-ες, -εῖς

19. *N.B.*—In the Third Declension, the α of the accusative singular, and the -ας of the accusative plural, are short; but in nouns in -ευς they are generally long.

20. οὐ or οὐκ means *not*.

πού means *where*, interrogative.

πού, with acute, or without accent, means *somewhere, anywhere*, indefinite.

ἐκεῖ means *there*.

ἐνθάδε means *here*.

EXERCISE XIII.

ὁ βασιλεύς ἐστι σεμνός. ὦ βασιλεῦ, ποῦ ἐστιν ἡ βασίλεια; ὁ νομεὺς καὶ ὁ ἱερεὺς ἐν τῷ τῆς γραὸς κήπῳ ἦσαν. οἱ Πέρσαι τοὺς* βασιλέας (βασιλεῖς) θαυμάζουσι. ὁ νομεὺς εἰς τὸν βασιλέα ἐπιστολὴν γράφει. οἱ νομεῖς ἐνθάδε εἰσί. ἡ τοῦ βασιλέως κόρη ἐκεῖ ἐστι. ποῦ εἰσιν οἱ ἱερεῖς; βοῦν ἄγριον οἱ νομεῖς διώκουσιν εἰς τὴν ὕλην. τὸν μέγαν βοῦν θαυμάζει ἡ γραῦς. ἡ ναῦς οὐκ ἦν ἐν τῷ λιμένι. ἐκεῖ ἦσαν οἱ ἱππεῖς. τοὺς ἱππέας ἐνθάδε λείπει ὁ στρατηγός. ὁ νομεὺς σὺν τοῖς βουσὶ ἐν τῷ λειμῶνί που ἦν. τὴν μεγάλην βοῦν ἐσθίει ὁ λέων. ἡ κόρη τοὺς γονέας (γονεῖς) ἐνθάδε λείπει. τὰ κέρατα τοῦ βοὸς μακρά ἐστι. οἱ στρατιῶται τὴν γέφυραν φυλάττουσι.

Old-woman! why do you run to the city? The shepherd pursues a gazelle into the wood. The force of habit is great. The horseman's chest is broad. The old-woman writes a letter to her daughter's child.

---

* The article is often equal to the possessive pronoun, so here we translate τοὺς *their*.

The barber shaves the king. Where are the cavalry of the king? The king's ship is here in the harbour. The horseman pursues the shepherd out of the city towards the mountain. The prophet sees a certain portion of the city. Where were the boy's parents? The two priests are somewhere in the city. The two boys are throwing balls down the mountain. The giant stalks down from the mountain towards the sea. A certain man had a black dog.

21. Besides the *seven classes* above enumerated, there are a few irregular nouns, which cannot be reduced to any class. They will be found in the Grammar, or will be met with in the course of reading.

SECTION V.
CONTRACTION.

1. When two vowels (belonging to different syllables) meet in the same word, they are usually (in the Attic dialect) combined either into a diphthong or a long vowel. This is called *Contraction.* The meeting of two vowels is called a *concursus.*

2. GENERAL RULE.—*The former member of the concursus absorbs the latter;* as, ἔαρ = ἦρ; ἀέκων = ἄκων; τιμήεν = τιμῆν.

> *Exceptions.*—(1.) Two vowels that can form a diphthong are contracted by *synæresis,*— *i.e.,* by simply removing the *diæresis;* as, πάϊς = παῖς; βασιλέϊ = βασιλεῖ; Λητόϊ = Λητοῖ.

(2.) Two short vowels, if identical, are contracted into their kindred diphthong; if not, into -ου; as, βασιλέ-ες = βασιλεῖς;[*] αἰδόος = αἰδοῦς; φιλέομεν = φιλοῦμεν; δηλόετε = δηλοῦτε.

(3.) ε before ω, and α before ο or ω, reverse the rule; as, φιλέω = φιλῶ; τιμάομεν = τιμῶμεν; τιμάω = τιμῶ.

3. SPECIAL RULE.—*When the latter member of the concursus is a diphthong, its* prepositive[†] *unites with the former member, and its* subjunctive *with the result, ι being subscribed;* as, τιμάεις = τιμᾷς; τιμάοιμι = τιμῷμι.

Exceptions.—(1.) ου after α drops its subjunctive; as, τιμάουσα = τιμῶσα; τιμάουσι = τιμῶσι.

(2.) ο before a diphthong expels the prepositive and unites with the subjunctive; as, δηλόει = δηλοῖ; δηλόῃ = δηλοῖ.

(3.) ε before a diphthong disappears; as, φιλέεις = φιλεῖς; φιλέουσα = φιλοῦσα; φιλέῃς = φιλῇς.

4. In the Third Declension—

(1.) Nouns like ἰχθύς (Class II.) contract in the nominative, vocative, and accusative plural.

(2.) Nouns like μάντις (VI.) contract in the dative singular, and nominative, vocative, and accusative plural.

---

[*] But εε sometimes make η.   [†] See Section I., 7.

(3.) Nouns like τεῖχος (VI.) contract in all cases where two vowels meet.

(4.) Nouns like βασιλεύς (VII.) contract in the dative singular, and nominative, vocative, and accusative plural.

(5.) Nouns like βοῦς (VII.) contract in the nominative, vocative, and accusative plural.

5. (SYNTAX) RULE X.—*The relative agrees with its antecedent in gender, number, and person.*

The relative pronoun, ὅς, ἥ, ὅ, *who, which, that:*—

	SINGULAR.			DUAL.			PLURAL.		
	Masc.	Fem.	Neut.	Masc.	Fem.	Neut.	Masc.	Fem.	Neut.
N.	ὅς	ἥ	ὅ	ὤ	ἅ	ὤ	οἵ	αἵ	ἅ
G.	οὗ	ἧς	οὗ	οἷν	αἷν	οἷν	ὧν	ὧν	ὧν
D.	ᾧ	ᾗ	ᾧ	οἷν	αἷν	οἷν	οἷς	αἷς	οἷς
A.	ὅν	ἥν	ὅ	ὤ	ἅ	ὤ	οὕς	ἅς	ἅ

EXERCISE XIV.

τὰ τῆς πόλεως τείχη ὑψηλά ἐστιν. οἱ ὄφεις τὰ ὄρη λείπουσι. κατὰ τῆς τοῦ ὄρους κορυφῆς θέουσιν οἱ ποιμένες. οἱ κύνες οὓς βλέπεις λαγὼν ἀνὰ τὰ ἄλση διώκουσιν. ἐν τῷ ὄρει, ὃ θαυμάζετε, ὄφεις εἰσὶ πολλοί. ἰχθῦς τινας καλοὺς ἐν τῷ ποταμῷ, ὃς ἀνὰ τὸ ἄλσος ῥεῖ, βλέπουσιν οἱ παῖδες. ἡ σφαῖρα ἣν ῥίπτεις χρυσῆ ἐστι. νεανίας τις πολλὰ βέλη ἔχει. τὰ χείλη τῆς κόρης ὠχρά ἐστιν. χρυσοῦς ἐστιν ὁ πέλεκυς. χρυσοῖ εἰσιν οἱ πελέκεις. ὁ βασιλεὺς τοὺς μάντεις* πείθει.

---

* The accusative plural of the Third Declension contracts like the nominative plural, contrary to the Rule; thus μάντεας should become μάντης by the General Rule, but it is actually contracted into μάντεις.

τὰ μῆλα ἃ ἐσθίομεν ἐν μέρει τινὶ τοῦ ἄλσους εὑρίσκει ὁ δοῦλος. τοὺς τοῦ γεωργοῦ βοῦς ὁ τοῦ γείτονος κύων ἐκ τοῦ χόρτου διώκει. ἔν τε τοῖς ἄλσεσι καὶ βάθεσι τῶν ὑλῶν ἄνθη ἐστὶ πολλά.

Some parts of the city are visible. The weapons of the soldiers are bright. The parents of the boy write to the king. The lips of the girl are white. He admires the white lips of the infant. The slave shaves the horseman's beard. The horsemen who are descending from the mountain are throwing their javelins against the lines of infantry in the plain. There are many wicked men in the city.

SECTION VI.
ADJECTIVE NOUNS.

1. Adjectives may be divided into three classes:—

   (1.) Those which have three forms, one for each gender; as, σεμνός, *masc.*; σεμνή, *fem.*; σεμνόν, *neut.*: εὐρύς, *masc.*; εὐρεῖα, *fem.*; εὐρύ, *neut.* To this class belong all participles.

   (2.) Those which have two forms—one for the masculine and feminine in common, and one for the neuter; as, σώφρων, *masc.*; σώφρων, *fem.*; σῶφρον, *neut.*: ἀληθής, *masc.*; ἀληθής, *fem.*; ἀληθές, *neut.*

   (3.) Those which have only one form for all genders; as, ἅρπαξ, *masc.*; ἅρπαξ, *fem.*;

ἅρπαξ, neut.: μάκαρ, masc.; μάκαρ, fem.; μάκαρ, neut.

2. In adjectives of three forms, the feminine is declined like substantives of the First Declension; and the masculine and neuter like those of the Second or Third, according to termination. Thus, σεμνός (masc.) is declined like δοῦλος; σεμνή (fem.) like αὐλή; and σεμνόν (neut.) like μῆλον: εὐρύς (masc.) is declined like πῆχυς, or βαρύς (p. 44); εὐρεῖα, like σκιά; and εὐρύ (neut.) like ἄστυ (neut.), or βαρύ (p. 44).

3. Adjectives of two forms, and those of one form, generally belong to the Third Declension; except such as end (1.) in -ως, as ἵλεως (masc. and fem.) like λαγώς, and ἵλεων like ἀνώγεων; or (2.) in -ος, as ἄλογος (masc. and fem.) like δοῦλος, and ἄλογον (neut.) like μῆλον. But participles in -ως, as τετυφώς (masc.) and τετυφός (neut.), belong to the Third Declension; while the feminine, τετυφυῖα, belongs to the First.

CLASS I.—THREE FORMS.

SINGULAR.

	Masc.	Fem.	Neut.
4. N.	σεμν-ός, venerable.	σεμν-ή	σεμν-όν
G.	σεμν-οῦ	σεμν-ῆς	σεμν-οῦ
D.	σεμν-ῷ	σεμν-ῇ	σεμν-ῷ
A.	σεμν-όν	σεμν-ήν	σεμν-όν
V.	σεμν-έ	σεμν-ή	σεμν-όν

DUAL.

N. A. & V.	σεμν-ώ	σεμν-ά	σεμν-ώ
G. & D.	σεμν-οῖν	σεμν-αῖν	σεμν-οῖν

	Masc.	PLURAL. Fem.	Neut.
N. & V.	σεμν-οί	σεμν-αί	σεμν-ά
G.	σεμν-ῶν	σεμν-ῶν	σεμν-ῶν
D.	σεμν-οῖς	σεμν-αῖς	σεμν-οῖς
A.	σεμν-ούς	σεμν-άς	σεμν-ά

	Masc.	SINGULAR. Fem.	Neut.
N.	βαρ-ύς, heavy.	βαρ-εῖα	βαρ-ύ
G.	βαρ-έος*	βαρ-είας	βαρ-έος
D.	βαρ-έϊ, -εῖ	βαρ-είᾳ	βαρ-έϊ, -εῖ
A.	βαρ-ύν	βαρ-εῖαν	βαρ-ύ
V.	βαρ-ύ	βαρ-εῖα	βαρ-ύ

		DUAL.	
N. A. & V.	βαρ-έε	βαρ-εία	βαρ-έε
G. & D.	βαρ-έοιν	βαρ-είαιν	βαρ-έοιν

		PLURAL.	
N. & V.	βαρ-έες, -εῖς	βαρ-εῖαι	βαρ-έα
G.	βαρ-έων	βαρ-ειῶν	βαρ-έων
D.	βαρ-έσι	βαρ-είαις	βαρ-έσι
A.	βαρ-έας, -εῖς	βαρ-είας	βαρ-έα

	Masc.	SINGULAR. Fem.	Neut.
N.	χαρίεις (for χαρίεντς)† beautiful.	χαρίεσσ-α	χαρίεν
G.	χαρίεντ-ος	χαρίεσσ-ης	χαρίεντ-ος
D.	χαρίεντ-ι	χαρίεσσ-ῃ	χαρίεντ-ι
A.	χαρίεντ-α	χαρίεσσ-αν	χαρίεν
V.	χαρίεν	χαρίεσσ-α	χαρίεν

---

* Adjectives have the genitive in -εος, but substantives, as πῆχυς, in -εως. Neuters, however, like ἄστυ, very seldom take -εως.

† See note to declension of λεών, p. 31.

	Masc.	DUAL. Fem.	Neut.
N. A. & V.	χαρίεντ-ε	χαριέσσ-ᾱ	χαρίεντ-ε
G. & D.	χαριέντ-οιν	χαριέσσ-αιν	χαριέντ-οιν

PLURAL.

	Masc.	Fem.	Neut.
N. & V.	χαρίεντ-ες	χαρίεσσ-αι	χαρίεντ-α
G.	χαριέντ-ων	χαριεσσ-ῶν	χαριέντ-ων
D.	χαρίεσ-ι	χαριέσσ-αις	χαρίεσ-ι
A.	χαρίεντ-ας	χαριέσσ-ας	χαρίεντ-α

5. Like χαρίεις are declined all participles in -είς, -εῖσα, -έν; as, τιθείς, τιθεῖσα, τιθέν; except that (1.) In participles the vocative masculine is the *same* as the nominative; and (2.) The dative plural has -εισι, not εσι.*

SINGULAR.

	Masc.	Fem.	Neut.
N. & V.	πᾶς, every, all	πᾶσ-α	πᾶν
G.	παντ-ός	πάσ-ης	παντ-ός
D.	παντ-ί	πάσ-ῃ	παντ-ί
A.	πάντ-α	πᾶσ-αν	πᾶν

DUAL.

	Masc.	Fem.	Neut.
N. A. & V.	πάντ-ε	πάσ-α	πάντ-ε
G. & D.	πάντ-οιν	πάσ-αιν	πάντ-οιν

PLURAL.

	Masc.	Fem.	Neut.
N. & V.	πάντ-ες	πᾶσ-αι	πάντ-α
G.	πάντ-ων	πασ-ῶν	πάντ-ων
D.	πᾶσι	πάσ-αις	πᾶσι
A.	πάντ-ας	πάσ-ας	πάντ-α

6. So the adjective μέλας, μέλαινα, μέλαν, and all participles in -ας, -ασα, -αν; as, στάς, στᾶσα, στάν;

---

* See note to declension of λέων, p 31.

τύψας, τυψᾶσα, τύψαν. The masculine belongs to Class V. (Third Declension), the neuter to Class IV., and the feminine to the First Declension, like ἄκανθα.

The adjectives πολύς, *much*, and μέγας, *great*, are irregular in the nominative, accusative, and vocative singular, masculine and neuter.

SINGULAR.

	Masc.	Fem.	Neut.
N.	πολ-ύς, much, many.	πολλ-ή	πολ-ύ
G.	πολλ-οῦ	πολλ-ῆς	πολλ-οῦ
D.	πολλ-ῷ	πολλ-ῇ	πολλ-ῷ
A.	πολ-ύν	πολλ-ήν	πολ-ύ
V.	πολ-ύ	πολλ-ή	πολ-ύ

PLURAL.

N. & V.	πολλ-οί	πολλ-αί	πολλ-ά
G.	πολλ-ῶν	πολλ-ῶν	πολλ-ῶν
D.	πολλ-οῖς	πολλ-αῖς	πολλ-οῖς
A.	πολλ-ούς	πολλ-άς	πολλ-ά

SINGULAR.

	Masc.	Fem.	Neut.
N.	μέγ-ας, great, large.	μεγάλ-η	μέγ-α
G.	μεγάλ-ου	μεγάλ-ης	μεγάλ-ου
D.	μεγάλ-ῳ	μεγάλ-η	μεγάλ-ῳ
A.	μέγ-αν	μεγάλ-ην	μέγ-α
V.	μέγ-α	μεγάλ-η	μέγ-α

PLURAL.

N. & V.	μεγάλ-οι	μεγάλ-αι	μεγάλ-α
G.	μεγάλ-ων	μεγάλ-ων	μεγάλ-ων
D.	μεγάλ-οις	μεγάλ-αις	μεγάλ-οις
A.	μεγάλ-ους	μεγάλ-ας	μεγάλ-α

CLASS II.—TWO FORMS.

SINGULAR.

	Masc. and Fem.	Neut.
7. N.	ἀληθ-ής, true, genuine.	ἀληθ-ές
G.	ἀληθ-έος, -οῦς	ἀληθ-έος, -οῦς
D.	ἀληθ-έϊ, -εῖ	ἀληθ-έϊ, -εῖ
A.	ἀληθ-έα, -ῆ	ἀληθ-ές
V.	ἀληθ-ές	ἀληθ-ές

DUAL.

N. A. & V.	ἀληθ-έε, -ῆ	ἀληθ-έε, -ῆ
G. & D.	ἀληθ-έοιν, -οῖν	ἀληθ-έοιν, -οῖν

PLURAL.

N. & V.	ἀληθ-έες, -εῖς	ἀληθ-έα, -ῆ
G.	ἀληθ-έων, -ῶν	ἀληθ-έων, -ῶν
D.	ἀληθ-έσι	ἀληθ-έσι
A.	ἀληθ-έας, -εῖς	ἀληθ-έα, -ῆ

8. Adjectives like σώφρων are declined, in masculine and feminine, as substantives of Class III. (Third Declension); and their neuter in -ον, like σῶφρον, as those of Class I. Those in -ος, -ον, are of the Second Declension, and are regular. All those of other terminations may be easily referred to their proper classes.

CLASS III.—ONE FORM.

9. The adjectives of this class require no paradigm. They are almost all of the Third Declension, and may be readily referred to their proper classes. Thus μάκαρ, μάκαρ-ος, belongs to Class I. of substantives;

φυγάς, φυγάδος, to Class V. The great majority of one-form adjectives have no neuter.

SECTION VII.

COMPARISON OF ADJECTIVES.

1. GENERAL RULE.—*To form the comparative and superlative degrees add -τερος and -τατος, respectively, to the simple stem of the positive; as,—*

POSITIVE.	COMPARATIVE.	SUPERLATIVE.
μάκαρ	μακάρ-τερος	μακάρ-τατος
μέλας (stem μέλαν)	μελάν-τερος	μελάν-τατος
φίλ-ος*	φίλ-τερος	φίλ-τατος
γεραι-ός	γεραί-τερος	γεραί-τατος

2. *Exception.*—But adjectives in -υς retain the substituted vowel of the nominative† (*i.e.*, υ instead of ε, as in γλυκ-έ-ος; see Class VI. of substantives, Third Declension); as, γλυκύ-ς (for γλυκές), γλυκύ-τερος, γλυκύ-τατος.

3. Some adjectives insert a euphonic or strengthening syllable between the stem and the comparative termination:—

(a) ο‡ is inserted when the last syllable of the stem of the positive is long; as,—

---

* Φίλος has four forms: φιλώτερος, φιλαίτερος, φιλίων, and that given above.

† Most of the peculiarities which are observable in the addition of the comparative terminations to the radical syllable of the adjective are also found in the formation of compound words; thus, as we have γλυκ-ύ-τερος, and not γλυκ-έ-τερος, so we find ἡδ-υ-λόγος, not ἡδ-ε-λόγος; and ἀστ-υ-νόμος, not ἀστ-ε-νόμος. See following notes.

‡ Compare the compounds ῥιζ-ο-τόμος, λογ-ο-γράφος, λειπ-ό-ταξις, &c.

κοῦφ-ος   κουφ-ό-τερος   κουφ-ό-τατος
σεμν-ός   σεμν-ό-τερος   σεμν-ό-τατος

(β) ω* is inserted when the last syllable of the stem is short; as,—

σοφ-ός   σοφ-ώ-τερος   σοφ-ώ-τατος
ἄξι-ος   ἀξι-ώ-τερος   ἀξι-ώ-τατος
ἐπίχαρις, (stem ἐπιχαριτ-) } ἐπιχαριτ-ώ-τερος   ἐπιχαριτ-ώ-τατος
πορφύρεος,   πορφυρε-ώ-τερος,   πορφυρε-ώ-τατος,
contracted   contracted   contracted
πορφυροῦς   πορφυρ-ώ-τερος   πορφυρ-ώ-τατος

(γ) αι† is inserted; as,—

μέσ-ος   μεσ-αί-τερος   μεσ-αί-τατος
φίλ-ος   φιλ-αί-τερος   φιλ-αί-τατος
ἥσυχ-ος   ἡσυχ-αί-τερος   ἡσυχ-αί-τατος

(δ) A few insert ς, or -ες, or -ις;‡ as,—

ἀληθής   ἀληθέ-σ-τερος   ἀληθέ-σ-τατος
σώφρων   σωφρον-έσ-τερος   σωφρον-έσ-τατος
ἄφθον-ος   { ἀφθον-έσ-τερος,   ἀφθον-έσ-τατος,
                  but also   but also
                  ἀφθον-ώ-τερος   ἀφθον-ώ-τατος
λάλ-ος   λαλ-ίσ-τερος   λαλ-ίσ-τατος

---

* Compare the compounds ὀρε-ω-κόμος, κρε-ω-πώλης.
† Compare the compounds μεσ-αι-πόλιος, μαλακ-αί-πους.
‡ Compare the compounds σακε-σ-φόρος, ὀρέ-σ-βιος, ὀρέ-σ-τερος, θέ-σ-φατος, παυ-σ-άνεμος, φω-σ-φόρος, φερ-έσ-βιος, λιπ-εσ-ήνωρ, αἰχ-ι-βάτης. Some scholars consider the -αι- and -εσ- in such forms as μεσ-αί-τερος and σωφρον-έσ-τερος to be double comparatives, and they think the germs of these syllables are readily found in Sanscrit (see Jelf's Greek Grammar, I. p. 130). But it is not easy to explain how a comparative or superlative termination could find a place in such compound nouns as those given in the notes above. Whatever the *origin* of the syllables -αι- and -εσ- may be, it seems evident that they were used in the *compounds* and the *comparatives* for the *same purpose*. The objections to the Sanscrit theory are many, but this is not the place to advance them.

Also, χαρίεις = χαρίεντς, makes χαριέ-σ-τερος, χαριέ-σ-τατος, the ν and τ being thrown out before ς, and compensation (see note, p. 31) being neglected, as in the dative plural (see declension of χαρίεις, pp. 44 and 45).

4. Some adjectives add -ίων and -ιστος to form the comparative and superlative; as,—

ἡδ-ύς   ἡδ-ίων   ἥδ-ιστος
αἰσχ-ρός   αἰσχ-ίων   αἴσχ-ιστος
καλ-ός   καλλ-ίων   κάλλ-ιστος,

in which last the final λ of the stem is doubled.

_{5. This mode of comparison is used principally by adjectives in υς; but many of these have also the other terminations, -τερος and -τατος.}

6. The comparative and superlative notions are also expressed by joining the adverbs μᾶλλον (*magis*), and μάλιστα (*maxime*), with the simple adjective; as, θνητὸς μᾶλλον, *more liable to death*.

7. The following list contains those irregular comparatives and superlatives which most frequently occur:—

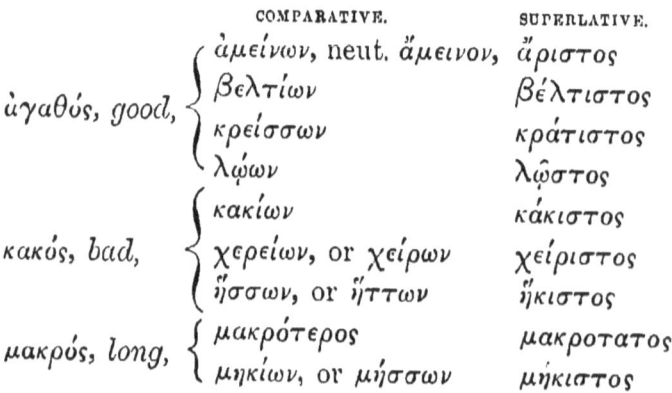

	COMPARATIVE.	SUPERLATIVE.
ἀγαθός, *good*,	ἀμείνων, neut. ἄμεινον,	ἄριστος
	βελτίων	βέλτιστος
	κρείσσων	κράτιστος
	λώων	λῷστος
κακός, *bad*,	κακίων	κάκιστος
	χερείων, or χείρων	χείριστος
	ἥσσων, or ἥττων	ἥκιστος
μακρός, *long*,	μακρότερος	μακρότατος
	μηκίων, or μήσσων	μήκιστος

	COMPARATIVE.	SUPERLATIVE.
μικρός,	μικρότερος ἐλάσσων μείων	μικρότατος ἐλάχιστος
πολύς, *much*,	πλείων, or πλέων	πλεῖστος
ῥᾴδιος, *easy*,	ῥᾴων	ῥᾷστος
μέγας, *great*,	μείζων	μέγιστος

8. The preposition ἀμφί means *on both sides of, around, about*. It governs the accusative, genitive, and dative, but in prose, most usually the accusative.

9. (SYNTAX) RULE XI.—*The comparative degree governs the genitive of the object with which comparison is instituted;* as, γλυκίων μέλιτος, sweeter than honey.

EXERCISE XV.

ὁ υἱὸς μείζων ἐστὶ τοῦ πατρός. ἡ κόρη καλλίων ἐστὶ τῆς μητρός. ἡ βασίλεια τλημονεστάτη ἐστὶ πασῶν γυναικῶν. ἡ θεὰ σεμνοτάτη ἐστίν. τὰ ἀμφὶ τὴν κώμην ὄρη ὑψηλότατά ἐστιν. ὁ λέων θαρσύτερός ἐστι τοῦ θωός. οἱ ὄρτυγες τὰς οὐρὰς βραχυτάτας ἔχουσιν. ἡ κέρκος τοῦ ταῶ λαμπροτάτη ἐστίν. ἡ γέφυρα εὐρυτέρα ἐστὶ τῆς ὁδοῦ. ἡ ὁδὸς εὐρυτέρα ἐστὶ τῆς γεφύρας. ἡ λέαινα ἀγριωτέρα ἐστὶ τοῦ λέοντος. οἱ κύνες σοφώτεροί εἰσι τῶν βοῶν. τὰ τοῦ ἰατροῦ ξυρὰ ὀξύτατά ἐστιν. τὰ μῆλα ἐν τῷ τοῦ βασιλέως κήπῳ γλυκύτατά ἐστι. ἐν τῇ ὕλῃ, τῇ πρὸς τῷ ποταμῷ, πλεῖσται ἦσαν αἴγειροι. τίς ἐστι σοφώτατος πάντων; πότερός ἐστι σοφώτερος; ἡ φήμη ἀληθεστάτη ἐστίν. ὁ παῖς λαλίστατός ἐστιν.

αἱ στολαὶ τῆς ἐμῆς μητρὸς χαριέσταταί εἰσιν. ὦ
λῷστε Σώκρατες! μελάντατοι οἱ Ἰνδοὶ καὶ δειλότατοί
εἰσιν. ὁ βαθύτατος ὕπνος ἥδιστός ἐστιν. ῥᾴων τίς
ἐστι καὶ βραχυτέρα πρὸς τὸ ἄστυ ὁδός.

Through* the city there flows a very beautiful†
river. My father has some very ferocious dogs.
Which of the rivers is the deepest? All the boys
are striking at the largest ball. The army of Cyrus
was very great. The waves of the sea were very
long. The slaves carry very light wallets. The
wallets of the slave are lighter than those of his
master. The army is guarding a very narrow
bridge. The crane has a very long neck. The
wine is very old. The master is teaching a very
ignorant boy. The boys and the dogs are pursuing
a very savage bear into the thickest part of the
forest.

SECTION VIII.

THE NUMERALS.

1. The Numerals are in reality adjectives. The
two principal classes are the Cardinals and the
Ordinals. The first four Cardinals are declinable, but
from 5 to 100 they are all indeclinable. The
Ordinals, however, are regular adjectives of three
forms.

---

* Διά, *through*, governs sometimes the accusative, but more usually the genitive.
In this case use the genitive.
† Use the superlative degree.

FIRST GREEK READER.

εἷς, ONE.

	Masc.	Fem.	Neut.
N.	εἷς	μία	ἕν
G.	ἑν-ός	μιᾶς	ἑν-ός
D.	ἑν-ί	μιᾷ	ἑν-ί
A.	ἕνα	μίαν	ἕν

δύο, TWO.

δύ-ο (for all genders)
δυ-οῖν
δυ-οῖν
δύ-ο

τρεῖς, THREE.

	Masc.	Fem.	Neut.
N.	τρεῖς	τρεῖς	τρία
G.	τριῶν	τριῶν	τριῶν
D.	τρισί	τρισί	τρισί
A.	τρεῖς	τρεῖς	τρία

τέσσαρες, FOUR.

N.	τέσσαρες	τέσσαρες	τέσσαρα
G.	τεσσάρων	τεσσάρων	τεσσάρων
D.	τέσσαρσι	τέσσαρσι	τέσσαρσι
A.	τέσσαρας	τέσσαρας	τέσσαρα

Like εἷς are declined its compounds, οὐδείς and μηδείς, no-one.

CARDINALS.	ORDINALS.	MULTIPLICATIVES.
1. εἷς, μία, ἕν, one.	πρῶτος, first.	ἅπαξ, once.
2. δύο	δεύτερος	δίς
3. τρεῖς, τρεῖς, τρία	τρίτος,	τρίς
4. τέσσαρες	τέταρτος	τετράκις
5. πέντε	πέμπτος	πεντάκις
6. ἕξ	ἕκτος	ἑξάκις
7. ἑπτά	ἕβδομος	ἑπτάκις
8. ὀκτώ	ὄγδοος	ὀκτάκις
9. ἐννέα	ἔννατος	ἐννεάκις
10. δέκα	δέκατος	δεκάκις

CARDINALS.	ORDINALS.	MULTIPLICATIVES.
11. ἕνδεκα	ἑνδέκατος	ἑνδεκάκις
12. δώδεκα	δωδέκατος	δωδεκάκις
20. εἴκοσι	εἰκοστός	εἰκοσάκις
100. ἑκατόν	ἑκατοστός	ἑκατονάκις
1000. χίλιοι	χιλιοστός	χιλιάκις
10,000. μύριοι	μυριοστός	μυριάκις

For the intermediate numbers, see Greek Grammar.

SECTION IX.

PRONOUNS.

PERSONAL PRONOUNS.

SINGULAR.	DUAL.	PLURAL.
1. N. ἐγώ,	νώ,	ἡμεῖς,
I [ego].	we two.	we.
G. ἐμοῦ, or μοῦ,	νῷν,	ἡμῶν,
of me.	of us two.	of us.
D. ἐμοί, or μοί,	νῷν,	ἡμῖν,
to or for me.	to or for us two.	to or for us.
A. ἐμέ, or μέ,	νώ,	ἡμᾶς,
me.	us two.	us.

SINGULAR.	DUAL.	PLURAL.
N. σύ,	σφώ,	ὑμεῖς,
thou [tu].	you two.	you.
G. σοῦ	σφῷν	ὑμῶν
D. σοί	σφῷν	ὑμῖν
A. σέ	σφώ	ὑμᾶς

SINGULAR.	DUAL.	PLURAL.
N. —		σφεῖς
G. οὗ [sui]		σφῶν
D. οἷ [sibi]		σφίσι
A. ἕ [se]		σφᾶς

2. The parts μέ, μοῦ, μοί, σέ, σοῦ, σοί, οἷ, and σφίσι, are enclitics (see Appendix, on Accents); but the emphatic forms, ἐμοῦ, &c., retain their accent. οὗ and ἕ are non-Attic, at least in prose.

3. The pronoun αὐτός is a regular adjective like σεμνός (p. 43); except that (1.) The nominative and accusative neuter end in -ο, not -ον (see ὅς, p. 41); and (2.) The vocative is wanting. αὐτός serves as the adjunctive pronoun *ipse*, in the nominative case, and when joined in agreement with a substantive; but when it stands alone (*i.e.*, without the article or a substantive) it answers to *is*, *ea*, *id*. ὁ αὐτός is equal to *idem*.

POSSESSIVE PRONOUNS.

4. The possessive pronouns are formed from the personals, and are regular adjectives like σεμνός (p. 43).

SINGULAR.			PLURAL.		
Masc.	Fem.	Neut.	Masc.	Fem.	Neut.
ἐμός, my, mine.	ἐμή,	ἐμόν,	ἡμέτερ-ος, our.	-α,	-ον,
σός, thy, thine	σή,	σόν,	ὑμέτερ-ος, your.	-α,	-ον,
(ὅς,* his.	ἥ,	ὅν,)	σφέτερ-ος, their.	-α,	-ον,

REFLEXIVE PRONOUNS.

5. These pronouns are compounded of the accusatives singular of the personal pronouns and the oblique cases of αὐτός (*self*). From their peculiar meaning and use they can have no nominative.

---
* The genitive of αὐτός is generally used instead of this possessive.

FIRST GREEK READER.

	SINGULAR.		PLURAL.	
	Masc.	Fem.	Masc.	Fem.
G.	ἐμαυτ-οῦ, of myself.	-ῆς	ἡμῶν αὐτ-ῶν, of ourselves.	-ῶν
D.	ἐμαυτ-ῷ	-ῇ	ἡμῖν αὐτ-οῖς	-αῖς
A.	ἐμαυτ-όν	-ήν	ἡμᾶς αὐτ-ούς	-άς

	Masc.	Fem.	Masc.	Fem.
G.	σεαυτοῦ, of thyself.	-ῆς,	ὑμῶν αὐτ-ῶν, of yourselves.	-ῶν
D.	σεαυτῷ	-ῇ	ὑμῖν αὐτ-οῖς	-αῖς
A.	σεαυτόν	-ήν	ὑμᾶς αὐτ-ούς	-άς

	Masc.	Fem.	Neut.	Masc.	Fem.	Neut.
G.	ἑαυτοῦ, of himself.	-ῆς herself.	-οῦ itself.	ἑαυτ-ῶν	-ῶν	-ῶν
D.	ἑαυτῷ	-ῇ	-ῷ	ἑαυτ-οῖς	-αῖς	-οῖς
A.	ἑαυτόν	-ήν	-ό	ἑαυτ-ούς	-άς	-ά

Observe, (1.) That the first two reflexives have no neuter; and, (2.) That their plurals are made up of two words. σεαυτόν and ἑαυτόν in their several cases often abbreviate into σαυτόν and αὑτόν, &c.

6. The RECIPROCAL PRONOUN, ἀλλήλους, *one another*, has no singular and no nominative case.

	DUAL.			PLURAL.		
	Masc.	Fem.	Neut.	Masc.	Fem.	Neut.
G.	ἀλλήλοιν	-αιν	-οιν	ἀλλήλων	-ων	-ων
D.	ἀλλήλοιν	-αιν	-οιν	ἀλλήλοις	-αις	-οις
A.	ἀλλήλω	-α	-ω	ἀλλήλους	-ας	-α

DEMONSTRATIVE PRONOUNS.

7. The demonstrative pronouns are, οὗτος (generally equal to *iste*), ὅδε, ἥδε, τόδε (equal to *hic*), and

ἐκεῖνος, η, ο (equal to *ille*). The article ὁ, ἡ, τό was originally a demonstrative; αὐτός is sometimes a demonstrative. Besides these, there are τόσος, η, ον, τοσοῦτος = *tantus*; τοῖος, τοιοῦτος = *talis*, &c.

	SINGULAR.			DUAL.		
	Masc.	Fem.	Neut.	Masc.	Fem.	Neut.
N.	οὗτος*	αὕτη	τοῦτο	τούτω	(ταύτᾱ)	τούτω
G.	τούτου	ταύτης	τούτου	τούτοιν	ταύταιν	τούτοιν
D.	τούτῳ	ταύτῃ	τούτῳ	τούτοιν	ταύταιν	τούτοιν
A.	τοῦτον	ταύτην	τοῦτο	τούτω	(ταύτᾱ)	τούτω

	PLURAL.		
	Masc.	Fem.	Neut.
N.	οὗτοι	αὗται	ταῦτα
G.	τούτων	τούτων	τούτων
D.	τούτοις	ταύταις	τούτοις
A.	τούτους	ταύτας	ταῦτα

8. For the indefinite and interrogative τίς see p. 33; and for the relative ὅς, see p. 41.

9. *The Dative case denotes,—*

(1.) The individual (person or thing) to which anything is given or communicated.

(2.) The individual (person or thing) which is benefited or injured in any way.

---

* Learned men differ as to the origin of this pronoun, but one thing seems plain, that the first part of it is the article ὁ, ἡ, τό. It will be observed, that, like the article, it loses τ in the nominative singular and plural, masculine and feminine; and that wherever the article has the vowels ο, ω, or the diphthong ου (in the masculine and neuter forms), this pronoun has -ου in its first syllable; and that wherever the article has α, η, or the diphthong αι (in the feminine forms), οὗτος has -αυ in its first syllable: as, τόν (*accus.*), τοῦτον; τήν, ταύτην. The only part of the feminine which has τουτ-, as its first syllable, is the genitive plural, because the genitive plural feminine of the article is τῶν, not τᾶν or τῆν.

(3.) The cause why something is done; the manner or circumstances in which it is done; the instrument by which it is done, or the agent by whom it is done.

(4.) Belief in, or obedience to.

(5.) Intercourse with, whether friendly or the opposite.

(6.) Likeness, or equality, or coincidence.

(7.) The place where.

(8.) The time when.

10. When the subject of a verb is a personal pronoun, it is seldom expressed, except when particularly emphatic, as when one individual is to be put in strong contrast to another.

11. μέν (which in derivation is connected with the first numeral, εἷς, μία, ἕν) means, (1.), *In the first place;* (2.), *On the one hand;* (3.), *For my (thy, his, &c.) part.* It is answered by δέ (connected with the second numeral, δύο); which means, (1.), *In the second place;* (2.), *On the other hand;* (3.), *On my (thy, his, &c.) part.*

EXERCISE XVI.

ἐγὼ μὲν φεύγω, σὺ δὲ διώκεις. σὲ θαυμάζω. ἡμεῖς μὲν θαυμάζομεν αὐτόν, ὑμεῖς δὲ οὐ θαυμάζετε. ὁ δοῦλος τὴν κόμην μοι κείρει. ὁ νεανίας πρὸς τὸν ἑαυτοῦ πατέρα ἐπιστολὴν πέμπει. οἱ στρατιῶται ἀλλήλους κελεύουσιν. ὁ παῖς πέντε μῆλα ἔχει. τί τοῦτό ἐστι; ταῦτα μὲν σὺ θαυμάζεις, ἐκεῖνα δὲ ἐγώ ἡ κόρη στέφανόν τινα ἑαυτῇ πλέκει. ταύτῃ τῇ ἡμέρᾳ οἱ Ἕλληνες τὰς Ἀθήνας οὐ λείπουσιν. ὁ κλέπτης τὸν χρυσὸν ἐν τῇ ὕλῃ κρύπτει. οἱ πολῖται καλόν τινα στέφανον τῷ βασιλεῖ πλέκουσιν. ἡμᾶς μὲν πείθει, αὐτὸν δὲ οὔ. ταῦτα τοῖς αὐτοῦ μαθηταῖς διδάσκει. δώδεκά εἰσι μῆνες τοῦ* ἔτους. τὰ Ἑλληνικὰ γράμματά εἰσι τέσσαρα καὶ εἴκοσι.

I indeed (*for my part*) admire him; but my father (*does*) not. The boy strikes the ball with his hand. The slave strikes the dog with a large stone. These things are beautiful. The soldier wounds himself with his sword. On the same day the Persians send ambassadors to Athens. The wild-beast bites the boy with his teeth. The master has† twenty-five slaves. In the tenth month he writes a letter to the king. On the third day the king sends ten ambassadors to Athens. The farmer catches twenty-five hares in one day. The farmer has seven horses, and nine asses. The king is friendly to us. I persuade my dear father with my words. With these words the daughter persuades her mother. We two are guarding our father's house. The two of us are plaiting a wreath for our mother. The slave is hiding our slings for us. My father is friendly to the good.‡

---

* The article is often used in a *distributive* sense; as, τοῦ μηνός, *every month*, i.e., by the month; τοῦ ἔτους, *every year*, i.e., in each year.

† Or, There are to the master twenty-five slaves; the verb εἰμί being used with the dative, as *sum* in Latin.

‡ The substantive is often omitted in Greek, as in Latin, the adjective standing alone.

SECTION X.

THE VERB.

1. There are *two* Conjugations of Greek Verbs— (1.), The First, in which the first singular present indicative ends in -ω; (2.), The Second, which ends in -μι.

2. Verbs in -ω are divided into three classes— *Pure, Mute*, and *Liquid*, according as the last letter of their stem is a *vowel*, a *mute* consonant, or a *liquid*. Thus, λύ-ω is called *pure;* λέγ-ω, *mute;* and μέν-ω, *liquid*.

3. The Greek Verb has three *Voices*—the *Active*, the *Passive*, and the *Middle*. The *middle voice* has always reference to *self*, signifying what one does, or gets done, for or in reference to himself. It thus holds a *middle* position between the active and the passive.

4. There are six Tenses, three of which (the *Present, Future*, and *Perfect*) are called *principal* or *leading* tenses; and three (the *Imperfect, Aorist*, and *Pluperfect*) are called *secondary* or *historical* tenses.

5. It will be noticed that each *leading* tense has a corresponding *secondary*, which takes the same stem, and has a certain connection in meaning.[*] Thus :—

---

[*] The more advanced student should consult on this subject Donaldson's "Cratylus," p. 562, second edition.

LEADING.

| γράφ-ω (*present*). | γράψ-ω (*future*). | γέγραφ-α (*perfect*). |

SECONDARY.

| ἔ-γραφ-ον (*imperfect*). | ἔ-γραψ-α (*aorist*). | ἐ-γεγράφ-ειν (*pluperfect*). |

6. There are *five Moods*—the *Indicative, Subjunctive, Optative, Imperative,* and *Infinitive*.

7. There are three Numbers—*Singular, Dual,* and *Plural*.

8. In conjugating a Greek verb, three kinds of changes must be attended to:—

(1.) The termination is varied.

(2.) In the secondary tenses a prefix is added.

(3.) In certain tenses the radical vowel is modified.

9. The *first* and *third* of these changes are best learned by practice in conjugation; but the second, which is called the *augment*, requires a detailed explanation.

10. The principal varieties of augment are as follows:—

(1.) When a verb begins with a consonant, ε is prefixed; and as this letter forms a syllable in itself, it is called the *syllabic augment;* as, γράφ-ω, ἔ-γραφ-ον.

(2.) When a verb begins with a short vowel, the initial letter is changed into its corresponding long; and as the *time* (*tempus*) or *quantity* of the syllable is thus lengthened, this kind of increase is called the *temporal augment;* as ἐλπίζω, ἤλπιζον.

Exception.—But ἔχω, *I have*, and some other verbs, change ε into ει; as, imperfect εἶχον.

(3.) When a verb begins with a *proper* or *genuine diphthong,* the augment is made by changing the proper diphthong into its corresponding *improper;* as, αἰτέω, ᾔτεον (ᾔτουν).

Note.—When a verb begins with a long vowel, or an improper diphthong, no change takes place.*

11. Verbs beginning with a *single* consonant, or with two consonants (*provided* they are a mute and a liquid, with the mute first), take, in the perfect and pluperfect, the initial consonant, together with the usual syllabic augment; as, γέ-γραφ-α. This is called reduplication.

Note.—But if a verb begin with an *aspirate,* the corresponding *Light* is used in the reduplication; as, φιλέω, πε-φίληκα, not φεφίληκα.

---

* There are numerous peculiarities in the verbal augment, which will be found at one view in any Greek Grammar, and which will be introduced in the after-part of this work, as occasion may require.

SECTION XI.

CLASS I.—PURE VERBS.

1. Pure Verbs are the most simple in their conjugation. They have no second aorist, nor second perfect. But observe,—

(1.) That most pure verbs insert ς in the first aorist, perfect, and pluperfect passive.

(2.) That those in -αω, -εω, -οω, contract concurrent vowels in the present and imperfect. But dissyllabic verbs in -έω contract only εε and εει into ει ; as, πλέ-εις, πλεῖς. The concursus εο is not contracted ; as, πλέομεν.

(3.) That those in -εω and -αω make the future in -ησω; and those in -οω, in -ωσω. But there are many exceptions.

Observe (1.) That the indicative adopts short vowels in its inflexions, while the subjunctive takes long ones, and the optative diphthongs ; as, λύ-ε-τον (indicative), λύ-η-τον (subjunctive), λύ-οι-τον (optative.)

(2.) That each leading tense and its corresponding secondary have a stem peculiar to themselves. The letter pointing out the tense, and ending this *secondary* stem, is called the "tense characteristic ;" thus, σ is the tense characteristic of the future, λύ-σ-ω, and of the first aorist, ἔ-λυ-σ-α, and κ (or in some verbs ά) of the perfect and pluperfect. While λυ- is the stem proper of the whole verb, λυσ- may be taken as a *secondary* stem of the future and aorist 1, and λελυκ- of the perfect.

(3.) There is also a special termination for each person ; and thus we have several elements in one verbal form,—*e.g.*, in λυ-σ-ω-μεν (first aorist subjunctive), λυ- is the stem, σ the tense characteristic, ω the modal (mood) vowel, and μεν the person ending. A careful distinction of these will be of much service to the student in learning the Greek verb.

PURE

The student will observe that λυ-, the radical syllable marked. The double line indicates a

ACTIVE

INDICATIVE.	SUBJUNCTIVE.	OPTATIVE.
Pres.—(I am loosing, &c.) S. λύ-ω, -εις, -ει D. —, λύ-ετον, -ετον P. λύ-ομεν, -ετε, -ουσι	(I may loose, &c.) λύ-ω, -ῃς, -ῃ —, λύ-ητον, -ητον λύ-ωμεν, -ητε, -ωσι	(I might loose, &c.) λύ-οιμι, -οις, -οι —, λύ-οιτον, -οίτην λύ-οιμεν, -οιτε, -οιεν
Imperf.—(I was loosing &c.) S. ἔ-λῦ-ον, -ες, -ε D. —, ἐλύ-ετον, -έτην P. ἐλύ-ομεν, -ετε, -ον	wanting	wanting
Fut.—(I shall or will loose, &c.) S. λύσ-ω, -εις, -ει D. —, λύσ-ετον, -ετον P. λύσ-ομεν, -ετε, -ουσι	wanting	(I might be about to loose, &c.) λύσ-οιμι, -οις, -οι —, λύσ-οιτον, -οίτην λύσ-οιμεν, -οιτε, -οιεν
Aor.—(I loosed, &c.) S. ἔ-λῦσ-α, -ας, -ε D. —, ἐλύσ-ατον, -άτην P. ἐλύσ-αμεν, -ατε, -αν	(I may have loosed, &c.) λύσ-ω, -ῃς, -ῃ —, λύσ-ητον, -ητον λύσ-ωμεν, -ητε, -ωσι	(I might have loosed, &c.) λύσ-αιμι, -ειας, (-αις,) -ειε, (-αι) —, λύσ-αιτον, -αίτην λύσ-αιμεν, -αιτε, -ειαν, (-αιεν)
Perf.—(I have loosed, &c.) S. λέ-λῦκ-α, -ας, -ε D. —, λελύκ-ατον, -ατον P. λελύκ-αμεν, -ατε, -άσι	(I may have loosed, &c.) λελύκ-ω, -ῃς, -ῃ —, λελύκ-ητον, -ητον λελύκ-ωμεν, -ητε, -ωσι	(I might have loosed, &c.) λελύκ-οιμι, -οις, -οι —, λελύκ-οιτον, -οίτην λελύκ-οιμεν, -οιτε, -οιεν
Plup.—(I had loosed, &c.) S. ἐ-λε-λύκ-ειν, -εις, -ει D. —, ἐλελύκ-ειτον, -είτην P. ἐλελύκ-ειμεν, -ειτε, -εισαν, or -εσαν	wanting	wanting

VERBS.

of λύ-ω, is long in some tenses and short in others, as change of stem. See Section X. 4, 5.

VOICE.

IMPERATIVE.	INFINITIVE.	PARTICIPLE.
(Be thou loosing, &c.) —, λῦ-ε, -έτω —·, λύ-ετον, -έτων —, λύ-ετε, -όντων (or -έτωσαν)	(To be loosing, &c.) λύ-ειν	(Loosing, &c.) λύ-ων, gen. -οντος λύ-ουσα, gen. -ούσης λῦ-ον, gen. -οντος
wanting	wanting	wanting
wanting	(To be about to loose, &c.) λύσ-ειν	(About to loose, &c.) λύσ-ων, gen. -οντος λύσ-ουσα, gen. -ούσης λῦσ-ον, gen. -οντος
(Loose thou, &c.) —, λῦσ-ον, -άτω —·, λῦσ-ατον, -άτων —, λῦσ-ατε, -άντων (or -άτωσαν)	(To loose, &c.) λῦσ-αι	(Having loosed, &c.) λύσ-ας, gen. -αντος λύσ-ασα, gen. -άσης λῦσ-αν, gen. -αντος
(Have thou loosed, &c.) —, λέλυκ-ε, -έτω —, λελύκ ετον, -έτων —, λελύκ-ετε, -έτωσαν (found only in those verbs whose perfect is used as a present.)	(To have loosed, &c.) λελυκ-έναι	(Having loosed, &c.) λελυκ-ώς, gen. -ότος λελυκ-υῖα, gen. -υίας λελυκ-ός, gen. -ότος
wanting	wanting	wanting

PURE VERBS
PASSIVE

INDICATIVE.	SUBJUNCTIVE.	OPTATIVE.
Pres.—(I am loosed, or set free, &c.) S. λύ-ο-μαι, -ει (or -ῃ), -ε-ται D. λυ-ό-μεθον, -ε-σθον, -ε-σθον P. λυ-ό-μεθα, -ε-σθε, -ο-νται	(I may be set free, &c.) λύ-ω-μαι, -ῃ, -η-ται λυ-ώ-μεθον, -η-σθον, -η-σθον λυ-ώ-μεθα, -η-σθε, -ω-νται	(I might be set free, &c.) λυ-οί-μην, -οι-ο, -οι-το λυ-οί-μεθον, -οι-σθον, -οί-σθην λυ-οί-μεθα, -οι-σθε, -οί-ντο
Imperf.—(I was being set free, &c.) S. ἐ-λῡ-ό-μην, -ου, -ε-το D. ἐλυ-ό-μεθον, -ε-σθον, -έ-σθην P. ἐλυ-ό-μεθα, -ε-σθε, -ο-ντο	wanting	wanting
Fut.—(I shall or will be set free, &c.) S. λυθήσ-ο-μαι, -ει (or ῃ), -ε-ται D. λυθησ-ό-μεθον, -ε-σθον, -ε-σθον P. λυθησ-ό-μεθα, -ε-σθε, -ο νται	wanting	(I might be about to be set free, &c.) λυθησ-οί-μην, -οι-ο, -οι-το λυθησ-οί-μεθον, -οι-σθον, -οί-σθην λυθησ-οί-μεθα, -οι-σθε, -οί-ντο
Aor.—(I was set free, &c.) S. ἐ-λύθ-ην, -ης, -η D. —, ἐλύθ-η-τον, -ή-την P. ἐλύθ-η-μεν, -η-τε, -η-σαν	(I may be set free, &c.) λυθ-ῶ, -ῇς, -ῇ —, λυθ-ῆ-τον, -ῆ-τον λυθ-ῶ-μεν, -ῆ-τε, -ῶ-σι	(I might be set free, &c.) λυθ-εί-ην, -εί-ης, -εί-η —, λυθ-εί-ητον, -εί-ήτην λυθ-εί-ημεν, -εί-ητε, -εῖεν, (-εί-ησαν)
Perf.—(I have been set free, &c.) S. λέλῠ-μαι, -σαι, -ται D. λελύ-μεθον, -σθον, -σθον P. λελύ-μεθα, -σθε, -νται	(I may have been set free, &c.) λελυ-μένος ᾦ, ᾖς, ᾖ —, λελυ-μένω, ἦτον, ἦτον λελυ-μένοι ὦμεν, ἦτε, ὦσι	(I might have been set free, &c.) λελυ-μένος εἴην, εἴης, εἴη —, λελυ-μένω, εἴητον, εἰήτην λελυ-μένοι εἴημεν, εἴητε, εἶεν (or εἴησαν)
Plup.—(I had been set free, &c.) S. ἐ-λελύ-μην, -σο, -το D. ἐλελύ-μεθον, -σθον, -σθην P. ἐλελύ-μεθα, -σθε, -ντο	wanting	wanting

— continued.
VOICE.

IMPERATIVE.	INFINITIVE.	PARTICIPLE.
(Be thou set free, &c.)	(To be set free, &c.)	(Being set free, &c.)
—, λύ-ου, -έ-σθω	λύ-ε-σθαι	λυ-ό-μενος, gen. -ου
—, λύ-ε-σθον, -έ-σθων		λυ-ο-μένη, gen. -ης
—, λύ-ε-σθε, -έ-σθων (or -έ-σθωσαν)		λυ-ό-μενον, gen. -ου
wanting	wanting	wanting
wanting	(To be about to be set free, &c.) λυθήσ-ε-σθαι	(About to be set free, &c.) λυθησ-ό-μενος, gen. -ου
		λυθησ-ο-μένη, gen. -ης
		λυθησ-ό-μενον, gen. -ου
(Be thou set free, &c.) —, λύθ-η-τι, -ή-τω —, λύθ-η-τον, -ή-των —, λύθ-η-τε, -έντ-ων (or -ήτωσαν)	(To be set free, &c.) λυθ-ῆ-ναι	(Set free, &c.) λυθ-είς, gen. -έντος λυθ-εῖσα, gen. -είσης λυθ-έν, gen. -έντος
(Be thou set free, &c.) —, λέλυ-σο, -σθω	(To have been set free, &c.) λελύ-σθαι	(Having been set free, &c.) λελυ-μένος, gen. -ου
—, λέλυ-σθον, -σθων		λελυ-μένη, gen. -ης
—, λέλυ-σθε, -σθων (or -σθωσαν)		λελυ-μένον, gen. -ου
wanting	wanting	wanting

PURE VERBS
PASSIVE VOICE

INDICATIVE.	SUBJUNCTIVE.	OPTATIVE.
Fut. III. or Fut. Perf.—(I shall have been set free, &c.) S. λελύσ-ο-μαι, -ει (or -ῃ), -ε-ται D. λελυσ-ό-μεθον, -ε-σθον, -ε-σθον P. λελυσ-ό-μεθα, -ε-σθε, -ο-νται	wanting	(I might have been about to be set free, &c.) λελυσ-οί-μην, -οι-ο, -οι-το λελυσ-οί-μεθον, -οι-σθον, -οί-σθην λελυσ-οί-μεθα, -οι-σθε, -οι-ντο

MIDDLE

INDICATIVE.	SUBJUNCTIVE.	OPTATIVE.
Pres.—(I loose for myself, &c.) S. λύ-ο-μαι,-ει(or -ῃ),-εται, &c., same as Pres. Pass.	λύ-ω-μαι, &c.	λυ-οί-μην, &c.
Imperf.—(I was loosing for myself, &c.) S. ἐ-λυ-ό-μην, &c.	wanting	wanting
Fut.—(I shall loose for myself, &c.) S. λύσ-ο-μαι, -ει (or -ῃ), -εται D. λυσ-ό-μεθον, -ε-σθον, -ε-σθον P. λυσ-ό-μεθα, -ε-σθε, -ο-νται	wanting	λυσ-οί-μην, -οι-ο, -οι-το λυσ-οί-μεθον, -οι-σθον, -οί-σθην λυσ-οί-μεθα, -οι-σθε, -οι-ντο
Aor.—(I loosed for myself, &c.) S. ἐ-λυσ-ά-μην, -ω, -α-το D. ἐλυσ-ά-μεθον, -α-σθον, -ά-σθην P. ἐλυσ-ά-μεθα, -α-σθε, -α-ντο	λύσ-ω-μαι, -ῃ, -η-ται λυσ-ώ-μεθον, -η-σθον, -η-σθον λυσ-ώ-μεθα, -η-σθε, -ω-νται	λυσ-αί-μην, -αι-ο, -αι-το λυσ-αί-μεθον, -αι-σθον, -αί-σθην λυσ-αί-μεθα, -αι-σθε, -αι-ντο

Verbal Adjectives:—λυ-τός, -τή, -τόν, loosed, or capable of

NOTE.—The Fut., Aor., and Perf. Pass.

—*continued.*
—*continued.*

IMPERATIVE.	INFINITIVE.	PARTICIPLE.
wanting	(To have been about to be set free, &c.) λελύσ-ε-σθαι	(Having been about to be set free, &c.) λελυσ-ό-μενος, *gen.* -ου λελυσ-ο-μένη, *gen.* -ης λελυσ-ό-μενον, *gen.* -ου

VOICE.

IMPERATIVE.	INFINITIVE.	PARTICIPLE.
—, λύ-ου, &c.	λύ-ε-σθαι	λυ-ό-μενος, -η, -ον, &c.
wanting	wanting	wanting
wanting	λύσ-ε-σθαι	λυσ-ό-μενος, *gen.* -ου λυσ-ο-μένη, *gen.* -ης λυσ-ό-μενον, *gen.* -ου
—, λῦσ-αι, -ά-σθω —, λύσ-α-σθον, -ά-σθων —, λύσ α-σθε, -ά-σθων (or -ά-σθωσαν)	λύσ-α-σθαι	λυσ-ά-μενος, *gen.* -ου λυσ-α-μένη, *gen.* -ης λυσ-ά-μενον, *gen.* -ου

being loosed : λῠ-τέος, -τέα, -τέον, deserving to be loosed.

are often used in a *Middle* sense.

FIRST GREEK READER.

Rule XII.—*Time* when *is put in the genitive, and sometimes in the dative.*

EXERCISE XVII.

ὁ δοῦλος τὸν ὄνον τῷ δεσπότῃ λύει. οἱ ἄνθρωποι λαγὼς καὶ ἐλάφους ἐθήρευον. ἐν τοῖς δόναξι παρὰ τὸν ποταμὸν ὄρτυγας θηρεύει ὁ παῖς. τὸ παιδίον μέλιτταν ἀνὰ τὸν κῆπον ἐθήρευσε. ὁ πατὴρ τὸν υἱὸν ἐκέλευσε. ἡ μήτηρ τὴν ἑαυτῆς θυγατέρα κελεύσει. κελεύσομεν τοὺς ποιμένας. τὴν κόρην ἐκέλευσα. πάντας ὁ θάνατος λύσει. ἀκούσατε πάντες. ὁ Κύριος τὴν τοῦ κωφοῦ γλῶτταν ἔλυσε. οἱ γεωργοὶ τοὺς δούλους κελεύσουσι. τί ἀκούεις; δεινόν τι ἀκούω. ἀκούειν. ἀκούειν ἐθέλω. τὸ παιδίον τὴν τροφὸν καλεῖ. αἱ κόραι τοὺς γονεῖς ἐκάλεσαν. ὁ ναύτης τὸν τοῦ πλοίου κάλων λέλυκε. ὁ κυβερνήτης τοὺς ναύτας τὸν κάλων λῦσαι ἐκέλευσε. ὁ ἱπποκόμος τὴν τοῦ ἵππου κριθὴν ἐπώλει.* ζητεῖτε καὶ εὑρήσετε. τὴν κριθὴν τὴν τοῦ ἵππου, ἱπποκόμε, μὴ πώλει.† δύο παῖδε ὀπτᾶτον‡ κοχλίας. παῖς τις κοχλίας ὤπτα (ὤπταε). ὁ παῖς καὶ ἡ κόρη κοχλίας πολλοὺς ὤπτων (ὤπταον). τοὺς θεοὺς κέκληκε ὁ μάντις.

We ordered our servants. We shall order the servant to loose (*aorist*) the horse. Do not loose the horses. The sailors are letting-go the cable. The king desired his groom not to sell the horse's barley. The father wishes his son to be good. The king ruled with prudence. Who is calling on the gods?

---

* Contracted for ἐπώλεε, *imperf.* See Rules of Contraction, p. 39.
† Πώλει, contracted for πώλεε, *imperative pres.*
‡ Contracted for ὀπτάετον.

The two sailors have let-go the rope. Death has set free the slave. The deaf do not hear. The kings are taking counsel. The king and the queen were consulting. Why do you not believe? The groom is riding along the road, in company with his master. The two grooms were riding towards the bridge. The farmer rode to the town by night.

EXERCISE XVIII.

ὁ ὄνος τῷ Κυρίῳ λύεται. μέλιτταί τινες ἀνὰ τὴν ὕλην ὑπὸ τοῦ παιδὸς ἐθηρεύθησαν. ἡ τοῦ ἵππου κριθὴ ὑπὸ τοῦ κακοῦ ἱπποκόμου ἀεὶ ἐπωλεῖτο. ἐν τοῖς δόναξι παρὰ τῷ ποταμῷ ἐθηρεύοντο ὄρτυγες πολλοί. ὁ παῖς παρὰ τῷ ποταμῷ εὑρίσκεται. οἱ ἵπποι ἐξ ἁρμάτων ἐλύθησαν. τὼ ἵππω ὑπὸ τοῦ ἱπποκόμου τῷ δεσπότῃ ἐλυέσθην. ὁ ποιμὴν ἐθέλει τοὺς κύνας λυθῆναι. οἱ παῖδες παρὰ τῷ κίονι εὑρίσκονται. ὁ τοῦ πλοίου κάλως ὑπὸ τῶν ναυτῶν λέλυται. λέλυνται οἱ δοῦλοι. ὑπὸ τῶν στρατιωτῶν ἐλύθημεν. λυθήσεσθε, ὦ ἵπποι, ἐξ ἅρματος.

The servants were desired by their masters to unyoke the horses. The slave was set free by death. The nurse was called by the child. The two children were found near the temple of Athena. The tongue of the dumb man was loosed by the Lord. All slaves will be liberated by death. The two slaves are about to be set free by their master. The snails were being roasted by the boys and the girls. The apples were roasted (*aor.* 1) by the child's nurse. Slaves! you have been set free!

SECTION XII.

The simple stem of τύπτω is τυπ-, which is strengthened in the Pres. Perf. II., and it is only in these tenses that the pure stem occurs. running through *that* tense, by attaching the first letter of the ter- has τυπτ-, the Fut. and Aor. τυψ-, the Perf. τυφ-, or τετυφ-, as

ACTIVE

INDICATIVE.	SUBJUNCTIVE.	OPTATIVE.
Pres.—(I strike, &c.) S. τύπτ-ω, -εις, -ει, &c., same as in λύω.	τύπτ-ω, -ῃς, -ῃ, &c.	τύπτ-οιμι, -οις, -οι, &c.
Imperf.—(I was striking, &c.) S. ἔ-τυπτ-ον, -ες, -ε, &c.	wanting	wanting
Fut.—(I shall strike, &c.) S. τύψ-ω, -εις, -ει, &c.	wanting	τύψ-οιμι, -οις, -οι, &c.
Aor. I.—(I struck, &c.) S. ἔ-τυψ-α, -ας, -ε, &c.	τύψ-ω, -ῃς, -ῃ, &c.	τύψ-αιμι, -ειας (-αις), -ειε (-αι), &c.
Perf. I.—(I have struck, &c.) S. τέ-τυφ-α, -ας, -ε D.—, τετύφ-ατον, -ατον P. τετύφ-αμεν, -ατε, -ᾱσι	τετύφ-ω, -ῃς, -ῃ —, τετύφ-ητον, -ητον τετύφ-ωμεν, -ητε, -ωσι	τετύφ-οιμι, -οις, -οι —, τετύφ οιτον, -οίτην τετύφ-οιμεν, -οιτε, -οιεν
Plup. I.—(I had struck, &c.) S. ἐ-τε-τύφ-ειν, -εις, -ει D.—, ἐτετύφ-ειτον, -είτην P. ἐτετύφ-ειμεν, -ειτε, -εισαν (or -εσαν)	wanting	wanting
Aor. II.—(I struck, &c.) S. ἔ-τυπ-ον, -ες, -ε D.—, ἐτύπ-ετον, -έτην P. ἐτύπ-ομεν, -ετε, -ον	τύπ-ω, -ῃς, &c., like the Present.	τύπ-οιμι, -οις, &c., like the Present.
Perf. II.—(I have struck, &c.) S. τέ-τυπ-α, -ας, -ε D.—, τετύπ-ατον, -ατον P. τετύπ-αμεν, -ατε, -ᾱσι	τετύπ-ω, &c., like Perfect I.	τετύπ-οιμι, like Perfect I.
Plup. II.—(I had struck, &c.) S. ἐ-τε-τύπ-ειν, -εις, -ει D.—, ἐτετύπ-ειτον, -είτην P. ἐτετύπ-ειμεν, -ειτε, -εισαν (or -εσαν)	wanting	wanting

MUTE VERBS.

by the insertion of τ. The verb, therefore, forms an Aor. II. and
Each of the other tenses, however, may be assigned a *secondary* stem,
mination, *i.e.*, the tense characteristic, to the simple stem; thus the Pres.
secondary stems; and so in λύω and other verbs. (See p. 63, Obs. 2.)

VOICE.

IMPERATIVE.	INFINITIVE.	PARTICIPLE.
—, τύπτ-ε, -έτω, &c.	τύπτ-ειν	τύπτ-ων, -ουσα, -ον, &c.
wanting	wanting	wanting
wanting	τύψ-ειν	τύψ-ων, -ουσα, -ον, &c.
—, τύψ-ον, -άτω, &c.	τύψ-αι	τύψ-ᾱς, -ᾱσα, -αν, &c.
—, τέτυφ-ε, -έτω, &c., like the Present.	τετυφ-έναι	τετυφ-ώς, *gen.* -ότος τετυφ-υῖα, *gen.* -υίας τετυφ-ός, *gen.* -ότος
wanting	wanting	wanting
—, τύπ-ε, -έτω, &c., like the Present.	τυπ-εῖν	τυπ-ών, -οῦσα, -όν, &c.
—, τέτυπ-ε, &c., like Perfect 1.	τετυπ-έναι	τετυπ-ώς, -υῖα, -ός, &c., like Perfect 1.
wanting	wanting	wanting

MUTE VERBS

PASSIVE

INDICATIVE.	SUBJUNCTIVE.	OPTATIVE.
Pres.—(I am being struck, &c.) S. τύπτ-ο-μαι -ει (or -ῃ), -ε-ται D. τυπτ-ό-μεθον, -ε-σθον, -ε-σθον P. τυπτ-ό-μεθα, -ε-σθε, -ο-νται	τύπτ-ω-μαι, -ῃ, -η-ται τυπτ-ώ-μεθον, -η-σθον, -η-σθον τυπτ-ώ-μεθα, -η-σθε, -ω-νται	τυπτ-οί-μην, -οι-ο, -οι-το τυπτ-οί-μεθον, -οι-σθον, -οί-σθην τυπτ-οί-μεθα, -οι-σθε, -οι-ντο
Imperf.—(I was being struck, &c.) S. ἐ-τυπτ-ό-μην, -ου, -ε-το D. ἐτυπτ-ό-μεθον, -ε-σθον, -έ-σθην P. ἐτυπτ-ό-μεθα, -ε-σθε, -ο-ντο	wanting	wanting
Fut. I.—(I shall be struck, &c.) S. τυφθήσ-ο-μαι, -ει (or -ῃ), -ε-ται D. τυφθησ-ό-μεθον, -ε-σθον, -ε-σθον P. τυφθησ-ό-μεθα, -ε-σθε, -ο-νται	wanting	τυφθησ-οί-μην, -οι-ο, -οι-το τυφθησ-οί-μεθον, -οι-σθον, -οί-σθην τυφθησ-οί-μεθα, -οι-σθε, -οιντο
Aor. I.—(I was struck, &c.) S. ἐ-τύφθ-ην, -ης, -η D. —, ἐτύφθ-η-τον, -ή-την P. ἐτύφθ-η-μεν, -η-τε, -η-σαν	τυφθ-ῶ, -ῇς, -ῇ —, τυφθ-ῆ-τον, -ῆ-τον τυφθ-ῶ-μεν, -ῆ-τε, -ῶ-σι	τυφθ-εί-ην, -εί-ης, -εί-η —, τυφθ-εί-ητον, -ει-ή-την τυφθ-εί-ημεν, -εῖμεν, -εί-ητε, -εῖτε, (-εί-η-σαν), -εῖεν
Perf.—(I have been struck, &c.) S. τέ-τυμ-μαι, τέτυψαι, τέτυπ-ται D. τετύμ-μεθον, τέτυφ-θον, τέτυφ-θον P. τετύμ-μεθα, τέτυφ-θε, τετυμ-μένοι (τι, α), εἰσί	τετυμ-μένος, ᾦ, ῇς, ῇ, &c., as in Perf. Pass. of λύομαι	τετυμ-μένος, εἴην, &c., as in Perf. Pass. of λύομαι
Plup.—(I had been struck, &c.) S. ἐ-τε-τύμ-μην, ἐτέτυψο, ἐτέτυπ-το. D. ἐτετύμ-μεθον, ἐτέτυφ-θον,		

—*continued.*

VOICE.

IMPERATIVE.	INFINITIVE.	PARTICIPLE.
—, τύπτ-ου, -έ·σθω —, τύπτ-ε-σθον, -έ-σθων —, τύπτ-ε-σθε, -έ·σθωσαν (or -έ-σθων)	τύπτ-ε-σθαι	τυπτ-ό-μενος, -ο-μένη, -ό-μενον
wanting	wanting	wanting
wanting	τυφθήσ-ε-σθαι	τυφθησ-ό-μενος, -ο-μένη, -ό-μενον
—, τύφθ-η-τι, -ή-τω —, τύφθ-η-τον, -ή-των —, τύφθ-η-τε, -ή-τωσαν	τυφθ-ῆ-ναι	τυφθ-είς, -εῖσα, -έν
—, τέτυψο, τετύφ-θω —, τέτυφ-θον, τετύφ-θων —, τέτυφ-θε, τετύφ θωσαν (or -θων)	τετύφ-θαι	τετυμ-μένος, -μένη, -μένον

ἐτετύφ-θην. P. ἐτετύμ-μεθα, ἐτέτυφ-θε, τετυμ-μένοι (αι, α), ἦσαν

MUTE VERBS
PASSIVE VOICE

INDICATIVE.	SUBJUNCTIVE.	OPTATIVE.
Aor. II.—(I was struck, &c.) S. ἐ-τύπ-ην, -ης, &c., like Aorist I.	τυπ-ῶ, -ῇς, &c., like Aorist I.	τυπ-εί-ην, -εί-ης, &c., like Aorist I.
Fut. II.—(I shall be struck, &c.) S. τυπήσ-ο-μαι, -ει (or -ῃ), &c., like Future I.	wanting	τυπησ-οί-μην, -οι-ο, &c., like Future I.
Fut. III.—(I shall have been struck, &c.) S. τε-τύψ-ομαι, -ει (or -ῃ), -εται, &c., like Future I.	wanting	τετυψ-οί-μην, -οι-ο, -οι-το, &c., like Future I.

MIDDLE

INDICATIVE.	SUBJUNCTIVE.	OPTATIVE.
Pres.—(I strike myself, &c.) τύπτ-ο-μαι, &c. as in Pass.	τύπτ-ω-μαι, as in Pass.	τυπτ-οί-μην, as in Pass.
Imperf.—(I was striking myself, &c.) ἐ-τυπτ-ό-μην, &c. as in Pass.	wanting	wanting
Fut.—(I shall strike myself, &c.) S. τύψ-ομαι, -ει (or -ῃ), &c., as in Pres. Pass.	wanting	τυψ-οί-μην, -οι-ο, &c., as in Pres. Pass.
Aor. I.—(I struck myself, &c.) S. ἐ-τυψ-ά-μην, -ω, -α-το D. ἐτυψ-ά-μεθον, -α-σθον, -άσθην P. ἐτυψ-ά-μεθα, -α-σθε, -α-ντο	τύψ-ω-μαι, -ῃ, -η-ται τυψ-ώ-μεθον, -η-σθον, -η-σθον τυψ-ώ-μεθα, -η-σθε, -ω-νται	τυψ-αί-μην, -αι-ο, -αι-το τυψ-αί-μεθον, -αι-σθον, -αί-σθην τυψ-αί-μεθα, -αι-σθε, -αι-ντο
Aor. II.—(I struck myself, &c.) S. ἐ-τυπ-ό-μην, -ου, -ε-το, &c., as in Imperf. Pass.	τύπ-ω-μαι, -ῃ, &c., as Pres. Pass.	τυπ-οί-μην, -οι-ο, &c., as in Pres. Pass.

Verbal Adjectives:—

FIRST GREEK READER.

—*continued.*
—*continued.*

IMPERATIVE.	INFINITIVE.	PARTICIPLE.
—, τύπ-η-θι, -ή-τω, &c., like Aorist I.	τυπ-ῆ-ναι	τυπ-είς, -εῖσα, -έν
wanting	τυπήσ-ε-σθαι	τυπησ-ό-μενος, -ο-μένη, -ό-μενον
wanting	τετύψ-ε-σθαι	τετυψ-ό-μενος, ο-μένη, -ό-μενον

VOICE.

IMPERATIVE.	INFINITIVE.	PARTICIPLE.
—-, τύπτ-ου	τύπτ-ε-σθαι	τύπτ-ο-μενος, &c.
wanting	wanting	wanting
wanting	τύψ-εσθαι	τυψ-ό-μενος, -ο-μένη, -ό-μενον
—, τύψ-αι, -ά-σθω —, τύψ-α-σθον, -ά-σθων —, τύψ-α-σθε, -ά-σθωσαν (or -ά-σθων)	τύψ-α-σθαι	τυψ-ά-μενος, -α-μένη, -ά-μενον
—, τυπ-οῦ, -έ-σθω, &c., as in Pres. Pass.	τυπ-έ-σθαι	τυπ-ό-μενος, -ο-μένη, -ό-μενον

τυπ-τός and τυπ-τέος.

N.B.—In forming the future of Mute Verbs, it must be remembered,—
(1.) That τ, δ, θ, and ν are rejected before ς; as, ἀνύτ-ω, *fut.* ἀνύ-σω.
(2.) That π, β, or φ, when united with ς, forms ψ; as, λείπ-ω, *fut.* λείψω (λείπ-σω): τρίβ-ω, *fut.* τρίψω (τρίβ-σω): γράφ-ω, γράψω (γράφ-σω).
(3.) That κ, γ, or χ, when united with ς, forms ξ; as, πλέκ-ω, πλέξω (πλέκ-σω): λέγ-ω, λέξω (λέγ-σω): ἄρχ-ω, ἄρξω (ἄρχ-σω).

RULE XIII.—*Time how long is put in the accusative.*

EXERCISE XIX.

ἱπποκόμοι τινὲς τοὺς τοῦ βασιλέως ἵππους πάσας ἡμέρας ἔτριβον. ἡ κριθὴ τοὺς ἵππους καὶ τοὺς ὄνους τρέφει. τὸ κρύος τοὺς ὄφεις ἔπηξε. τί ταῦτα τρέφεις; τὼ κόρα τὰς κόμας πᾶσαν τὴν ἡμέραν κτενίζουσι. τοῦτο τὸ βιβλίον πρός σε πέμψω. ἐπιστολὰς πολλὰς πρὸς τοὺς γονεῖς γέγραφε ὁ παῖς. ταῦτα ἔλεξαν οἱ γέροντες. τὸν γέροντα καὶ τὴν γραῦν ἐδίωξαν οἱ κύνες. ὁ ποιμὴν τοὺς αὑτοῦ κύνας ἐν τῇ σκηνῇ λέλοιπε. ἀνὰ τὸ πεδίον τοὺς θῆρας ἐδίωξα. μή με κρύψῃς ταῦτα.* ἔκρυψε τὸ αὑτοῦ γένος. αἱ κόραι πάντα ταῦτα τοὺς γονεῖς ἔκρυψαν. ἡμᾶς τὰ βιβλία τρέφει.

The wicked groom sells the horse's barley. The daughter of the king has written many letters to her

---
* Verbs of concealing govern two accusatives—one of the person, the other of the thing concealed.

mother. What did the poet write? Why did the judge write this (*i.e.*, these things)? Who wrote the letter? The ball hit my head. Why do you strike the dog? The shepherds hunted the wolf into the river. The boys have left the balls in the garden. Two husbandmen were pursuing a hare through the fields. Why did the shepherd pursue the two boys?

SECTION XIII.

CLASS III.—LIQUID VERBS.

1. In reference to Liquid Verbs, it must be noted—
   (1.) That they have no ς in the inflexion of the future and aorist, and that the termination -εω (*i.e.* -εσω) is contracted into ω; as, μένω, *fut.* μεν-έ(σ)ω, μενῶ.
   (2.) That they shorten the penult in the future (when possible), by omitting the second of two vowels or consonants; as, στέλλω, *fut.* στελῶ; σπείρω, *fut.* σπερῶ.
   (3.) That they lengthen the penult of the first aorist, α into η or ᾱ; φαίνω, φανῶ, ἔφηνα: ε into ει; as, σπείρω, *fut.* σπερῶ, *aor.* ἔσπειρα: ῐ into ῑ; as, κρίνω, κρῐνῶ, ἔκρῑνα: ῠ into ῡ; as, ἀμύνω, ἀμῠνῶ, ἤμῡνα.
   (4.) That many of them change the vowel of the stem in the perfect; as, στ-έ-λλω, *perf.* ἔστ-α-λκα.

LIQUID
ACTIVE

INDICATIVE.	SUBJUNCTIVE.	OPTATIVE.
Pres.—(I report, &c.) S. ἀγγέλλ-ω, -εις, -ει, &c.	ἀγγέλλ-ω, -ῃς, -ῃ, &c.	ἀγγέλλ-οι-μι, -οις, &c.
Imperf.— S. ἤγγελλ-ον, -ες, -ε, &c.	wanting	wanting
Fut.— S. ἀγγελ-ῶ, -εῖς, -εῖ D. —, ἀγγελ-εῖτον, -εῖτον P. ἀγγελ-οῦμεν, -εῖτε, -οῦσι	wanting	ἀγγελ-οῖμι,* -οῖς, -οῖ —, ἀγγελ-οῖτον, -οί-την ἀγγελ-οῖμεν, -οῖτε, -οῖεν
Aor. 1.— S. ἤγγειλ-α, -ας, -ε, &c.	ἀγγείλ-ω, -ῃς, ῃ, &c.	ἀγγείλ-αιμι, -αις, -αι, &c.
Perf.— S. ἤγγελκ-α, -ας, -ε, &c.	ἠγγέλκ-ω, -ῃς, &c.	ἠγγέλκ-οιμι, -οις, &c.
Plup.— S. ἠγγέλκ-ειν, -εις, &c.	wanting	wanting
Aor. II.— S. ἤγγελ-ον, -ες, -ε, &c.	ἀγγέλ-ω, -ῃς, &c.	ἀγγέλ-οιμι, -οις, &c.

* In Liquid Verbs, Pure Verbs, and Verbs in -μι, the Optative

PASSIVE

INDICATIVE.	SUBJUNCTIVE.	OPTATIVE.
Pres.—(I am reported of, &c.) S. ἀγγέλλ-ο-μαι, -ῃ, &c.	ἀγγέλλ-ω-μαι, -ῃ, &c.	ἀγγελλ-οί-μην, -οιο, &c.
Imperf.— S. ἠγγελλ-ό-μην, -ου, &c.	wanting	wanting
Fut. I.— S. ἀγγελθήσ-ο-μαι, -ῃ, &c.	wanting	ἀγγελθησ-οί-μην, -οι-ο, &c.
Aor. I.— S. ἠγγέλθ-ην, -ης, &c.	ἀγγελθ-ῶ, -ῇς, &c.	ἀγγελθ-εί-ην, -εί-ης, &c.

VERBS.
VOICE.

IMPERATIVE.	INFINITIVE.	PARTICIPLE.
—, ἄγγελλ-ε, -έτω, &c.	ἀγγέλλ-ειν	ἀγγέλλ-ων, -ουσα, -ον
wanting	wanting	wanting
wanting	ἀγγελ-εῖν	ἀγγελ-ῶν, -οῦσα, -οῦν, gen. -οῦντος
—, ἄγγειλ-ον, -ά-τω, &c.	ἀγγεῖλ-αι	ἀγγείλ-ας, -ασα, ''
wanting	ἠγγελκ-έναι	ἠγγελκ-ώς, -υῖα, -ός
wanting	wanting	wanting
—, ἄγγελ-ε, -έτω, &c.	ἀγγελ-εῖν	ἀγγελ-ών, οὖσα, -όν

is frequently made in -οιην, -οιης, &c., instead of -οιμι, &c.

VOICE.

IMPERATIVE.	INFINITIVE.	PARTICIPLE.
—, ἀγγέλλ-ου, -έ-σθω, &c.	ἀγγέλλ-ε-σθαι	ἀγγελλ ό-μενος, -ο-μένη, -ό-μενον
wanting	wanting	wanting
wanting	ἀγγελθήσ-ε-σθαι	ἀγγελθησ-ό-μενος, -ο-μένη, -ό μενον
—, ἀγγέλθ-η-τι, -ή-τω, &c.	ἀγγελθ-ῆ-ναι	ἀγγελθ-είς, -εῖσα, -έν

LIQUID VERBS

PASSIVE VOICE

INDICATIVE.	SUBJUNCTIVE.	OPTATIVE.
Perf.— S. ἤγγελ-μαι, -σαι, -ται, &c.	ἠγγελ-μένος (-η, -ον), ὦ, ῇς, ῇ, &c.	ἠγγελ-μένος (-η, -ον), εἴην, εἴης, &c.
Plup.— S. ἠγγέλ-μην, -σο, -το, &c.	wanting	wanting
Aor. II.— S. ἠγγέλ-ην, -ης, &c.	ἀγγελ-ῶ, -ῇς, &c.	ἀγγελ-εί-ην, -εί-ης, &c.
Fut. II.— S. ἀγγελήσ-ο-μαι, -ει (or -ῃ), &c.	wanting	ἀγγελησ-οί-μην, -οι-ο, &c.
Fut. III.— wanting	wanting	wanting

MIDDLE

INDICATIVE.	SUBJUNCTIVE.	OPTATIVE.
Fut.—(I shall report myself, &c.) S. ἀγγελ-οῦ-μαι, -εῖ (or -ῇ), -εῖται D. ἀγγελ-ού-μεθον, -εῖ-σθον, -εῖ-σθον P. ἀγγελ-ού-μεθα, -εῖ-σθε, -οῦ-νται	wanting	ἀγγελ-οί-μην, -οῖ-ο, -οῖ-το ἀγγελ-οί-μεθον, -οῖ-σθον, -οί-σθην ἀγγελ-οί-μεθα, -οῖ-σθε, -οῖ-ντο
Aor. I.— S. ἠγγειλ-ά-μην, -ω, -α-το, &c.	ἀγγείλ-ω-μαι, -ῃ, -η-ται, &c.	ἀγγειλ-αί-μην, -αι-ο, -αι-το, &c.
Aor. II.— S. ἠγγελ-ό-μην, -ου, -ε-το, &c.	ἀγγέλ-ω μαι, -ῃ, -η-ται, &c.	ἀγγελ-οί-μην, -οι-ο, -οι-το, &c.

Verbal Adjectives

— *continued.*

—*continued.*

IMPERATIVE.	INFINITIVE.	PARTICIPLE.
—, ἤγγελ-σο, -θω, &c.	ἠγγέλ-θαι	ἠγγελ-μένος, -μένη, -μενον
wanting	wanting	wanting
—, ἀγγέλ-η-θι, -ή-τω, &c.	ἀγγελ-ῆ-ναι	ἀγγελ-είς, -εῖσα, -έν
wanting	ἀγγελήσ-ε-σθαι	ἀγγελησ-ό-μενος
wanting	wanting	wanting

VOICE.

IMPERATIVE.	INFINITIVE.	PARTICIPLE.
wanting	ἀγγελ-εῖ-σθαι	ἀγγελ-ού-μενος, -ου-μένη, -ού-μενον
—, ἀγγειλ-αι, -ά-σθω, &c.	ἀγγείλ-α-σθαι	ἀγγειλ-ά-μενος, -α-μένη, -ά-μενον
—, ἀγγέλ-ου, -έ-σθω, &c.	ἀγγελ-έ-σθαι	ἀγγελ-ό-μενος, -ο-μένη, -ο-μενον

ἀγγελ-τός and ἀγγελ-τέος.

EXERCISE XX.

οἱ ναῦται τὴν ἄγκυραν εἰς τὴν θάλατταν βάλλουσι. ὁ ποιμὴν τὸν αὑτοῦ υἱὸν εἰς μάχην ἔστειλε. πρός σε τὴν σφαῖραν βάλλω. πρός σε τὴν σφαῖραν βαλῶ. οἱ παῖδες τοὺς ὄφεις λίθοις ἔβαλλον. οἱ ποιμένες τὸν λύκον βακτηρίαις ἔβαλον. ὅλην τὴν ἡμέραν ἐν τῷ κήπῳ ἔμειναν αἱ κόραι. ὁ δεσπότης τὸν κακὸν δοῦλον εἰς φυλακὴν βέβληκε. διὰ τί με λίθῳ ἔβαλες; βάλλετε τὰς σφαίρας εἰς τὸ ὕδωρ. μεῖνον μεθ᾽ ἡμῶν, ἡ ἡμέρα γὰρ ἤδη κέκλικε. τίς μοι τὴν ὁδὸν πρὸς τὴν θάλατταν φανεῖ; τὴν κεφαλήν μου τέτμηκας λίθῳ. τὸν δοῦλον, ὃς τὸν ἐμοῦ ἵππον ἔκλεψε, εἰς φυλακὴν βέβληκεν ὁ κριτής. πολλοὺς τῶν πολεμίων ἀποκτενοῦμεν. αἱ γυναῖκες τὰς τοῦ γέροντος κόμας ἔτιλλον. τὰς τοῦ κριτοῦ κόμας μὴ κεῖρε. τὰς τοῦ κριτοῦ κόμας μὴ κείρῃς.

Do not throw the anchor into the sea. Two sailors were casting an anchor into the sea. Mothers! do not send your sons to the war. Some one has struck the old man with a stone. Do not throw the balls into the air. The shepherds will strike the dog with sticks. My father has put his slave in prison. The boys will stay the livelong day in the wood. Boys! do not remain all day in the forest. Stay with us, my friend. The shepherds sent their sons to the war. The two boys were throwing stones into the sea. Sailors! do not throw the dog into the sea. We shall cast the wicked thieves into prison. I shall remain the livelong day in the temple.

SECTION XIV.

PASSIVE VOICE.

EXERCISE XXI.

λύονται οἱ ὄνοι ἀπὸ τῶν κιόνων. οἱ λαγῷ ἡρέθησαν ὑπὸ τῶν τοῦ γεωργοῦ κυνῶν. οἱ ἵπποι ἐκ τοῦ ἅρματος ἐλύθησαν. οἱ κάλῳ λέλυνται ὑπὸ τῶν ναυτῶν. κοχλίαι πολλοὶ ὑπὸ τοῖν δυοῖν παίδοιν τοῦ ἱπποκόμου ὠπτήθησαν. ἡ οἰκία καίεται. αἱ ἐν τῇ κώμῃ οἰκίαι καίονται. μάχαιραι εὑρίσκονται ἐν ταῖς τῆς κώμης οἰκίαις. οἱ πολῖται πιστεύονται ὑπὸ τῶν στρατιωτῶν. Ξενοφῶν ὑπὸ τῶν πολιτῶν θαυμάζεται ἕνεκα τῆς ἀρετῆς. οἱ λαγῷ ἐδιώκοντο. ἡ τοῦ Ξενοφῶντος σκηνὴ ὑπὸ τῶν βαρβάρων ταχὺ ἐκαίετο. τὰ ὑποζύγια ἠλαύνετο. οἱ ἵπποι διὰ τοῦ πεδίου ἠλαύνοντο. οἱ σοφοὶ τιμῶνται, οἱ δὲ αἰσχροὶ οὐ τιμῶνται. οἱ πονηροὶ οὐκ ἄξιοί εἰσι φιλεῖσθαι. ἀργυρᾶ* κύπελλα ἐν τῇ οἰκίᾳ εὑρίσκεται. οἱ τῶν ἀρίστων Περσῶν παῖδες ἐπὶ ταῖς βασιλέως θύραις παιδεύονται. οἱ παῖδες ὑπὸ τοῦ αὐτοῦ διδασκάλου ἐπαιδεύθησαν. τὼ κόρα ὑπὸ τοῦ αὐτοῦ διδασκάλου ἐπαιδευθήτην. ὑπὸ πάντων τῶν πολιτῶν ἀκουσθήσῃ, ὦ ῥῆτορ.

Some swords were found in the citizen's garden. The farmer's horses have been unyoked from the waggon. The boys have been educated by their own father. The soldiers' tents were quickly burned

---

* In the First and Second Declensions, ε before α, of the dual and plural, and ο before anything but a short vowel, reverse the general rule of contraction (see p. 39); as, ὀστέα, ὀστᾶ; διπλόη, διπλῆ; διπλόῳ, διπλῷ.

by the enemy. A silver cup was found in the shepherd's tent. The serpents were struck by the boys with sticks. The worthless slave was cast into prison by his master. Many of the enemy were slain. The majority of the enemy were slain by the Greeks. My head has been cut with a stone. Cyrus was sent for from his province by his brother, Artaxerxes. The poet was admired for (*i.e.*, on account of) his learning.

MIDDLE VOICE AND DEPONENT VERBS.

RULE XIV.—Measure of distance *is put in the accusative;* as, ἀπέχει δέκα σταδίους, *it is ten stadia distant.*

EXERCISE XXII.

οἱ στρατιῶται ἀνδρείως ἐμάχοντο. Δαρεῖος Κῦρον μεταπέμπεται ἀπὸ τῆς ἀρχῆς, ἧς αὐτὸν σατράπην ἐποίησε καὶ στρατηγὸν δὲ αὐτὸν ἀπέδειξε πάντων ὅσοι εἰς Καστωλοῦ πεδίον ἀθροίζονται.

ὁ Κῦρος ἐπὶ τὸν ἀδελφὸν ἐστρατεύετο. οἱ στρατηγοὶ τοὺς ἀγγέλους μεταπέμψονται. ὁ βασιλεὺς ἐβουλεύσατο περὶ τῆς σωτηρίας τῆς ἀρχῆς. ἐν τῷ τρίτῳ σταθμῷ Κῦρος ἐξέτασιν ποιεῖται τῶν Ἑλλήνων περὶ μέσας νύκτας. περὶ τῆς πατρίδος μαχώμεθα. βουλευώμεθα περὶ τῆς τῶν πολιτῶν σωτηρίας. Ἀρταξέρξης συλλαμβάνει Κῦρον, ὡς ἀποκτενῶν· ἡ δὲ μήτηρ, ἐξαιτησαμένη αὐτόν, ἀποπέμπει ἐπὶ τὴν ἀρχήν. πρὸ τοῦ ἔργου εὖ βούλευσαι. πάντες τιμῆς γεύσασθαι βούλονται. ἀπόκριναί μοι, τίνος ἕνεκα χρὴ θαυμάζειν ἄνδρα ποιητήν; οἱ στρατιῶται εἰς μάχην ἐτάξαντο.

The king sent-for his brother from his government (province). The queen wishes to send for her son from his province. Cyrus took the field against Artaxerxes. The king reviewed his soldiers about midnight. Let us consult about the safety of the city. Before (we take) action let us carefully deliberate. All of us wish to taste liberty. The mother of Cyrus begged him off (for herself), and sent him away to his province. The citizens arranged themselves for battle. Let us beg off our friends. Do not send for (to yourselves) the wicked citizens.

MISCELLANEOUS SENTENCES.

Prepositions, when compounded with Verbs, retain generally their proper signification; as, ἀπέχειν, for ἀπὸ ἔχειν, to keep from,—i.e., to refrain; ἀνὰ βαίνω, to go up,—i.e., ascend, mount.

EXERCISE XXIII.

ὅτε αἱ οἰκίαι ἐκαίοντο, οἱ πολῖται ἀπέφευγον. ὁ Κῦρος ἐξελαύνει διὰ τῆς Λυδίας σταθμοὺς τρεῖς. οἱ πολῖται πλοῖα οὐκ εἶχον. τὰ θηρία ἔτρεχεν. ὅτε αἱ Ἀθῆναι ἐκαίοντο οἱ πολῖται ἐπὶ τὰ πλοῖα ἀνέβαινον. ἀφ' ἵππου ἐθήρευε ὁ Πέρσης.

ἡ οἰκία ἀνώγεω ἔχει πολλά. μὴ διώκετε, ὦ παῖδες, τοὺς λαγώς. τῶν αἰσχρῶν ἡδονῶν ἀπέχου. ἐπὶ τὸν ἵππον ἀναβαίνει ὁ νεανίας. ὁ πολίτης τὸν ἀδελφὸν βουλεύσεται. οἱ πολῖται βουλεύσονται. Δαρεῖος, ὁ ἀδελφός, τὸν Κῦρον μεταπέμψεται ἀπὸ τῆς ἀρχῆς. οἱ πολέμιοι ἐπὶ τὸν βασιλέα ἐστρατεύσαντο. ὁ στρατηγὸς σὺν τοῖς στρατιώταις ἔθυσε τῇ Ἀθηνᾷ. οἱ πολῖται τὸν κριτὴν ἔπεισαν. Κλέαρχος μὲν τοῦ δεξιοῦ κέρως ἡγεῖται, Μένων δὲ τοῦ εὐωνύμου. ὁ ἱπποκόμος κατεπήδησεν ἀπὸ τοῦ ἅρματος. γυμνάζετε τὰ σώματα, ὦ παῖδες. πολλάκις βραχεῖα ἡδονὴ μακρὰν τίκτει λύπην. πίστευε τοῖς σώφροσι. Κῦρος ἐκάλεσε τοὺς φυγάδας, καὶ ἐκέλευσεν αὐτοὺς στρατεύεσθαι σὺν αὐτῷ. οἱ μὲν οὖν ἄνευ σακῶν φεύγουσι· οἱ δὲ ἐν τοῖς ξίφεσι πίπτουσι· οἱ δ' ἔτι ἐκ τῶν τειχῶν μάχονται· ἀνὰ δὲ τὰ ὄρη κεῖται ξίφη τε, καὶ ἔγχη, καὶ δὴ καὶ μελῶν μέρη. ἡ Νῖνος μέν, ὦ πορθμεῦ, ἀπόλωλεν ἤδη, καὶ οὐδὲν ἴχνος ἔτι λοιπὸν αὐτῆς· ἀποθνήσκουσι γὰρ καὶ αἱ πόλεις, ὥσπερ ἄνθρωποι.

The soldiers were fleeing without their shields. Two swords were found in the shepherd's hut. The farmers have found two silver cups in the slave's cottage. The master sent for his servant from the field. The slaves wished to taste liberty. The father begged his son off, and sent him away to the war. The generals reviewed the soldiers about midnight. The citizens are about to take the field against the enemies of their king. Do not send for the boy from the wood. The soldiers' children are fleeing with their fathers' shields. The king's generals review the soldiers in the garden of the palace. The two shepherds will remain the livelong night in the snow.

SECTION XV.

SECOND CONJUGATION—VERBS IN -μι.

1. Verbs in -μι are of a more ancient formation than verbs in -ω, but are much less numerous. They differ in inflexion from verbs in -ω, in the Present, Imperfect (Active, Passive, and Middle), and Aorist II. (Active and Middle).

2. The stems which adopt this mode of conjugation end in one of the vowels, α, ε, ο, or υ. In the Present and Imperfect a reduplication is prefixed, consisting of the initial consonant of the stem, with ι; thus, the stem δο-, *I give*, is lengthened into δω-, which, with the person ending, -μι, makes δω-μι, and this again, with the reduplication, δί-δω-μι. So θε-, lengthened into θη-, with person ending, θη-μι, and with reduplication, τί-θη-μι. (See p. 62, 11, on Reduplication.)

3. If the stem begin with σ, or an aspirated vowel, the reduplication is made by prefixing ι aspirated; thus, stem στα-, lengthened στη-, with person ending, στη-μι, and with reduplication, ἵ-στη-μι. Compare *sto* and *si-sto*, in Latin.

4. The three verbs, τίθημι, *I place*, δίδωμι, *I give*, and ἵημι, *I send*, have the inflexion -κα, instead of -σα, in the first aorist indicative active; as, ἔθηκα, ἔδωκα, ἧκα; but this form is used almost solely in the singular. For these and other minor peculiarities, consult the paradigms.

VERBS

The student will remember that the stem of ἵστημι is στᾰ-; of τίθημι, θε-; that of the inflexion, as, τιθῶμεν for τιθέ-ωμεν, the hyphen has declension. The parts not here given are regularly declined, like

ACTIVE

INDICATIVE.	SUBJUNCTIVE.	OPTATIVE.
Pres.—(I set up or erect, &c.) S. ἵστ-ημι, -ης, -ησι D. —, ἵστ-ᾰτον, -ᾰτον P. ἵστ-ᾰμεν, -ᾰτε, -ᾱσι(ν)	ἱστ-ῶ, -ῇς, -ῇ —, ἱστ-ῆτον, -ῆτον ἱστ-ῶμεν, -ῆτε, -ῶσι(ν)	ἱστ-αίην, -αίης, -αίη —, ἱστ-αίητον, -αιήτην* ἱστ-αίημεν, -αίητε, (-αίησαν), -αῖεν
Imperf.—(I was erecting, &c.) S. ἵστ-ην, -ης, -η D. —, ἵστ-ᾰτον, -ᾰτην P. ἵστ-ᾰμεν, -ᾰτε, -ᾰσαν	wanting	wanting
Aor. II.—(I stood, &c.) S. ἔστ-ην, -ης, -η D. —, ἔστ-ητον, -ήτην P. ἔστ-ημεν, -ητε, -ησαν	στ-ῶ, -ῇς, -ῇ —, στ-ῆτον, -ῆτον στ-ῶμεν, -ῆτε, -ῶσι(ν)	στ-αίην, -αίης, -αίη —, στ-αίητον, -αιήτην στ-αίημεν, -αίητε, (-αίησαν) -αῖεν

MIDDLE

Pres.—(I erect myself, or stand, &c.) S. ἵστ-ᾰμαι, -ᾰσαι, -ᾰται D. ἱστ-άμεθον, -ασθον, -ασθον P. ἱστ-άμεθα,-ασθε,-ανται	ἱστ-ῶμαι, -ῇ, -ῆται ἱστ-ώμεθον, -ῆσθον, -ῆσθον ἱστ-ώμεθα, -ῆσθε, -ῶνται	ἱστ-αίμην, -αιο, -αιτο ἱστ-αίμεθον, -αισθον, -αίσθην ἱστ-αίμεθα, -αισθε, -αιντο
Imperf.—(I was erecting myself, &c.) S. ἱστ-ᾰμην, -ασο, -ατο D. ἱστ-άμεθον, -ασθον, -ασθην P. ἱστ-άμεθα, -ασθε, -αντο	wanting	wanting
Aor. II.— wanting	wanting	wanting

* The Dual and Plural Optative are usually

IN -μι.

and of δίδωμι, δο- : but since the vowel of the stem is often united with
been placed with a regard, not to the pure stem, but to convenience of
λύω; as, *fut.* στήσω ; *aor.* ἔστησα; *perf.* ἕστηκα, &c. (See p. 96.)

VOICE.

IMPERATIVE.	INFINITIVE.	PARTICIPLE.
—, ἵστ-η (ἱστ-άθι), -άτω —, ἵστ-άτον, -ότων —, ἵστ-ᾶτε, -άντων (-άτω-σαν)	ἱστ-άναι	ἱστ-άς, -άντος ἱστ-ᾶσα, -άσης ἱστ-άν, -άντος
wanting	wanting	wanting
—, στ-ῆθι, -ήτω —, στ-ῆτον, -ήτων —, στ-ῆτε, -άντων (or -ήτωσαν)	στ-ῆναι	στ-άς, -άντος στ-ᾶσα, -άσης στ-άν, -άντος

VOICE.

—, ἵστ-ω (ἱστ-άσο), -άσθω —, ἵστ-ασθον, -άσθων	ἵστ-ασθαι	ἱστ-άμενος, -αμένου ἱστ-αμένη, -αμένης
—, ἵστ-ασθε, -άσθων (-άσθωσαν)		ἱστ-άμενον, -αμένου
wanting	wanting	wanting
wanting	wanting	wanting

contracted into -αῖτον, -αίτην, &c.
(128)

VERBS IN -μι

ACTIVE

INDICATIVE.	SUBJUNCTIVE.	OPTATIVE.
Pres.—(I place, &c.) S. τίθ-ημι, -ης, -ησι D. —, τίθ-ετον, -ετον P. τίθ-εμεν, -ετε, -έᾱσι(ν), and -εῖσι(ν)	τιθ-ῶ, -ῇς, -ῇ —, τιθ-ῆτον, -ῆτον τιθ-ῶμεν, -ῆτε, -ῶσι(ν)	τιθ-είην, -είης, -είη —, τιθ-είητον, -ειήτην* τιθ-είημεν, -είητε, -εῖεν (-είησαν)
Imperf.—(I was placing, &c.) S. ἐτίθ-ην, -ης, -η D. —, ἐτίθ-ετον, -έτην P. ἐτίθ-εμεν, -ετε, -εσαν	wanting	wanting
Aor.—(I placed, &c.) S. ἔθη-κα, -κας, -κε D. —, ἔθ-ετον, -έτην P. ἔθ-εμεν, -ετε, -εσαν, or ἔθηκαν	θ-ῶ, -ῇς, -ῇ —, θ-ῆτον, -ῆτον θ-ῶμεν, -ῆτε, -ῶσι(ν)	θ-είην, -είης, -είη —, θ-είητον, -ειήτην θ-είημεν, -είητε, -εῖεν (-είησαν)

MIDDLE

Pres.—(I place myself, &c.) S. τίθ-εμαι, -εσαι, -εται D. τιθ-έμεθον, -εσθον, -εσθον P. τιθ-έμεθα, -εσθε, -ενται	τιθ-ῶμαι, -ῇ, -ῆται† τιθ-ώμεθον, -ῆσθον, -ῆσθον τιθ-ώμεθα,-ῆσθε,-ῶνται	τιθ-είμην, -ειο, -ειτο τιθ-είμεθον, -εισθον, -είσθην τιθ-είμεθα,-εισθε,-ειντο
Imperf.—(I was placing myself, &c.) S. ἐτιθ-έμην, -εσο, -ετο D. ἐτιθ-έμεθον, -εσθον, -ίσθην P. ἐτιθ-έμεθα, -εσθε, -εντο	wanting	wanting
Aor. II.—(I placed myself, &c.) S. ἐθ-έμην, ἔθου (-εσο), -ετο D. ἐθ-έμεθον, -εσθον, -έσθην P. ἐθ-έμεθα, -εσθε, -εντο	θ-ῶμαι, -ῇ, -ῆται θ-ώμεθον, -ῆσθον, -ῆσθον θ-ώμεθα, -ῆσθε, -ῶνται	θ-είμην, -εῖο, -εῖτο θ-είμεθον, -εῖσθον, -είσθην θ-είμεθα, -εῖσθε, -εῖντο

* These forms are usually contracted
† Otherwise accented.

—*continued.*
VOICE.

IMPERATIVE.	INFINITIVE.	PARTICIPLE.
—, τίθ-ει (τίθ-εθι), -έτω —, τίθ-ετον, -έτων —, τίθ-ετε, -έντων (-έτω-σαν)	τιθ-έναι	τιθ-είς, -έντος τιθ-εῖσα, -είσης τιθ-έν, -έντος
wanting	wanting	wanting
—, θ-ές (for θέθι), -έτω —, θ-έτον, -έτων —, θ-έτε, -έντων (-έτωσαν)	θ-εῖναι	θ-είς, -έντος θ-εῖσα, -είσης θ-έν, -έντος

VOICE.

— τίθ-ου (for τίθ-εσο), -έσθω —, τίθ-εσθον, -έσθων	τίθ-εσθαι	τιθ-έμενος, -εμένου τιθ-εμένη, -εμένης
—, τίθ-εσθε, -έσθων (-έσ-θωσαν)		τιθ-έμενον, -εμένου
wanting	wanting	wanting
—, θ-οῦ (for θέσο), -έσθω —, θ-έσθον, -έσθων	θ-έσθαι	θ-έμενος, -εμένου θ-εμένη, -εμένης
—, θ-έσθε, -έσθων (-έσθω-σαν)		θ-έμενον, -εμένου

into -εῖτον, -είτην, &c.
τίθωμαι, τίθῃ, &c.

VERBS IN -μι
ACTIVE

INDICATIVE.	SUBJUNCTIVE.	OPTATIVE.
Pres.—(I give, &c.) S. δίδ-ωμι, -ως, -ωσι D. —, δίδ-οτον, -οτον P. δίδ-ομεν, -οτε, -όᾱσι(ν) (or δίδ-οῦσι)	διδ-ῶ, -ῷς, -ῷ —, διδ-ῶτον, -ῶτον διδ-ῶμεν, -ῶτε, -ῶσι(ν)	διδ-οίην, -οίης, -οίη —, διδ-οίητον, -οιήτην διδ-οίημεν, -οίητε, -οῖεν (-οίησαν)
Imperf.—(I was giving, &c.) S. ἐδίδ-ων, -ως, -ω D. —, ἐδίδ-οτον, -ότην P. ἐδίδ-ομεν, -οτε, -οσαν	wanting	wanting
Aor. II.—(I gave, &c.) S. ἔδω-κα, -κας, -κε D. —, ἔδ-οτον, -ότην P. ἔδ-ομεν, -οτε, -οσαν, or ἔδωκαν	δ-ῶ, -ῷς, -ῷ —, δ-ῶτον, -ῶτον δ-ῶμεν, -ῶτε, -ῶσι(ν)	δ-οίην, -οίης, -οίη —, δ-οίητον, -οιήτην δ-οίημεν, -οίητε, -οῖει (-οίησαν)

MIDDLE

Pres.—(I give myself, &c.) S. δίδ-ομαι, -οσαι, -οται D. διδ-όμεθον, -οσθον, -οσθον P. διδ-όμεθα, -οσθε, -ονται	διδ-ῶμαι, -ῷ, -ῶται διδ-ώμεθον, -ῶσθον, -ῶσθον διδ-ώμεθα, -ῶσθε, -ῶνται	διδ-οίμην, -οιο, -οιτο διδ-οίμεθον, -οισθον, -οίσθην διδ-οίμεθα, -οισθε, -οιντο
Imperf.—(I was giving myself, &c.) S. ἐδιδ-όμην, -ου (-οσο), -οτο D. ἐδιδ-όμεθον, -οσθον, -όσθην P. ἐδιδ-όμεθα, -οσθε, -οντο	wanting	wanting
Aor. II.—(I gave myself, &c.) S. ἐδ-όμην, -ου, (-οσο), -οτο D. ἐδ-όμεθον, -οσθον, -όσθην P. ἐδ-όμεθα, -οσθε, -οντο	δ-ῶμαι, -ῷ, -ῶται δ-ώμεθον, -ῶσθον, -ῶσθον δ-ώμεθα, -ῶσθε, -ῶνται	δ-οίμην, -οῖο, -οῖτο δ-οίμεθον, -οῖσθον, -οίσθην δ-οίμεθα, -οῖσθε, -οῖντο

—*continued.*

VOICE.

IMPERATIVE.	INFINITIVE.	PARTICIPLE.
—, δίδ-ου (δίδ-οθι), -ότω —, δίδ-οτον, -ότων —, δίδ-οτε, -όντων (-ότωσαν)	διδ-όναι	διδ-ούς, -όντος διδ-οῦσα, -ούσης διδ-όν, -όντος
wanting	wanting	wanting
—, δ-ός, -ότω —, δ-ότον, -ότων —, δ-ότε, -όντων (-ότωσαν)	δοῦναι	δούς, δόντος δοῦσα, δούσης δόν, δόντος

VOICE.

IMPERATIVE.	INFINITIVE.	PARTICIPLE.
—, δίδ-ου (-οσο), -όσθω —, δίδ-οσθον, -όσθων	δίδ-οσθαι	διδ-όμενος, -ομένου διδ-ομένη, -ομένης
—, δίδ-οσθε, -όσθων (-όσθωσαν)		διδ-όμενον, -ομένου
wanting	wanting	wanting
—, δοῦ (δόσο), δόσθω —, δόσθον, δόσθων	δόσθαι	δόμενος, δομένου δομένη, δομένης
—, δόσθε, δόσθων δόσθωσαν)		δόμενον, δομένου

VERBS IN -μι

ACTIVE

INDICATIVE.	SUBJUNCTIVE.	OPTATIVE.
Pres.—(I show, &c.) S. δείκνῡ-μι, -s, -σι D. —, δείκνῠ-τον, -τον P. δείκνῠ-μεν, -τε, -ᾱσι(ν) [or δεικνῦσι(ν)]	δεικνύ-ω, -ῃς, -ῃ, &c., (formed regularly from δεικνύω)	δεικνύ-οιμι, -οις, &c., (from δεικνύω)
Imperf.—(I was showing, &c.) S. ἐδείκνῡ-ν, -s, ἐδείκνῡ D. —, ἐδείκνῠ-τον, -την P. ἐδείκνῠ-μεν, -τε, -σαν	wanting	wanting

MIDDLE

Pres.—(I show myself, &c.) S. δείκνῠ-μαι, -σαι, -ται D. δεικνύ-μεθον, -σθον, -σθον P. δεικνύ-μεθα, -σθε, -νται	δεικνύ-ωμαι, -ῃ, &c., (from δεικνύω)	δεικνυ-οίμην, -οιο, &c., (from δεικνύω)
Imperf.—(I was showing myself, &c.) S. ἐδεικνῡ́-μην, -σο, -το D. ἐδεικνύ-μεθον, -σθον, -σθην P. ἐδεικνύ-μεθα, -σθε, -ντο	wanting	wanting

The parts of these Verbs which do not appear in the foregoing Tables are

ACTIVE.

Pres.	Imperf.	Fut.	Aor. 1.	Aor. II.	Perf.	Plup.	Pres.	Imperf.
ἵστημι	ἵστην	στήσω	ἔστησα	ἔστην	ἕστηκα	εἱστήκειν	ἵσταμαι	ἱστάμην
τίθημι	ἐτίθην	θήσω	ἔθηκα	(ἔθην)	τέθεικα	ἐτεθείκειν	τίθεμαι	ἐτιθέμην
δίδωμι	ἐδίδων	δώσω	ἔδωκα	(ἔδων)	δέδωκα	ἐδεδώκειν	δίδομαι	ἐδιδόμην
δείκνυμι	ἐδείκνυν	δείξω	ἔδειξα	—	δέδειχα	ἐδεδείχειν	δείκνυμαι	ἐδεικνύμην

—continued.
VOICE.

IMPERATIVE.	INFINITIVE.	PARTICIPLE.
—, δείκνῡ (δείκνυθι), δεικ-νῠ́-τω —, δείκνυ-τον, -των —, δείκνῠ-τε, -ντων (-τω-σαν)	δεικνῠ́-ναι	δεικνύ-s, -ντος δεικνῦ-σα, -σης δεικνύ-ν, -ντος
wanting	wanting	wanting

VOICE.

—, δείκνῠ-σο, -σθω —, δείκνυ-σθον, -σθων —, δείκνυ-σθε, -σθων (-σθω-σαν)	δείκνυ-σθαι	δεικνύ μενος, -μένου δεικνυ μένη, -μένης δεικνύ μενον, -μένου
wanting	wanting	wanting

declined regularly. All the Tenses are seen in the following scheme:—

PASSIVE.				MIDDLE.	
Fut.	Aor. I.	Perf.	Plup.	Fut.	Aor.
σταθήσομαι	ἐστάθην	ἔσταμαι	ἐστάμην	Pres. and Imperf. same as in Passive.	στήσομαι ἐστησάμην
τεθήσομαι	ἐτέθην	τέθειμαι	ἐτεθείμην		θήσομαι ἐθέμην
δοθήσομαι	ἐδόθην	δέδομαι	ἐδεδόμην		δώσομαι ἐδόμην
δειχθήσομαι	ἐδείχθην	δέδειγμαι	ἐδεδείγμην		δείξομαι ἐδειξάμην

ACTIVE VOICE.

EXERCISE XXIV.

οἱ στρατιῶται τρόπαιον ἔστησαν (1 aor.) οἱ ἱππεῖς εἰς χιλίους παρὰ Κλέαρχον ἔστησαν (2 aor.) τοῖς ἀνθρώποις θεὸς πολλὰ ἀγαθὰ τίθησιν. οἱ θεοὶ πάντα τὰ ἀγαθὰ διδόασι. Κῦρος ἔδωκε Κλεάρχῳ μυρίους δαρεικούς. δὸς ποῦ στῶ, καὶ τὸν κόσμον κινήσω. δότε ἡμῖν τὰ ξίφη. ἡ νῆσος φαίνεται πῦρ ἀναδιδοῦσα νυκτός. οἱ πολέμιοι εἶπον, ὅτι οὐκ ἀποδοῖεν τοὺς νεκρούς. οἱ ἄρχοντες τοὺς νόμους τεθείκασιν. κατάθες μισθὸν τοῖς δούλοις. ὑμεῖς τοὺς Ἀθηναίους εἰάσατε τὰ μακρὰ στῆσαι τείχη. οἱ στρατηγοὶ ἆθλα τοῖς στρατιώταις ἔθεσαν. πῇ στῶ. οὐκ ἔχω ὅτι ἑκάστῳ τῶν φίλων δῶ. οὐκ ἔξεστιν ἀνδρὶ Θηβαίῳ ἐκθεῖναι παιδίον. Λυκοῦργος, ὁ θεὶς Λακεδαιμονίοις νόμους, σοφώτατος ἦν. ὑμῖν εὐτυχεῖν δοῖεν οἱ θεοί. στήλη ἔστηκε παρὰ τὸν ναὸν γράμματα ἔχουσα.

The father gave (1 aor.) the book to his son. Give the shepherd his staff again.* The Greeks have given Cyrus ten thousand soldiers. Where shall we stand? (2 aor. subj.) The island revolted from the Athenians. (I pray that) God would grant (2 aor. opt.) me faithful friends. We very much admire Lycurgus, who made (lit. the person having made,— 2 aor. part. act.) laws for the Lacedæmonians. Ye rich! give some part of your goods to the poor. The general has given thirty* days' pay (say, the pay of thirty days) to the soldiers.

---
* Use ἀποδίδωμι when the meaning is to give back, or to give what is due, &c.

MIDDLE AND PASSIVE VOICES.

EXERCISE XXV.

οἱ στρατιῶται σὺν πολλῇ σπουδῇ καθίσταντο. μηδένα κακὸν ἂν θείμην στρατηγόν. τῇ στρατιᾷ τότε μισθὸς τεττάρων μηνῶν ὑπὸ Κύρου ἀπεδόθη. ἑκάστῳ τῶν στρατιωτῶν στέφανος χρουσοῦς δέδοται. Κῦρος, πρὸς βασιλέα πέμπων, ἠξίου δοθῆναί οἱ (to him) ταύτας τὰς πόλεις, μᾶλλον ἢ Τισσαφέρνην ἄρχειν αὐτῶν. Δάφνιν τὸν βουκόλον λέγουσι τεχθέντα ἐκτεθῆναι ἐν δάφνῃ, ὅθεν καὶ τὸ ὄνομα ἔλαβεν. Πλάτων πρὸς Ἀρίστιππον εἶπε, σοὶ μόνῳ δέδοται καὶ χλαμύδα εὖ φορεῖν καὶ ῥάκος. Πυθαγόρας ἔλεγε, δύο ταῦτα ἐκ τῶν θεῶν τοῖς ἀνθρώποις δεδόσθαι κάλλιστα, τό τε ἀληθεύειν καὶ τὸ εὐεργετεῖν. ὁ οἶνος εἰς τὴν ἰατρικὴν χρησιμώτατος, πολλάκις γὰρ τοῖς ποτοῖς φαρμάκοις κεράννυται.

His own cutlass was returned to the sailor. A silver crown was given to each of the slaves. Six days' pay was given by Tissaphernes to his soldiers. The soldiers of (*King*) Perses post themselves (*i.e.*, fall into position) in great haste. Socrates used-to-say (*imperf.*) that many blessings have been given by the gods to men. The infant was exposed on a high mountain. Plato used-to-say to Aristippus that to him only it had been granted to wear becomingly both the robe-of-wealth (χλαμύς) and the-garment-of-poverty (ῥάκος). The soldiers were put in position with great haste.

SECTION XVI.

The following Irregular Verbs in -μι are those most frequently met consult the Greek Grammar, and Buttmann's or Veitch's "Irregular in its inflexions from τίθημι. The compounds, ἀφίημι, &c., are more compounds.

ACTIVE

INDICATIVE.	SUBJUNCTIVE.	OPTATIVE.
Pres.—(I throw, or send, &c.) S. ἵ-ημι, -ης, -ησι, &c., [the 3d pl. is ἱ-ᾶσι(ν)]	ἱ-ῶ, -ῇς, -ῇ, &c.	ἱ-είην, -είης, -είη, &c.
Imperf.— S. ἵ-ουν* or -ειν, -ης or -εις, -η or -ει, -ετον, -έτην, &c.	wanting	wanting
Fut.— S. ἥ-σω, &c.	wanting	wanting
Aor.— S. ἧκα,† ἧκας, ἧκε P. εἷμεν, εἷ-τε, εἷ-σαν	ὧ, ᾗς, ᾗ, &c.	εἷ-ην, -ης, -η, &c.
Perf.— S. εἷ κα, -κας, &c.	wanting	wanting
Plup.— S. εἷ-κειν, -κεις, &c.	wanting	wanting

* ἵουν, as in ἀφίουν, or ἠφίουν: and ἵειν, as in

PASSIVE

Pres.—(I am sent, &c.) S. ἵ-εμαι, -εσαι or -ῃ, -εται, &c.	ἵ-ωμαι, &c.	ἱ-είμην, &c. or -οίμην
Imperf.— S. ἱ-έμην, -εσο (or -ου), -ετο, &c.	wanting	wanting
Perf.— S. εἷ-μαι, -σαι, &c.	wanting	wanting

IRREGULAR VERBS IN -μι.

with in the course of reading. For the others, the learner must Greek Verbs." — The verb ἵημι (stem ἑ), I throw, differs but slightly frequently used than the simple verb. Many of the parts occur only in

VOICE.

IMPERATIVE.	INFINITIVE.	PARTICIPLE.
—, ἵ-ει, -έτω, -ετον, &c.	ἱ-έναι	ἱ-είς, -εῖσα, -έν
wanting	wanting	wanting
wanting	wanting	wanting
—, ἕ-s, -τω, -τον, &c.	εἷ-ναι	εἵς, εἷσα, ἕν
wanting	wanting	wanting
wanting	wanting	wanting

ἠφίειν, προίειν.   † See aorist active of τίθημι.

VOICE.

—, ἵ-εσο (or -ου), -έσθω, &c.	ἵ-εσθαι	ἱέμεν-ος, -η, -ον
wanting	wanting	wanting
—, εἷ-σο, &c.	εἷ-σθαι	εἱμέν-ος, -η, -ον

IRREGULAR VERBS
PASSIVE VOICE

INDICATIVE.	SUBJUNCTIVE.	OPTATIVE.
Plup.— S. εἴ-μην, &c.	wanting	wanting
Fut. I.- S. ἐθήσ-ομαι, &c.	wanting	wanting
Aor. I.— S. εἴ-θην or ἔθην, &c.	ἑ-θῶ, &c.	ἑ-θείην, &c.

MIDDLE

Fut.— S. ἤ-σομαι, &c.	wanting	ἡ-σοίμην, &c.
Aor. I.— S. (ἠ-κάμην, &c.)	wanting	wanting
Aor. II. - S. εἴ-μην (or ἔμην), &c.	ὦμαι, &c.	wanting

Verbal Adjectives :

ΕΙΜΊ,

Some of the forms of εἰμί, *I am*, which is defective, differ from those

Pres.— S. εἰ-μί, εἶ, ἐσ-τί(ν) D. —, ἐσ-τόν, -τόν P. ἐσ-μέν, -τέ, εἰ-σί(ν)	ὦ, ᾖ-s, ᾖ —, ἦ-τον, -τον ὦ-μεν, ἦτε, ὦ-σί(ν)	εἴ-ην, -ης, -η —, εἴ-ητον or εἶτον, -ήτην or εἴτην εἴημεν or εἶμεν, εἴητε or εἶτε, εἴ-ησαν, εἶεν
Imperf. - S. ἦ-ν (ἦ), -σθα, -ν D. —, (ἦ-τον) ἦσ-τον, (ἦ-την), ἦσ-την P. ἦ-μεν, -τε or -στε, -σαν	wanting	wanting
Fut.— S. ἔσ-ομαι, -ει or -ῃ, -ται D. ἐσ-όμεθον, -εσθον, -ε-σθον P. ἐσ-όμεθα, -εσθε, -ονται	wanting	ἐσοίμην, &c.

FIRST GREEK READER. 103

IN -μι—*continued.*
—*continued.*

IMPERATIVE.	INFINITIVE.	PARTICIPLE.
wanting	wanting	wanting
wanting	wanting	wanting
—, ἔ-θητι, &c.	ἐ-θῆναι	ἐ-θείς, &c.

VOICE.

wanting	ἤ-σεσθαι	wanting
wanting	wanting	wanting
—, οὗ, ἔσθω	ἔ-σθαι	ἔ-μενος, -η, -ον

ἐ-τός and ἐ-τέος.

I am.
of ἵημι only in the breathing. ὑπάρχω, &c., supply the parts deficient.

—, ἴσ-θι, ἔσ-τω —, ἔσ-τον, -των —, ἔσ-τε, -τωσαν, -των	εἶ-ναι	ὤν, οὖσα, ὄν
wanting	wanting	wanting
wanting	ἔσεσθαι	ἐσόμεν-ος, -η, -ον

IRREGULAR VERBS

Εἶμι (stem ἰ), has a Future meaning, *I shall go.* Like εἰμί, *I am*, it is
by the accent, or

INDICATIVE.	SUBJUNCTIVE.	OPTATIVE.
Pres.—(I shall go, &c.) S. εἶ-μι, εἶ, εἶ-σι(ν) D. —, ἴ-τον, -τον P. ἴ-μεν, -τε, -ᾱσι(ν)	ἴ-ω, -ῃς, -ῃ —, (ἴ-ητον), (-ητον) ἴ-ωμεν, -ητε, -ωσι(ν)	ἴ-οιμι or ἴ-οίην, ἴ-οις, -οι —, (ἴ-οιτον), (ἰ-οίτην) ἴ-οιμεν, -οιτε, -οιεν
Imperf.— S. ᾔ-ειν or ᾖ-α, ᾔ-εις or -εισθα, -ει or -ειν D. —, ᾔ-ειτον or ᾖ-τον, ᾔ εἴτην or ᾔ-την P. ᾖ ειμεν or ᾖ-μεν, ᾔ-ειτε or ᾖ-τε, ᾖ-εσαν	wanting	wanting

The verb Φημί (stem φα), *I say*, is conjugated much like

Pres.—(I say, &c.) S. φη-μί, φή-ς, φη-σί(ν) D. —, φᾱ-τόν, -τόν P. φα-μέν, -τέ, φᾱ-σί(ν)	φῶ, φῇς, φῇ, &c.	φαί-ην, -ης, -η, &c.
Imperf.— S. ἔ-φη-ν, (-s) -σθα, -φη D. —, ἐφᾱ-τον, ἐφά-την P. ἔφα-μεν, -τε, -σαν	wanting	[The Future, φήσω, are regular.]

Οἶδα (stem ἰδ, Lat. *vid*) *I know*, is a preteritive verb.

Perf.—(I know, &c.) S. οἶδ-α, οἶ-σθα, οἶδ-ε(ν) D. —, ἴσ-τον, -τον P. ἴσ-μεν, -τε, -ᾱσι(ν)	εἰδ-ῶ, -ῇς, &c.	εἰδ-είην, -είης, &c.
Plup.— S. ᾔδ-ειν or -η, -εισθα or -ησθα, -εις or -ης, -ει or -ειν, or -η D. —, ᾔδ-ειτον, ᾔδ-είτην P. ᾔδ-ειμεν, -ειτε, -εσαν (-εισαν)	wanting	wanting
Aor. II.— S. εἶδον, &c.	ἴδω, &c.	ἴδοιμι, &c.

IN -μι—continued.

very defective, and in some forms is distinguished from the latter only an iota subscript.

IMPERATIVE.	INFINITIVE.	PARTICIPLE.
—, ἴ-θι(εἶ), -τω —, ἴ-τον, -των —, ἴ-τε, -τωσαν or ἰόντων	ἰ-έναι	ἰ-ών, -οῦσα, -όν
wanting	wanting	wanting

ἵστημι, but wants the reduplication, and is defective.

—, φα-θί or φά-θι, φά-τω —, φά-τον, -των —, φά-τε, -τωσαν or -ντων	φά-ναι	(φάς, -ᾶσα, -άν)
and the 1st Aorist, ἔφησα,	wanting	wanting

Its conjugation is much like that of verbs in -μι.

—, ἴσ-θι, -τω, &c.	εἰδ-έναι	εἰδ-ώς, -υῖα, -ός
wanting	wanting	wanting
—, ἰδέ	ἰδεῖν	ἰδών, &c.

IRREGULAR VERBS IN -μι—continued.

Κεῖμαι (stem κε), *I am lying* (*I have laid myself*), is originally a perfect passive.

INDICATIVE.	SUBJUNCTIVE.	OPTATIVE.
Pres.—(I am lying, &c.) S. κεῖ-μαι, -σαι, -ται D. κεί-μεθον, -σθον, -σθον P. κεί-μεθα, -σθε, -νται	(κέ-ωμαι), (κέ-ῃ), κέ-ηται wanting —, —, κέ-ωνται	(κε-οίμην), (κέ-οιο), κέ-οιτο wanting —, —, κέ-οιντο

IMPERATIVE.	INFINITIVE.	Imperf.—
Pres.— S. —, κεῖ-σο, -σθω D. —, κεῖ-σθον, -σθων P. wanting	κεῖ-σθαι PARTICIPLE. κείμεν-ος, -η, -ον	S. ἐκεί-μην, -σο, -το D. ἐκεί-μεθον, -σθον, -σθην P. ἐκεί-μεθα, -σθε, -ντο

The verb Ἧμαι (stem ἑ), *I sit* (*I have seated myself*), is originally a perfect passive. It is used in Attic prose only in the compound κάθημαι, *I sit*, or *sit down*.

INDICATIVE.	SUBJUNCTIVE.	OPTATIVE.
Pres.—(I sit, &c.) S. ἧ-μαι, -σαι, -σται D. ἧ-μεθον, -σθον, -σθον P. ἧ-μεθα, -σθε, -νται	wanting	wanting

IMPERATIVE.	INFINITIVE.	Imperf.—
Pres.— S. —, ἧ-σο, -σθω D. —, ἧ-σθον, -σθων P. —, ἧ-σθε, -σθωσαν	ἧ-σθαι PARTICIPLE. ἥμεν-ος, -η, -ον	S. ἥ-μην, -σο, -στο D. ἥ-μεθον, -σθον, -σθην P. ἥ-μεθα, -σθε, -ντο

PART II.
EXTRACTS FOR READING.

SECTION I.
THE WITTICISMS (OF HIEROCLES).

1. Σχολαστικὸς κολυμβᾶν βουλόμενος παρὰ μικρὸν ἐπνίγη· ὤμοσεν οὖν μὴ ἅψασθαι ὕδατος, ἐὰν μὴ πρῶτον μάθῃ κολυμβᾶν.

2. Σχολαστικὸς φίλῳ συναντήσας εἶπε, Καθ' ὕπνους σε ἰδὼν προσηγόρευσα. Ὁ δέ,—Σύγγνωθί μοι, ὅτι οὐ προσέσχον.

3. Σχολαστικός, νοσοῦντα ἐπισκεπτόμενος, ἠρώτα περὶ τῆς ὑγιείας· ὁ δὲ οὐκ ἠδύνατο ἀποκριθῆναι· ὀργισθεὶς οὖν ἐξήλεγξεν,—Ἐλπίζω κἀμὲ νοσῆσαι, καὶ ἐλθόντι σοι μὴ ἀποκριθῆναι.

4. Σχολαστικὸς ἰατρῷ συναντήσας,—Συγχώρησόν μοι, εἶπε, καὶ μή μοι μέμψῃ, ὅτι οὐκ ἐνόσησα.

5. Σχολαστικὸς θέλων τὸν ἵππον αὐτοῦ διδάξαι μὴ τρώγειν πολλά, οὐ παρέβαλεν αὐτῷ τροφάς. Ἀποθανόντος δὲ τοῦ ἵππου τῷ λιμῷ, ἔλεγε,—Μέγα ἐζημιώθην, ὅτε γὰρ ἔμαθε μὴ τρώγειν, τότε ἀπέθανε.

6. Σχολαστικός, οἰκίαν πωλῶν, λίθον ἀπ' αὐτῆς εἰς δεῖγμα περιέφερε.

7. Σχολαστικὸς θέλων εἰδέναι, εἰ πρέπει αὐτῷ κοιμᾶσθαι, καμμύσας εἰσοπτρίζετο.

8. Σχολαστικός, ἰατρῷ συναντήσας, ὑπὸ τοίχου ἐκρύβη. Τινὸς δὲ πυθομένου τὴν αἰτίαν, ἔφη,—Καιρὸν ἔχω μὴ ἀσθενήσας, καὶ αἰσχύνομαι εἰς ὄψιν ἐλθεῖν τοῦ ἰατροῦ.

9. Σχολαστικὸς Ἀμιναῖαν ἔχων, ἐσφράγισεν αὐτήν. Τοῦ δὲ δούλου κάτωθεν τρήσαντος, καὶ τὸν οἶνον αἴροντος, ἐθαύμαζεν ὅτι, τῶν σημάντρων σώων ὄντων, ὁ οἶνος ἐλαττοῦτο· ἕτερος εἶπεν,—Ὅρα, μὴ κάτωθεν ἀφῃρέθη. Ὁ δὲ εἶπεν,—Ἀμαθέστατε, οὐ τὸ κάτωθεν λείπει, ἀλλὰ τὸ ἄνωθεν μέρος.

10. Σχολαστικός, ἰδὼν στρουθία ἐπὶ δένδρου, λάθρα ὑπεισελθὼν ὑφαπλώσατο τὸν κόλπον, καὶ ἔσειε τὸ δένδρον, ὡς ὑποδεξόμενος τὰ στρουθία.

11. Σχολαστικὸς σχολαστικῷ συναντήσας εἶπεν,— Ἔμαθον ὅτι ἀπέθανες· κἀκεῖνος,—Ἀλλ' ὁρᾷς με ἔτι, ἔφη, ζῶντα· καὶ ὁ σχολαστικός,—Καὶ μὴν ὁ εἰπών μοι πολλῷ σου ἀξιοπιστότερος ὑπάρχει.

12. Σχολαστικός, ἐν τῷ ἰδίῳ ἀγρῷ ἐξιών, ἠρώτα πιεῖν ὕδωρ, εἰ καλὸν ἐν τῷ αὐτόθι φρέατι· τῶν δὲ φησάντων ὅτι καλόν, καὶ γὰρ οἱ γονεῖς αὐτοῦ ἐξ αὐτοῦ ἔπινον· Καὶ πηλίκους, ἔφη, εἶχον τραχήλους, ὅτι εἰς τοσοῦτον βάθος πίνειν ἠδύναντο.

13. Σχολαστικὸς μαθὼν ὅτι ὁ κόραξ ὑπὲρ τὰ διακόσια ἔτη ζῇ, ἀγοράσας κόρακα εἰς ἀπόπειραν ἔτρεφε.

14. Σχολαστικὸς εἰς χειμῶνα ναυαγῶν, καὶ τῶν συμπλεόντων ἑκάστου περιπλεκομένων σκεύους πρὸς τὸ σωθῆναι, ἐκεῖνος μίαν τῶν ἀγκυρῶν περιεπλέξατο.

15. Διδύμων ἀδελφῶν εἷς ἐτελεύτησε. Σχολαστικὸς οὖν ἀπαντήσας τῷ ζῶντι ἠρώτα,—Σὺ ἀπέθανες, ἢ ὁ ἀδελφός σου;

16. Σχολαστικός, ναυαγεῖν μέλλων, πινακίδας ᾔτει, ἵνα διαθήκας γράφῃ· τοὺς δὲ οἰκέτας ὁρῶν ἀλγοῦντας διὰ τοῦ κινδύνου, ἔφη,—Μὴ λυπεῖσθε, ἐλευθερῶ γὰρ ὑμᾶς.

17. Σχολαστικὸς ποταμὸν βουλόμενος περᾶσαι, ἀνῆλθεν ἐς τὸ πλοῖον ἔφιππος· πυθομένου δέ τινος τὴν αἰτίαν, ἔφη σπουδάζειν.

18. Σχολαστικὸς ἀπορῶν δαπανημάτων, τὰ βιβλία αὐτοῦ ἐπίπρασκε, καί, γράφων πρὸς τὸν πατέρα, ἔλεγε,—Σύγχαιρε ἡμῖν, πάτερ· ἤδη γὰρ ἡμᾶς τὰ βιβλία τρέφει.

19. Σχολαστικοῦ υἱός, ὑπὸ τοῦ πατρὸς εἰς πόλεμον ἐκπεμπόμενος, ὑπέσχετο ἑνὸς τῶν ἐχθρῶν κεφαλὴν ἀγάγειν. Ὁ δὲ ἔφη,—Εὔχομαι καὶ χωρὶς κεφαλῆς σε ἐλθόντα, μόνον ὑγιῆ ὄντα, ἰδεῖν, καὶ εὐφρανθῆναι.

20. Σχολαστικῷ φίλος ἔγραψεν ἐν Ἑλλάδι ὄντι, βιβλία αὐτῷ ἀγοράσαι· τοῦ δὲ ἀμελήσαντος, ὡς, μετὰ χρόνον, τῷ φίλῳ συνώφθη, εἶπε,—Τὴν ἐπιστολὴν ἣν περὶ βιβλίων ἀπέστειλάς μοι, οὐκ ἐκομισάμην.

21. Σχολαστικὸς μῦν ἐθέλων πιάσαι, συνεχῶς τὰ βιβλία τρώγοντα, κρέας δακὼν ἐναντία ἐκάθισε.

22. Σχολαστικὸς κατ᾽ ὄναρ ἰδὼν ἧλον πεπατηκέναι, καὶ δόξας ἀλγεῖν τὸν πόδα, περιεδήσατο. Ἕτερος δὲ μαθὼν τὴν αἰτίαν ἔφη,—Διατὶ γὰρ ἀνυπόδητος καθεύδεις;

SECTION II.

ANECDOTES.

1. ANECDOTES OF PHILOSOPHERS.

ZENO.

1. Ζήνων δοῦλον ἐπὶ κλοπῇ ἐμαστίγου. Τοῦ δὲ εἰπόντος, εἵμαρτό μοι κλέψαι,—καὶ δαρῆναι, ἔφη. 2. Πρὸς τὸ φλυαροῦν μειράκιον,—Διὰ τοῦτο, εἶπε, δύο ὦτα ἔχομεν, στόμα δὲ ἕν, ἵνα πλείω μὲν ἀκούωμεν, ἥττονα δὲ λέγωμεν. 3. Νεανίσκου πολλὰ λαλοῦντος, Ζήνων ἔφη,—Τὰ ὦτά σου εἰς τὴν γλῶτταν συνερρύηκεν.

ARISTOTLE.

4. Ἀριστοτέλης ὀνειδιζόμενός ποτε, ὅτι πονηρῷ ἀνθρώπῳ ἐλεημοσύνην ἔδωκεν,—Οὐ τὸν τρόπον, ἔφη, ἀλλὰ τὸν ἄνθρωπον ἠλέησα. 5. Τοὺς Ἀθηναίους ἔφασκεν εὑρηκέναι πυροὺς καὶ νόμους· ἀλλὰ πυροῖς μὲν χρῆσθαι, νόμοις δὲ μή. 6. Πρὸς τὸν καυχώμενον, ὡς ἀπὸ μεγάλης πόλεως εἴη,—Οὐ τοῦτο, ἔφη, δεῖ σκοπεῖν, ἀλλ' εἴ τις μεγάλης πατρίδος ἄξιός ἐστιν.

7. Ἀριστοτέλης ἐνοχλούμενος ὑπ' ἀδολέσχου, καὶ κοπτόμενος ἀτόποις τισὶ διηγήμασι, πολλάκις αὐτοῦ λέγοντος, οὐ θαυμαστὸν ὅ τι λέγω;—Οὐ τοῦτο, φησί, θαυμαστόν, ἀλλ' εἴ τις πόδας ἔχων σὲ ὑπομένει.

PLATO.

8. Πλάτων θρασυνόμενον ἰδών τινα πρὸς τὸν ἑαυτοῦ πατέρα,—Οὐ παύσῃ, μειράκιον, εἶπε, τούτου κατα-

φρονῶν, δι' ὃν μέγα φρονεῖν ἀξιοῖς; 9. Πλάτων ὀργιζόμενός ποτε τῷ οἰκέτῃ, ἐπιστάντος Ξενοκράτους, —Λαβών, ἔφη, τοῦτον, μαστίγωσον· ἐγὼ γὰρ ὀργίζομαι.

SOCRATES.

10. Σωκράτης πρὸς Ξανθίππην, πρότερον μὲν λοιδοροῦσαν, ὕστερον δὲ καὶ περιχέασαν αὐτῷ,—Οὐκ ἔλεγον, εἶπεν, ὅτι Ξανθίππη βροντῶσα καὶ ὕδωρ πέμψει; 11. Πρὸς Ἀλκιβιάδην εἰπόντα, Οὐκ ἀνεκτὴ ἡ Ξανθίππη λοιδοροῦσα,—Οὐ καὶ σύ, εἶπε, χηνῶν βοώντων ἀνέχῃ

DIOGENES.

12. Διογένης πρὸς τὸν εἰπόντα, κακὸν εἶναι τὸ ζῆν, —οὐ τὸ ζῆν, εἶπεν, ἀλλὰ τὸ κακῶς ζῆν. 13. Διογένης ὁ Σινωπεύς, ὁ κύων ἐπικαλούμενος, παντὶ τόπῳ ἐχρῆτο εἰς πάντα, ἀριστῶν τε καὶ καθεύδων καὶ διαλεγόμενος. Βακτηρίᾳ ἐπηρείσατο ἀσθενήσας· ἔπειτα μέντοι καὶ διαπαντὸς ἐφόρει αὐτήν. Καὶ πήραν ἐκομίσατο, ἔνθα αὐτῷ τὰ σιτία ἦν. Ἐπιστείλας δέ τινι οἰκίδιον αὐτῷ προνοήσασθαι, καὶ βραδύνοντος, πίθον τινὰ ἔσχεν οἰκίαν.

14. Θεασάμενός ποτε παιδίον ταῖς χερσὶ πῖνον, ἐξέρριψε τῆς πήρας τὴν κοτύλην, εἰπών,—Παιδίον με νενίκηκεν εὐτελείᾳ. Ἐξέβαλε δὲ καὶ τὸ τρυβλίον, ὁμοίως παιδίον θεασάμενος, ἐπειδὴ κατέαξε τὸ σκεῦος, τῷ κοίλῳ ἄρτῳ τὴν φακῆν ὑποδεχόμενον.

15. Μοχθηροῦ τινος ἀνθρώπου ἐπιγράψαντος ἐπὶ τὴν οἰκίαν, Μηδὲν εἰσίτω κακόν·—Ὁ οὖν κύριος τῆς οἰκίας, ἔφη, ποῦ εἰσέλθοι ἄν; 16. Πρὸς τοὺς ἐρπύσαντας ἐπὶ τὴν τράπεζαν μῦς,—Ἰδού, φησί, καὶ Διογένης παρασίτους τρέφει. 17. Πρὸς τὸν πυθόμενον, ποίᾳ

ὥρᾳ δεῖ ἀριστᾶν,—Εἰ μὲν πλούσιος, ἔφη, ὅταν θέλῃ, εἰ δὲ πένης, ὅταν ἔχῃ. 18. Πλάτωνος ὁρισαμένου,— "Ἄνθρωπός ἐστι ζῶον δίπουν, ἄπτερον·—καὶ εὐδοκιμοῦντος, τίλας ἀλεκτρυόνα εἰσήνεγκεν εἰς τὴν σχολὴν αὐτοῦ, καὶ ἔφη,—Οὗτός ἐστιν ὁ Πλάτωνος ἄνθρωπος.

ANTISTHENES.

19. Ἀντισθένης ποτὲ ἐπαινούμενος ὑπὸ πονηρῶν,— Ἀγωνιῶ, ἔφη, μή τι κακὸν εἴργασμαι. 20. Ἐρωτηθείς, τί αὐτῷ περιγέγονεν ἐκ φιλοσοφίας, ἔφη,—Τὸ δύνασθαι ἑαυτῷ ὁμιλεῖν.
21. Αἱρετώτερον εἶπεν εἶναι, εἰς κόρακας ἐμπεσεῖν, ἢ εἰς κόλακας· τοὺς μὲν γὰρ ἀποθανόντος τὸ σῶμα, τοὺς δὲ ζῶντος τὴν ψυχὴν λυμαίνεσθαι.

SOLON. GORGIAS.

22. Σόλων ἀποβαλὼν υἱὸν ἔκλαυσεν. Εἰπόντος δέ τινος πρὸς αὐτόν, ὡς οὐδὲν προὔργου ποιεῖ κλαίων,— Δι' αὐτὸ γάρ τοι τοῦτο, ἔφη, κλαίω. 23. Γοργίας ὁ Λεοντῖνος ἐρωτηθείς, ποίᾳ διαίτῃ χρώμενος εἰς μακρὸν γῆρας ἦλθεν,—Οὐδὲν οὐδέποτε, ἔφη, πρὸς ἡδονὴν οὔτε φαγών, οὔτε δράσας. 24. Γοργίας ἤδη γηραιὸς ὑπάρχων, ἐρωτηθείς, εἰ ἡδέως ἀποθνήσκοι,—Μάλιστα, εἶπεν· ὥσπερ γὰρ ἐκ σαπροῦ καὶ ῥέοντος οἰκιδίου ἀσμένως ἀπαλλάττομαι.

PITTACUS. XENOPHON.

25. Πιττακὸς ἀδικηθεὶς ὑπό τινος, καὶ ἔχων ἐξουσίαν αὐτὸν κολάσαι, ἀφῆκεν, εἰπών,—Συγγνώμη τιμωρίας ἀμείνων· τὸ μὲν γὰρ ἡμέρου φύσεως ἐστί, τὸ δὲ

θηριώδους. 26. Γρύλλος, ὁ Ξενοφῶντος υἱός, ἐν τῇ μάχῃ περὶ Μαντίνειαν ἰσχυρῶς ἀγωνισάμενος ἐτελεύτησεν. Ἐν ταύτῃ τῇ μάχῃ καὶ Ἐπαμινώνδας ἔπεσε. Τηνικαῦτα δὴ καὶ τὸν Ξενοφῶντά φασι θύειν ἐστεμμένον· ἀπαγγελθέντος δὲ αὐτῷ τοῦ θανάτου τοῦ παιδός, ἀποστεφανώσασθαι· ἔπειτα μαθόντα ὅτι γενναίως, πάλιν ἐπιθέσθαι τὸν στέφανον. Ἔνιοι δὲ οὐδὲ δακρῦσαί φασιν αὐτόν, ἀλλὰ γὰρ εἰπεῖν, ᾔδειν θνητὸν γεγεννηκώς.

2. ANECDOTES OF STATESMEN AND KINGS.

ARCHELAUS. DIONYSIUS.

27. Χαριέντως ὁ βασιλεὺς Ἀρχέλαος, ἀδολέσχου κουρέως περιβαλόντος αὐτῷ τὸ ὠμόλινον, καὶ πυθομένου,—Πῶς σε κείρω, βασιλεῦ;—Σιωπῶν, ἔφη. 28. Ὁ νεώτερος Διονύσιος ἔλεγε πολλοὺς τρέφειν σοφιστάς, οὐ θαυμάζων ἐκείνους, ἀλλὰ δι' ἐκείνων θαυμάζεσθαι βουλόμενος.

PHILIP, KING OF MACEDON.

29. Φίλιππος ἔλεγε, κρεῖττον εἶναι στρατόπεδον ἐλάφων, λέοντος στρατηγοῦντος, ἢ λεόντων, ἐλάφου στρατηγοῦντος. 30. Φίλιππος, ὁ Ἀλεξάνδρου πατήρ, Ἀθηναίους μακαρίζειν ἔλεγεν, εἰ καθ' ἕκαστον ἐνιαυτὸν αἱρεῖσθαι δέκα στρατηγοὺς εὑρίσκουσιν· αὐτὸς γὰρ ἐν πολλοῖς ἔτεσιν ἕνα μόνον στρατηγὸν εὑρηκέναι, Παρμενίωνα. 31. Φίλιππος ἐρωτώμενος, οὕστινας μάλιστα φιλεῖ, καὶ οὕστινας μάλιστα μισεῖ,—Τοὺς μέλλοντας, ἔφη, προδιδόναι μάλιστα φιλῶ, τοὺς δ' ἤδη προδεδωκότας μάλιστα μισῶ.

32. Ἐν Χαιρωνείᾳ τοὺς Ἀθηναίους μεγάλῃ νίκῃ ἐνίκησε Φίλιππος. Ἐπαρθεὶς δὲ τῇ εὐπραγίᾳ, ᾤετο δεῖν αὐτὸν ὑπομιμνήσκεσθαι, ὅτι ἄνθρωπός ἐστιν, καὶ προσέταξε παιδί τινι τοῦτο ἔργον ἔχειν. Τρὶς δὲ ἑκάστης ἡμέρας ὁ παῖς ἔλεγεν αὐτῷ,—Φίλιππε ἄνθρωπος εἶ.

ALEXANDER THE GREAT.

33. Ὁ Ἀλέξανδρος Διογένει εἰς λόγους ἐλθών, οὕτω κατεπλάγη τὸν βίον καὶ τὸ ἀξίωμα τοῦ ἀνδρός, ὥστε πολλάκις αὐτοῦ μνημονεύων λέγειν, εἰ μὴ Ἀλέξανδρος ἤμην, Διογένης ἂν ἤμην. 34. Ἀλέξανδρος Ἀναξάρχου περὶ κόσμων ἀπειρίας ἀκούων ἐδάκρυε, καὶ τῶν φίλων ἐρωτησάντων αὐτόν, τί δακρύει;—Οὐκ ἄξιον, ἔφη, δακρύειν, εἰ κόσμων ὄντων ἀπείρων, ἑνὸς οὐδέπω κύριοι γεγόναμεν;

THE SUCCESSORS OF ALEXANDER.

35. Πτολεμαῖόν φασι τὸν Λάγου, καταπλουτίζοντα τοὺς φίλους αὐτοῦ ὑπερχαίρειν· ἔλεγε δέ, ἄμεινον εἶναι πλουτίζειν ἢ πλουτεῖν. 36. Ἀντίγονος πρός τινα μακαρίζουσαν αὐτὸν γραῦν,—Εἰ ᾔδεις, ἔφη, ὦ μῆτερ, ὅσων κακῶν μεστόν ἐστι τουτὶ τὸ ῥάκος, δείξας τὸ διάδημα, οὐκ ἂν ἐπὶ κοπρίας κείμενον αὐτὸ ἐβάστασας.

THEMISTOCLES.

37. Θεμιστοκλῆς ἐρωτηθεὶς πότερον Ἀχιλλεὺς ἐβούλετ' ἂν εἶναι ἢ Ὅμηρος; Σὺ δὲ αὐτός, ἔφη, πότερον ἤθελες ὁ νικῶν ἐν Ὀλυμπιάσιν ἢ ὁ κηρύσσων τοὺς νικῶντας εἶναι;

38. Θεμιστοκλῆς πρὸς τὸν Εὐρυβιάδην τὸν Λακεδαιμόνιον ἔλεγέ τι ὑπεναντίον, καὶ ἀνέτεινεν αὐτῷ τὴν βακτηρίαν ὁ Εὐρυβιάδης. Ὁ δέ, πάταξον μέν, ἔφη, ἄκουσον δέ· ᾔδει δέ, ὅτι ἃ μέλλει λέγειν τῷ κοινῷ λυσιτελεῖ. 39. Σεριφίου τινὸς πρὸς αὐτὸν εἰπόντος, ὡς οὐ δι' αὐτόν, ἀλλὰ διὰ τὴν πόλιν ἔνδοξός ἐστιν, ἀληθῆ λέγεις, εἶπεν, ἀλλ' οὔτ' ἂν ἐγὼ Σερίφιος ὢν ἐγενόμην ἔνδοξος, οὔτε σύ, Ἀθηναῖος.

EPAMINONDAS.

40. Ἐπαμινώνδας ἕνα εἶχε τρίβωνα· εἰ δέ ποτε αὐτὸν ἔδωκεν εἰς γναφεῖον, αὐτὸς ὑπέμενεν οἴκοι δι' ἀπορίαν ἑτέρου. 41. Ἐπαμινώνδας, ὁ Θηβαῖος, ἰδὼν στρατόπεδον μέγα καὶ καλόν, στρατηγὸν οὐκ ἔχον,— Ἡλίκον, ἔφη, θηρίον, καὶ κεφαλὴν οὐκ ἔχει.

PERICLES.

42. Ὁ Περικλῆς ἐν τῷ λοιμῷ τοὺς παῖδας ἀποβαλών, ἀνδρειότατα τὸν θάνατον αὐτῶν ἤνεγκε, καὶ πάντας Ἀθηναίους ἔπεισε τοὺς τῶν φιλτάτων θανάτους εὐθυμότερον φέρειν.

SECTION III.

FABLES OF ÆSOP.

1. THE WOLF.

Λύκος ἰδὼν ποιμένας ἐσθίοντας ἐν σκηνῇ πρόβατον, ἐγγὺς προσελθών,—Ἡλίκος, ἔφη, ἂν ἦν θόρυβος, εἰ ἐγὼ τοῦτο ἐποίουν!

2. THE LIONESS.

Λέαινα, ὀνειδιζομένη ὑπ' ἀλώπεκος, ἐπὶ τὸ διὰ παντὸς ἕνα τίκτειν,—Ἕνα, ἔφη, ἀλλὰ λέοντα.

3. THE GNAT AND THE OX.

Κώνωψ ἐπὶ κέρᾶτος βοὸς ἐκαθέσθη καὶ ηὔλει· εἶπε δὲ πρὸς τὸν βοῦν,—Εἰ βαρῶ σου τὸν τένοντα, ἀναχωρήσω. Ὁ δὲ ἔφη,—Οὔτε ὅτε ἦλθες ἔγνων, οὔτε ἐὰν μένῃς, μελήσει μοι.

4. THE HUSBANDMAN AND THE SNAKE.

Γεωργὸς χειμῶνος ὥρᾳ ὄφιν εὑρὼν ὑπὸ κρύους πεπηγότα, τοῦτον λαβὼν ὑπὸ κόλπου κατέθετο. Θερμανθεὶς δὲ ἐκεῖνος, καὶ ἀναλαβὼν τὴν ἰδίαν φύσιν, ἔπληξε τὸν εὐεργέτην.

5. THE FOX AND THE BUNCH OF GRAPES.

Βότρυας πεπείρους ἀλώπηξ κρεμαμένους ἰδοῦσα, τούτους ἐπειρᾶτο καταφαγεῖν. Πολλὰ δὲ καμοῦσα καὶ μὴ δυνηθεῖσα ψαῦσαι, τὴν λύπην παραμυθουμένη, ἔλεγεν,—Ὄμφακες ἔτι εἰσίν.

6. THE KID AND THE WOLF.

Ἔριφος ἐπί τινος δώματος ἑστώς, ἐπειδὴ λύκον παριόντα εἶδεν, ἐλοιδόρει καὶ ἔσκωπτεν αὐτόν. Ὁ δὲ λύκος ἔφη,—Ὦ οὗτος, οὐ σύ με λοιδορεῖς, ἀλλὰ ὁ τόπος.

7. THE BOY BATHING.

Παῖς λουσάμενος ἐν ποταμῷ ἐκινδύνευε πνιγῆναι· καὶ ἰδὼν τινα παροδίτην, ἐπεφώνει,—βοήθησον. Ὁ δε εμέμφετο τῷ παιδὶ τὴν τολμηρίαν. Τὸ δὲ παιδίον εἶπεν,—Ἀλλὰ νῦν μοι βοήθησον, ὕστερον δὲ σωθέντι μέμφου.

8. THE HOUND AND THE FOX.

Κύων θηρευτικὸς λέοντα ἰδών, τοῦτον ἐδίωκεν· ὡς δὲ ἐπιστραφεὶς ἐκεῖνος ἐβρυχήσατο, ὁ κύων φοβηθεὶς εἰς τὰ ὀπίσω ἔφυγεν. Ἀλώπηξ δὲ θεασαμένη αὐτὸν ἔφη,—Ὦ κακὴ κεφαλή, σὺ λέοντα ἐδίωκες, οὕτινος οὐδὲ τὸν βρυχηθμὸν ὑπήνεγκας;

9. THE WOLF AND THE LAMB.

Λύκος ἀμνὸν ἐδίωκεν, ὁ δὲ εἰς ναὸν κατέφυγε. Προσκαλουμένου δὲ τοῦ λύκου τὸν ἀμνόν, καὶ λέγοντος, ὅτι θυσιάσει αὐτὸν ὁ ἱερεὺς τῷ θεῷ, ἐκεῖνος ἔφη πρὸς αὐτόν,—Ἀλλ' αἱρετώτερόν μοί ἐστι θεῷ θυσίαν εἶναι, ἢ ὑπὸ σοῦ διαφθαρῆναι.

10. THE ASS IN THE LION'S SKIN.

Ὄνος δορὰν λέοντος ἐπενδυθείς, λέων ἐνομίζετο πᾶσι, καὶ φυγὴ μὲν ἦν ἀνθρώπων, φυγὴ δὲ ποιμνίων. Ὡς δὲ ἄνεμος βιαιότερον πνεύσας ἐγύμνου αὐτὸν τοῦ προκαλύμματος, τότε πάντες ἐπιδραμόντες ξύλοις καὶ ῥοπάλοις αὐτὸν ἔπαιον.

11. THE WOMAN AND THE HEN.

Γυνή τις χήρα ὄρνιν εἶχε, καθ' ἑκάστην ἡμέραν ᾠὸν αὐτῇ τίκτουσαν. Νομίσασα δέ, ὡς, εἰ πλείους τῇ ὄρνιθι κριθὰς παραβάλοι, δὶς τέξεται τῆς ἡμέρας, τοῦτο πεποίηκεν. Ἡ δὲ ὄρνις πιμελὴς γενομένη οὐδ' ἅπαξ τῆς ἡμέρας τεκεῖν ἠδύνατο.

12. THE BIRDS AND THE PEACOCK.

Τῶν ὀρνίθων βουλομένων ποιῆσαι βασιλέα, ταὼς ἑαυτὸν ἠξίου διὰ τὸ κάλλος χειροτονεῖν. Αἱρουμένων δὲ τοῦτον τῶν ἄλλων, ὁ κολοιὸς ὑπολαβὼν ἔφη,— Ἀλλ' εἰ, σοῦ βασιλεύοντος, ὁ ἀετὸς ἡμᾶς καταδιώκειν ἐπιχειρήσει, πῶς ἡμῖν ἐπαρκέσεις;

13. THE BOY AND THE SNAILS.

Γεωργοῦ παῖς ὤπτα κοχλίας· ἀκούσας δὲ αὐτῶν τρυζόντων, ἔφη,—Ὦ κάκιστα ζῶα, τῶν οἰκιῶν ὑμῶν ἐμπιπραμένων, αὐτοὶ ᾄδετε;

14. THE HORSE AND HIS GROOM.

Κριθὴν τὴν τοῦ ἵππου ὁ ἱπποκόμος κλέπτων καὶ πωλῶν, τὸν ἵππον ἔτριβε καὶ ἐκτένιζε πάσας ἡμέρας· ἔφη δὲ ὁ ἵππος,—Εἰ θέλεις ἀληθῶς καλὸν εἶναί με, τὴν κριθὴν τὴν τρέφουσαν μὴ πώλει.

15. THE HEN AND THE SWALLOW.

Ὄρνις ὄφεως ᾠὰ εὑροῦσα, ἐπιμελῶς ἐκθερμάνασα ἐξεκόλαψε· χελιδὼν δέ, θεασαμένη αὐτήν, ἔφη,—Ὦ ματαία, τί ταῦτα τρέφεις, ἅπερ αὐξηθέντα ἀπὸ σοῦ πρώτης τοῦ ἀδικεῖν ἄρξεται;

16. THE FLY.

Μυῖα, ἐμπεσοῦσα εἰς χύτραν κρέατος, ἐπειδὴ ὑποπνίγεσθαι ἔμελλεν, ἔφη πρὸς ἑαυτήν· Ἀλλ' ἔγωγε καὶ βέβρωκα, καὶ πέπωκα, καὶ λέλουμαι, κἂν ἀποθάνω οὐδὲν μέλει μοι.

17. THE FOX AND THE MASK.

Ἀλώπηξ εἰς οἰκίαν ἐλθοῦσα ὑποκριτοῦ, καὶ ἕκαστα τῶν αὐτοῦ σκευῶν διερευνωμένη, εὗρε καὶ κεφαλὴν μορμολυκείου εὐφυῶς κατεσκευασμένην· ἣν καὶ ἀναλαβοῦσα ταῖς χερσίν, ἔφη,—Ὦ οἵα κεφαλή, καὶ ἐγκέφαλον οὐκ ἔχει!

18. THE RAVEN AND HIS DAM.

Κόραξ νοσῶν ἔφη τῇ μητρί,—Μῆτερ, εὔχου τῷ θεῷ, καὶ μὴ θρήνει. Ἡ δ' ὑπολαβοῦσα ἔφη,—Τίς σε, ὦ τέκνον, τῶν θεῶν ἐλεήσει; τίνος γὰρ κρέας ὑπὸ σοῦ γε οὐκ ἐκλάπη;

19. THE DOG AND HIS SHADOW.

Κύων, κρέας φέρων, ποταμὸν διέβαινε· θεασάμενος δὲ τὴν ἑαυτοῦ σκιὰν ἐπὶ τοῦ ὕδατος, ὑπέλαβεν ἕτερον κύνα εἶναι κρέας κατέχοντα· καὶ, ἀφεὶς τὸ ἴδιον, ὥρμησε τὸ ἐκείνου λαβεῖν· ἀπώλεσε δὲ ἀμφότερα· τὸ μὲν οὖν οὐκ ἦν· ὃ δὲ κατεῖχεν ὑπὸ τοῦ ῥεύματος κατεσύρετο.

20. THE HORSE AND THE STAG.

Ἵππος κατεῖχε λειμῶνα μόνος· ἐλθόντος δ' ἐλάφου, καὶ διαφθείροντος τὴν νομήν, βουλόμενος τιμωρήσασθαι τὸν ἔλαφον, ἠρώτα τιν' ἄνθρωπον, εἰ δύναιτο μετ' αὐτοῦ κολάσαι τὸν ἔλαφον· ὁ δ' ἔφησεν, ἐὰν λάβῃ χαλινόν, καὶ αὐτὸς ἀναβῇ ἐπ' αὐτόν, ἔχων ἀκόντια· συνομολογήσαντος δέ, καὶ ἀναβάντος, ἀντὶ τοῦ τιμωρήσασθαι, αὐτὸς ἐδούλευσεν ἤδη τῷ ἀνθρώπῳ.

21. THE GRASSHOPPER AND THE ANTS.

Χειμῶνος ὥρᾳ τῶν σίτων βραχέντων, οἱ μύρμηκες ἔψυχον· τέττιξ δὲ λιμώττων ᾔτει αὐτοὺς τροφήν· οἱ δὲ μύρμηκες εἶπον αὐτῷ,—Διὰ τί τὸ θέρος οὐ συνῆγες τροφήν; Ὁ δὲ εἶπεν,—Οὐκ ἐσχόλαζον, ἀλλ' ᾖδον μουσικῶς· Οἱ δὲ γελάσαντες εἶπον,—Ἀλλ' εἰ θέρους ὥραις ηὔλεις, χειμῶνος ὀρχοῦ.

22. THE OLD MAN AND DEATH.

Γέρων ποτὲ ξύλα τεμὼν ἐξ ὄρους, κἀπὶ τῶν ὤμων ἀράμενος, ἐπειδὴ πολλὴν ὁδὸν ἐπηχθισμένος ἐβάδισεν, ἀπειρηκώς, ἀπέθετό τε τὰ ξύλα, καὶ τὸν θάνατον ἐλθεῖν ἐπεκαλεῖτο· τοῦ δὲ θανάτου εὐθὺς ἐπιστάντος, καὶ τὴν αἰτίαν πυνθανομένου δι' ἣν αὐτὸν καλοίη, ὁ γέρων ἔφη, —Ἵνα τὸν φόρτον τοῦτον ἄρας ἐπιθῇς μοι.

23. THE DOG AND HIS MASTER.

Ἔχων τις κύνα Μελιταῖον καὶ ὄνον, διετέλει τῷ κυνὶ προσπαίζων· καὶ εἴ ποτε ἔξω δεῖπνον εἶχεν, ἐκόμιζέ τι αὐτῷ καὶ προσιόντι παρέβαλεν· ὁ δὲ ὄνος ζηλώσας προέδραμεν αὐτός, καὶ σκιρτῶν ἐλάκτισε τὸν δεσπότην· καὶ οὗτος ἀγανακτήσας ἐκέλευσε παίοντα αὐτὸν ἀναγαγεῖν πρὸς τὸν μυλῶνα, καὶ τοῦτον δῆσαι.

24. THE WOLF AND THE CRANE.

Λύκου λαιμῷ ὀστέον ἐπεπήγει· ὁ δὲ γεράνῳ μισθὸν παρέξειν εἶπεν, εἰ τὴν κεφαλὴν αὐτῆς ἐπιβαλοῦσα, τὸ ὀστοῦν ἐκ τοῦ λαιμοῦ αὐτοῦ ἐκβάλοι· ἡ δὲ τοῦτ' ἐκβαλοῦσα, δολιχόδειρος οὖσα, τὸν μισθὸν ἐπεζήτει·

ὅστις γελάσας, καὶ τοὺς ὀδόντας θήξας,—Ἀρκεῖ σοι μισθός, ἔφη, τοῦτο καὶ μόνον, ὅτι ἐκ λύκου στόματος καὶ ὀδόντων ἐξεῖλες κάρα σῶον, μηδὲν παθοῦσα.

25. THE LION AND THE ASS.

Λέων καὶ ὄνος κοινωνίαν θέμενοι, ἐξῆλθον ἐπὶ θήραν· γενομένων δὲ αὐτῶν κατά τι σπήλαιον, ἐν ᾧ αἶγες ἄγριαι, ὁ μὲν λέων πρὸ τοῦ στομίου στάς, ἐξιούσας τὰς αἶγας συνελάμβανεν· ὁ δὲ ὄνος ἔνδον εἰσελθὼν ἐνήλατο αὐταῖς, καὶ ὠγκᾶτο ἐκφοβεῖν βουλόμενος· τοῦ δὲ λέοντος τὰς πλείστας συλλαβόντος, ἐξελθὼν ἐκεῖνος ἐπυνθάνετο αὐτοῦ εἰ γενναίως ἠγωνίσατο, καὶ τὰς αἶγας ἐξεδίωξεν· ὁ δὲ εἶπεν,—Ἀλλ' εὖ ἴσθι ὅτι κἀγὼ ἄν σε ἐφοβήθην, εἰ μὴ ᾔδειν σε ὄνον ὄντα.

26. THE STAG AT THE FOUNTAIN.

Ἔλαφος διψήσας ἐπὶ πηγὴν ἦλθεν· ἰδὼν δὲ τὴν ἑαυτοῦ σκιάν, τοὺς μὲν πόδας ἐμέμφετο ὡς λεπτοὺς καὶ ἀσθενεῖς ὄντας· τὰ δὲ κέρατα αὐτοῦ ἐπῄνει, ὡς μέγιστα καὶ εὐμήκη· μηδέπω πιών, κυνηγοῦ καταλαβόντος, ἔφευγεν· ἐπὶ πολὺν δὲ τόπον δραμὼν καὶ εἰς ὕλην ἐμβάς, τοῖς κέρασιν ἐμπλακεὶς ἐθηρεύθη· ἔφη δέ,—Ὢ μάταιος ἐγώ! ὃς ἐκ μὲν τῶν ποδῶν ἐσώθην, οἷς ἐμεμφόμην, ἐκ δὲ τῶν κεράτων προεδόθην, οἷς ἐκαυχώμην.

27. THE FOX AND THE RAVEN.

Κόραξ, κρέας ἁρπάσας, ἐπί τινος δένδρου ἐκάθισεν· ἀλώπηξ δὲ τοῦτον ἰδοῦσα, καὶ βουληθεῖσα περιγενέσθαι τοῦ κρέατος, στᾶσα κάτωθεν ἐπῄνει αὐτόν, ὡς εὐμεγεθὲς καὶ καλὸν ὄρνεον καὶ θηρευτικὸν καὶ εὔμορφον· καὶ λέγουσα, Ὅτι ἥρμοζέ σοι βασιλέα εἶναι ὀρνέων, εἰ καὶ φωνητικὸς ὑπῆρχες· ἀλλ' ὦ ποῖον ὄρνεον, καὶ ἄλαλον ὑπάρχεις· Ὁ δὲ κόραξ, ἀκούσας ταῦτα, καὶ χαυνωθεὶς τοῖς ἐπαίνοις, ῥίψας τὸ κρέας, μεγάλως ἐκεκράγει· ἡ δ' ἀλώπηξ, δραμοῦσα καὶ λαβοῦσα τὸ κρέας, ἔφη πρὸς αὐτόν· Ἔχεις, κόραξ, ἅπαντα, νοῦς δέ σοι λείπει.

28. THE CITY MOUSE AND THE COUNTRY MOUSE.

Μῦς ἀρουραῖος ἀστικῷ γίνεται φίλος μυΐ, καὶ τὴν φιλίαν πιστούμενος, πρῶτος εἰς ἀγρὸν τὸν ἀστικὸν παρελάμβανεν, καὶ ξενίαν αὐτῷ παρετίθει καὶ τράπεζαν, ἃ φέρειν οἶδε τοῖς ἐνοικοῦσιν ἀγρόν· ἀμειβόμενος δὲ τὴν ξενίαν ὁ ἀστικός, εἰς ἄστυ τὸν ἀρουραῖον ἐκόμιζεν, καὶ εἰς ἀνδρὸς εὐπόρου παρελάμβανεν οἶκον· ὡς δὲ τῶν ὄντων ἤδη προσάπτεσθαι ἤθελον, προσιών τις ἀνέκοπτε· καὶ τοσαυτάκις τῆς ἐν τοῖς ὄψοις ἀπηλαύνοντο πείρας, ὁσάκις ἐπειρῶντο μεταλαμβάνειν· καὶ τελευταῖον ὁ ἀρουραῖος, Ἄπειμι, ἔφη, τὴν ἐν ἀγροῖς προτιμῶν μετριότητα τῆς ἐν ἄστει τρυφῆς.

29. THE FROGS ASKING A KING.

Βάτραχοι, λυπούμενοι περὶ τῆς ἑαυτῶν ἀναρχίας, πρέσβεις ἔπεμψαν πρὸς τὸν Δία, βασιλέα αὐτοῖς παρασχεῖν· ὁ δὲ συνιδὼν αὐτῶν τὴν εὐήθειαν, ξύλον εἰς τὴν λίμνην καθῆκεν· καὶ οἱ βάτραχοι, τὸ μὲν πρῶτον καταπλαγέντες τὸν ψόφον, εἰς τὰ βάθη τῆς λίμνης ἔδυσαν· ὕστερον δέ, ὡς ἀκίνητον ἦν τὸ ξύλον, ἀναδύντες, εἰς τοσοῦτον καταφρονήσεως ἦλθον, ὡς καὶ ἐπιβαίνοντες αὐτῷ ἐπικαθέζεσθαι· ἀναξιοπαθοῦντες δὲ τοιοῦτον ἔχειν βασιλέα, ἧκον ἐκ δευτέρου πρὸς τὸν Δία, καὶ τοῦτον παρεκάλουν ἀλλάξαι αὐτοῖς τὸν ἀρχηγόν· τὸν γὰρ πρῶτον λίαν εἶναι νωχελῆ καὶ ἀδόκιμον· ὁ δὲ Ζεύς, ἀγανακτήσας κατ' αὐτῶν, ὕδρον αὐτοῖς ἔπεμψεν, ὑφ' οὗ συλλαμβανόμενοι κατησθίοντο.

30. MERCURY AND THE STATUARY.

Ἑρμῆς γνῶναι βουλόμενος ἐν τίνι τιμῇ παρ' ἀνθρώποις ἐστίν, ἧκεν εἰς ἀγαλματοποιοῦ, ἑαυτὸν εἰκάσας ἀνθρώπῳ· καὶ θεασάμενος ἄγαλμα τοῦ Διός, ἠρώτα, πόσου τις αὐτὸ πρίασθαι δύναται; τοῦ δὲ εἰπόντος,—δραχμῆς· γελάσας,—Πόσου τὸ τῆς Ἥρας, ἔφη· εἰπόντος δέ,—πλείονος, ἰδὼν καὶ τὸ ἑαυτοῦ ἄγαλμα, καὶ νομίσας, ὡς ἐπειδὴ ἄγγελός ἐστι θεῶν καὶ κερδῷος, πολὺν αὐτοῦ παρὰ τοῖς ἀνθρώποις εἶναι τὸν λόγον, ἤρετο περὶ αὐτοῦ· ὁ δ' ἀγαλματοποιὸς ἔφη,— Ἐὰν τούτους ὠνήσῃ, καὶ τοῦτον προσθήκην σοι δίδωμι.

SECTION IV.
DIALOGUES OF LUCIAN.
1. DIALOGUES OF THE DEAD.

DIALOGUE I.—CHARON, MENIPPUS, AND HERMES,
(*Mercury.*)

ΧΑ. Ἀπόδος, ὦ κατάρατε, τὰ πορθμεῖα.
ΜΕ. Βόα, εἰ τοῦτό σοι ἥδιον, ὦ Χάρων.
ΧΑ. Ἀπόδος, φημί, ἀνθ' ὧν σε διεπορθμευσάμην.
ΜΕ. Οὐκ ἂν λάβοις παρὰ τοῦ μὴ ἔχοντος.
ΧΑ. Ἔστι δέ τις ὀβολὸν μὴ ἔχων; 5

ΜΕ. Εἰ μὲν καὶ ἄλλος τις, οὐκ οἶδα· ἐγὼ δὲ οὐκ ἔχω.

ΧΑ. Καὶ μὴν ἄγξω σε, νὴ τὸν Πλούτωνα, ὦ μιαρέ, ἢν μὴ ἀποδῷς.

10 ΜΕ. Κἀγὼ τῷ ξύλῳ σου πατάξας διαλύσω τὸ κρανίον.

ΧΑ. Μάτην οὖν ἔσῃ πεπλευκὼς τοσοῦτον πλοῦν;

ΜΕ. Ὁ Ἑρμῆς ὑπὲρ ἐμοῦ σοι ἀποδότω, ὅς με παρέδωκέ σοι.

15 ΕΡ. Νὴ Δία, ὠνάμην γε, εἰ μέλλω καὶ ὑπερεκτίνειν τῶν νεκρῶν.

ΧΑ. Οὐκ ἀποστήσομαί σου.

ΜΕ. Τούτου γε ἕνεκα νεωλκήσας τὸ πορθμεῖον, παράμενε· πλὴν ἀλλ' ὅ γε μὴ ἔχω, πῶς ἂν λάβοις;

20 ΧΑ. Σὺ δ' οὐκ ᾔδεις ὡς κομίζεσθαι δέον;

ΜΕ. Ἤιδειν μέν, οὐκ εἶχον δέ· τί οὖν; ἐχρῆν διὰ τοῦτο μὴ ἀποθανεῖν;

ΧΑ. Μόνος οὖν αὐχήσεις προῖκα πεπλευκέναι;

ΜΕ. Οὐ προῖκα, ὦ βέλτιστε· καὶ γὰρ ἤντλησα.
25 καὶ τῆς κώπης συνεπελαβόμην, καὶ οὐκ ἔκλαον μόνος τῶν ἄλλων ἐπιβατῶν.

ΧΑ. Οὐδὲν ταῦτα πρὸς τὰ πορθμεῖα· τὸν ὀβολὸν ἀποδοῦναί σε δεῖ· οὐ γὰρ θέμις ἄλλως γενέσθαι·

ΜΕ. Οὐκοῦν ἀπάγαγέ με αὖθις ἐς τὸν βίον.

30 ΧΑ. Χάριεν λέγεις, ἵνα καὶ πληγὰς ἐπὶ τούτῳ παρὰ τοῦ Αἰακοῦ προσλάβω.

ΜΕ. Μὴ ἐνόχλει οὖν.

ΧΑ. Δεῖξον τί ἐν τῇ πήρᾳ ἔχεις.

ΜΕ. Θέρμους, εἰ θέλεις, καὶ τῆς Ἑκάτης τὸ δεῖπνον.

35 ΧΑ. Πόθεν τοῦτον ἡμῖν, ὦ Ἑρμῆ, τὸν κύνα ἤγαγες;

οἷα δὲ καὶ ἐλάλει παρὰ τὸν πλοῦν, τῶν ἐπιβατῶν τῶν
ἁπάντων καταγελῶν, καὶ ἐπισκώπτων, καὶ μόνος ᾄδων,
οἰμωζόντων ἐκείνων;
ΕΡ. Ἀγνοεῖς, ὦ Χάρων, ὅντινα ἄνδρα διεπορθμεύ-
σας; ἐλεύθερον ἀκρῑβῶς, κοὐδενὸς αὐτῷ μέλει· οὗτός 40
ἐστιν ὁ Μένιππος.
ΧΑ. Καὶ μὴν ἄν σε λάβω ποτέ—
ΜΕ. Ἂν λάβῃς, ὦ βέλτιστε· δὶς δὲ οὐκ ἂν λάβοις.

DIALOGUE 2.—CRŒSUS, PLUTO, MENIPPUS, MIDAS,
AND SARDANAPALUS.

ΚΡ. Οὐ φέρομεν, ὦ Πλούτων, Μένιππον τουτονὶ
τὸν κύνα παροικοῦντα· ὥστε ἢ ἐκεῖνόν ποι μετάστησον,
ἢ ἡμεῖς μετοικήσομεν εἰς ἕτερον τόπον.
ΠΛ. Τί δ' ὑμᾶς δεινὸν ἐργάζεται, ὁμόνεκρος ὤν;
ΚΡ. Ἐπειδὰν ἡμεῖς οἰμώζωμεν, καὶ στένωμεν, 5
ἐκείνων μεμνημένοι τῶν ἄνω, Μίδας μὲν οὑτοσὶ τοῦ
χρυσίου, Σαρδανάπαλος δὲ τῆς πολλῆς τρυφῆς, ἐγὼ
δὲ τῶν θησαυρῶν, ἐπιγελᾷ καὶ ἐξονειδίζει, ἀνδράποδα
καὶ καθάρματα ἡμᾶς ἀποκαλῶν. ἐνίοτε δὲ καὶ ᾄδων,
ἐπιταράττει ἡμῶν τὰς οἰμωγάς· καὶ ὅλως, λυπηρός ἐστι. 10
ΠΛ. Τί ταῦτά φασιν, ὦ Μένιππε;
ΜΕ. Ἀληθῆ, ὦ Πλούτων· μισῶ γὰρ αὐτούς, ἀγεννεῖς καὶ ὀλεθρίους ὄντας, οἷς οὐκ ἀπέχρησε βιῶναι
κακῶς, ἀλλὰ καὶ ἀποθανόντες ἔτι μέμνηνται, καὶ περιέχονται τῶν ἄνω. χαίρω τοιγαροῦν ἀνιῶν αὐτούς. 15
ΠΛ. Ἀλλ' οὐ χρή· λυποῦνται γὰρ οὐ μικρῶν
στερούμενοι.
ΜΕ. Καὶ σὺ μωραίνεις, ὦ Πλούτων, ὁμόψηφος
ὢν τοῖς τούτων στεναγμοῖς;

ΠΛ. Οὐδαμῶς· ἀλλ' οὐκ ἂν ἐθέλοιμι στασιάζειν ὑμᾶς.

ΜΕ. Καὶ μήν, ὦ κάκιστοι Λυδῶν, καὶ Φρυγῶν, καὶ Ἀσσυρίων, οὕτω γινώσκετε, ὡς οὐδὲ παυσομένου μου· ἔνθα γὰρ ἂν ἴητε, ἀκολουθήσω, ἀνιῶν, καὶ καταδῶν, καὶ καταγελῶν.

ΚΡ. Ταῦτα οὐχ ὕβρις;

ΜΕ. Οὔκ· ἀλλ' ἐκεῖνα ὕβρις ἦν, ἃ ὑμεῖς ἐποιεῖτε, προσκυνεῖσθαι ἀξιοῦντες, καὶ ἐλευθέροις ἀνδράσιν ἐντρυφῶντες, καὶ τοῦ θανάτου τὸ παράπαν οὐ μνημονεύοντες· τοιγαροῦν οἰμώξεσθε, πάντων ἐκείνων ἀφῃρημένοι.

ΚΡ. Πολλῶν γε, ὦ θεοί, καὶ μεγάλων κτημάτων.

ΜΙ. Ὅσου μὲν ἐγὼ χρυσοῦ.

ΣΑ. Ὅσης δὲ ἐγὼ τρυφῆς.

ΜΕ. Εὖγε, οὕτω ποιεῖτε. ὀδύρεσθε μὲν ὑμεῖς ἐγὼ δέ, τὸ " Γνῶθι σαυτὸν" πολλάκις συνείρων, ἐπάσομαι ὑμῖν. πρέποι γὰρ ἂν ταῖς τοιαύταις οἰμωγαῖς ἐπᾳδόμενον.

DIALOGUE 3.—ZENOPHANTUS AND CALLIDEMIDES.

ΖΗ. Σὺ δέ, ὦ Καλλιδημίδη, πῶς ἀπέθανες; ἐγὼ μὲν γάρ, ὅτι παράσιτος ὢν Δεινίου, πλέον τοῦ ἱκανοῦ ἐμφαγών, ἀπεπνίγην, οἶσθα· παρῆς γὰρ ἀποθνήσκοντί μοι.

ΚΑ. Παρῆν, ὦ Ζηνόφαντε· τὸ δ' ἐμὸν παράδοξόν τι ἐγένετο· οἶσθα γὰρ καὶ σύ που Πτοιόδωρον τὸν γέροντα.

ΖΗ. Τὸν ἄτεκνον, τὸν πλούσιον, ᾧ σε τὰ πολλὰ ᾔδειν συνόντα;

ΚΑ. Ἐκεῖνον αὐτὸν ἀεὶ ἐθεράπευον, ὑπισχνούμενος
ἐπ' ἐμοὶ τεθνήξεσθαι. ἐπεὶ δὲ τὸ πρᾶγμα ἐς μήκιστον
ἐπετείνετο, καὶ ὑπὲρ τὸν Τιθωνὸν ὁ γέρων ἔζη, ἐπίτομόν τινα ὁδὸν ἐπὶ τὸν κλῆρον ἐξηῦρον· πριάμενος γὰρ
φάρμακον, ἀνέπεισα τὸν οἰνοχόον, ἐπειδὰν τάχιστα ὁ
Πτοιόδωρος αἰτήσῃ πιεῖν—πίνει δ' ἐπιεικῶς ζωρότερον
—ἐμβαλόντα ἐς κύλικα, ἕτοιμον ἔχειν αὐτό, καὶ ἐπιδοῦναι αὐτῷ· εἰ δὲ τοῦτο ποιήσει, ἐλεύθερον ἐπωμοσάμην ἀφήσειν αὐτόν.

ΖΗ. Τί οὖν ἐγένετο; πάνυ γάρ τι παράδοξον ἐρεῖν
ἔοικας.

ΚΑ. Ἐπεὶ τοίνυν λουσάμενοι ἥκομεν, δύο ἤδη ὁ
μειρακίσκος κύλικας ἑτοίμους ἔχων, τὴν μὲν τῷ Πτοιοδώρῳ, τὴν ἔχουσαν τὸ φάρμακον, τὴν δ' ἑτέραν ἐμοί,
σφαλεὶς οὐκ οἶδ' ὅπως, ἐμοὶ μὲν τὸ φάρμακον,
Πτοιοδώρῳ δὲ τὴν ἀφάρμακτον ἐπέδωκεν· εἶτα ὁ μὲν
ἔπινεν· ἐγὼ δὲ αὐτίκα μάλα ἐκτάδην ἐκείμην ὑποβολιμαῖος ἀντ' ἐκείνου νεκρός. Τί τοῦτο; γελᾷς, ὦ
Ζηνόφαντε; καὶ μὴν οὐκ ἔδει γε ἑταίρῳ ἀνδρὶ ἐπιγελᾶν.

ΖΗ. Ἀστεῖα γάρ, ὦ Καλλιδημίδη, πέπονθας. ὁ
γέρων δέ, τί πρὸς ταῦτα;

ΚΑ. Πρῶτον μὲν ὑπεταράχθη πρὸς τὸ αἰφνίδιον.
εἶτα συνείς, οἶμαι, τὸ γεγενημένον, ἐγέλα καὶ αὐτὸς
οἷά με ὁ οἰνοχόος εἴργασται.

ΖΗ. Πλὴν ἀλλ' οὐδὲ σὲ τὴν ἐπίτομον ἐχρῆν τραπέσθαι· ἧκε γὰρ ἄν σοι διὰ τῆς λεωφόρου ἀσφαλέστερον, εἰ καὶ ὀλίγῳ βραδύτερον.

DIALOGUE 4.—PLUTO, PROTESILAUS, AND PERSEPHONE
(*Proserpine*).

ΠΡ. Ὦ δέσποτα, καὶ βασιλεῦ, καὶ ἡμέτερε Ζεῦ, καὶ σύ, Δήμητρος θύγατερ, μὴ ὑπερίδητε δέησιν ἐρωτικήν.

ΠΛ. Σὺ δὲ τίνων δέῃ παρ' ἡμῶν; ἢ τίς ὢν τυγ-
5 χάνεις;

ΠΡ. Εἰμὶ μὲν Πρωτεσίλαος ὁ Ἰφίκλου, Φυλάκιος, συστρατιώτης τῶν Ἀχαιῶν, καὶ πρῶτος ἀποθανὼν τῶν ἐπ' Ἰλίῳ· δέομαι δέ, ἀφεθεὶς πρὸς ὀλίγον, ἀναβιῶναι πάλιν.

10 ΠΛ. Τοῦτον μὲν τὸν ἔρωτα, ὦ Πρωτεσίλαε, πάντες νεκροὶ ἐρῶσι· πλὴν οὐδεὶς ἂν αὐτῶν τύχοι.

ΠΡ. Ἀλλ' οὐ τοῦ ζῆν, Ἀϊδωνεῦ, ἐρῶ ἔγωγε, τῆς γυναικὸς δέ, ἣν νεόγαμον ἔτι ἐν τῷ θαλάμῳ καταλιπών, ᾠχόμην ἀποπλέων· εἶτα ὁ κακοδαίμων ἐν τῇ ἀποβάσει
15 ἀπέθανον ὑπὸ τοῦ Ἕκτορος· ὁ οὖν ἔρως τῆς γυναικὸς οὐ μετρίως ἀποκναίει με, ὦ δέσποτα· καὶ βούλομαι, κἂν πρὸς ὀλίγον ὀφθεὶς αὐτῇ, καταβῆναι πάλιν.

ΠΛ. Οὐκ ἔπιες, ὦ Πρωτεσίλαε, τὸ Λήθης ὕδωρ;

ΠΡ. Καὶ μάλα, ὦ δέσποτα· τὸ δὲ πρᾶγμα ὑπέρ-
20 ογκον ἦν.

ΠΛ. Οὐκοῦν περίμεινον· ἀφίξεται γὰρ ἐκείνη ποτέ, καὶ οὐδέν σε ἀνελθεῖν δεήσει.

ΠΡ. Ἀλλ' οὐ φέρω τὴν διατριβήν, ὦ Πλούτων· ἠράσθης δὲ καὶ αὐτὸς ἤδη, καὶ οἶσθα οἷον τὸ ἐρᾶν
25 ἐστιν.

ΠΛ. Εἶτα τί σε ὀνήσει μίαν ἡμέραν ἀναβιῶναι, μετ' ὀλίγον τὰ αὐτὰ ὀδυρούμενον;

ΠΡ. Οἶμαι πείσειν κἀκείνην ἀκολουθεῖν παρ' ὑμᾶς· ὥστε ἀνθ' ἑνός, δύο νεκροὺς λήψῃ μετ' ὀλίγον.

ΠΛ. Οὐ θέμις γενέσθαι ταῦτα, οὐδὲ γέγονε 30 πώποτε.

ΠΡ. Ἀναμνήσω σε, ὦ Πλούτων· Ὀρφεῖ γὰρ, δι' αὐτὴν ταύτην τὴν αἰτίαν τὴν Εὐρυδίκην παρέδοτε, καὶ τὴν ὁμογενῆ μου Ἄλκηστιν παρεπέμψατε, Ἡρακλεῖ χαριζόμενοι. 35

ΠΛ. Θελήσεις δέ, οὕτω κρανίον γυμνὸν ὤν, καὶ ἄμορφον, τῇ καλῇ σου ἐκείνῃ νύμφῃ φανῆναι; πῶς δὲ κἀκείνη προσόψεταί σε, οὐδὲ διαγνῶναι δυναμένη; φοβήσεται γάρ, εὖ οἶδα, καὶ φεύξεταί σε· καὶ μάτην ἔσῃ τοσαύτην ὁδὸν ἀνεληλυθώς. 40

ΠΕ. Οὐκοῦν, ὦ ἄνερ, σὺ καὶ τοῦτο ἴασαι, καὶ τὸν Ἑρμῆν κέλευσον, ἐπειδὰν ἐν τῷ φωτὶ ἤδη ὁ Πρωτεσίλαος ᾖ, καθικόμενον τῇ ῥάβδῳ, νεανίαν εὐθὺς καλὸν ἀπεργάσασθαι αὐτόν, οἷος ἦν ἐκ τοῦ παστοῦ.

ΠΛ. Ἐπεὶ Περσεφόνῃ συνδοκεῖ, ἀναγαγὼν τοῦ- 45 τον αὖθις, ποίησον νυμφίον· σὺ δὲ μέμνησο μίαν λαβὼν ἡμέραν.

DIALOGUE 5.—ÆACUS, PROTESILAUS, MENELAUS, AND PARIS.

ΑΙ. Τί ἄγχεις, ὦ Πρωτεσίλαε, τὴν Ἑλένην προσπεσών;

ΠΡ. Ὅτι διὰ ταύτην, ὦ Αἰακέ, ἀπέθανον, ἡμιτελῆ μὲν τὸν δόμον καταλιπών, χήραν δὲ τὴν νεόγαμον γυναῖκα. 5

ΑΙ. Αἰτιῶ τοίνυν τὸν Μενέλαον, ὅστις ὑμᾶς ὑπὲρ τοιαύτης γυναικὸς ἐπὶ Τροίαν ἤγαγεν.

ΠΡ. Ευ λέγεις· εκείνον μοι αιτιατέον.

ΜΕ. Ουκ εμέ, ώ βέλτιστε, αλλά δικαιότερον τον Πάριν, ος εμού του ξένου την γυναίκα παρά πάντα τα δίκαια ώχετο αρπάσας· ούτος γάρ ουχ υπό σού μόνου, αλλ' υπό πάντων Ελλήνων τε και Βαρβάρων άξιος άγχεσθαι τοσούτοις θανάτου αίτιος γεγενημένος.

ΠΡ. Άμεινον ούτω· σε τοιγαρούν, ώ Δύσπαρι, ουκ αφήσω ποτε εκ των χειρών.

ΠΑ. Άδικα ποιών, ώ Πρωτεσίλαε, και ταύτα, ομότεχνον όντα σοι, ερωτικός γάρ και αυτός ειμι, και τω αυτώ θεώ κατέσχημαι· οίσθα δε ως ακούσιόν τι εστί, και τις ημάς δαίμων άγει, ένθα αν εθέλη· και αδύνατόν εστιν αντιτάττεσθαι αυτώ.

ΠΡ. Ευ λέγεις· είθε ουν μοι τον Έρωτα ενταύθα λαβείν δυνατόν ην.

ΑΙ. Εγώ σοι και υπέρ του Έρωτος αποκρινούμαι τα δίκαια· φήσει γάρ αυτός μεν του εράν τω Πάριδι ίσως γεγενήσθαι αίτιος· του θανάτου δέ σοι ουδένα άλλον, ώ Πρωτεσίλαε, ή σε αυτόν, ος εκλαθόμενος της νεογάμου γυναικός, επεί προσεφέρεσθε τη Τρωάδι, ούτω φιλοκινδύνως και απονενοημένως προεπήδησας των άλλων, δόξης ερασθείς, δι' ην πρώτος εν τη αποβάσει απέθανες.

ΠΡ. Ουκούν και υπέρ εμαυτού σοι, ώ Αιακέ, αποκρινούμαι δικαιότερα; ου γάρ εγώ τούτων αίτιος, αλλ' η μοίρα, και το εξ αρχής ούτως επικεκλώσθαι.

ΑΙ. Ορθώς. τί ουν τούτους αιτιά;

DIALOGUE 6.—HERMES AND CHARON.

ΕΡ. Λογισώμεθα, ὦ Πορθμεῦ, εἰ δοκεῖ, ὁπόσα μοι ὀφείλεις ἤδη, ὅπως μὴ αὖθις ἐρίζωμέν τι περὶ αὐτῶν.

ΧΑ. Λογισώμεθα, ὦ Ἑρμῆ· ἄμεινον γὰρ ὡρίσθαι περὶ αὐτῶν, καὶ ἀπραγμονέστερον.

ΕΡ. Ἄγκυραν ἐντειλαμένῳ ἐκόμισα πέντε δραχμῶν.

ΧΑ. Πολλοῦ λέγεις.

ΕΡ. Νὴ τὸν Ἀϊδωνέα, τῶν πέντε ὠνησάμην, καὶ τροπωτῆρα δύο ὀβολῶν.

ΧΑ. Τίθει πέντε δραχμάς, καὶ ὀβολοὺς δύο.

ΕΡ. Καὶ ἀκέστραν ὑπὲρ τοῦ ἱστίου,—πέντε ὀβολοὺς ἐγὼ κατέβαλον.

ΧΑ. Καὶ τούτους προστίθει.

ΕΡ. Καὶ κηρὸν ὡς ἐπιπλάσαι τοῦ σκαφιδίου τὰ ἀνεῳγότα, καὶ ἥλους δέ, καὶ καλώδιον, ἀφ' οὗ τὴν ὑπέραν ἐποίησας—δύο δραχμῶν ἅπαντα.

ΧΑ. Εὖγε, ἄξια ταῦτα ὠνήσω.

ΕΡ. Ταῦτά ἐστιν, εἰ μή τι ἄλλο ἡμᾶς διέλαθεν ἐν τῷ λογισμῷ· πότε δ' οὖν ταῦτ' ἀποδώσειν φής;

ΧΑ. Νῦν μέν, ὦ Ἑρμῆ, ἀδύνατον· ἢν δὲ λοιμός τις ἢ πόλεμος καταπέμψῃ ἀθρόους τινάς, ἐνέσται τότε ἀποκερδᾶναι ἐν τῷ πλήθει παραλογιζόμενον τὰ πορθμεῖα.

ΕΡ. Νῦν οὖν ἐγὼ καθεδοῦμαι τὰ κάκιστα εὐχόμενος γενέσθαι, ὡς ἂν ἀπὸ τούτων ἀπολαύοιμι.

ΧΑ. Οὐκ ἔστιν ἄλλως, ὦ Ἑρμῆ· νῦν δ' ὀλίγοι, ὡς ὁρᾷς, ἀφικνοῦνται ἡμῖν· εἰρήνη γάρ.

ΕΡ. Ἄμεινον οὕτως, εἰ καὶ ἡμῖν παρατείνοιτο ὑπὸ
σοῦ τὸ ὄφλημα. πλὴν ἀλλ' οἱ μὲν παλαιοί, ὦ Χάρων,
οἶσθα οἷοι παρεγίνοντο, ἀνδρεῖοι ἅπαντες, αἵματος
ἀνάπλεῳ, καὶ τραυματίαι οἱ πολλοί· νῦν δέ, ἢ φαρμάκῳ
τις ὑπὸ τοῦ παιδὸς ἀποθανών, ἢ ὑπὸ τῆς γυναικός, ἢ
ὑπὸ τρυφῆς ἐξῳδηκὼς τὴν γαστέρα, καὶ τὰ σκέλη·
ὠχροὶ γὰρ ἅπαντες, καὶ ἀγεννεῖς, οὐδὲ ὅμοιοι ἐκείνοις·
οἱ δὲ πλεῖστοι αὐτῶν, διὰ χρήματα ἥκουσιν, ἐπιβουλ-
εύοντες ἀλλήλοις, ὡς ἐοίκασι.

ΧΑ. Πάνυ γὰρ περιπόθητά ἐστι ταῦτα.

ΕΡ. Οὐκοῦν οὐδ' ἐγὼ δόξαιμι ἂν ἁμαρτάνειν, πικρῶς ἀπαιτῶν τὰ ὀφειλόμενα παρὰ σοῦ.

2. DIALOGUES OF THE GODS.

DIALOGUE 7.—ZEUS AND HERMES.

ΖΕ. Τὴν τοῦ Ἰνάχου παῖδα τὴν καλὴν οἶσθα, ὦ
Ἑρμῆ;

ΕΡ. Ναί· τὴν Ἰὼ λέγεις.

ΖΕ. Οὐκ ἔτι παῖς ἐκείνη ἐστίν, ἀλλὰ δάμαλις.

ΕΡ. Τεράστιον τοῦτο· τῷ τρόπῳ δ' ἐνηλλάγη;

ΖΕ. Ζηλοτυπήσασα ἡ Ἥρα, μετέβαλεν αὐτήν·
ἀλλὰ καὶ καινὸν ἄλλο τι δεινὸν ἐπιμεμηχάνηται τῇ
κακοδαίμονι· βουκόλον τινὰ πολυόμματον, Ἄργον
τοὔνομα, ἐπέστησεν, ὃς νέμει τὴν δάμαλιν, ἄϋπνος ὤν.

ΕΡ. Τί οὖν ἡμᾶς χρὴ ποιεῖν;

ΖΕ. Καταπτάμενος ἐς τὴν Νεμέαν—ἐκεῖ δέ που ὁ
Ἄργος βουκολεῖ—ἐκεῖνον μὲν ἀπόκτεινον· τὴν δὲ Ἰὼ
διὰ τοῦ πελάγους ἐς τὴν Αἴγυπτον ἀπαγαγών, Ἶσιν
ποίησον. καὶ τοιλοιπὸν ἔστω θεὸς τοῖς ἐκεῖ· καὶ τὸν

Νεῖλον ἀναγέτω, καὶ τοὺς ἀνέμους ἐπιπεμπέτω, καὶ 15
σωζέτω τοὺς πλέοντας.

DIALOGUE 8.—HEPHÆSTUS (*Vulcan*) AND ZEUS (*Jupiter*).

"ΗΦ. Τί με, ὦ Ζεῦ, χρὴ ποιεῖν; ἥκω γάρ, ὡς
ἐκέλευσας, ἔχων τὸν πέλεκυν ὀξύτατον, εἰ καὶ λίθον
δέοι μιᾷ πληγῇ διατεμεῖν.
ΖΕ. Εὖγε, ὦ "Ηφαιστε. ἀλλὰ δίελέ μου τὴν κεφαλὴν εἰς δύο, κατενεγκών. 5
"ΗΦ. Πειρᾷ μου, εἰ μέμηνα; πρόσταττε δ᾽ οὖν
τἀληθές, ὅπερ θέλεις σοι γενέσθαι.
ΖΕ. Τοῦτο αὐτό—διαιρεθῆναί μοι τὸ κρανίον· εἰ
δὲ ἀπειθήσεις, οὐ νῦν πρῶτον ὀργιζομένου πειράσῃ
μου· ἀλλὰ χρὴ καθικνεῖσθαι παντὶ τῷ θυμῷ, μηδὲ 10
μέλλειν· ἀπόλλυμαι γὰρ ὑπὸ ὠδίνων, αἵ μοι τὸν
ἐγκέφαλον ἀναστρέφουσιν.
"ΗΦ. Ὅρα, ὦ Ζεῦ, μὴ κακόν τι ποιήσωμεν· ὀξὺς
γὰρ ὁ πέλεκύς ἐστι, καὶ οὐκ ἀναιμωτί, οὐδὲ κατὰ τὴν
Εἰλήθυιαν, μαιώσεταί σε. 15
ΖΕ. Κατένεγκε μόνον, ὦ "Ηφαιστε, θαρρῶν· οἶδα
γὰρ ἐγὼ τὸ συμφέρον.
"ΗΦ. Ἄκων μέν, κατοίσω δέ· τί γὰρ χρὴ ποιεῖν,
σοῦ κελεύοντος;—τί τοῦτο; κόρη ἔνοπλος; μέγα, ὦ
Ζεῦ, κακὸν εἶχες ἐν τῇ κεφαλῇ· εἰκότως γοῦν ὀξύθυμος 20
ἦσθα, τηλικαύτην ὑπὸ τῇ μήνιγγι παρθένον ζωογο-
νῶν, καὶ ταῦτα ἔνοπλον· ἦπου στρατόπεδον, οὐ κεφαλὴν ἐλελήθεις ἔχων· ἡ δὲ πηδᾷ, καὶ πυρριχίζει, καὶ τὴν
ἀσπίδα τινάσσει, καὶ τὸ δόρυ πάλλει, καὶ ἐνθουσιᾷ·
καὶ τὸ μέγιστον, καλὴ πάνυ καὶ ἀκμαία γεγένηται ἤδη 25
ἐν βραχεῖ· γλαυκῶπις μέν, ἀλλὰ κοσμεῖ καὶ τοῦτο ἡ

κόρυς· ὥστε, ὦ Ζεῦ, μαίωτρά μοι ἀπόδος ἐγγυήσας ἤδη αὐτήν.

ΖΕ. Ἀδύνατα αἰτεῖς, ὦ Ἥφαιστε· παρθένος γὰρ
30 ἀεὶ ἐθελήσει μένειν· ἐγὼ δ' οὖν τό γε ἐπ' ἐμοὶ οὐδὲν ἀντιλέγω.

ΗΦ. Τοῦτ' ἐβουλόμην. ἐμοὶ μελήσει τὰ λοιπά· καὶ ἤδη συναρπάσω αὐτήν.

ΖΕ. Εἴ σοι ῥᾴδιον, οὕτω ποίει· πλὴν οἶδα ὅτι
35 ἀδυνάτων ἐρᾷς.

DIALOGUE 9.—ZEUS, ÆSCULAPIUS, AND HERACLES
(Hercules).

ΖΕ. Παύσασθε, ὦ Ἀσκληπιὲ καὶ Ἡράκλεις, ἐρίζοντες πρὸς ἀλλήλους ὥσπερ ἄνθρωποι· ἀπρεπῆ γὰρ ταῦτα, καὶ ἀλλότρια τοῦ συμποσίου τῶν θεῶν.

ΗΡ. Ἀλλὰ ἐθέλεις, ὦ Ζεῦ, τουτονὶ τὸν φαρμακέα
5 προκατακλίνεσθαί μου;

ΑΣ. Νὴ Δία· καὶ ἀμείνων γάρ εἰμι.

ΗΡ. Κατὰ τί, ὦ ἐμβρόντητε; ἢ διότι σε ὁ Ζεὺς ἐκεραύνωσεν, ἃ μὴ θέμις ποιοῦντα, νῦν δὲ κατ' ἔλεον αὖθις ἀθανασίας μετείληφας;

10 ΑΣ. Ἐπιλέλησαι γὰρ καὶ σύ, ὦ Ἡράκλεις, ἐν τῇ Οἴτῃ καταφλεγείς, ὅτι μοι ὀνειδίζεις τὸ πῦρ;

ΗΡ. Οὔκουν ἴσα καὶ ὅμοια βεβίωται ἡμῖν· ὃς Διὸς μὲν υἱός εἰμι, τοσαῦτα δὲ πεπόνηκα ἐκκαθαίρων τὸν βίον, θηρία καταγωνιζόμενος, καὶ ἀνθρώπους ὑβριστὰς
15 τιμωρούμενος· σὺ δὲ ῥιζοτόμος εἶ καὶ ἀγύρτης, νοσοῦσι μὲν ἴσως ἀνθρώποις χρήσιμος εἰς ἐπίθεσιν τῶν φαρμάκων, ἀνδρῶδες δὲ οὐδὲν ἐπιδεδειγμένος.

ΑΣ. Εὖ λέγεις· ὅτι σου τὰ ἐγκαύματα ἰασάμην, ὅτι πρώην ἀνῆλθες ἡμίφλεκτος ὑπ' ἀμφοῖν διεφθαρ-

μένος το σώμα, και του χιτώνος, και μετά τούτο του 20
πυρός· εγώ δε εἰ καὶ μηδὲν ἄλλο, οὔτε ἐδούλευσα
ὥσπερ σύ, οὔτε ἔξαινον ἔρια ἐν Λυδίᾳ πορφυρίδα
ἐνδεδυκώς, καὶ παιόμενος ὑπὸ τῆς Ὀμφάλης χρυσῷ
σανδάλῳ· ἀλλ' οὐδὲ μελαγχολήσας ἀπέκτεινα τὰ τέκνα
καὶ τὴν γυναῖκα. 25

ΗΡ. Εἰ μὴ παύσῃ λοιδορούμενός μοι, αὐτίκα
μάλα εἴσῃ, ὡς οὐ πολύ σε ὀνήσει ἡ ἀθανασία· ἐπεὶ
ἀράμενός σε, ῥίψω ἐπὶ κεφαλὴν ἐκ τοῦ οὐρανοῦ, ὥστε
μηδὲ τὸν Παιῶνα ἰάσασθαί σε, τὸ κρανίον συντριβέντα. 30

ΖΕ. Παύσασθε, φημί, καὶ μὴ ἐπιταράττετε ἡμῖν
τὴν συνουσίαν, ἢ ἀμφοτέρους ἀποπέμψομαι ὑμᾶς τοῦ
συμποσίου· καίτοι εὔγνωμον, ὦ Ἡράκλεις, προκατακλίνεσθαί σου τὸν Ἀσκληπιόν, ἅτε καὶ πρότερον
ἀποθανόντα. 35

DIALOGUE 10.—HERMES AND MAIA.

ΕΡ. Ἔστι γάρ τις, ὦ μῆτερ, ἐν οὐρανῷ θεὸς
ἀθλιώτερος ἐμοῦ;

ΜΑ. Μὴ λέγε, ὦ Ἑρμῆ, τοιοῦτον μηδέν.

ΕΡ. Τί μὴ λέγω, ὃς τοσαῦτα πράγματα ἔχω,
μόνος κάμνων, καὶ πρὸς τοσαύτας ὑπηρεσίας διασπώ- 5
μενος; ἕωθεν μὲν γὰρ ἐξαναστάντα σαίρειν τὸ συμπόσιον δεῖ· καὶ διαστρώσαντα τὴν κλισίαν, εὐθε-
τήσαντά τε ἕκαστα, παρεστάναι τῷ Διΐ, καὶ διαφέρειν
τὰς ἀγγελίας τὰς παρ' αὐτοῦ ἄνω καὶ κάτω ἡμεροδρο-
μοῦντα· καὶ ἐπανελθόντα ἔτι κεκονιμένον παρατιθέναι 10
τὴν ἀμβροσίαν· πρὶν δὲ τὸν νεώνητον τοῦτον οἰνοχόον
ἥκειν, καὶ τὸ νέκταρ ἐγὼ ἐνέχεον· τὸ δὲ πάντων δεινό-

τατον, ὅτι μηδὲ νυκτὸς καθεύδω μόνος τῶν ἄλλων,
ἀλλὰ δεῖ με καὶ τότε τῷ Πλούτωνι ψυχαγωγεῖν, καὶ
15 νεκροπομπὸν εἶναι, καὶ παρεστάναι τῷ δικαστηρίῳ· οὐ
γὰρ ἱκανά μοι τὰ τῆς ἡμέρας ἔργα, ἐν παλαίστραις
εἶναι, κἂν ταῖς ἐκκλησίαις κηρύττειν, καὶ ῥήτορας
ἐκδιδάσκειν, ἀλλ᾽ ἔτι καὶ νεκρικὰ συνδιαπράττειν με-
μερισμένον· καίτοι τὰ μὲν τῆς Λήδας τέκνα, παρ᾽
20 ἡμέραν ἑκάτερος ἐν οὐρανῷ ἢ ἐν ᾅδου εἰσίν· ἐμοὶ δὲ
καθ᾽ ἑκάστην ἡμέραν καὶ ταῦτα κἀκεῖνα ποιεῖν ἀναγ-
καῖον. καὶ οἱ μὲν Ἀλκμήνης καὶ Σεμέλης υἱοί, ἐκ
γυναικῶν δυστήνων γενόμενοι, εὐωχοῦνται ἀφρόντιδες·
ὁ δὲ Μαίας τῆς Ἀτλαντίδος διακονοῦμαι αὐτοῖς· καὶ
25 νῦν ἄρτι ἥκοντά με ἀπὸ Σιδῶνος παρὰ τῆς Κάδμου
θυγατρός, ἐφ᾽ ἣν πέπομφέ με ὀψόμενον ὅ τι πράττει
ἡ παῖς, μηδὲ ἀναπνεύσαντα, πέπομφεν αὖθις ἐς τὸ
Ἄργος ἐπισκεψόμενον τὴν Δανάην. εἶτ᾽ ἐκεῖθεν ἐς
Βοιωτίαν, φησίν, ἐλθών, ἐν παρόδῳ τὴν Ἀντιόπην ἰδέ.
30 καὶ ὅλως ἀπηγόρευκα ἤδη. εἰ γοῦν μοι δυνατὸν ἦν,
ἡδέως ἂν ἠξίωσα πεπρᾶσθαι, ὥσπερ οἱ ἐν γῇ κακῶς
δουλεύοντες.

ΜΑ. Ἔα ταῦτα, ὦ τέκνον· χρὴ γὰρ πάντα ὑπηρ-
ετεῖν τῷ πατρί, νεανίαν ὄντα· καὶ νῦν ὥσπερ ἐπέμ-
35 φθης, σόβει εἰς Ἄργος, εἶτα ἐς τὴν Βοιωτίαν, μὴ καὶ
πληγὰς βραδύνων λάβοις· ὀξύχολοι γὰρ οἱ ἐρῶντες.

DIALOGUE 11.—THE CYCLOP POLYPHEMUS AND POSEIDON
(*Neptune*).

ΚΥ. Ὦ πάτερ, οἷα πέπονθα ὑπὸ τοῦ καταράτου
ξένου, ὃς μεθύσας ἐξετύφλωσέ με, κοιμωμένῳ ἐπιχει-
ρήσας.

ΠΟ. Τίς δ' ἦν ὁ ταῦτα τολμήσας, ὦ Πολύφημε;
ΚΥ. Τὸ μὲν πρῶτον Οὖτιν αὑτὸν ἀπεκάλει· ἐπεὶ δὲ διέφυγε, καὶ ἔξω ἦν βέλους, Ὀδυσσεὺς ὀνομάζεσθαι ἔφη.
ΠΟ. Οἶδα ὃν λέγεις, τὸν Ἰθακήσιον· ἐξ Ἰλίου δ' ἀνέπλει.. Ἀλλὰ πῶς ταῦτ' ἔπραξεν, οὐδὲ πάνυ εὐθαρσὴς ὤν;
ΚΥ. Κατέλαβον ἐν τῷ ἄντρῳ, ἀπὸ τῆς νομῆς ἀναστρέψας, πολλούς τινας, ἐπιβουλεύοντας δῆλον ὅτι τοῖς ποιμνίοις· ἐπεὶ γὰρ ἐπέθηκα τῇ θύρᾳ τὸ πῶμα (πέτρα δέ ἐστι παμμεγέθης) καὶ τὸ πῦρ ἀνέκαυσα, ἐναυσάμενος ὃ ἔφερον δένδρον ἀπὸ τοῦ ὄρους, ἐφάνησαν ἀποκρύπτειν αὑτοὺς πειρώμενοι· ἐγὼ δὲ συλλαβὼν αὐτῶν τινας, ὥσπερ εἰκὸς ἦν, κατέφαγον, λῃστάς γε ὄντας. Ἐνταῦθα ὁ πανουργότατος ἐκεῖνος, εἴτε Οὖτις, εἴτε Ὀδυσσεὺς ἦν, δίδωσί μοι πιεῖν φάρμακόν τι ἐγχέας, ἡδὺ μὲν καὶ εὔοσμον, ἐπιβουλότατον δὲ καὶ ταραχωδέστατον· ἅπαντα γὰρ εὐθὺς ἐδόκει μοι περιφέρεσθαι πιόντι, καὶ τὸ σπήλαιον αὐτὸ ἀνεστρέφετο, καὶ οὐκέτι ὅλως ἐν ἐμαυτῷ ἤμην· τέλος δὲ ἐς ὕπνον κατεσπάσθην. Ὁ δέ, ἀποξύνας τὸν μοχλόν, καὶ πυρώσας γε προσέτι, ἐτύφλωσέ με καθεύδοντα· καὶ ἀπ' ἐκείνου τυφλός εἰμι σοί, ὦ Πόσειδον.
ΠΟ. Ὡς βαθὺν ἐκοιμήθης, ὦ τέκνον, ὃς οὐκ ἐξέθορες μεταξὺ τυφλούμενος. Ὁ δ' οὖν Ὀδυσσεὺς πῶς διέφυγεν; οὐ γὰρ ἄν, εὖ οἶδ' ὅτι, ἐδυνήθη ἀποκινῆσαι τὴν πέτραν ἀπὸ τῆς θύρας.
ΚΥ. Ἀλλ' ἐγὼ ἀφεῖλον, ὡς μᾶλλον αὐτὸν λάβοιμι ἐξιόντα· καὶ καθίσας παρὰ τὴν θύραν ἐθήρων τὰς χεῖρας ἐκπετάσας, μόνα παρεὶς τὰ πρόβατα ἐς τὴν

νομήν, ἐντειλάμενος τῷ κριῷ, ὁπόσα ἐχρῆν πράττειν
35 αὐτὸν ὑπὲρ ἐμοῦ.

ΠΟ. Μανθάνω,—ὑπ' ἐκείνοις ἔλαθον ὑπεξελθόντες·
σὲ δὲ τοὺς ἄλλους Κύκλωπας ἔδει ἐπιβοήσασθαι ἐπ'
αὐτόν.

ΚΥ. Συνεκάλεσα, ὦ πάτερ, καὶ ἧκον· ἐπεὶ δὲ
40 ἤροντο τοῦ ἐπιβουλεύοντος τοὔνομα, κἀγὼ ἔφην,
ὅτι Οὖτίς ἐστι, μελαγχολᾶν οἰηθέντες με, ᾤχοντο
ἀπιόντες. Οὕτω κατεσοφίσατό με ὁ κατάρατος τῷ
ὀνόματι. Καὶ ὃ μάλιστα ἠνίασέ με, ὅτι καὶ ὀνειδί-
ζων ἐμοὶ τὴν συμφοράν, Οὐδ' ὁ πατήρ, φησίν, ὁ
45 Ποσειδῶν, ἰάσεταί σε.

ΠΟ. Θάρρει, ὦ τέκνον, ἀμυνοῦμαι γὰρ αὐτόν, ὡς
μάθῃ, ὅτι, εἰ καὶ πήρωσίν μοι ὀφθαλμῶν ἰᾶσθαι ἀδύ-
νατον, τὰ γοῦν τῶν πλεόντων ἐπ' ἐμοί ἐστι· πλεῖ δὲ ἔτι

DIALOGUE 12.—PANOPE AND GALENE.

ΠΑ. Εἶδες, ὦ Γαλήνη, χθὲς οἷα ἐποίησεν ἡ Ἔρις
παρὰ τὸ δεῖπνον ἐν Θετταλίᾳ, διότι μὴ καὶ αὐτὴ
ἐκλήθη ἐς τὸ συμπόσιον;

ΓΑ. Οὐ συνειστιώμην ὑμῖν ἔγωγε· ὁ γὰρ Ποσειδῶν
5 ἐκέλευσέ με, ὦ Πανόπη, ἀκύμαντον ἐν τοσούτῳ φυλάτ-
τειν τὸ πέλαγος. Τί δ' οὖν ἐποίησεν ἡ Ἔρις μὴ
παροῦσα;

ΠΑ. Ἡ Θέτις μὲν ἤδη καὶ ὁ Πηλεὺς ἀπεληλύθε-
σαν ἐς τὸν θάλαμον, ὑπὸ τῆς Ἀμφιτρίτης καὶ τοῦ
10 Ποσειδῶνος παραπεμφθέντες. Ἡ Ἔρις δ' ἐν τοσούτῳ
λαθοῦσα πάντας, (ἐδυνήθη δὲ ῥᾳδίως, τῶν μὲν πινόντων, ἐνίων δὲ κροτούντων, ἢ τῷ Ἀπόλλωνι κιθαρίζοντι
ἢ ταῖς Μούσαις ᾀδούσαις προσεχόντων τὸν νοῦν,)

ἐνέβαλεν ἐς τὸ συμπόσιον μῆλόν τι πάγκαλον, χρυσοῦν ὅλον, ᾧ Γαλήνη· ἐπεγέγραπτο δέ, Ἡ καλὴ λαβέτω. Κυλινδόμενον δὲ τοῦτο, ὥσπερ ἐξεπίτηδες, ἧκεν ἔνθα Ἥρα τε, καὶ Ἀφροδίτη, καὶ Ἀθηνᾶ κατεκλίνοντο. Κἀπειδὴ ὁ Ἑρμῆς ἀνελόμενος ἐπελέξατο τὰ γεγραμμένα, αἱ μὲν Νηρηΐδες ἡμεῖς ἀπεσιωπήσαμεν· τί γὰρ ἔδει ποιεῖν, ἐκείνων παρουσῶν; αἱ δὲ ἀντεποιοῦντο ἑκάστη, καὶ αὑτῆς εἶναι τὸ μῆλον ἠξίουν. Καὶ εἰ μή γε ὁ Ζεὺς διέστησεν αὐτάς, καὶ ἄχρι χειρῶν ἂν προὐχώρησε τὸ πρᾶγμα. Ἀλλ' ἐκεῖνος, Αὐτὸς μὲν οὐ κρινῶ, φησί, περὶ τούτου, (καίτοι ἐκεῖναι αὐτὸν δικάσαι ἠξίουν,) ἄπιτε δὲ ἐς τὴν Ἴδην παρὰ τὸν Πριάμου παῖδα· ὃς οἶδέ τε διαγνῶναι τὸ κάλλιον, φιλόκαλος ὤν, καὶ οὐκ ἂν ἑκὼν κρίναι κακῶς.

ΓΑ. Τί οὖν αἱ θεαί, ὦ Πανόπη;

ΠΑ. Τήμερον, οἶμαι, ἀπίασιν ἐς τὴν Ἴδην, καί τις ἥξει μετὰ μικρὸν ἀπαγγελῶν ἡμῖν τὴν κρατοῦσαν.

ΓΑ. Ἤδη σοί φημι, οὐκ ἄλλη κρατήσει, τῆς Ἀφροδίτης ἀγωνιζομένης, ἢν μὴ πάνυ ὁ διαιτητὴς ἀμβλυώττῃ.

NOTES TO PART II.

SECTION I.—'ΑΣΤΕΙΑ.

THESE 'Αστεῖα, or "Joe Millers," are commonly, but erroneously, attributed to Hierocles, a philosopher of the Platonic school, who flourished at Alexandria about the middle of the fifth century.

1. ὤμοσεν, 1 aorist of ὄμνυμι. § ἄψασθαι ὕδατος: observe that the aorist infinitive is used where a future might rather be expected, (so also νοσῆσαι, in No. 3;) and that verbs of *touching, holding on by*, &c., govern the genitive. § μάθῃ, 2 aorist subjunctive of μανθάνω.

2. σύγγνωθι, 2 aorist imperative of συγγιγνώσκω. § After προσέσχον (2 aorist of προσέχω) supply τὸν νοῦν, making the phrase equal to *animadvertere*, in Latin.

3. Observe that the verbs δύναμαι, βούλομαι, and μέλλω, often take η as their *temporal augment*, instead of ε. δύναμαι is inflected like ἵσταμαι. § ἐξήλεγξεν, from ἐξελέγχω.

4. μέμψῃ: the aorist subjunctive, when used for the imperative, as here, commands the doing of an action on *one particular occasion;* whereas the present imperative enjoins the *habitual practice*. So μὴ μέμφου, "do not be always blaming;" μὴ μέμψῃ, "do not blame on this occasion." In prohibitions, μή is rarely joined to the aorist imperative, but to the subjunctive.

5. ἀποθανόντος, 2 aorist participle, from ἀποθνήσκω. § μέγα, "greatly," the neuter of the adjective, used as an adverb.

6. εἰς δεῖγμα, "as a sample." § περιέφερε, "used to carry:" the imperfect tense is used to express a *continued action* or a *habitual action*; so ἠρώτα, in No. 3, "went on to ask," or "began to ask."

7. εἰδέναι, from οἶδα (see *Irregular Verbs*). § εἰσοπτρίζετο: we should rather expect εἰσωπτρίζετο.

8. ἐκρύβη, 2 aorist passive of κρύπτω. § πυθομένου, 2 aorist participle of πυνθάνομαι. § καιρόν, " for a season ;" *i.e.*, for a long time, the accusative of *duration of time*. § ἔχω μὴ ἀσθενήσας, " I continue free from sickness." ἔχω, signifying "to have one's self," *i.e.*, "to be," when joined with a participle, implies the continuance of the state indicated by the participle; so here the whole phrase means, "I continue now for a long time in a state of non-sickness."

9. 'Αμιναίαν, "a cask of Aminean wine." The Aminæi, a Thessalian tribe, are said to have introduced into Italy the vines which furnished this wine. It was produced near Naples in greatest quantity. (Con-

sult *Vocabulary.*) §τρήσαντος, 1 aorist participle of τετραίνω. §Instead of ἐλαττοῦτο we should expect ἠλαττοῦτο.

10. ὑπεισελθών, 2 aorist participle of ὑπεισέρχομαι. § ἔσειε, "began to shake." (See note on 6, περιέφερε.) § ὡς ὑποδεξόμενος, "with the intention of catching," or "expecting to receive." § ὑπό, like *sub* in Latin, means properly, "from beneath;" *i.e.*, in a lower position. The future participle is used to express a *purpose* or *intention*, or an *expectation*.

11. Observe πολλῷ, in the dative, after the comparative adjective, expressing the *measure of difference*. The accusative is sometimes used in this sense.

12. ἠρώτα ὕδωρ πιεῖν, "asked *about* water for drinking;" literally, "to drink." The infinitive mood is a kind of verbal substantive, and often takes the place of a noun. Here it is equal to the accusative of the Latin *gerund* with *ad*; *i.e.*, *ad bibendum*. § καὶ γάρ: this phrase is often used like our "moreover," and the sense may easily be discovered by supplying the ellipse; so here we may read, "and *(they alleged it was good)*, for his parents drank out of it."

13. τὰ διακόσια ἔτη: the article joined thus with the numeral, signifies "the space of two hundred years," looked on as a *whole*. § ξῇ, contracted for ξάει. The contracted form would, if regular, be ξᾷ, but χράομαι, διψάω, πεινάω, ξάω, κνάω, σμάω, and a few others, generally contract αε and αει into η and ῃ (instead of α and ᾳ).

14. εἰς χειμῶνα ναυαγῶν, "being shipwrecked in a storm." Here we should rather expect ἐν χειμῶνι, but verbs signifying *rest in a place* are very often followed by a preposition denoting *motion*, with *an accusative*, the phrase thus suggesting the movement that preceded and led to the state of rest. So here the preposition εἰς, with the accusative, suggests the sailing into the line of storm; and ναυαγῶν relates the result. § τῶν συμπλεόντων ἑκάστου, "his fellow-passengers, each for himself, clasping;" ἑκάστου being in apposition to τῶν συμπλ. § σκεύους, contracted for σκεύεος, genitive singular of σκεῦος, neuter. This is what is called the partitive genitive—"clasping *part of* the tackling." "Tackling" is properly expressed by the plural τὰ σκεύη, but the Greek of these *asteia* is not the most correct or elegant. § Observe that the penult of ἄγκυρα is long, while the corresponding syllable of *ancŏra* is short. In later Greek, however, the penult was short, ἄγκὔρα.

15. σὺ ἀπέθανες: observe that the personal pronouns are expressed in Greek, as in Latin, only when *personality* is to be strongly brought out; as when one person is to be contrasted with another.

16. As ᾔτει is a *historical tense*, we should expect γράφοι, the optative, and not γράφῃ, the subjunctive; but the subjunctive is often used, as here, to give vividness to the story, by introducing us to the events as if passing before us.

17. περᾶσαι, "to cross." The penult is long in the future and aorist of περάω, to "pass over" or "cross," while the corresponding tenses of πιπράσκω (viz., περάσω and ἐπέρασα) have the a short.

18. τρέφει, a verb singular, with a neuter plural subject, βιβλία.

19. ὑπέσχετο, 2 aorist indicative of ὑπισχνέομαι. § ἀγαγεῖν, 2 aorist (reduplicated) of ἄγω. § χωρὶς κεφαλῆς must be translated, "without *the* head," (not "your head,") so as to preserve the ambiguity.

20. συνώφθη, 1 aorist passive of συνόπτομαι.

21. δακών, 2 aorist participle active of δάκνω.
22. Observe πόδα in the accusative, after the intransitive verb ἀλγεῖν. This is called "*the accusative of reference or limitation.*" § ἕτερος, *scil.* σχολαστικός, "another simpleton."

SECTION II.—ANECDOTES.

1. εἵμαρτο, from μείρομαι. § δαρῆναι, 2 aorist infinitive passive of δέρω.
2. φλυαροῦν, contracted for φλυαρέον, neuter participle of φλυαρέω. Observe the use of the article where we might expect the indefinite, τίς.
3. συνερρύηκεν, perfect of συρρέω.
4. The *point* of this sentence is in the similarity of sound between τρόπον and the latter part of ἄν-θρωπον. We can bring out the play on the words by making a slight inversion, and translating, "the *man*, but not the *man*-ner." "Manner," however, is not the most appropriate term here for the expression of the idea, and yet it is the only meaning of τρόπος that is at all suitable for translating the pun. Indeed, it is seldom possible to transfer into another language those puns which are mere play upon words or sounds.
5. χρῆσθαι governs the dative (of the instrument), as *utor* in Latin is followed by the ablative.
7. αὐτοῦ, *i.e.*, the talkative person, ἀδολέσχου.
10. Xantippe, wife of Socrates, is compared to Jupiter, to whom was assigned the duty of sending thunder and rain.
13. εἰς πάντα, "for all purposes." § ἐπηρείσατο, from ἐπερείδω. § βραδύνοντος, *i.e.*, the person to whom the commission had been given "being tardy." § ἔσχεν, 2 aorist of ἔχω.
14. πῖνον, neuter participle of πίνω, agreeing with παιδίον. § πήρας is governed in the genitive by ἐξέρριψε, the preposition in composition being followed by the same case, as if ἐξ stood alone. § κατέαξε, from κατάγνυμι. Note the peculiarity of augment, the *syllabic* being employed where the *temporal* only should be found.
15. εἰσίτω, from εἴσειμι, "to enter." (See *Irregular Verbs.*)
18. ὁρισαμένου, "having defined." ʔ εὐδοκιμοῦντος is the genitive singular neuter—"it (the definition) being approved of;" *i.e.*, Diogenes approving of it, or adopting it for the time. ʔ τίλας, 1 aorist participle of τίλλω. ʔ εἰσήνεγκεν, 2 aorist of εἰσφέρω.
21. Note the play on the words κόρακας and κόλακας. The similarity of sound is more evident when the words are pronounced quickly, as in conversation. The phrase εἰς κόρακας, "to the crows," is like our "to the mischief," "to perdition."
22. ἔκλαυσεν, from κλαίω. 23. Observe the repetition of negatives in this sentence.
25. The genitive, τιμωρίας, "than vengeance," is governed by the comparative, ἀμείνων. This is another instance in which the Greek genitive is equivalent to the Latin ablative.
26. ἐστεμμένον, perfect participle passive of στέφω. § ἔπεσεν, 2 aorist of πίπτω. § γεγεννηκώς, perfect participle active, from γεννάω. Our idiom would require an infinitive here rather than a participle.
32. ἐπαρθείς, 1 aorist participle passive, from ἐπαίρω.
33. κατεπλάγη, 2 aorist passive of καταπλήσσω. § Note that βίον and

ἀξίωμα are *accusatives of reference* after the passive verb. § αὐτοῦ is governed by μνημονεύων.

35. The article is used with the genitive of a proper noun to denote *the son of*; as τὸν Λάγου, " the son of Lagus."

36. τουτί, " this, here," = τοῦτοί. The letter ῑ is appended to all the parts of οὗτος, to give a stronger demonstrative force; as, οὑτοσί (*hicce*), αὑτηί, τουτί. This ῑ has three peculiarities:—(1.) It is always long, and always has the accent; (2.) It absorbs a preceding short vowel, as τουτο-ί, τουτί; (3.) It shortens a preceding long vowel or diphthong, as τουτοΐ.

SECTION III.—FABLES OF ÆSOP.

Little is known of the private history of Æsop. The place and the date of his birth are uncertain. There is no doubt, however, that he was a slave, and that his parents were slaves. Having been liberated by his master, the philosopher Iadmon, on account of his great mental qualities, he travelled through many countries, and among the rest, Greece. The Athenians prized so highly his wisdom and talents that they erected a statue to him, as we are told by Phædrus. He sojourned some time at the court of Crœsus, king of Lydia, on the invitation of that monarch, who had heard of his great fame. Having been sent by him to present an offering to Apollo at Delphi, he gave offence to the Delphians, and was hurled headlong by them down the Hyampeian Rock in 563 B.C.

" Whether Æsop left any written works at all is a question which affords considerable room for doubt, though it is certain that Fables bearing Æsop's name were popular at Athens in its most intellectual age. We find them frequently noticed by Aristophanes. They were in prose, and were turned into poetry by several writers. Socrates turned some of them into verse during his imprisonment (399 B.C.), and Demetrius Phalereus (320 B.C.) imitated his example. The only Greek versifier of Æsop, of whose writings any whole Fables are preserved, is Babrius. Of the Latin writers of Æsopean Fables, Phædrus is the most celebrated." —*Smith's Dictionary of Biography.*

---

1. ἂν ἦν, " would have been."
2. ἐπὶ τὸ τίκτειν, " upon the bearing;" *i.e.*, that she bore. § ἕνα, " one cub," σκύμνον being understood. § διὰ παντός. " always."
3. ἐκαθέσθη, 1 aorist passive of καθέζομαι. § ἔγνων, 2 aorist from γιγνώσκω.
4. εὑρών, 2 aorist participle of εὑρίσκω.
6. ἑστώς for ἑστηκώς, perfect participle of ἵστημι.
7. ἀλλά, supply, " all very well," but.
8. ὑπήνεγκας, aorist of ὑποφέρω. § ἐπιστραφείς, from ἐπιστρέφω.
9. διαφθαρῆναι, 2 aorist passive of διαφθείρω.
10. πνεύσας, from πνέω. § ἐπιδραμόντες, 2 aorist participle of ἐπιτρέχω.
11. τέξεται, from τίκτω. § δὶς τῆς ἡμέρας. " twice in the day." Ad-

verbs of place likewise govern the genitive ; as, ποῖ γῆς : so in Latin *ubi terrarum*. § τεκεῖν, 2 aorist infinitive of τίκτω.

12. αἱρουμένων τῶν ἄλλων, " the others being inclined to choose him ;" or, " being on the point of choosing him."

13. κοχλίας, " some snails." Snails were considered rather a dainty by the ancients ; so much so that a Roman country seat was hardly complete without its *cochlearium*, or " snail-preserve."

14. πάσας ἡμέρας, " during all days ;" *i.e.*, " every day." Observe that *duration of time* is put in the accusative.

15. τοῦ ἀδικεῖν : here again we find the article with the infinitive mood, the latter being in fact a verbal noun, governed in the genitive by ἄρξεται. § ἄπερ, a neuter plural, has its verb, ἄρξεται, in the singular.

16. ἐμπεσοῦσα, 2 aorist participle active of ἐμπίπτω. § ἀλλ' for ἀλλά, " well, but." ἀλλά often begins a clause having reference to something not expressed, but uppermost in the mind of the speaker. Here the fly ponders with itself, " I am going to die, certainly. *Well, well ! but* it is some consolation that I have had a hearty meal, a satisfying draught, and a comfortable bath." § βέβρωκα, from βιβρώσκω ; and πέπωκα, from πίνω.

17. κεφαλὴν μορμ., " the head of a hobgoblin." The masks of the ancients were not faces, but *whole heads*. § ἥν should rather be τήν, or else the καί ought to be removed.

18. τῇ μητρί : the article is here equal to the possessive pronoun, " *his* mother." § ὑπολαβοῦσα, *scil.* τὸν λόγον : so in the Scriptures, " He took up his parable, and said." § ἐκλάπη, from κλέπτω : translate, " For from which of them has not the flesh (of the sacrifices) been stolen by you ?"

19. εἶναι κατέχοντα, &c. : " that there was (*i.e.*, existed) another dog, which possessed (literally, possessing) a piece of flesh ;" or, εἶναι κατέχοντα may be taken as equal to κατέχειν. But the former is preferable. § ἀφείς, 2 aorist participle of ἀφίημι. § ὁ δὲ κατεῖχεν, " and that, on the other hand, which he held." ὅ is the accusative singular neuter of the relative pronoun ὅς, ἥ, ὅ, governed by κατεῖχεν.

20. ἐλθόντος, διαφθείροντος : observe that the former is the aorist,— " when a stag had come ;" and the latter the present,—" and was spoiling," *i.e.*, was going to spoil. § ἔφησεν, " said, yes ;" *i.e.*, ὁ, the man. § αὐτός means the man, and αὐτόν the horse.

21. βραχέντων, 2 aorist passive of βρέχω. § θέρος is the accusative, expressing *duration of time*,—" during the summer ;" while ὥρᾳ is the dative, indicating a *point, time when*, or a *space of time*, in some part of which an action takes place. § With χειμῶνος ὀρχοῦ, supply ὥραις.

22. πολλὴν ὁδόν is in the accusative, expressing *motion along* or *throughout a space ;* just as action *during*, or *throughout* a certain *time*, is put in the accusative. § ἀπειρηκώς, from ἀπεῖπον, (which see in the *Vocabulary*.) § ἐπιστάντος, from ἐφίστημι. § καλοίη, the forms -οίην, -οίης, &c., are generally adopted, in Attic, in the singular of contracted verbs in -αω, -εω, and -οω, instead of the common inflexions, -οιμι, -οις, &c.

23. Μελιταῖον, from Melite, *i.e.*, Malta. § προέδραμεν, from προτρέχω.

24. ἐξεῖλες, 2 aorist indicative of ἐξαιρέω. § παθοῦσα, 2 aorist participle of πάσχω.

25. θέμενοι, 2 aorist participle middle of τίθημι, " having entered into

partnership." § στάς, 2 aorist participle active of ἵστημι. § ἐνήλατο, 1 aorist middle of ἐνάλλομαι. § ἴσθι and ᾔδειν, from οἶδα.
26. καταλαβόντος, "having surprised him." § ἐμβάς, 2 aorist participle active of ἐμβαίνω. § ἐμπλακείς, from ἐμπλέκω.
27. λέγουσα ὅτι, &c.: there is a sudden change here from the *indirect* to the *direct* mode of speech, σοί being used where we should expect αὐτῷ, and the other *second* persons supplying the place of *thirds*. § ἐκέκραγει, from κράζω.
28. πιστούμενος, "giving a pledge of," or "sealing," friendship. § παρετίθει: the imperfect of τίθημι is often ἐτίθουν, ἐτίθεις, ἐτίθει. § ἃ φέρειν: observe that the relative ἃ is *neuter plural*, though referring, in syntax, to two feminine nouns. It is the σῖτα, or viands, which the writer is thinking of, and he therefore uses ἃ in reference, *not* to the *table* and the *hospitality*, but to the *eatables* and *drinkables* (σῖτα and ποτά), which were set forward before the guest. § τῶν ὄντων, "the things that were there." The genitive follows verbs of *touching, clinging to*, and such like. § τρυφῆς, the genitive governed by προτιμῶν, which implies a comparison;—the comparative in Greek being followed by a genitive, as it is in Latin by an ablative.
29. The article is joined to Δία, as pointing to a *well-known* deity. § παρασχεῖν, 2 aorist infinitive of παρέχω. § συνιδών, from συνοῖδα, "being well aware of." § καθῆκεν, 1 aorist of καθίημι. § καταπλαγέντες, from καταπλήσσω. § τὸν ψόφον, "at the noise,"—the *accusative of reference*. The accusative is often used after intransitive and passive verbs, and even after adjectives, to express the object in *reference* to which the meaning of the governing word (verb or adjective) is specially applicable. Sometimes such an accusative *limits* the signification of the verb, and it is then called the *accusative of limitation;* thus, in the phrase ἀλγεῖν πόδα, ἀλγεῖν means to *feel pain* generally, but when πόδα is added it *limits* the pain to *one part*. § ἔδυσαν, 2 aorist of δύω, or δύνω.
30. γνῶναι, 2 aorist infinitive of γιγνώσκω. § After εἰς supply οἶκον, or ἐργαστήριον, "to the workshop, or studio, of a statuary." So we say, "To St. Paul's,"—*i.e.*, Cathedral understood—where the preposition *seems* to govern the possessive case. § εἰκάσας, from εἰκάζω. Note that here we have the active voice with the reflexive pronoun, instead of the middle voice by itself. § πόσου, the *genitive of price*, "for how much." So δραχμῆς, next line, "for a drachma;" and πλείονος, "for a larger sum." The *drachma* of the Athenians was worth about 9¾d. of our money. § προσθήκην, in apposition to τοῦτον, "as an addition,"—*i.e.*, "into the bargain."

SECTION IV.—DIALOGUES OF LUCIAN.

Lucian was a native of Samosata, in the province of Commagene, Syria. He was born probably about 120 A.D., and is believed to have lived till near the end of the century. For details of his life and writings, consult *Smith's Dictionary of Biography.*

DIALOGUE 1.—*Line* 1. ἀπόδος, 2 aorist imperative of ἀποδίδωμι. 3. ἀνθ' ὧν, "because." 4. οὐκ ἂν λάβοις, "you could not by any means get it," (the fare.) As ἄν implies a condition, and therefore uncertainty, when joined with the optative in negative clauses it strengthens the negation. 5. ὀβολόν, an *obol* = 1½d. English. As Charon's fare for the ferrying a spirit over Styx was an obol, relatives put into the mouth of the deceased, before sepulture, an obol to pay the boat, and a cake to appease the watch-dog Cerberus, which kept guard on the other side of Styx. 15. ὠνάμην, from ὀνίνημι. 34. θέρμους, "lupines." Menippus, being a Cynic philosopher, carried some lupines about with him in a bag or wallet. Lupines were the cheapest food of the very poor. *Hecate's supper* was a meal supplied by the rich Athenians to their poorer fellow-citizens once a month. It was set out at the point where three ways met; and as the poor carried it off so soon as it appeared, they said that " Hecate had devoured it." Hecate was a goddess of a three-fold nature, having different attributes, different names, and different places of abode. She was Σελήνη (Moon), in heaven ; Ἄρτεμις (Diana), on earth ; and Hecate in the infernal regions. 36. ἐλάλει, "he kept jabbering." 40. κοὐδενός, &c., "and he cares for nobody." 41. ὁ Μένιππος, "the *well-known* Menippus." Observe the force of the article ὁ.

DIALOGUE II.—*Line* 1. τουτονί, "this here." The demonstrative ι is added to all the parts of οὗτος, to give strong emphasis to the pronoun. On its peculiarities see note, Section II., 36 (of Notes). 4. Observe ἐργάζεται governing *two* accusatives, τί and ὑμᾶς. 15. περιέχονται, "cling to." 23. ὡς οὐδέ, &c., "that I shall never cease;" more literally, "how that I am not going to leave off, either." This is a peculiar construction ; another remarkable example of which will be found in *Xen. Anab.*, I. 3. 6. It is usually called the *genitive absolute*, the ὡς being added to show that the action implied by the participle does not really exist, but is only *thought of* or *intended*. But this so-called *genitive absolute* (a term which is self-contradictory, and which has been adopted to get easily quit of a difficulty) can always be referred to some recognised grammatical *principle* and some general *rule*, and is very often used to express the *time*, or *cause*, or *manner*. Here, then, we regard the participle in the genitive as the *cause* of the state indicated by the verb γινώσκετε. We would therefore translate, "make up your mind to this, (or, come to this conclusion,) because (*i.e.*, for this reason, that) I shall never cease." Instead of this genitive, we should have expected the infinitive with an accusative before it. 26. ταῦτα οὐχ ὕβρις, "is not this insolence *itself?*" *i.e.*, "is not this the very essence of insolence?" 36. τὸ Γνῶθι, &c., "that *well known* saying, 'Know thyself.'" The article τό is joined to γνῶθι-σαυτόν, which is regarded as a compound noun. 36. συνείρων, literally "stringing together;" *i.e.*, forming into a connected strain. 37. πρέποι γάρ, &c., "for it would suit (admirably), being sung after, (as a chorus to) your lamentations."

DIALOGUE III.—*Line* 5. τὸ ἐμόν, "my case." "My affair happened in a very unexpected way." The indefinite pronoun τὶς, when appended to an adjective, increases the force of the adjective ; thus, μέγας τις, "very large;" μικρός τις, "very small." In some parts of our own country there is a similar use made of the indefinite, as in the phrase, " As big as anything,"—*i.e.*, very big; "As clear as anything,"—*i.e.*, very clear. 8. τὸν ἄτεκνον, τὸν πλούσιον, are in apposition to Πτοιόδωρον, in preceding sentence. § τὰ πολλά, an adverbial phrase, "for the most part," "generally." 11. ἐπ' ἐμοί, &c., "promising myself that he would die to my advantage, (in my favour;)" *i.e.*, that he would make me his heir. § ἐς μήκιστον, "and when the matter went on for a very long time," χρόνον being understood. 14. ἐπειδὰν τάχιστα, "as soon as," *quum primum*. 15. ἐπιεικῶς, "tolerably;" *i.e.*, pretty hard. 17. ἐπωμοσάμην, 1 aorist indicative middle of ἐπόμνυμι. 24. οὐκ οἶδ' ὅπως = *nescio quomodo*, "I don't know how." 30. ἀστεῖα, &c., "for you have had a comical fate;" literally, "you have suffered amusing things." 32. πρὸς τό, &c., "he was in considerable perturbation at the suddenness" (of the thing). 33. συνείς, 2 aorist participle of συνίημι. 34. οἷα, an adverbial accusative, "at what a clever (trick;)" literally, "at what things." οἷος means properly, "of what kind," but it generally implies *good, great, extraordinary*, like Latin *qualis*. We have expressed this by inserting *clever* in the translation of the phrase. 35. τραπέσθαι, literally, "turn yourself;" *i.e.*, "have recourse to the short cut," ὁδόν being understood. ἧκε ἄν, "it would have come."

DIALOGUE IV.—Line 1. ἡμέτερε Ζεῦ, "our Jove;" *i.e.*, Pluto, who was called so ("Jove with us") in the infernal regions. Proserpine was the daughter of Demeter. 4. τίνων δέῃ, "what do you want?" or *beg*: observe the genitive after a verb of entreating. § τίς ὤν, &c., "who may you be?" literally, "who do you happen to be?" 6. ὁ Ἰφίκλου, "the son of Iphiclus." The article is often used thus, υἱός or θυγάτηρ being understood. 8. ἀφεθείς, 1 aorist passive of ἀφίημι. § πρὸς ὀλίγον, "for a little." 10. Observe ἔρωτα in the accusative, after the cognate verb ἐρῶσι (contracted for ἐράουσι). 11. τύχοι, 2 aorist optative of τυγχάνω. 12. τοῦ ζῆν: the infinitive ζῆν, with τοῦ joined to it, is equal to a genitive, and is governed by ἐρῶ, a *verb of desiring*. γυναικός is also governed by ἐρῶ. 14. ᾠχόμην, &c., "*I went off* (at once), *sailing away;*" *i.e.*, I sailed hastily away. 17. ὀφθείς, 1 aorist passive of ὁράω: "I am willing to come down again, after having appeared (on earth) to her, even although (κἄν for καὶ ἐάν) it *were* but for a little time." 19. καὶ μάλα, "(yes, I drank of it), *and* (that too) *heartily*." § τὸ δὲ πρᾶγμα, &c., "but the case was an extraordinary one;" *i.e.*, my love was so strong that all the water of Lethe could not overpower it." 24. τὸ ἐρᾶν, another infinitive with the article, the two words forming the subject to ἐστί: "and *you* know what a *sore* thing it is to be in love." 29. λήψῃ, 2d singular future of λαμβάνω. 40. ὁδόν is the accusative, *motion along* or *throughout* being expressed. 41. ὦ ἄνερ, "my husband;" *i.e.*, Pluto. 43. καθικόμενον, &c., "striking him with his wand." 46. μέμνησο, imperative of μέμνημαι.

DIALOGUE V.—Line 1. προσπεσών, "having attacked;" literally, "fallen upon." 3. ἡμιτελῆ, accusative of ἡμιτελής, "half-complete;" *i.e.*, without its head, or master. 8. αἰτιατέον, *scil.* ἐστί, "I ought to blame him." Such verbal adjectives govern the same case as the verbs from which they come. 16. ἄδικα ποιῶν, "acting unjustly, Protesilaus, and that too (καὶ ταῦτα) towards a '*brother-chip*'" (ὁμότεχνον); *i.e.*, one of the same trade. The meaning is, "if you never let me go, you will act an unfair part." 18. θεῷ, by the same god, namely, Cupid. 24. τοῦ ἐρᾶν, and τῷ Πάριδι, both depend on αἴτιος. 28. προεπήδησας, &c., "leaped forth before the rest in a fool-hardy and unreflecting manner." 33. ἐπικεκλῶσθαι, perfect infinitive passive of ἐπικλώθω, "that it had been destined for me." § αἰτιᾷ is contracted for αἰτιάει, αἰτιάῃ, 2d singular present middle of αἰτιάομαι.

DIALOGUE VI.—*Line* 1. λογισώμεθα, "suppose we reckon," is not put here in the form of a command, but as a suggestion. This is the usual meaning of the first plural subjunctive when used *imperatively*, or rather in a *suggestively adhortatory* manner. 3. ὡρίσθαι, "to come to a distinct understanding." 6. ἐντειλαμένῳ, "for you having commissioned me;" *i.e.*, according to your commission. Observe the *genitives of price* which follow, δραχμῶν, πολλοῦ, &c. 9. τῶν πέντε, "the five," already named. 11. τίθει, "mark down." 12. ἀκέστραν is governed by ἐκόμισα, from former sentence. 13. κατέβαλον, "paid down;" literally, "threw down." 16. ἀνεῳγότα, "the seams," or "chinks;" the perfect participle of ἀνοίγνυμι, or ἀνοίγω. Observe that the verbs ἀνοίγω, ὁράω, and ἁλίσκομαι, take in their past tenses a *double* augment, both the *temporal* and the syllabic; thus:—

Present.   Imperfect.
ἀν-οίγω   ἀν-έ-ῳγον, which would regularly be ἄνῳγον.
ὁράω   ἑ-ώρων   ...   ...   ὥρων.
ἁλίσκομαι ἑ-άλων (2 aor.) ...   ...   ἅλων, or (*Att.*) ἥλων.

17. ἅπαντα refers to all the accusatives going before, and, as they are of different genders, it is neuter. 18. ὠνήσω, 2d singular 1 aorist middle of ὠνέομαι, "you have bought these cheap;" literally, "worthy," —*i.e.*, worth the money. 19. διέλαθεν, 2 aorist of διαλανθάνω, "has escaped our notice." 22. ἐνέσται, "it will be in my power." 25. καθεδοῦμαι, future of καθέζομαι, "I shall sit down." 32. ἀνάπλεῳ, nominative plural of ἀνάπλεως. 34. ἐξῳδηκώς (perfect participle of ἐξοιδέω), though intransitive, governs γαστέρα in the accusative [accusative of *reference* or *limitation*.] 37. ὡς ἐοίκασι, "as they appear;" *i.e.*, "to all appearance." 38. πάνυ, &c.: "(No wonder they try to ensnare one another), for these things (namely, riches) are very, very desirable." περί, like *per* in Latin, increases the force of the adjective; Charon, therefore, by using πάνυ and περί both, makes his statement very emphatic. This expression Hermes at once turns against Charon, by using it as a justification for himself, should he think fit to "demand payment sharply" of his "*little bill.*"

DIALOGUE VII.—*Line* 5. ἐνηλλάγη, 2 aorist passive from ἐναλλάσσω. § τῷ (for τίνι) τρόπῳ, "in what way." 11. καταπτάμενος, 2 aorist participle middle of καθίπταμαι.

DIALOGUE VIII.—*Line* 1. ἥκω, "I have come," and οἴχομαι, "I have gone," though presents, are translated as perfects; their imperfects, therefore, become pluperfects. 2. ὀξύτατον, "very sharp (ay, sharp enough), even if it were necessary to cut through stones at one stroke." 4. δίελε,

150 NOTES.

2 aorist imperative of διαιρέω. 5. κατενεγκών, 2 aorist participle of καταφέρω. 6. πειρᾷ, contracted for πειράῃ, 2d singular of πειράομαι, "are you testing me whether I am mad or no?" § μέμηνα, 2d perfect of μαίνομαι. 18. κατοίσω, from καταφέρω. 21. ἦσθα, 2d singular imperfect of εἰμί. The syllable -θα was frequently added in the early language to the 2d singular: in Attic it is retained in six verbs—οἶσθα (from οἶδα); ᾔδεισθα or ᾔδησθα (imperfect of οἶδα); ἦσθα (εἰμί, to be); ἔφησθα (imperfect of φημί); ἤεισθα (εἶμι, to go); and χρῆσθα (χρῆς.) 23. ἐλελήθεις (from λανθάνω) ἔχων, "you escaped your own notice, having a camp and not a head;" i.e., "you had, unawares to yourself, a camp, and not a head." When λανθάνω and τυγχάνω are joined in syntax with a participle, it is best to translate the participle as if it were the indicative (or other) mood, and the part of λανθάνω or τυγχάνω as if an adverb. So here, ἔχων, "you had," ἐλελήθεις, "unawares." § πυρριχίζει, "is dancing the Pyrric dance." The Pyrric was a war-dance, rapid in step, and performed, to the sound of the flute, by men under arms. It was therefore suitable to Minerva, goddess of war. 25. τὸ μέγιστον, "greatest wonder of all." 26. ἐν βραχεῖ, "in a short time,"—so *brevi* for *brevi tempore*. § κοσμεῖ, "sets off." 30. τό γε ἐπ' ἐμοί, "as far at least as depends on me."

DIALOGUE IX.—*Line* 1. παύσασθε ἐρίζοντες, "leave off quarrelling with one another, just like men; for this is unbecoming (*in itself*, or *to yourselves*), and foreign to the banquet of the gods." 3. ἀλλότρια: words that express or imply a *comparison* or a *difference* are followed by a genitive. 5. προκατακλίνεσθαι, "should have a more honourable place at table than I." The ancients reclined at table, as is well known. 6. Νὴ Δία: observe that Æsculapius, with comic freedom, swears by Jupiter to his very face. § καί, "and (*quite right I should take precedence of you*), for I am your superior." 7. ἦ, the interrogative of direct questions = "is it?" "In what respect (are you my superior), you crazy fool? Is it because Jupiter," &c. 8. ἃ μὴ θέμις, &c., "doing what was unlawful." This refers to Æsculapius being killed by lightning for restoring Glaucus to life again. 10. ἐπιλέλησαι γάρ, "(you need not talk so boldly), for have you too forgotten your being burned to a cinder (literally, *having been burned down*) on Mount Œta, that you cast up fire to me?" 12. οὔκουν, (accented thus), means "therefore not;" but in οὐκοῦν, (accented thus), the negative force seems to vanish, it being equal to "therefore," or "wherefore." § ἴσα and ὅμοια are neuter plurals, used adverbially. Translate, "Well, then, (*to take you on another topic,—not what has befallen us, but what we* have done), life has not been spent with equal benefit (to others) and in a similar way by you, and by me who, in the first place, am the son of Jupiter." Hercules means to say that he has benefited others more than Æsculapius has done, and has been engaged in more honourable and manly occupations. § βεβίωται, perfect passive of βιόω, used impersonally,—"it has been lived;" i.e., "Life has been spent." § ἡμῖν, "by us;" which is equal to "by you, and by *me*"—this "*me*," ἐμοί, being antecedent to ὅς which follows. 13. τοσαῦτα, &c., "have performed so many labours." 14. ἀνθρώπους, &c., "of use. perhaps. in applying (some) of your drugs to diseased folk, but a person who has exhibited no manly trait of character." ἄνθρωπος, like *homo*, means any human being—man or woman; hence often used as a term of *depreciation* or *contempt;* while ἀνήρ, like *vir*, implies *dignity* and *bravery*, or other merit. 16. τῶν φαρμάκων is the *partitive genitive*, meaning *some of*. 19. ὑπ' ἀμφοῖν, &c., "damaged in your body by both (calamities); by the tunic, and after that by the fire." Observe that χιτῶνος and πυρός are in the genitive, in apposition to ἀμφοῖν. § διεφθαρμένος, perfect participle passive of διαφθείρω. (See *Smith's Dictionary of Biography*, for Life of Hercules.) 22. πορφυρίδα depends on ἐνδεδυκώς, "clothed in purple;" *i.e.*, "having put on a purple robe." 29. ἰάσασθαι, aorist infinitive, for future. § κρανίον is another *accusative of reference or limitation*, depending on the passive form, συντριβέντα, "being crushed as to your skull;" *i.e.*, "having had your skull broken." 34. ἅτε is the accusative plural neuter of ὅστε, but is used adverbially, to introduce the reason or explanation of the foregoing clause. It may be translated, "forasmuch as." It is used much like Latin *quippe*, with the relative, *qui,—quippe qui*.

DIALOGUE X.—*Line* 1. γάρ refers to some previous conversation supposed to have taken place between Mercury and Maia. 3. Observe the two negatives, μή and μηδέν, which in Greek do *not destroy*, but *strengthen* each other. 4. λέγω is the subjunctive here—"the *subjunctive of deliberation*," as it is called: "Why may I not say so?" 5. διασπώμενος, "torn asunder;" *i.e.*, "distracted." So we say to "divide one's self." 9. ἡμεροδρομοῦντα, "posting up and down like a courier." The ἡμεροδρόμοι, or "day-runners," were men who were trained to run long distances without rest. (See *Corn. Nepos*, in *Life of Themistocles*.) 11. οἰνοχόον, *i.e.*, Ganymede. 18. μεμερισμένον, "divided as I am." 19. τὰ τέκνα, the sons of Leda, Castor and Pollux. 20. ἐν ᾅδου, *i.e.*, δόμῳ understood. § παρ' ἡμέραν, "day by day;" *i.e.*, "on alternate days." 21. ταῦτα κἀκεῖνα, affairs here (in Heaven), and affairs there (in Hades). 22. The sons of Alcmena and Semele were Hercules and Bacchus. 24. ὁ, "the son of Maia." 25. Lucian seems here to refer to Europa, who, however, was the daughter of Agenor, and the *sister* of Cadmus. 27. πέπομφε, perfect of πέμπω. 28. Danae, daughter of Acrisius, king of Argos. 30. ἀπηγόρευκα, "I am done out;" perfect of ἀπαγορεύω. 31. πεπρᾶσθαι, perfect infinitive passive of πιπράσκω. 33. ἔα ταῦτα, "never mind these things;" or, "let these things pass." § πάντα is an *accusative of reference or limitation,*—"as to all things ;" *i.e.*, "in all things."

DIALOGUE XI.—*Line* 1. οἷα, &c.: "what shameful treatment I have experienced at the hand of my accursed guest!" 9. οὐδέ, "by no means." 15. ὃ ἔφερον, &c., *i.e.*, τὸ δένδρον ὃ ἔφερον. 23. τέλος, "in fine," "at length." § ἤμην: see εἰμί, *Irregular Verbs*. 25. ἀπ' ἐκείνου, "from that time." 28. μεταξύ, &c., "while being blinded;" *i.e.*, "in the middle of (your) being blinded." 29. οὐ γὰρ ἄν, &c., "for I well know that he could not have moved," &c. 33. παρείς, 2 aorist participle of παρίημι. 36. μανθάνω, &c., "I understand,—that they (Ulysses and his companions) escaped your notice, going out secretly under them;" (*i.e.*, the ram, and other sheep.) 41. οἰηθέντες, 1 aorist passive, from οἴομαι. 48. τὰ τῶν πλεόντων, "the interests of those at sea (sailing) are in my keeping."

DIALOGUE XII.—*Line* 2. τὸ δεῖπνον, &c., " the banquet in Thessaly," at the marriage of Peleus and Thetis. 11. λαθοῦσα, " escaping the notice of." § τῶν πινόντων, and the other genitives, afford good examples of the so-called genitive absolute being used to express the *cause*. 18. ἀνελόμενος, 2 aorist middle of ἀναιρέω. 21. Observe αὐτῆς in genitive after εἶναι, " to belong to her." 22. ἄχρι χειρῶν, " even to blows." 26. ὅς = οὗτος γάρ. 28. What then did the goddesses *do?* 32. ἢν μή, " unless."

APPENDIX.

EUPHONY.

The concurrence of certain consonants was very offensive to a Greek ear, and was therefore systematically avoided. The following are the principal rules which must be observed in affixing a termination beginning with a consonant to a stem ending in a consonant:—

I. THE MUTES.

1. *In a concursus of mutes, the second must be a lingual dental*, τ, δ, or θ; *i.e.*, a labial is not followed by a palatal, nor a palatal by a labial. [The preposition ἐκ, in compound words, forms the only exception to this rule.]

2. *Cognate consonants come together*; *i.e.*, a light labial or palatal must precede a light lingual dental, an aspirate must precede an aspirate, and an intermediate, an intermediate: thus we cannot say γέγρα-φ-τ-αι, but γέγρα-π-τ-αι (from γράφ-ω); [so in Latin we do not say *scrib-tus*, but *scrip-tus*]; not ἐτύ-π-θ-ην, but ἐτύ-φ-θ-ην; not ὄκ-δοος (from ὀκ-τώ), but ὄγ-δοος.

3. *When two lingual dentals meet, the former is changed into* s: thus we cannot say ἐπεί-θ-θ-ην, but ἐπεί-σ-θ-ην (from πείθ-ω); not ἐρει-δ-θ-ῆναι, but ἐρει-σ-θ-ῆναι (from ἐρείδ-ω.)

4. If two successive syllables begin with an aspirate, the first aspirate is changed into its corresponding Light; as, πε-φί-ληκα, not φε-φί-ληκα; ἕ-χω, not ἔ-χω.

II. THE MUTES AND OTHER CONSONANTS.

5. The mutes π, β, φ, before μ, are changed into μ; as, γέγραμ-μαι, not γέγραφ-μαι (from γράφ-ω).

6. The mutes κ and χ, before μ, are changed into γ; as, βέβρεγ-μαι, not βέβρεχ-μαι (from βρέχ-ω). Except a few words like ἀκμή, δραχμή, &c.

7. The mutes τ, δ, θ, before μ, are changed into s; as, πέπεισ-μαι, not πέπειθ-μαι (from πείθω). Except a few words like σταθμός.

8. The mutes π, β, φ, before s, combine with s and form ψ; as, τύ-ψ-ω for τύ-πσ-ω.

9. The mutes κ, γ, χ, before s, combine with s and form ξ; as, λέ-ξ-ω, not λέ-γσ-ω. Except the preposition ἐκ, which remains unchanged.

10. The mutes τ, δ, θ (and the lingual ν) are rejected before s; as, σώμασι, not σώμα-τ-σι; πᾶσι, not πά-ντ-σι. (See note, p. 31.)

11. The letter ν, before π, β, φ (or ψ), is changed into μ; as, συμ-βάλλω, for συν-βάλλω.
12. The letter ν, before κ, γ, χ (or ξ), is changed into γ; as, ἐγχέω for ἐν-χέω; ἐγκέφαλον, for ἐν-κέφαλον.
13. The letter ν, before a liquid, assimilates itself to it; as, συλ-λέγω, for συν-λέγω.
14. Consonants are not doubled, except π, κ, τ, γ, and the semi-vowels λ, μ, ν, ρ, s, (π, κ, and γ very seldom.)
15. See note, p. 28, for another euphonic principle.

THE ACCENTS.*

1. There are three accent-marks in Greek:—
    (a) The *acute*, as on τιμή.
    (b) The *grave*, as on τινός.
    (c) The *circumflex*, as on αὐλῆς.
2. The acute may stand on any of the last three syllables of a word; and the circumflex on either of the last two.
3. Every syllable not otherwise accented is considered as having the *grave*; but the grave is never *written* except on the last syllable, and then only when no punctuation mark follows. The grave merely indicates that the acute is not to be admitted, for the time. Thus we write ἀνά, τούς, and ἀγρούς with an acute on the final syllable; but this acute is turned into a grave when the words meet in a sentence without any punctuation mark between; as, ἀνὰ τοὺς ἀγροὺς τῶν γεωργῶν.
4. The circumflex results from a combination of the acute and the grave; thus, -εά when contracted makes ῆ, or ῆ, or in cursive writing, ῆ. It can stand only on syllables *naturally* long, *i.e.*, containing a long vowel or diphthong; as, αὐλῆς, φεῦγε.
5. When the last syllable of a word is short, the acute *may* stand on the antepenult; as, ἄνθρωπος.
   N.B.—The terminations -οι and -αι (except in the optative mood), and the Attic inflexions -ως and -ων, are treated as short syllables; as, ἄκανθαι, πολῖται, ἄνθρωποι, πόλεως, ἀνώγεων.
6. When the last syllable of a word is long, the acute cannot stand farther back than the penult; as, ἀνθρώπου.
7. The circumflex can stand on the penult only when the last syllable is short (see No. 4.); as, μυῖα [but μυιᾶ, nominative dual], γλῶττα [but γλώττης]. So μῆτερ [but μήτηρ].
8. In contractions,—
    (1.) If the first member of the concursus have the acute, the contracted syllable will have the circumflex; as, φιλ-έο-μεν, φιλ-οῦ-μεν; βασιλ-έϊ, βασιλ-εῖ.
    (2.) If the second member have the acute, the contracted syllable will likewise have the acute; as, φιλ-εού-σης, φιλ-ού-σης. Except a few words like ἀργύρεος, ἀργυροῦς.

---

* It is only the leading principles of accentuation that are here given. For the theory and more minute details, the advanced student is referred to "The Laws of Greek Accentuation," by the Rev. R. J. Bryce, LL.D. Williams and Norgate: 1859.

(3.) If neither of the syllables have the acute, the contracted syllable will not be affected; as, μάντ-εε-s, μάντ-ει-s; τιμ-αο-μένη, τιμ-ω-μένη.

OF THE ACCENT IN THE INFLEXION OF NOUNS.

9. The position of the accent in the nominative singular of a declinable word must be learned by practice, or ascertained from the Lexicon; but when the tone-syllable of the nominative is once known, the accent of the oblique cases is easily fixed by the following rules:—

10. The accent remains throughout the oblique cases on the same syllable on which it stands in the nominative, so long as the quantity of the final syllable permits; as, αὐλ-ή, αὐλ-ήν; βασιλ-εύς, βασιλ-έα; παρθέν-ος, παρθέν-οι; λειμών, λειμῶν-ος; ποιμήν, ποιμέν-ος; αἴγειρος, αἰγείρον, but αἰγείρου.

11. *Exceptions.*—In the Third Declension, genitives and datives of two syllables take the accent on the inflexion; as, θήρ, θηρ-ός, θηρ-οῖν, θηρ-ῶν, θηρ-σί; but accusative θῆρ-α, nominative plural θῆρ-ες. So likewise syncopated nouns, as μήτηρ, genitive μητρ-ός (not μῆτρος); θυγάτηρ, genitive θυγατρός; and γυνή, genitive γυναικός, γυναικῶν, though not syncopated.

12. The inflexions of all genitives and datives, when long, are circumflexed, provided the tone be on the inflexion syllable (see 10); as, σκι-ά, σκι-άς, σκιᾷ, σκι-αῖν, σκι-αῖς; ἀετ-οῦ, ἀετ-ῶν; θηρ-οῖν, θηρ-ῶν; θε-ῷ, θε-οῖς. The other cases take the acute; as, σκι-αί, σκι-άς; θε-ούς; ἀετ-όν.

13. The genitive plural of the First Declension has always a circumflex on the last syllable, because -ων is contracted for -άων; as, σκι-ῶν for σκι-άων.

14. Vocatives in -ευ and -οι circumflex the last syllable; as βασιλ-εῦ, Λητ-οῖ.

THE ACCENT OF VERBS.

15. In verbs the accent stands as far back as the quantity of the final syllable permits; as, τύπτομεν, τύπτεται, τυπτοίσθην, βουλεύσαι (optative).

16. Those parts of verbs in which there was originally a contraction (or supposed contraction) follow the rules for contraction (8, above); as, ἀγγελῶ, *fut.*, for ἀγγελέω; μενεῖτον, *fut.*, for μενέετον; ἱστῶμεν, for ἱστάωμεν; λυθῇς (1 aorist passive).

17. *Exceptions.*—The accent of the following parts must be specially noted:—

ACTIVE.

(1.) 1 aorist infinitive on penult, λῦσ-αι.
2 aorist infinitive on final, λιπ-εῖν.
2 aorist participle on final, λιπ-ών.
Perfect infinitive on penult, λελυκ-έναι: and so all infinitives in -ναι; as, τιθέναι.

MIDDLE.

(2.) 2 aorist imperative on final, as λιπ-οῦ.
2 aorist infinitive on penult, λιπ-έσθαι.

156 APPENDIX.

PASSIVE.

(3.) Perfect infinitive on penult, λελύ-σθαι.
Perfect participle on penult, λελυ-μένος.

18. All participles of the Third Declension, ending in s, take an acute on the final syllable; as, λυθείς (1 aorist passive), τιθείς (present active). But the participle of 1 aorist active follows the rule; as, βουλεύσας.

PROCLITICS.

19. Some small words, οὐ, εἰ, ὡς, ἐν, εἰς (ἐς), ἐκ, ὁ, ἡ, οἱ, αἱ, throw forward their accent on the word following, if connected in syntax; as, ἐν μάχῃ, εἰς μάχην.

ENCLITICS.

20. Enclitics are small, unemphatic words, which throw back their accent on the preceding word (if connected in meaning), so that the two words form only one, as it were, in pronunciation; as, κόρη τις, νομεῖς τινες, βασιλεύς ἐστι, δοῦλός τις, βοῦν τινα. Compare *que*, *ne*, &c., in Latin; as, *omnemque*.

BRIEF SYNOPSIS OF THE SYNTAX OF SIMPLE SENTENCES.

I. SUBJECT AND PREDICATE.

1. RULE.—An adjective (whether article, pronoun, participle, or adjective proper) agrees with its own substantive in gender, number, and case; as, ἡ κόρη ἐστὶ καλή: οἱ πολῖταί εἰσι ἐλεύθεροι: τὰ πράγματά ἐστι καλά.

Obs. 1. When an adjective refers to substantives of different genders, it takes the gender of the masculine noun rather than that of the feminine, and of the feminine rather than of the neuter: ὁ πατὴρ καὶ ἡ μήτηρ ἀγαθοί εἰσι: ἡ μήτηρ καὶ τὸ παιδίον ἀγαθά εἰσι.

Obs. 2. When the substantives are names of inanimate objects, the adjective is put in the neuter; as, λίθοι τε καὶ πλίνθοι καὶ ξύλα ἐστὶ χρήσιμα,—*stones and bricks and beams of timber are useful (things)*.

THE ARTICLE.

2. The article was originally a demonstrative adjective pronoun, and hence it is used to point distinctly to an object, to render it prominent, and thus distinguish it from others, and oppose it to others.

(1.) It points to what is known, or supposed to be well known; as, ὁ Σωκράτης, that well-known person, Socrates; ὁ Ξενοφῶν, Xenophon, who was *mentioned* lately.

(2.) With singulars, it sometimes denotes a class; as, ὁ παῖς, children generally.

(3.) It is used with names of materials, virtues, and generic nouns; as, ὁ χρυσός, ἡ ἀρετή, gold, virtue.

(4.) It serves as a possessive pronoun; as, ὁ πατὴρ σὺν τῷ υἱῷ, the *father with his son*.

(5.) It has a distributive force; as, τοῦ μηνός, *by the month*,—i.e., *every month*.
(6.) It distinguishes the subject of a sentence from the predicate; as, ὁ ἀνὴρ ἀγαθός, *the man is good;* or, ἀγαθὸς ὁ ἀνήρ. But ὁ ἀγαθὸς ἀνήρ would simply mean, *the good man*.
(7.) It indicates what is *customary* or *deserved;* as, ἔλαβε τὰ παλτά, *he received the two spears usually given;* τὴν δίκην, *the deserved punishment*.

Obs. 1. The article, with a participle, is equal to a relative clause; as, ὁ πράττων = ἐκεῖνος ὃς πράττει, *he who does*. In this case it retains its primary demonstrative power.

Obs. 2.—It is used with the infinitive mood (in all cases), thus forming a kind of gerundival substantive; as, τὸ κλέπτειν, *stealing;* τοῦ κλέπτειν, *of stealing, of theft*.

AGREEMENT.

3. RULE.—A verb agrees with its subject in number and person; as, ἐγὼ γράφω; σὺ γράφεις; ἡμεῖς γράφομεν.

Exception.—But a *neuter plural* subject usually takes the verb in the singular; as, τὰ ζῶα τρέχει, *the animals run*.

N. B.—Since two singulars are equal to a plural, two singular subjects connected by a co-ordinative conjunction (καί, &c.) have a verb or adjective in the plural; ὁ παῖς καὶ ἡ κόρη σοφοί εἰσι, *the boy and the girl are wise*.

Exception. — But in a series of nominatives the verb often agrees with the subject nearest it; as, φιλεῖ σε ὁ πατὴρ καὶ ἡ μήτηρ καὶ οἱ ἀδελφοί, *your father loves you, and (so do) your mother and your brothers*.

APPOSITION.

4. RULE.—Substantives which stand in *apposition** to one another agree in case; as, Κῦρος, ὁ βασιλεύς, *Cyrus, the king;* Σωκράτην, τὸν σοφόν, θαυμάζομεν, *we admire Socrates the philosopher*.

Obs.—The same rule applies when the second substantive is used as a predicate; as, Κῦρος ἦν βασιλεύς, *Cyrus was king;* Πρόκνη ἐγένετο ἀηδών, *Procne was changed into a nightingale*. This kind of apposition occurs (1) with SUBSTANTIVE VERBS, (2) PASSIVE VERBS OF NAMING AND CHOOSING, and (3) VERBS OF GESTURE.

II. THE CASES.

NOMINATIVE AND VOCATIVE.

5. The nominative is used to express the subject of the sentence, or the substantival predicate, as shown in Art. 3 and 4 above.

6. The vocative is used in expressions of *address*, as in Latin; but the nominative often takes the place of the vocative, even in address.

---

* Two substantives are said to be in *apposition* when one is appended to the other to explain or limit it.

ACCUSATIVE.

7. The accusative case expresses the *direct object* of the action indicated by a transitive verb. It answers to the questions, *whom? what? to what place? during what time?*

8. RULE.—Transitive verbs govern the accusative; as, ὁ παῖς ῥίπτει τὴν σφαῖραν, *the boy throws the ball;* πείθει τὸν κριτήν, *he persuades the judge.* [But many transitive verbs govern the gen. or dat.]

9. Any verb, whether it be transitive or intransitive, may govern in the accusative a substantive of kindred signification; as, τοῦτον τὸν κίνδυνον κινδυνεύσω, *I shall incur this danger;* νόσον νοσεῖν, *to be ill of a disease.*

10. Many verbs in Greek are followed by *two* accusatives, the one expressing the person, the other the thing. Such are verbs of *concealing, teaching, asking, dividing, depriving, clothing,* and many others.

11. An accusative is often put after *passive verbs,* intransitive verbs, and adjectives, to define them and limit their application. This is called the *accusative of reference* or *limitation;* as, ἀλγεῖν τοὺς πόδας, *to be pained in the feet:* καλὸς τὰ ὄμματα, *beautiful in the eyes;* i.e., *having beautiful eyes:* Σωκράτης τὸ ὄνομα, *Socrates by name.*

12. The accusative is used to express *duration of time* and *extent of space;* as, πέντε ἡμέρας ἔμεινε, *he remained* (for) *five days;* ἀπέχει δέκα σταδίους, *it is distant ten stadia.*

THE GENITIVE.

13. The primary meaning of the genitive is *source* or *origin*. Hence it is employed to express (1.) The *point of separation (from, away from);* (2.) The *cause, material,* or *occasion;* (3.) The *time* at *which,* or *place in which* an action originates or occurs. Hence it signifies.—

(1.) The *author* or *possessor;* as, ὁ υἱὸς τοῦ Ξενοφῶντος, *Xenophon's son;* ἡ μάχαιρα τοῦ ναύτου, *the sailor's cutlass.* It thus answers to the questions, *whose? of whom? of what?*

Obs. 1. Thus arises the genitive of material; as, νόμισμα ἀργύρου, *a coin of silver.*

Obs. 2. εἰμί, like *sum* in Latin, is followed by the genitive to denote that something is the part, duty, or characteristic of; as, ἀνδρός ἐστιν ἀγαθοῦ εὖ ποιεῖν τοὺς φίλους, *it is the part* (or *duty*) *of a good man to benefit his friends.*

(2.) The *whole* of which anything is a part (*partitive genitive*); as, σοφώτατος πάντων, *the wisest of all;* σταγόνες ὕδατος, *drops of water;* ποῦ γῆς ἐστιν, *where on earth is he?* οὐκ ἐγὼ τούτων εἰμί, *I am not* ONE *of these;* ἔχεις τι τῶν χρημάτων, *you have some of the money.*

(3.) The *part affected.* Hence it is used with verbs which signify to *touch, take hold of, share, obtain,* &c.; as, ἅπτεται τοῦ χιτῶνος, *he takes hold of the robe;* μετέχειν τιμῶν, *to share in the honours.*

4.) The *operations of the senses* (except sight); as, ἤκουσα τῆς φωνῆς, *I heard the voice.* But ἤκουσα ταῦτα τοῦ πατρός, *I heard this* FROM *my father.* So verbs and verbal adjectives which signify an affection of the mind are followed by a genitive; as, ἄπειρος τῶν πραγμάτων, *inexperienced in business;* ἐπιθυμεῖ τῆς ἀρετῆς, *he aims at* (yearns after) *virtue.*

(5.) *The price* or *value*; as, ἀγοράζειν τι δραχμῆς, *to buy something for a drachma*; ἄξιος τῆς ἐλευθερίας, *worthy of freedom*.
(6.) *The crime*, or *ground of accusation*; as, καταδικεῖν τινα φόνου, *to condemn one on a charge of murder*.
(7.) *Abundance* or *scarceness*; as, ὕλη θηρίων πλήρης, *a forest full of wild beasts*.
(8.) *Separation*, or *removal from*; as, εἴκειν τῆς ὁδοῦ, *to withdraw from the road*.
(9.) *Cause* or *occasion*; as, τὸν παῖδα τῆς ἀρετῆς θαυμάζει ὁ κριτής, *the judge admires the boy for* (i.e., because of) *his merit*.
(10.) *Superiority* or *inferiority*; as, ὁ υἱὸς μείζων ἐστὶ τοῦ πατρός, *the son is taller than his father*; Ἀστυάγης Μήδων ἦρξεν, *Astyages ruled over the Medes*; ὁ υἱὸς μείων ἐστι τοῦ πατρός, *the son is less than his father*.
(11.) *Time when*, or *within which*, if spoken of indefinitely; as, νυκτός, *by night*; τοῦ ἔαρος, *in spring*.

THE DATIVE.

14. The dative case denotes,—
(1.) The individual (person or thing) to whom anything is given or communicated; as, αὐτῷ εἶπεν ὁ κύριος, *the master said to him*; διελέξαν ἀλλήλοις, *they conversed with one another*.
(2.) The individual who is benefited or injured in any way; as, ἡ βασίλεια ὑπῆρχε τῷ Κύρῳ, *the queen favoured Cyrus*; δίδωσι αὐτῷ ἵππον, *he gives him a horse*.
(3.) *Belief in*, or *obedience to*; as, τῷ ἡγεμόνι ἐπιστεύσαμεν, *we trusted to the guide*.
(4.) The *cause* why something is (done), the *manner* or *circumstances* in which it is (done), the *instrument* by which it is (done), and the *agent* by whom it is (done); as, ἀγάλλονται τῇ νίκῃ, *they are delighted at the victory*—i.e., *because* of the victory; βίᾳ εἰς οἰκίαν παριέναι, *to enter a house by force*; ἔβαλον λίθοις, *they struck with stones*; ἐκτείνοντο Ἀχαιοῖς, *they were slain by the Greeks*. [But ὑπό with the genitive is most usually employed in this sense.]
(5.) *Intercourse with*, whether *friendly* or the *opposite*; as, τοῖς ἀγαθοῖς ὁμίλει, *associate with the good*.
(6.) *Likeness*, or *equality*, or *coincidence*; as, πάθος ἴσον θανάτῳ, *a calamity equal to death*; ὅμοιος πατρί, *like* (one's) *father*.
(7.) *Time* or *place*; as, τῇ τρίτῃ ἡμέρᾳ, *on the third day*; Ἀθήναις, *at Athens*.

III. INFINITIVE MOOD.

15. The infinitive mood is a kind of verbal substantive, and is used with or without the article to express the *object* or *aim*; as, ἐλπίζω νικήσειν, *I hope to conquer*,—i.e., *I hope for victory*.

16. It often serves as the subject of a verb; as, ἡδύ ἐστι τὸ μανθάνειν, *to learn is pleasant*.

COMPARATIVE VIEW OF THE THIRD DECLENSION IN LATIN AND IN GREEK.

LATIN.
CLASS.
I. *Pure stem in the Nominative.*
Consul.   Honor.
Consul-is. Honor-is.

ADDITION.
II. *Letter added to stem.*
Urb-s.   Dux (= duc-s).
Urb-is. Duc-is.
Ret-e.   Ret-is, *n.*

III. *Vowel inserted.*
Nav-i-s. Clad-c-s.
Nav-is.   Clad-is.

SUBTRACTION.
IV. *Last letter of stem dropped.*
Sermo.   Lac, *n.*
Sermon-is. Lact-is.

V. *Letter thrown out before s.*
Aetas.   Laus.
Aetat-is. Laud-is.

SUBSTITUTION.
VI. *Last vowel of stem changed.*
Nomen, *n.* Caput, *n.*
Nomin-is.   Capit-is.

VII. *Last consonant of stem changed.*
Flos.   Arbos, or Arbor.
Flor-is. Arbor-is.

GREEK.
CLASS.
I. *Pure stem in the Nominative.*
λειμών.   θήρ.
λειμῶν-ος.   θηρ-ός.

ADDITION.
II. *Letter added to stem.*
ἥρω-s.   γύψ (*i.e.*, γύπ-s).
ἥρω-ος. γυπ-ός.

III. *Half a vowel inserted,*
(*i.e.*, a short vowel lengthened.)
ποιμήν.   δαίμων.
ποιμέν-ος. δαίμον-ος.

SUBTRACTION.
IV. *Last letter of stem dropped.*
Ξενοφῶν.   σῶμα, *n.*
Ξενοφῶντ-ος. σώματ-ος.
γάλα.   γάλακτ-ος, *n.*

V. *Letter thrown out before s.*
λέβης.   ὄρνις.
λέβητ-ος.   ὀρνιθ-ος.

SUBSTITUTION.
VI. *Last vowel of stem changed.*
μάντι-ς.   γλυκύ-s.
μάντε-ως.   γλυκέ-ος.

VII. *Last cons. of stem vocalized in some cases and omitted in others.*
βοῦ-ς (βο-F-ς). βασιλεύ-ς.
βο ός.   βασιλέ-ως.

NOUNS WITH PECULIARITIES OF MORE THAN ONE CLASS.

CLASSES.   STEM.   GEN.
(1.) II. & VI. Judex (judic-), judic-is.
(2.) IV. & VI. Homo (homin-), homin-is.
(3.) V. & VI. Miles (milit-), milit-is.
(4.) VI. & VII. Corpus (corpor-), corpor-is.

NOUNS WITH PECULIARITIES OF MORE THAN ONE CLASS.

CLASSES.   STEM.   GEN.
(1.) II. & III. αἰδώ-ς (αἰδο-),   αἰδό-ος.
     ἀλώπηξ (ἀλωπεκ-), ἀλώπεκ-ος.
(2.) III. & IV. λέων (λεοντ-), λέοντ-ος.
     κτείς (κτεν-),   κτεν-ός.
     ὀδούς (ὀδοντ-),   ὀδόντ-ος.

CONTRACTED VERBS IN -άω, -έω, AND -όω.

Certain Pure Verbs suffer contraction in the Pres. and Imperf. of all Voices and Moods. The other tenses have no concursus, and are declined like the corresponding parts of λύω. The verbs τιμάω, *I honour*; ποιέω, *I make*; and μισθόω, *I let out for hire*, will exhibit all the peculiarities of the contracted inflexions.

ACTIVE VOICE.

	Pres.—τιμ άω, I honour.		φιλ-έω, I love.		μισθ-όω, I let out for hire.	
INDICATIVE.	S. -άω	-ῶ	-έω	-ῶ	-όω	-ῶ
	-άεις	-ᾷς	-έεις	-εῖς	-όεις	-οῖς
	-άει	-ᾷ	-έει	-εῖ	-όει	-οῖ
	D. -άετον	-ᾶτον	-έετον	-εῖτον	-όετον	-οῦτον
	-άετον	-ᾶτον	-έετον	-εῖτον	-όετον	-οῦτον
	P. -άομεν	-ῶμεν	-έομεν	-οῦμεν	-όομεν	-οῦμεν
	-άετε	-ᾶτε	-έετε	-εῖτε	-όετε	-οῦτε
	-άουσι	-ῶσι	-έουσι	-οῦσι	-όουσι	-οῦσι
SUBJUNCTIVE.	S. -άω	-ῶ	-έω	-ῶ	-όω	-ῶ
	-άῃς	-ᾷς	-έῃς	-ῇς	-όῃς	-οῖς
	-άῃ	-ᾷ	-έῃ	-ῇ	-όῃ	-οῖ
	D. -άητον	-ᾶτον	-έητον	-ῆτον	-όητον	-ῶτον
	-άητον	-ᾶτον	-έητον	-ῆτον	-όητον	-ῶτον
	P. -άωμεν	-ῶμεν	-έωμεν	-ῶμεν	-όωμεν	-ῶμεν
	-άητε	-ᾶτε	-έητε	-ῆτε	-όητε	-ῶτε
	-άωσι	-ῶσι	-έωσι	-ῶσι	-όωσι	-ῶσι
OPTATIVE.	S. -άοιμι	-ῷμι	-έοιμι	-οῖμι	-όοιμι	-οῖμι
	-άοις	-ῷς	-έοις	-οῖς	-όοις	-οῖς
	-άοι	-ῷ	-έοι	-οῖ	-όοι	-οῖ
	D. -άοιτον	-ῷτον	-έοιτον	-οῖτον	-όοιτον	-οῖτον
	-αοίτην	-ῴτην	-εοίτην	-οίτην	-οοίτην	-οίτην
	P. -άοιμεν	-ῷμεν	-έοιμεν	-οῖμεν	-όοιμεν	-οῖμεν
	-άοιτε	-ῷτε	-έοιτε	-οῖτε	-όοιτε	-οῖτε
	-άοιεν	-ῷεν	-έοιεν	-οῖεν	-όοιεν	-οῖεν
IMPERATIVE.	S. -αε	-α	-εε	-ει	-οε	-ου
	-αέτω	-άτω	-εέτω	-είτω	-οέτω	-ούτω
	D. -άετον	-ᾶτον	-έετον	-εῖτον	-όετον	-οῦτον
	-αέτων	-άτων	-εέτων	-είτων	-οέτων	-ούτων
	P. -άετε	-ᾶτε	-έετε	-εῖτε	-όετε	-οῦτε
	-αέτωσαν	-άτωσαν	-εέτωσαν	-είτωσαν	-οέτωσαν	-ούτωσαν
INFIN.	-άειν	-ᾶν	-έειν	-εῖν	-όειν	-οῦν

ACTIVE VOICE—continued.

		Pres.—τίμ-άω.		φιλ-έω.		μισθ-όω.	
PART.		M. -άων	-ῶν	-έων	-ῶν	-όων	-ῶν
		F. -άουσα	-ῶσα	-έουσα	-οῦσα	-όουσα	-οῦσα
		N. -άον	-ῶν	-έον	-οῦν	-όον	-οῦν
INDICATIVE.		Imperf.— ἐτίμ-αον.		ἐφίλ-εον.		ἐμίσθ οον.	
	S.	-αον	-ων	-εον	-ουν	-οον	-ουν
		-αες	-ᾶς	-εες	-εις	-οες	-ους
		-αε	-ᾶ	-εε	-ει	-οε	-ου
	D.	-άετον	-ᾶτον	-έετον	-εῖτον	-όετον	-οῦτον
		-αέτην	-άτην	-εέτην	-είτην	-οέτην	-ούτην
	P.	-άομεν	-ῶμεν	-έομεν	-οῦμεν	-όομεν	-οῦμεν
		-άετε	-ᾶτε	-έετε	-εῖτε	-όετε	-οῦτε
		-αον	-ων	-εον	-ουν	-οον	-ουν

PASSIVE AND MIDDLE VOICES.

		Pres.—τίμ-άομαι.		φιλ-έομαι.		μισθ όομαι.	
INDICATIVE.	S.	-άομαι	-ῶμαι	-έομαι	-οῦμαι	-όομαι	-οῦμαι
		-άῃ	-ᾷ	-έῃ	-ῇ or -εῖ	-όῃ	-οῖ
		-άεται	-ᾶται	-έεται	-εῖται	-όεται	-οῦται
	D.	-αόμεθον	-ώμεθον	-εόμεθον	-ούμεθον	-οόμεθον	-ούμεθον
		-άεσθον	-ᾶσθον	-έεσθον	-εῖσθον	-όεσθον	-οῦσθον
		-άεσθον	-ᾶσθον	-έεσθον	-εῖσθον	-όεσθον	-οῦσθον
	P.	-αόμεθα	-ώμεθα	-εόμεθα	-ούμεθα	-οόμεθα	-ούμεθα
		-άεσθε	-ᾶσθε	-έεσθε	-εῖσθε	-όεσθε	-οῦσθε
		-άονται	-ῶνται	-έονται	-οῦνται	-όονται	-οῦνται
SUBJUNCTIVE.	S.	-άωμαι	-ῶμαι	-έωμαι	-ῶμαι	-όωμαι	-ῶμαι
		-άῃ	-ᾷ	-έῃ	-ῇ	-όῃ	-οῖ
		-άηται	-ᾶται	-έηται	-ῆται	-όηται	-ῶται
	D.	-αώμεθον	-ώμεθον	-εώμεθον	-ώμεθον	-οώμεθον	-ώμεθον
		-άησθον	-ᾶσθον	-έησθον	-ῆσθον	-όησθον	-ῶσθον
		-άησθον	-ᾶσθον	-έησθον	-ῆσθον	-όησθον	-ῶσθον
	P.	-αώμεθα	-ώμεθα	-εώμεθα	-ώμεθα	-οώμεθα	-ώμεθα
		-άησθε	-ᾶσθε	-έησθε	-ῆσθε	-όησθε	-ῶσθε
		-άωνται	-ῶνται	-έωνται	-ῶνται	-όωνται	-ῶνται
OPTATIVE.	S.	-αοίμην	-ῴμην	-εοίμην	-οίμην	-οοίμην	-οίμην
		-άοιο	-ῷο	-έοιο	-οῖο	-όοιο	-οῖο
		-άοιτο	-ῷτο	-έοιτο	-οῖτο	-όοιτο	-οῖτο
	D.	-αοίμεθον	-ῴμεθον	-εοίμεθον	-οίμεθον	-οοίμεθον	-οίμεθον
		-άοισθον	-ῷσθον	-έοισθον	-οῖσθον	-όοισθον	-οῖσθον
		-αοίσθην	-ῴσθην	-εοίσθην	-οίσθην	-οοίσθην	-οίσθην
	P.	-αοίμεθα	-ῴμεθα	-εοίμεθα	-οίμεθα	οοίμεθα	-οίμεθα
		-άοισθε	-ῷσθε	-έοισθε	-οῖσθε	-όοισθε	-οῖσθε
		-άοιντο	-ῷντο	-έοιντο	-οῖντο	-όοιντο	-οῖντο

PASSIVE AND MIDDLE VOICES—continued.

		Pres.- τιμ-άομαι.		φιλ-έομαι.		μισθ-όομαι.	
IMPERATIVE	S.	-άου	-ῶ	-έου	-οῦ	-όου	-οῦ
		-αέσθω	-άσθω	-εέσθω	-είσθω	-οέσθω	-ούσθω
	D.	-άεσθον	-ᾶσθον	-έεσθον	-εῖσθον	-όεσθον	-οῦσθον
		-αέσθων	-άσθων	-εέσθων	-είσθων	-οέσθων	-ούσθων
	P.	-άεσθε	-ᾶσθε	-έεσθε	-εῖσθε	-όεσθε	-οῦσθε
		-αέσθωσαν	-άσθωσαν	-εέσθωσαν	-είσθωσαν	-οέσθωσαν	-ούσθωσαν

INFIN.	-άεσθαι	-ᾶσθαι	-έεσθαι	-εῖσθαι	-όεσθαι	-οῦσθαι

PART.	M.	-αόμενος	-ώμενος	-εόμενος	-ούμενος	-οόμενος	-ούμενος
	F.	-αομένη	-ωμένη	-εομένη	-ουμένη	-οομένη	-ουμένη
	N.	-αόμενον	-ώμενον	-εόμενον	-ούμενον	-οόμενον	-ούμενον

		Imperf.— ἐτιμ αόμην.		ἐφιλ-εόμην.		ἐμισθ-οόμην.	
INDICATIVE		-αόμην	-ώμην	-εόμην	-ούμην	-οόμην	-ούμην
		-άου	-ῶ	-έου	-οῦ	-όου	-οῦ
		-άετο	-ᾶτο	-έετο	-εῖτο	-όετο	-οῦτο
		-αόμεθον	-ώμεθον	-εόμεθον	-ούμεθον	-οόμεθον	-ούμεθον
		-άεσθον	-ᾶσθον	-έεσθον	-εῖσθον	-όεσθον	-οῦσθον
		-αέσθην	-άσθην	-εέσθην	-είσθην	-οέσθην	-ούσθην
		-αόμεθα	-ώμεθα	-εόμεθα	-ούμεθα	-οόμεθα	-ούμεθα
		-άεσθε	-ᾶσθε	-έεσθε	-εῖσθε	-όεσθε	-οῦσθε
		-άοντο	-ῶντο	-έοντο	-οῦντο	-όοντο	-οῦντο

LISTS OF WORDS USED IN EACH EXERCISE.

I.
ἄγκυρ-α, *f.*, an anchor.
ἀδελφ-ή, *f.*, a sister.
αὐλ-ή, *f.*, a court, hall, palace.
βασίλει-α, *f.*, a queen.
δεξι-ά, *f.*, a right hand.
θε-ά, *f.*, a goddess.
θήκ-η, *f.*, a chest, box.
θύρ-α, *f.*, a door.
κόρ-η, *f.*, a girl, maiden, daughter.
λαι-ά, *f.*, a left hand.
μάχ-η, *f.*, a battle.
μυῖ-α, *f.*, a fly.
νύμφ-η, *f.*, a nymph; maiden.
παρει-ά, *f.*, a cheek.
πήρ-α, *f.*, a bag, wallet, purse.
πρῴρ-α, *f.*, a prow, fore part of a ship.
πύλ-η, *f.*, a gate.
σελήν-η, *f.*, the moon.
σκην-ή, *f.*, a tent, a hut, a cottage.
σκι-ά, *f.*, a shadow, a shade.
στρατι-ά, *f.*, an army.
σφαῖρ-α, *f.*, a ball.
σφενδόν-η, *f.*, a sling.
ὕλ-η, *f.*, a wood, a forest.
χηλ-ή, *f.*, a hoof, a claw, a talon.

ἐμ-ή, fem. of adj., means *my*.
ἐν, prep. governing dat., means *in, at, among, on*.
σύν, prep. governing dat., means *along with*.
ὁ, ἡ, τό, *the*. (See the Article, Second Declension.)

II.
ἄκανθ-α, ης, *f.*, a thorn.
γλῶττ-α, ης, *f.*, a tongue.
δεσπότ-ης, ου, *m.*, a master, lord, owner (*dominus*).
δόξ-α, ης, *f.*, glory.
λέαιν-α, ης, *f.*, a lioness.
μάζ-α, ης, *f.*, a cake.
Μοῦσ-α, ης, *f.*, the Muse.
ναύτ-ης, ου, *m.*, a sailor.
Πέρσ-ης, ου, *m.*, a Persian.
Πέρσ ης, ου, *m.*, Perses.
ποιητ-ής, οῦ, *m.*, a poet.
πολίτ-ης, ου, *m.*, a citizen.
Σκύθ-ης, ου, *m.*, a Scythian.
τράπεζ-α, ης, *f.*, a table.

ὦ, an interjection, O, joined to vocatives.

III.
SUBSTANTIVES.
ἀρότ-ης, ου, *m.*, a ploughman.
κόμ-η, ης, *f.*, hair.
νίκ-η, ης, *f.*, victory.
πέδ-η, ης, *f.*, a fetter.

ADJECTIVES.
ἁγί-α, holy.
δασεῖ-α, shaggy, bushy, dense.
εὑρεῖ-α, broad, wide.
καλ-ή, beautiful.
κεν-ή, empty.
κλειν-ή, famous, celebrated, glorious.
λεῖ α, smooth (to the touch), level.
μακρά, long, large.
μικρ-ά, small, little.
μωρ-ός, *m.* (see Decl. II.) foolish, silly.
νέ-α, new, fresh, recent.
ξανθ-ή, yellow, golden, fair, auburn.
ξηρ-ά, dry, parched, withered.
ὀξεῖ-α, sharp, keen, quick.

πολλ-ή, much, (in pl. many.)
σεμν-ή, venerable, revered.
σκληρ-ά, dry, rough, stiff, harsh.
σοφ-ή, wise, prudent.
τραχεῖ-α, rough.
φανερ-ά, plain, clear, bright.
ὠχρ-ά, pale, wan.

ἐστί, 3d sing., he, she, or it is.
εἰσί, 3d pl., they are.
ἐστόν, 3d dual, they two are.

IV.
SUBSTANTIVES.
ἀετ-ός, οῦ, m., an eagle.
δάκτυλ-ος, ου, m., a finger.
δεῖπν-ον, ου, n., a dinner, a supper.
δοῦλ-ος, ου, m., a slave, a servant.
δῶρ-ον, ου, n., a gift.
θε-ός, οῦ, m., a god, deity.
ἵππ-ος, ου, m. or f., a horse.
κῆπ-ος, ου, m., a garden.
μῆλ-ον, ου, n., an apple.
ξυρ-όν, οῦ, n., a razor.
πλοῖ-ον, ου, n., a ship, boat.
φύλλ-ον, ου, n., a leaf.
ᾠ-όν, οῦ, n., an egg.

ADJECTIVES.
καλ-ός, m.; καλ-ή, f.; καλ-όν, n., beautiful.
λευκ-ός, m.; λευκ-ή, f.; λευκ-όν, n., white.
μικρ-ός, ά, όν, small.

V.
SUBSTANTIVES.
ἀγρ-ός, οῦ, m., a field, land.
ἀγυι-ά, ᾶς, f., a street, road, way.
ἀδελφ-ός, οῦ, m., a brother.
Ἀθῆν-αι, ῶν, f. pl., Athens.
αἴγειρ-ος, ου, f., a poplar-tree.
ἄνθρωπ-ος, ου, m. (homo), man, mankind; a man.
βωμ-ός, οῦ, m., an altar.
γεωργ-ός, οῦ, m., a farmer, husbandman.
γνάθ-ος, ου, f., a jaw, cheek.
δάφν-η, ης, f., a bay-tree, laurel.
ἰατρ-ός, οῦ, m., physician, doctor.
κύρι-ος, ου, m., master.
μόσχ-ος, ου, m., a calf.

να-ός, οῦ, m., a temple.
ὁδ-ός, οῦ, f., a way, road.
οἰκί-α, ας, f., a house.
οἶκ-ος, ου, m., a house.
ὄν-ος, ου, m. or f., an ass.
ὀφθαλμ-ός, οῦ, m., an eye.
φύλλ-ον, ου, n., a leaf.
χαίτ-η, ης, f., a mane.

ADJECTIVES.
γλαυκ-ός, ή, όν, grey, blue.
γλυκ-ύς, γλυκεῖ-α, γλυκ-ύ, sweet, pleasant.
δασ-ύς, δασεῖ-α, δασ-ύ, thick; shaggy, bushy; rough, dense.
ἡδ-ύς, ἡδεῖ-α, ἡδ-ύ, sweet, pleasant.
ἱερ-ός, ά, όν, sacred, holy.
κεν-ός, ή, όν, empty.
λεῖ-ος, α, ον, smooth.
μακρ-ός, ά, όν, long, large.
μαλακ-ός, ή, όν, soft.
νήπι-ος, α, ον, foolish, ignorant.
ξηρ-ός, ά, όν, dry, parched, withered.
πιστ-ός, ή, όν, faithful.
σεμν-ός, ή, όν, venerable, revered.

ἀνά, up, along, accus., gen., dat.
ἄνευ, without, gen.
ἀπό, away from, gen.
διά, through, accus., gen.
εἰς, into, accus.
ἐκ, out of, gen.
ἕνεκα, on account of, because of, gen.
καί, and.
κατά, down, accus. and gen. (See p. 34.)

VI.
SUBSTANTIVES.
ἀλ-ώς, ώ, f., a thrashing-floor.
ἀνώγε-ων, ω, n., an upper chamber.
κάλ-ως, ω, m., a cable, a rope.
κέρκ-ος, ου, f., a tail, hare's scut.
κεφαλ-ή, ῆς, f., a head, source.
λαγ-ώς, ώ, m., a hare.
λε-ώς, ώ, m., a people.
νε-ώς, ώ, m., a temple.
οὐρ-ά, ᾶς, f., a tail.
τα-ώς, ῶ, m., a peacock.

ADJECTIVES.

βραχ-ύς, εῖα, ύ, short, little.
λαμπρ-ός, ά, όν, bright, brilliant.
παλαι-ός, ά, όν, old, ancient.
ὠκ-ύς, εῖα, ύ, swift, fleet, rapid.

VII.
SUBSTANTIVES.

Ἕλλην, m., a Greek.
θήρ, m., a wild beast.
λειμών, m., a meadow.
μήν, m., a month.
χήν, m. or f., a gander or goose.

VERBS.

διώκ-ω, I hunt, pursue, chase.
ἔχ-ω, I have.
λείπ-ω, I leave.

VIII.
SUBSTANTIVES.

ἄρτ-ος, ου, m., bread; a loaf.
γύψ, γυπ-ός, m., a vulture.
δμώ-ς, ός, m., a domestic servant.
ἥρω s, ος, m., a hero, warrior, demigod.
θάλαττ-α, ης, f., the sea.
θώ-ς, ός, m., a jackal.
ἰχθύ-ς, ος, m., a fish.
κλέπτ-ης, ου, m., a thief.
κλώψ, κλωπ-ός, m., a thief.
κόραξ, κόρακ-ος, m., a raven, crow.
μάχαιρ-α, ας, f., a cutlass, sword.
μυκτήρ, ος, m., a nostril.
μύρμηξ, μύρμηκ-ος, m., an ant.
μῦς, μυ-ός, m., a mouse.
πτέρυξ, πτέρυγ-ος, f., a wing.
σκύλαξ, σκύλακ-ος, m. or f., a young dog or whelp, a puppy.
σῦ-ς, συ-ός, m. or f., a pig, swine, boar.
φλέψ, φλεβ-ός, f., a vein.
φώρ, ος, m., a thief.

ADJECTIVES.

ἄγρι-ος, α, ον, fierce, savage.
ἐμ-ός, ή, όν, my or mine.
ξανθ-ός, ή, όν, yellow, golden; auburn, fair.
σκληρ-ός, ά, όν, dry; rough; stiff; harsh.

σοφ-ός, ή, όν, wise, prudent.
τραχ-ύς, εῖα, ύ, rough, rugged.

VERBS.

ἐσθί-ω, I eat.
κείρ-ω, I crop, cut, shave, shear.
τρώγ-ω, I eat, nibble.

IX.
SUBSTANTIVES.

ἀηδών, ἀηδόν-ος, f., a nightingale.
Ἀθήν-ᾶ, ᾶς, f., Athena (Minerva).
ἀλώπηξ, ἀλώπεκ-ος, f., a fox.
ἀνήρ, ἀνδρ-ός, m., a man (vir).
αὐχήν, αὐχέν-ος, m., the neck.
γειτών, γειτόν-ος, m. or f., a neighbour.
ἐπιστολ-ή, ῆς, f., a letter, epistle.
κίων, κίον-ος, m., a pillar.
κύων, κυν-ός, m. or f., a dog.
λιμήν, λιμέν-ος, m., a harbour, port.
μήτηρ, μητρ-ός, f., a mother.
οἶς, οἰ-ός, m. or f., a sheep.
πατήρ, πατρ-ός, m., a father.
ποιμήν, ποιμέν-ος, m., a shepherd.
ῥάβδ-ος, ου, f., a rod, wand.
τριήρ-ης, τριήρε-ος, f., a trireme.
φίλ-ος, ου, m., a friend.
φων ή, ῆς, f., a voice, sound.
χελιδών, χελιδόν-ος, f., a swallow.
χιών, χιόν-ος, f., snow.

ADJECTIVES.

ἀληθ-ής, ής, ές, (see p. 47,) true.
πολλοί, nom. pl., (see p. 46), many.

VERBS.

γράφ-ω, I write.
θαυμάζ-ω, I admire, wonder at.
πείθ-ω, I persuade.
ῥίπτ-ω, I throw, hurl.

X.
SUBSTANTIVES.

ἄγαλμα, τος, n., an image, statue.
ἅρμα, τος, n., a chariot, car.
ἄρχων, ἄρχοντ-ος, m., a ruler, commander.
βῆμα, τος, n., a step; judgment-seat.

γδλα,* γάλακτ-ος, n., milk.
γέρων, γέροντ-ος, m., an old man.
γῆ, γῆς, f., the earth ; a country; a land.
κῦμα, τος, n., a swell of the sea, wave.
λέων, λέοντ-ος, m., a lion.
μέλι, μέλιτ-ος, n., honey.
μέλιττ-α, ης, f., a bee.
Ξενοφῶν, m., Xenophon.
ποταμ-ός, οῦ, m., a river.
σῶμα, τος, n., a body, a corpse.
ὑπηρέτ-ης, ου, m., a servant, attendant.

ADJECTIVES.
ὄρθι-ος, α, ον, steep.
πολ-ύς, πολλ-ή, πολ-ύ, much. In pl. many. (See p. 46.)

VERBS.
βλέπ-ω, I see ; I look upon.
κελεύ-ω, I bid, order, command, desire.

XI.
SUBSTANTIVES.
ἄναξ, ἄνακτ-ος, m., a prince, king.
ἄντρ-ον, ου, n., a cave.
ἀσπίς, ἀσπίδ-ος, f., a shield.
γίγας, γίγαντ-ος, m., a giant.
δόμ-ος, ου, m., a building, a house.
κλείς, κλειδ-ός, f., a key.
κόρυς, κόρυθ-ος, f., a helmet.
κριτ-ής, οῦ, m., a judge.
λαμπάς, λαμπάδ-ος, f., a torch.
λέβης, λέβητ-ος, m., a caldron; ewer.
ὀδούς, ὀδόντ-ος, m., a tooth.
ὁλκάς, ὁλκάδ-ος, f., a ship of burden ; a merchant-man.
ὄρνις, ὄρνιθ-ος, m. or f., a bird, fowl, hen.
παῖς, παιδ-ός, m. or f., a child; boy; girl.
παράδεισ-ος, ου, m., a park ; pleasure-grounds.
ῥίς, ῥιν-ός, f., a nostril. In pl. the nose.

τίς, τίς, τί, interrog. pron., who ? which ? what ?
τὶς, τὶς, τί, indef. pron., some one, any one, a certain.
τρίβων, ος, m., a (coarse or threadbare) cloak.
χλαμύς, χλαμύδ-ος, f., a mantle.

VERBS.
βαίν-ω, I go.
ἦν, he was, or I was.
ἦσαν, they were.
λέγ-ω, I say.
πλέκ-ω, I plait, twine.
πλέ-ω, I sail.
τύπτ-ω, I strike, hit.

ADJECTIVES.
μέλας, (gen. μέλαν-ος), μέλαινα, μέλαν, black.
πᾶς, πᾶσα, πᾶν, all, every. (See πᾶς, p. 45.)

παρά, prep., beside. (See p. 34.)
ποῦ, interrog. adv., where ?
τέ, conj., and.   τέ—καί, both—and.

XII.
SUBSTANTIVES.
αἷμα, αἵματ-ος, n., blood.
ἄστ-υ, εος, n., a city.
δύναμ-ις, εως, f., power, force.
κορυφ-ή, ῆς, f., a top, summit.
κοχλί-ας, ου, m., a snail.
μάντ-ις, εως, m., a prophet, seer.
μέρ-ος, εος, n., a part, share.
ξίφ-ος, εος, n., a sword.
ὄροφ-ος, ου, m. a roof.
ὄρ-ος, εος, n., a mountain.
ὄφ-ις. εως, m., a serpent, snake.
ὄχλ-ος, ου, m., a crowd ; the populace.
πέλεκ-υς, εως, m., an axe, hatchet.
πόλ-ις, εως. f., a city, state.
πώγων, πώγων-ος, m., a beard.
σοφιστ-ής, οῦ, m., a learned man, teacher, sophist.

---

* As every genuine Greek word ends either in a vowel or in ν, ρ, ς, the κτ in which the stem of this word terminates must be left off, and so γαλακτ is reduced to γάλα.

στῆθ-ος, εος, n., the breast, chest.
τεῖχ-ος, εος, n., a wall.
υἱ ός, οῦ, m., a son.

ADJECTIVES.
βαρ-ύς, εῖα, ύ, heavy.
δειν-ός, ή, όν, dreadful, mighty.
δῆλ-ος, η, ον, evident, plain, visible.
ὀξ-ύς, εῖα, ύ, sharp, swift.

VERBS.
διδάσκ-ω, I teach.
ἕρπ-ω, I creep.
ῥέω, I flow.
φεύγ-ω, I flee, run away.

XIII.
SUBSTANTIVES.
βασιλ-εύς, έως, m., a king.
βοῦς. βο-ός, m. or f., an ox or cow.
γέφυρ-α, ας, f., a bridge.
γον-εύς, έως, m. or f., a parent.
γραῦς, γρα-ός, f., an old woman.
δορκ-άς, άδος, f., a gazelle.
ἔθ-ος, εος, n., habit, custom.
θυγάτηρ, θυγατρ-ός, f., a daughter.
ἱερ-εύς, έως, m., a priest.
ἱππ-εύς, έως, m., a horseman. In pl. cavalry.
κέρας, κέρατ-ος, n., a horn.
κουρ-εύς, έως, m., a barber.
ναῦς, νεώς, f., a ship.
νομ-εύς, έως, m., a shepherd.
στρατηγ-ός, οῦ, m., a general, commander.
στρατιώτ ης, ου, m., a soldier.

ADJECTIVES, ETC.
εὐρ-ύς, εῖα, ύ, broad, wide.
μέγ-ας, μεγάλ-η, μέγ-α, great; p. 46.
τί, why.

VERBS.
βαδίζ-ω, I stalk, walk in a stately manner.
φυλάττ-ω (or -σσω), I guard.
θέ-ω, I run.

XIV.
SUBSTANTIVES.
ἄλσ-ος, εος, n., a grove.
ἄνθ-ος, εος, n., a flower.
βάθ-ος, εος, n., a depth, a glen.
βέλ-ος, εος, n., a javelin, dart, weapon.
νεανί-ας, ου, m., a young man.
ὅπλ-ον, ου, n., a weapon; pl. arms.
παιδί-ον, ου, n., an infant.
πεδί-ον, ου, n., a plain.
πεζ-οί, ῶν, m., infantry.
τάξ-ις, εως, f., line (of troops).
χεῖλ-ος, εος, n., a lip.
χόρτ-ος, ου, m., an enclosure, a garden.

ADJECTIVES.
κακ-ός, ή, όν, bad, wicked, worthless. (See p. 50.)
ὅς, ἥ. ὅ, who, which, that.
πονηρ-ός, ά, όν, wicked.
ὑψηλ-ός, ή, όν, lofty, high.
χρύσ-εος, εα, εον, golden.
ὠχρ ός, ά, όν, pale, wan.

VERBS.
εὑρίσκ-ω, I find.
καταβαίν-ω, I descend.

XV.
SUBSTANTIVES.
ἄρκτ-ος, ου, m. or f., a bear.
γέραν-ος, ου, m., a crane.
γυνή, gen. γυναικ-ός, f. a woman, wife.
Ἰνδ-ός, οῦ, m., an Indian.
Κῦρ-ος, ου, m., Cyrus.
κώμ-η, ης, f., a village.
οἶν-ος, ου, m., wine.
ὄρτυξ, ὄρτυγ ος, m., a quail.
στολ-ή, ῆς, f., a robe.
ὕπν-ος, ου, m., sleep.
φήμ-η, ης, f., a rumour, report.

ADJECTIVES.
ἀμαθ-ής, ής, ές, unlearned, ignorant.
βαθ-ύς, εῖα, ύ, deep.
δειλ-ός, ή, όν, cowardly; wretched, miserable.
θαρσ-ύς, εῖα, ύ, bold, courageous.
κοῦφ-ος, η, ον, light.
λάλ-ος, ος, ον, talkative.
πότερ ος, α, ον, whether of the two.
ῥᾴδι-ος, α, ον, easy.
στεν-ός, ή, όν, narrow.
τλήμ-ων, ων, ον, patient; suffering; wretched.
χαρί-εις, εσσα, εν, beautiful, graceful.

LISTS OF WORDS.

VERB.
φέρ-ω, I carry.

PREPOSITIONS.
διά, through, *gen.* (sometimes *accus.*)
πρός, towards (with *accus.*) See *Vocabulary*.

XVI.
SUBSTANTIVES.
γράμμα, γράμματ-ος, *n.*, a letter.
ἔτ-ος, εος, *n.*, a year.
ἡμέρ-α, ας, *f.*, a day.
λίθ-ος, ου, *m.*, a stone.
λόγ-ος, ου, *m.*, a word; speech; reason.
μαθητ-ής, οῦ, *m.*, a disciple.
μῦθ-ος, ου, *m.*, a word.
πρέσβ-υς, υος, or εως, *m.*, an old man; an ambassador.
στέφαν-ος, ου, *m.*, a wreath, crown.
χείρ, χειρ-ός, *f.*, the hand.
χρυσ-ός, οῦ, *m.*, gold.

ADJECTIVES.
ἀγαθ-ός, ή, όν, good. (See p. 50.)
Ἑλληνικ-ός, ή, όν, Greek.
κωφ-ός, ή, όν, deaf.
φίλι-ος, α, ον, friendly.
φίλ-ος, η, ον, friendly, beloved.

VERBS.
δάκν-ω, I bite.
κρύπτ-ω, I conceal.
πέμπ-ω, I send.
πλέκ-ω, I plait, twine.
τιτρώσκ-ω, I wound.

XVII.
SUBSTANTIVES.
δόναξ, δόνακ-ος, *m.*, a reed.
ἔλαφ-ος, ου, *m.* or *f.*, a deer.
θάνατ-ος, ου, *m.*, death.
ἱπποκόμ-ος, ου, *m.*, a groom.
κριθ-ή, ῆς, *f.*, barley.
Κύρι-ος, ου, *m.*, the Lord.
κυβερνήτ-ης, ου, *m.*, a pilot, steersman.
νύξ, νυκτ-ός, *f.*, night; νυκτός, by night.
παιδί ον, ου, *n.*, a child, infant.
σοφί-α, ας, *f.*, wisdom, prudence; learning.

τροφ ός, οῦ, *f.*, a nurse.
φρόνησ-ις, εως, *f.*, wisdom, prudence
ἀεί (*adv.*), always.
ὑπό, *prep.*, under, by.

VERBS.
ἀκού-ω, I hear.
βασιλεύ-ω, I act the king, reign, rule.
βουλεύ-ω, I consult, take counsel, deliberate, advise.
ἐθέλ-ω, I wish.
ζητέ-ω, I seek.
θηρεύ-ω, I hunt.
ἱππεύ-ω, I ride.
καλέ-ω, I call, call on, invoke.
λύ-ω, I loose, unyoke, let go, set free.
ὀπτά-ω, I roast.
πιστεύ-ω, I believe.
πωλέ-ω, I sell, barter.

XVIII.
Same as preceding.

XIX.
SUBSTANTIVES.
βιβλί-ον, ου, *n.*, a book.
γέν-ος, εος, *n.*, race, origin, family.
κρύ-ος, εος, *n.*, cold.

VERBS.
κτενίζ-ω, I comb.
πήγνυ-μι, F. πήξω, I fasten, stiffen.
τρέφ-ω, I nourish, support.
τρίβ-ω, I rub.

XX.
SUBSTANTIVES.
ἀήρ, ἀέρ-ος, *m.*, the air.
βακτηρί-α, ας, *f.*, a stick, cudgel.
λύκ-ος, ου, *m.*, a wolf.
πολέμι-ος, ου, *m.*, an enemy.
πόλεμ-ος, ου, *m.*, war.
ὕδωρ, ὕδατ-ος, *n.*, water.
φυλακ-ή, ῆς, *f.*, guard, prison.
μεθ' for μετά, *prep.*, among, with.
ὅλ-ος, η, ον, *adj.*, whole, entire.
γάρ, *conj.*, for, because.
ἤδη, *adv.*, already, now.

VERBS.

ἀποκτείν-ω, I kill, slay.
βάλλ-ω, I throw, cast, hit.
κλέπτ-ω, I steal.
κλίν-ω, I bend; (of the sun,) to set.
μέν-ω, I remain, stay.
στέλλ-ω, I send, equip.
τέμν-ω, I cut.
τίλλ-ω, I pluck, pull out.
φαίν-ω, I show, point out.

XXI.

SUBSTANTIVES.

ἅμαξ-α, ης, f., a waggon.
ἀρετ-ή, ῆς, f., virtue, merit.
Ἀρταξέρξ-ης, ου, m., Artaxerxes.
ἀρχ-ή, ῆς, f., government, province.
βάρβαρ-ος, ου, m., a barbarian.
διδάσκαλ-ος, ου, m. or f., a teacher.
κύπελλ-ον, ου, n., a cup.
λόγ-ος, ου, m., a word; book, treatise.
οἰκί-α, ας, f., a house.
ῥήτωρ, ῥήτορ-ος, m., an orator.
ὑποζύγι-ον, ου, n., a beast of burden.

ADJECTIVES.

αἰσχρ-ός, ά, όν, base, worthless.
ἄξι-ος, α, ον, worthy, deserving.
ἀργύρε-ος (οῦς), α, ον, made of silver; silver.
ἄριστ-ος, η, ον, best.

ἔμπροσθεν, adv., formerly; used adjectively, former.
ὑπό, prep., by. (See Vocabulary.)

VERBS.

αἱρέ-ω, I take, choose, catch.
δηλό-ω, I make plain, detail.
ἐλαύν-ω, I drive, ride.
καί-ω, I set on fire, burn.
παιδεύ-ω, I teach, educate.
πορεύ-ομαι, I go, journey, advance.
τιμά-ω, I honour.
φιλέ-ω, I love.

XXII.

SUBSTANTIVES.

ἄγγελ-ος, ου, m., a messenger.
Δαρεῖ-ος, ου, m., Darius.

ἐλευθερί-α, ας, f., freedom, liberty.
ἐξέτασ-ις, εως, f., a review; ποιεῖσθαι ἐξέτασιν, to review.
ἔργ-ον, ου, n., a work, action.
Καστωλ-ός, οῦ, m., Castolus.
πατρίς, πατρίδ-ος, f., native country.
σατράπ-ης, ου, m., a satrap, or Persian governor.
σταθμ-ός, οῦ, m., a halting-place, a stage.
σωτηρί-α, ας, f., safety.
τιμ-ή, ῆς, f., honour.

ADJECTIVES.

μέσ-ος, η, ον, middle.
ὅσ-ος, η, ον, how much, how great.

VERBS.

ἀθροίζ-ω, I collect, assemble.
ἀποδείκνυ-μι, I set forth, exhibit, declare.
ἀποκρίν-ομαι, I reply.
ἀποπέμπ-ω, I send away, despatch.
βούλ-ομαι, I wish.
γεύ-ομαι, I taste, (with gen.)
ἐξαιτέ-ομαι, I beg off (for myself.)
μάχ-ομαι, I fight.
μεταπέμπ-ομαι, I send for (to myself.)
ποιέ-ω, I make; I do.
στρατεύ-ομαι, I take the field, go on a military expedition.
συλλαμβάν-ω, I seize, apprehend.
τάττ-ω (τάσσ-ω), F. τάξω, I marshal, arrange.
χρή (impers. verb), it is necessary.

ἀνδρείως, manfully, bravely.
ἐπιμελῶς, carefully.
περί, around, about. (See Vocabulary.)
πρό, before, for.

XXIII.

SUBSTANTIVES.

ἔγχ-ος, εος, n., a spear.
ἡδον-ή, ῆς, f., pleasure.
θηρί-ον, ου, n., a wild beast.
ἴχν-ος, εος, n., a track, trace, footprint.
Κλέαρχ-ος, ου, m., Clearchus.

LISTS OF WORDS.

Λυδί-α, ας, f., Lydia.
λύπ-η, ης, f., grief.
μέλ ος, εος, n., a limb, member.
Μένων, ος, m., Menon.
μέρ ος, εος, n., a part, share.
Νῖν-ος, ου, f., Nineveh.
πορθμ-εύς, έως, m., a ferryman, boatman.
σάκ-ος, εος, n., a shield.
φυγ-άς, φυγάδ-ος, m. or f., an exile.

ADJECTIVES.
βραχ-ύς, εῖα, ύ, short.
δεξι-ός, ά, όν, the right hand; favourable, fortunate.
εὐώνυμ-ος, ος, ον, the left, lucky.
λοιπ-ός, ή, όν, remaining; the rest.
σώφρ-ων, ων, ον, self-controlling; wise, prudent.

ὅτε, conj., when.
πολλάκις, adv., often.
ὥσπερ, as, as if.

VERBS.
ἀναβαίν-ω, I go up, ascend.
ἀπέχ-ομαι. I keep myself from, refrain.
ἀποθνήσκ-ω, I die.
ἀπόλλυ-μι, I perish, I die.
ἀποφεύγ-ω, I flee away, retreat.
γυμνάζ-ω, I exercise.
ἐξελαύν-ω, I ride forth, march forward.
ἡγέ-ομαι, I lead the way, guide.
θύ-ω, I sacrifice.
καταπηδά-ω, I leap down.
κεῖμ-αι, I lie.
πείθ-ω, I persuade.
πίπτ-ω, I fall.
τίκτ-ω, I beget, produce.
τρέχ-ω, I run.

XXIV.
SUBSTANTIVES.
ἀγαθ-ά, ῶν, neut. pl., goods, blessings.
ἆθλ-ον, ου, n., a prize of a contest, a reward.
ἄρχων, ἄρχοντ-ος, m., a ruler.
γράμμα, γράμματ-ος, n., a letter; pl. an inscription.

δαρεικ-ός, οῦ, m., a daric (a Persian coin).
κόσμ-ος, ου, m., the world.
Λυκοῦργ-ος, ου, m., Lycurgus.
μισθ-ός, οῦ, m., pay, wages.
νεκρ-ός, οῦ, m., a dead body, corpse.
νόμ-ος, ου, m., a law.
πῦρ, πυρ-ός, n., fire.
στήλ-η, ης, f., a pillar, a tombstone.
τρόπαι-ον, ου, n., a trophy.

ADJECTIVES.
ἕκαστ-ος, η, ον, each, every.
Θηβαῖ-ος, α, ον, Theban.
μύρι-οι, αι, α, ten thousand; a very great number.
ὅστις, ἥτις, ὅτι, whoever, whichever; who, what.
χίλι-οι, αι, α, a thousand.

VERBS.
ἀναδίδω-μι, I give forth, yield, send up.
ἀποδίδω-μι, I give back, return, pay.
ἀφίστη-μι, I revolt.
δίδω-μι, I give, grant.
ἐά-ω, I allow, permit.
εἶπ-ον (2 aor. of φημί), I said.
ἐκτίθη-μι, I expose.
ἔξεστ-ιν, impers., it is lawful; it is permitted.
εὐτυχέ-ω, I am fortunate.
ἵστη-μι, I cause to stand, I erect.
κατατίθη μι, I put down, I pay.
κινέ-ω, I move.
τίθη-μι, I place; τίθημι νόμον, I make a law.
φαίν-ω, I show; mid. and pass., I appear.

ὅτι, conj., that.
μάλιστα, adv., very much; especially.

XXV.
SUBSTANTIVES.
Ἀρίστιππ-ος, ου, m., Aristippus.
βουκόλ-ος, ου, m., a cowherd, herdsman.
δάφν-η, ης, f., a bay-tree, laurel.

Δάφνις, Δάφνιδ-ος, m., Daphnis.
οἱ (i.e., οἵ), to him. (See p. 54.)
ὄνομα, ὀνόματ-ος, n., a name.
Πλάτων, ος, m., Plato.
Πυθαγόρ-ας, α, m., Pythagoras.
ῥάκ-ος, εος, n., a rag; a coarse or ragged garment.
σπουδ-ή, ῆς, f., haste, eagerness.
Τισσαφέρν-ης, ου, m., Tissaphernes.
φάρμακ-ον, ου, n., a drug, medicine.
χλαμύς, χλαμύδ-ος, f., a mantle, cloak.

ADJECTIVES.

ἰατρική (scil. τέχνη), fem. of ἰατρικός, the healing art, medicine, surgery.
κάλλιστ-ος, η, ον (superl. of καλός), most beautiful, or excellent.
μηδείς, μηδεμία, μηδέν (see εἷς, p. 53), no one, none.
μόν-ος, η, ον, only, alone.
ποτ-ός, ή, όν, drinkable; ποτὸν φάρμακον, a potion.
χρήσιμ-ος, η, ον, useful.

VERBS.

ἀληθεύ-ω, I am truthful, I speak truth.
ἀξιό-ω, I deem myself worthy; I demand.
ἄρχ-ω, I rule, govern.
εὐεργετέ-ω, I benefit, show kindness to.
καθίστη-μι, I establish; mid. I take up my position, post myself.
κεράννυ-μι, I mix.
λαμβάν-ω (2 aor. ἔλαβον), I take, receive.
τίκτ-ω (1 aor. pass. ἐτέχθην), I produce, bring forth, bear.
φορέ-ω, I carry, wear.

ἄν, adv., perchance, if. (See Greek Vocabulary.)
εὖ, adv., well, becomingly.
μᾶλλον, adv., more, rather.
ὅθεν, adv., whence.
τότε, adv., then.

GREEK VOCABULARY.

m. stands for Masculine, *f.* for Feminine, and *n.* for Neuter. Proper names begin with capitals. In Verbs, F. stands for Future, P. for Perfect.

A

ἀγαθ-ός, ή, όν, good; brave; noble; wise, &c.: τὸ ἀγαθόν, advantage, a blessing: τὰ ἀγαθά, goods, wealth. (For *Comparatives* and *Superlatives*, see p. 50.)

ἄγαλμα, ἀγάλματ-ος, *n.*, delight; honour; gift; statue; picture.

ἀγαλματοποι-ός, ός, όν, making statues: as a *subst. m.*, a statuary.

ἄγαν, *adv.*, very, very much.

ἀγανακτ-έω, F. ήσω, to feel violent irritation; to be vexed; to be angry, &c. Governs dative, and sometimes accusative, or is followed by a preposition and case. From ἄγαν, and perhaps ἄγω (which see); or ἄχθος (grief, distress).

ἀγγελί-α, ας, *f.*, a message; news; command.

ἄγγελ-ος, ου, *m.* or *f.*, a messenger, bearer of tidings.

ἀγγέλ-λω, F. ἀγγελ-ῶ, to announce, proclaim. (See *Liquid Verbs*.)

ἀγεν-ής (or ἀγεννής), ής, ές, low-born, ignoble; low-minded, mean: from ἀ, not, and γένος, race, descent.

ἅγι-ος, α, ον (Lat. *sacer*), devoted (to the gods), sacred, holy; *also* accursed.

ἄγκυρ-α, ας, *f.* (Lat. *ancŏra*), an anchor.

ἀγνο-έω, F. ήσω, to be ignorant of, not to observe.

ἀγοράζ-ω, F. ἀγοράσω, to attend market; to buy.

ἄγρι-ος, α, ον, wild, savage, fierce.

ἀγρ-ός, οῦ, *m.* (Lat. *ager*), a field, land, the country (opposed to the town).

ἀγυι-ά, ᾶς, *f.*, a way, street, road; from ἄγω. In *pl.*, a town.

ἀγύρτ-ης, ου, *m.* (from ἀγείρω), a gatherer, beggar; mountebank, quack, cheat.

ἄγχω, F. ἄγξω (Lat. *ango*), to press tight; *hence*, to throttle, strangle.

ἄγω, F. ἄξω, P. ἦχα, 2 aor. (reduplicated), ἤγαγον, with *inf.* ἀγαγεῖν, to lead, take with one, carry, take away, drive; consider (like *duco*); spend (as time, life, &c.).

ἀγων-άω, F. ἀσω, to strive eagerly; to be distressed; to be anxious.

ἀγωνίζομαι, F. ἀγωνίσομαι (Attic, ἀγωνιοῦμαι), to contend for a prize, to struggle, to fight.

ἀδελφ-ή, ῆς, *f.*, a sister.

ἀδελφ-ός, οῦ, *m.*, a brother; a near relative.

ᾅδ-ης, ου, *m.*, Hades, Pluto, the lower world; the grave, death. The derivation from ἀ, *not*, and ἰδεῖν, *to see*, is doubtful.

ἀδικ-έω, F. ήσω, to be ἄδικος, to do wrong, to violate the laws; to injure, to do wrong to.

ἄδῐκ-ος, ος, ον (ἀ, not, and δίκη, justice), unrighteous, unjust.
ἀδόκῐμ-ος, ος, ον, unproved; disreputable; ignoble, mean.
ἀδολέσχ-ης, ου, m. (or ἀδόλεσχ-ος, ος, ον), a prating fellow, a babbler.
ἀδύνᾰτ-ος, ος, ον, (active), unable to do (a thing), powerless; (passive), impossible.
ᾄδ-ω, F. ᾄσω, or ᾄσομαι (contracted for ἀείδω, which is principally poetic in use), to sing, to chant; to praise.
ἀεί, adv., always, ever, for ever.
ἀετ-ός, οῦ, m., an eagle.
ἀηδών, ἀηδόν-ος, f., a songstress; the nightingale.
ἀθᾰνᾰσί-α, ας, f., immortality.
Ἀθην-ᾶ, ᾶς, f., Athena (Minerva).
Ἀθῆν-αι, ῶν, f. pl., Athens.
Ἀθηναῖ-οι, ων, m. pl., the Athenians; sing. Ἀθηναῖος.
ἄθλῐ-ος, α, ον, or ἄθλιος, ος, ον, toilsome, painful; wretched, miserable.
ἆθλον (for ἄεθλον), ου, n., the prize of a contest; a reward, gift, &c.
ἀθροίζ-ω, F. ἀθροίσω, to collect, assemble.
ἀθρό-ος, α, ον (rarely ἀθρόος, ος, ον), crowded together, set thick, numerous.
Αἰακ-ός, οῦ, Æacus (one of the judges in Hades).
αἴγειρ-ος, ου, f., the black poplar.
Αἰγύπτ-ος, ου, f., Egypt.
Αἰδων-εύς, έος, m., Pluto (See ᾅδης.)
αἷμα, αἵματ-ος, n., blood.
αἴξ, αἰγός, m. or f., a goat.
αἱρετ-ός, ή, όν, desirable, eligible.
αἱρέ-ω, F. αἱρήσω, P. ᾕρηκα, 2 aor. (from root, ἕλω), εἷλον, inf. ἑλεῖν, I take with the hand, receive, catch, win, conquer; understand, detect, convict; mid. αἱρέομαι, to take to one's self, choose, prefer.
αἴρ-ω, F. ἀρῶ, 1 aor. ἦρα, P. ἦρκα, to raise, lift up; carry, bear; exalt; take away: and in mid.

to lift or take for one's self, or what is one's own; to gain.
αἰσχ-ρός, ά, όν, or αἰσχ-ρός, ρός, ρόν, ugly, ill-looking; hence, disgraceful, base, immoral. Comparative and superlative, αἰσχ-ίων, αἴσχ-ιστος.
αἰσχῡν-ω, F. αἰσχῠνῶ, P. ᾔσχυγκα, to disfigure, dishonour; pass. αἰσχύνομαι, to be ashamed of, to blush.
αἰτέ-ω, F. αἰτήσω, to ask, beg, request, &c.
αἰτί-α, ας, f., a cause, reason, occasion; fault, charge.
αἰτιά-ομαι, αἰτιάσομαι, deponent mid., to allege as the cause; hence, to blame, charge, find fault with.
αἰτιατ-έον, verb adj., one must, or ought to accuse.
αἴτι-ος, α, ον (rarely αἴτι-ος, ος, ον), causing, or giving cause for blame; culpable, blamable: as subst., an author.
αἰφνίδι-ος, ος, ον, sudden, unexpected. Neuter used as an adverb.
ἄκανθ-α, ης, f., a thorn, prickle; thorny shrub.
ἀκέστρ-α, ας, f., a needle.
ἀκίνητ-ος, ος, ον, also ος, η, ον, unmoved, immovable, motionless, steady; idle, sluggish.
ἀκμαῖ-ος, α, ον, in full bloom, in the flower of youth; vigorous.
ἀκολουθέ-ω, to follow or go with a person, accompany.
ἀκόντι-ον, ου, n. (diminutive from ἄκων), a dart, javelin.
ἀκούσι-ος, ον, unwilling, forced.
ἀκού-ω, F. ἀκούσομαι (ἀκούσω, late), P. ἀκήκοα, P. pass. ἤκουσμαι, to hear, listen to, obey. Governs usually the accusative of the thing heard, and the genitive of the person from whom heard; but see Liddell and Scott's Greek Lexicon.
ἀκρῑβῶς, adv., exactly, thoroughly, strictly; from adj. ἀκρῑβής, exact, &c.

ἀκύμαντ-ος, ος, ον, waveless, calm.
ἄκ-ων, ἄκουσα, ἆκον (contracted for ἀέκων), unwilling, against one's will.
ἀλαλ-ος, ος, ον, speechless, dumb; (from ἀ, not, and λάλος, talkative.)
ἀλγ-έω, ήσω, to be pained in body or mind ; hence, to be sick, to grieve, to be sorry for.
ἀλεκτρυ-ών, όνος, m., a cock; sometimes f., a hen.
Ἀλέξανδρ-ος, ου, m., Alexander ; applied to Paris, son of Priam.
ἀληθεύ-ω, σω, to speak truth ; from the following.
ἀληθ-ής, ής, ές (from ἀ, not, and λαθεῖν, to lie hid), unconcealed, open ; true, candid, genuine.
ἀληθῶς, adv., truly, in truth, &c.
Ἄλκηστ-ις, ιδος, f., Alcestis, daughter of Pelias, and wife of Admetus.
Ἀλκιβιάδ-ης, ου, m., Alcibiades, a famous Athenian.
Ἀλκμήν-η, ης, f., Alcmena, mother of Hercules.
ἀλλ', for ἀλλά.
ἀλλά, conj., but, but then, nay.
ἀλλὰ γάρ (enimvero), but really, however : this combination implies an ellipsis, as explained in the notes.
ἀλλάττ-ω, or ἀλλάσσ-ω, f. ἀλλάξ-ω, p. ἤλλαχα, to make other than it is, to change, alter ; to exchange.
ἀλλήλων, gen. pl. (see p. 56), of one another, mutually, reciprocally.
ἄλλ-ος, η, ο (Lat. alius), another, other ; ἄλλοι, others ; but οἱ ἄλλοι, the rest.
ἀλλότρι-ος, α, ον (Lat. alienus), belonging to another, foreign, strange ; inconsistent with, unsuitable to.
ἄλλως, adv., in another way, otherwise ; heedlessly, at random ; in vain : from ἄλλος ; ἄλλως τε καὶ, especially.
ἄλσ-ος, εος, n., a grove, lawn, wood.
ἀλώπηξ, ἀλώπεκ-ος, f., a fox.

ἄλως, gen. ἄλω, or ἄλωος, f., a threshing-floor.
ἅμα, adv., together, at the same time.
ἀμαθ-ής, ής, ές, unlearned, ignorant; stupid.
ἁμαρτάν-ω, F. ἁμαρτήσομαι, to miss the mark, fail ; go wrong, sin, mistake, offend.
ἀμβλυώττ-ω, or ἀμβλυώσσ-ω, ἀμβλυώξω, to be dim-sighted, to be purblind ; to want power of discrimination.
ἀμβροσί-α, ας, f., ambrosia, the food of the gods.
ἀμείβω, F. ἀμείψω, to exchange, change ; mid. to give in return, to recompense, to answer.
ἀμείν-ων, ων, ον, gen. -ονος, better ; comp. of ἀγαθός, for which see p. 50.
ἀμελ-έω, ήσω, to be careless, to neglect.
Ἀμιναῖ-ος, α, ον, f., Aminean : as a subst. f., "a cask of Aminean wine." Both Aminea in Campania and Aminaeum in Thessaly were famed for wine.
ἀμν-ός, οῦ (the oblique cases are generally borrowed, being ἀρνός, ἀρνί, ἄρνα, &c.), m. or f., a lamb.
ἄμορφ-ος, ος, ον, misshapen, ugly, unseemly.
ἀμύν-ω, F. ἀμύν-ῶ, to ward off, defend ; to help : mid. to defend or avenge one's self.
ἀμφί, prep., with accusative, genitive, and dative, on both sides, around, about; concerning;—used sometimes as an adverb, all round.
Ἀμφιτρίτ-η, ης, f., daughter of Nereus and wife of Poseidon (Neptune).
ἀμφότερ-ος, α, ον, both, (seldom used in singular).
ἀμφ-ω, gen. and dat. ἀμφοῖν, both, both parties (whether individuals or aggregates). (Lat. ambo.)
ἄν, adv., perchance, haply, &c. It cannot be easily translated by one word, but always implies a

condition, and so refers to a verb either expressed or understood. It never begins a sentence. (See Grammar, and Liddell and Scott's Greek Lexicon.)

ἀνά, *prep.*, *with accusative, genitive, and dative*, up, upon—*opposed to* κατά. Its meaning varies with the case governed by it.

ἀναβαίν-ω, F. ἀναβήσομαι, to go up, ascend, climb; to embark.

ἀναβι-όω, -ώσομαι, aor. ἀνέβιων, *inf.* ἀναβιῶναι, to come to life again, revive.

ἀναγκαῖ-ος, α, ον, *also* ος, ος, ον, by force, using force ; necessary : οἱ ἀναγκαῖοι, relatives. (Lat. *necessarii.*)

ἀνάγω, F. ἀνάξω, to lead up; to bring up (from the dead), to raise ; to bring back, to withdraw.

ἀναδίδωμι, F. ἀναδώσω, to give up, give forth or yield; to distribute; give back.

ἀναδύνω, to come out of, emerge.

ἀναδύομαι, F. ἀναδύσομαι, 2 aor. act. ἀνέδυν, to come up, rise, emerge (as from beneath a surface), to ascend ; to embark.

ἀναιμωτί, *adv.*, without shedding blood, bloodless.

ἀναιρέω, F. ἀναιρήσω, P. ἀνῄρηκα, 2 aor. ἀνεῖλον, to take up or away, to overturn ; destroy, kill : *mid.* to gain; *i.e.*, to procure for one's self.

ἀνακαίω, F. ἀνακαύσω, to kindle, light up.

ἀνακόπτω, F. ἀνακόψω, to beat back, repulse ; stop ; cut off.

ἀναλαμβάνω, F. ἀναλήψομαι, to take up; receive ; resume.

ἀναμιμνῄσκω, F. ἀναμνήσω, to remind one of a thing, to recall to memory, to remember; to suggest; admonish.

Αναξ, ἄνακτ-ος, *m.*, a lord, master; prince, king.

Αναξαγόρ-ας, ου, *m.*, Anaxagoras, a philosopher of Clazomenæ in Ionia.

ἀναξιοπαθ-έω, -ήσω, to suffer undeservedly ; to be indignant : from ἀνάξιος, unworthy, and ἔπαθον.

ἀναπείθ-ω, F. ἀναπείσω, to bring over to a different opinion, to persuade; to incite to.

ἀναπλέω, F. ἀναπλεύσομαι, or ἀναπλευσοῦμαι, to sail upwards or up the stream; to sail back again.

ἀνάπλε-ως, ως, ων, *gen.*, ἀνάπλεω (see p. 22), full to the brim, full.

ἀναπνέω, F. ἀναπνεύσω, to breathe again ; take breath, breathe, respire.

ἀναρχί-α, as, *f.*, want of government ; lawlessness, anarchy.

ἀναστρέφω, F. ἀναστρέψω, F. ἀνέστροφα, to turn upside down ; to turn back, turn round, return.

ἀνατείν-ω, F. ἀνατενῶ, to stretch or lift up, raise, hold forth.

ἀναχωρ-έω, ησω, to retreat, retire, return to.

ἀνδράποδ-ον, ου, *n.*, a slave (captive in war) ; from ἄνδρα ἀποδόσθαι: or, according to others, from ἀνδρός and πούς, the captive falling at the *feet* of his *conqueror.*

ἀνδρεῖ-ος, α, ον (ἀνήρ), belonging to a man ; manly, courageous.

ἀνδρειότατα, *n.*, *pl.* of *superlative* of ἀνδρεῖος, used as *adv.*. most manfully, most bravely, &c.

ἀνδρείως, *adv.*, in a manly way, manfully.

ἀνδρώδ-ης, ης, ες, like a man, manly.

ἄνεμ-ος, ου, *m.*, a current of air, wind ; from ἄω, ἄημι, to blow.

ἀνέρχομαι, F. ἀνελεύσομαι, aor. ἀνῆλθον or ἀνήλυθον, P. ἀνελήλυθα, to go up; go or come back, return.

ἄνευ, *prep. with gen.*, without, away from, except, besides.

ἀνέχω (see ἔχω), to hold up, lift up ; maintain, support ; endure.

ἀνήρ, *gen.* ἀνδρός, *voc.* ἄνερ, a man (as opposed to a woman, like *vir*; whereas ἄνθρωπος means a man, as opposed to a beast, like *homo*), a husband, a warrior, &c.

ἀνθ' for ἀντί.
ἄνθ-ος, εος, n., a blossom, flower; shoot.
ἄνθρωπ-ος, ου, m., a man (as opposed to a beast), mankind; sometimes f., when used of a woman (contemptuously).
ἀνιάω, ἀνιάσω, to grieve, distress; vex, annoy.
ἀνοίγνυμι and ἀνοίγω, F. ἀνοίξω, imperf., with double augment, ἀνέῳγον, F. ἀνέῳγα, to open, unfold, disclose.
ἀντ' for ἀντί.
ἀντί, prep. with gen., over against, opposite; equivalent to, instead of; at the price of, in return for.
'Αντίγον-ος, ου, m., Antigonus, king of Asia.
ἀντιλέγω (see λέγω), to speak against, gainsay.
'Αντιόπ-η, ης, f., Antiope, mother of Amphion and Zethus.
ἀντιποιέω, to do in return: in mid. to exert one's self about a thing; to lay claim to, pretend to.
'Αντισθέν-ης, ους (εος), m., Antisthenes, an Athenian, founder of the sect of Cynic philosophers.
ἀντιτάττω, or ἀντιτάσσω, F. ἀντιτάξω, to range in order of battle; mid. to strive against, oppose.
ἀντλ-έω, ήσω, to bale out bilgewater, to drain, dry; exhaust.
ἄντρ-ον, ου, n. (antrum), a cave, cavern, hole.
ἀνυπόδητ-ος, ος, ον (ἄν, not; ὑπό, under; δέω, to bind), unshod, barefoot.
ἄνω, adv. (ἀνά), up, upwards, above, on high; inland: ἄνω καὶ κάτω, up and down.
ἀνώγαι-ον, ου (ἄνω and γαῖα, earth), anything elevated above the ground; the upper storey or floor of a house.
ἀνώγεων, gen. ἀνώγεω (see p. 22), n.; also ἀνώγεως, gen. ἀνώγεω, m. and f., same as ἀνώγαιον.
ἄνωθεν, adv., from above, on high; from the beginning.

ἀξιόπιστ-ος, ος, εν, worthy of credit, trustworthy.
ἄξι-ος, a, ον, worth, worthy (literally, weighing as much; from ἄγω, in the sense, to weigh), deserved, meet, fit.
ἀξιόω, F. ἀξιώσω, imperf. ἠξίουν, to deem worthy of, to think fit; require, demand; think, suppose.
ἀξίωμα, gen. ἀξιώματ-ος, n., that of which a person is thought worthy, an honour; worth, high character, dignity; an axiom.
ἀπ' for ἀπό.
ἀπαγγέλλω, F. ἀπαγγελῶ (see Liquid Verbs), to bring tidings, to report, relate, announce.
ἀπαγορεύ-ω, σω, to forbid; to bid farewell to, to renounce; to fail (through fatigue—see ἀπείρηκα).
ἀπάγω (see ἄγω), to lead away, carry off; bring back.
ἀπαιτ-έω, ήσω, to demand back, seek payment of.
ἀπαλλάττ-ω, or ἀπαλλάσσω, F. ἀπαλλάξω, to set free, release; to remove: intrans. to escape, get off; to give over, cease, &c.
ἅπαξ, adv., once, once for all (semel).
ἅπας, ἅπασα, ἅπαν (ἅμα, πᾶς), all together (cuncti).
ἀπειθ-έω, ήσω, to be disobedient, to disobey.
ἄπειμι (see εἶμι, Irregular Verbs), to go away: pres. used as fut., "I shall go away;" depart.
ἀπεῖπον (2 aor.), F. ἀπερῶ, P. ἀπείρηκα, to speak out, declare; to deny, refuse; but usually it means to fail, to be wearied, to sink from exhaustion.
ἀπείρηκα. (See foregoing word.)
ἀπειρί-α, as, f., infinity, immensity; it also means, inexperience, ignorance.
ἄπειρ-ος, ος, ον, infinite, boundless; also, unused to, ignorant.
ἀπελαύνω (see ἐλαύνω), to drive away, expel, &c.
ἀπεργάζομαι, F. ἀπεργάσομαι, P.

ἀπείργασμαι, to finish off, complete.
ἀπέρχομαι (see ἔρχομαι), to go away, depart, go out of.
ἀπέχω, F. ἀφέξω (see ἔχω), to hold or keep off from : mid. ἀπέχομαι, to hold one's self off from, to abstain, desist from : intrans. to be away or distant from.
ἀπό, prep., governing genitive only, from, away from, far from; of time—from, after, since. It is sometimes used also to express the instrument, the cause, or the material.
ἀποβάλλω (see βάλλω), to throw off or away, to reject; to lose (e.g., to lose children by death).
ἀπόβασ-ις, εως, f. (ἀποβαίνω), a stepping off, landing, disembarking.
ἀποδείκνυμι (see Verbs in -μι), to point away from (other objects, to one specially); hence, to show forth, exhibit, produce; to declare, appoint, create.
ἀποδίδωμι (see Verbs in -μι), to give back, return, repay; give away.
ἀποθνήσκω (see θνήσκω), F. ἀποθανοῦμαι, 2 aor. ἀπέθανον, to be put to death, to die.
ἀποκαλ-έω, F. -έσω, to call back, call away or aside ; miscall, to call by a disparaging title.
ἀποκερδ-αίνω, F. -ἀνῶ and -ήσω, to derive benefit or enjoyment from something.
ἀποκιν-έω, F. ήσω, to remove from.
ἀποκναίω, or ἀποκνάω, to scrape off; to wear (a person) out, to worry, annoy.
ἀποκρίν-ω, F. ἀποκρινῶ, to separate, distinguish, choose out; mid. ἀποκρίνομαι, to give answer, to reply.
ἀποκρύπτω, F. ἀποκρύψω, to hide from, conceal.
ἀποκτείνω, F. ἀποκτενῶ, 1 aor. ἀπέκτεινα, to slay, condemn.
ἀπολαύ-ω, F. -σω, to benefit from, enjoy.
ἀπόλλυμι, ἀπολέσω, and ἀπολῶ, to destroy utterly, to kill; mid. ἀπόλλυμαι, to perish, to be undone.
Ἀπόλλων, Ἀπόλλων-ος, m., Apollo.
ἀπονενοημένως, adv. (from perf. part. pass. of ἀπονοέομαι), without regard for life, desperately, foolishly.
ἀπ-οξύνω (ἀπό, ὀξύνω from ὀξύς), to bring to a point, to sharpen.
ἀπόπειρ-α, as, f., a trial, venture, risk.
ἀποπέμπω (see πέμπω), to send away, dismiss; send back, return.
ἀποπλέω (see πλέω), to sail away, set sail; sail back.
ἀποπνίγω (see πνίγω), to choke, throttle; pass., to be choked, throttled, drowned.
ἀπορ-έω, F. ήσω, to be in perplexity; to be at a loss for, to be in want.
ἀπορί-α, as, f., perplexity, difficulty, doubt; need, poverty.
ἀποσιωπ-άω, F. -ήσω, trans. to keep secret; intrans. to be silent (after speaking).
ἀποστέλλω (see στέλλω), to send off or away, despatch; 2 aor. pass. ἀπεστάλην.
ἀποστεφαν-όω, ώσω, to deprive of a crown, or garland.
ἀποτίθημι (see Verbs in -μι), to put away, or stow away; mid. to put away from one's self, to put off (as clothes), to lay past for one's self.
ἀποφεύγω (see φεύγω), to flee away from, escape.
ἀποχράω, inf. ἀποχρῆν, imperf. ἀπέχρην, to suffice, be sufficient.
ἀπόχρη (3d sing. pres. of preceding verb), used impersonally, it is enough, sufficient, &c.
ἀπράγμων, ων, ον, gen. -ονος, free from occupation, disengaged: hence, free from trouble, easy, quiet; lazy.
ἀπρεπ-ής, ής, ές, unbecoming, unseemly.
ἄπτερ-ος, ος, ον, without wings, unfledged, callow.
ἅπτω, F. ἅψω, to fasten, bind, tie; to kindle or set fire to: more usual in mid. ἅπτομαι; perf.

pass. ἧμμαι, to fasten one's self to, cling to, to grasp; set upon, attack; to overtake, gain.

'Αργ-ος, ου, m., Argus, son of Agenor, called the " hundred-eyed."

'Αργ-ος, ους (εος), n., Argos, a town in the Peloponnese.

ἀργύρεος, contracted ἀργυροῦς, ᾶ, οῦν, (made) of silver.

ἀρετ-ή, ῆς, f., excellence, merit (of any kind); bravery, (moral) virtue; skill.

ἀριστ-άω, ήσω, to take the ἄριστον, or mid-day meal; to lunch, to dine.

'Αρίστιππ-ος, ου, m., Aristippus, a philosopher from Cyrene.

ἄριστ-ος, η, ον, best. (See irregular comparison, p. 50, under ἀγαθός.)

'Αριστοτέλ-ης, εος, m., Aristotle, tutor of Alexander the Great.

ἀρκ-έω, F. -έσω (Lat. arceo), to ward off; to assist, to be of service, to avail; to suffice: impersonal, ἀρκεῖ, it is sufficient, I am content.

ἅρμα, ἅρματος, n., a chariot (especially war-chariot), car.

ἁρμόζω, Attic, ἁρμόττ-ω, F. ἁρμόσω, to fit together; join, arrange, suit; intrans. to fit, suit, be adapted for.

ἀρότης, ου, m., a ploughman.

ἄρουρα, ας, f., a field.

ἀρουραί-ος, α, ον, from the country, rustic.

ἁρπάζω, F. ἁρπάσομαι [ἁρπάξω], to snatch away, carry off; to seize greedily, to plunder.

Ἀρταξέρξης, ου, m., Artaxerxes, king of Persia.

ἄρτι, adv., just, exactly; just now.

ἄρτ-ος, ου, m., bread, a loaf (wheaten); in pl., loaves, bread (generally). Barley bread is μᾶζα.

'Αρχέλα-ος, ου, m., Archelaus, king of Macedonia.

ἀρχή, ῆς, f., beginning, origin; first place or power, dominion, sovereignty, magistracy.

ἀρχηγ-ός, ός, όν, used substantively,
leader, founder; prince, chief, general.

ἄρχ-ω, ἄρξω, to be first, to begin (usually mid. in this sense); to lead, govern, command.

ἄρχων, ἄρχοντ-ος, m. (participle of ἄρχω, used as a subst.), a ruler, commander, chief magistrate.

ἀσθεν-έω, ήσω, to be ἀσθενής,—i.e., weak, feeble, sickly.

ἀσθεν-ής, ής, ές (ἀ, σθένος), without strength, weak, sickly; insignificant.

'Ασκληπι-ός, οῦ, m., Æsculapius, son of Apollo, and god of medicine.

ἀσμένως, adv., willingly, gladly.

ἀσπίς, ἀσπίδος, f., a round shield.

'Ασσύρι-οι, ων, m. pl., the Assyrians.

ἀστεῖ-ος, ος, ον, and ος, α, ον (from ἄστυ), of the town, polite (urbanus), comical.

ἀστικ-ός, ή, όν, of the city, or town.

ἄστ-υ, εος, n., a city, town.

ἀσφαλ-ής, ής, ές, not tottering; safe, secure, sure, steadfast.

ἄτε, conj., inasmuch as, seeing that, because.

ἄτεκν-ος, ος, ον, without children, childless.

'Ατλαντ-ίς, -ίδος, f., a daughter of Atlas.

"Ατλας, "Ατλαντ-ος, m., Atlas (who bears heaven on his shoulders).

ἄτοπ-ος, ος, ον, out of place, extraordinary, strange; absurd, monstrous.

αὖθις, adv., back, back again, again, afresh, hereafter.

αὐλ-έω, ήσω (αὐλός), to play on the flute, to pipe.

αὐλ-ή, ῆς, f., the open court-yard, a court or hall; palace, dwelling, country house (villa).

αὐξάνω, or αὔξω, F. αὐξήσω (Lat. augeo), to make large, increase; honour, extol.

ἄυπν-ος, ος, ον, sleepless, wakeful.

αὐτίκα, adv., immediately, forthwith, presently, at once.

αὐτόθι, adv., on the spot, here, there.

αὐτ-ός, ή, ό, *reflexive pronoun*, self; but in oblique cases often used for personal pronoun (see p. 55), myself, thyself, &c.: ὁ αὐτός, the very one, the same (contracted αὑτός).

αὑτοῦ, αὑτῆς, αὑτοῦ, for ἑαυτοῦ, &c. (see p. 56), himself, herself, itself.

αὐχ-έω, ήσω, to boast, plume one's self; declare, avow.

αὐχήν, αὐχέν-ος, *m.*, the neck, throat.

ἀφαιρέω (see αἱρέω), to take away from, remove, deprive; *mid. more usual*, to take for one's self, carry off.

ἀφάρμακτ-ος, ος, ον, unmixed with drugs, free from poison.

ἀφίημι (see ἵημι, and *Verbs* in -μι), to send forth or away, let go, set free, give up.

ἀφικνέομαι, F. ἀφίξομαι, F. *pass.* ἀφῖγμαι, to arrive at, come to, reach.

ἀφίστημι (see ἵστημι, and *Verbs* in -μι), F. ἀποστήσω, F. ἀφέστηκα, to make to sta d off from, to put away, remove; *mid.*, *and intrans. tenses of act.*, to stand aloof from, shun, revolt.

Ἀφροδίτ-η, ης, *f.*, Aphroditê (*Venus*) goddess of love.

ἄφροντ-ις, ις, *gen.* ἀφρόντιδ-ος, free from care (*securus*).

Ἀχαι-ός, ά, όν, Achaian ; *pl.* οἱ Ἀχαιοί, the Achaeans.

Ἀχιλλ-εύς, έως, *m.*, Achilles, son of Peleus and Thetis.

ἄχρι, or ἄχρις (before a vowel), *prep. governing gen.*, until, up to, as far as; *as conj.*, until.

B

βαδίζω, F. (βαδίσω), βαδιοῦμαι, and βαδίσομαι, to go; to walk, or go slowly.

βάθ-ος, εος (ους), *n.*, depth, height; deep place, valley.

βαθ-ύς, εῖα, ύ, deep, high (like *altus*).

βαίνω, F. βήσομαι, F. βέβηκα (F. βήσω, will cause to go), 2 *aor.* ἔβην, *inf.* βῆναι, to go, walk, advance.

βακτηρί-α, ας, *f.*, a staff, cane, walking stick, sceptre.

βάλλω, F. βαλῶ or βαλλήσω, F. βέβληκα, 2 aor. ἔβαλον, to throw at, or hit (opposed to τύπτω, to strike), to throw, cast, fling.

βάρβαρ-ος, ος, ον, barbarous (*i.e.*, not Greek), strange, foreign ; outlandish, rude, boorish, uncivilized.

βαρ-έω, ήσω, to weigh down, oppress.

βαρ-ύς, εῖα, υ, heavy, weighty ; oppressive, troublesome.

βασίλει-ἀ, ας, *f.*, a queen, a princess.

βασιλεί-ἀ, ας, *f.*, sovereign power, kingdom, dominion.

βασιλ-εύς, έως, *m.*, a king, chief, sovereign, prince. (See p. 37.)

βασιλεύ-ω, to be king, to rule.

βαστάζω, F. βαστάσω, to lift, raise, exalt, support; carry off.

βάτραχ-ος, ου, *m.*, a frog.

βέλ-ος, εος, *n.*, a missile ; a dart, arrow ; a weapon.

βέλτιστος, η, ον, the best; *irregular superlative of* ἀγαθός.

βῆμα, βήματ-ος, *n.*, a step, pace ; a platform or tribunal (to speak from).

βίαι-ος, α, ον, forcible, violent.

βιαιότερον, *adv.*, *compar. of foregoing*, more forcible, with considerable force or violence.

βιβλί-ον, ου, *n.*, a paper, letter ; a little book.

βιβρώσκω, F. βρώσομαι, F. βέβρωκα, to eat, eat up.

βίος, ου, *m.*, life (Lat. *vita*) ; way of life, livelihood ; common life.

βιόω, ώσομαι, 2 aor. ἐβίων, inf. βιῶναι, part. βιούς, to live.
βλέπω, F. (βλέψω) βλέψομαι, to have the power of sight, see; to look on or towards.
βοάω, ήσομαι, to cry aloud, to shout; to call on (a person).
βοηθέω, ήσω, to succour, assist, help, come to the rescue.
Βοιωτί-α, ας, f., Bœotia, a district of Greece.
βότρυ-ς, ος, m., a bunch of grapes.
βουκολέω, to act as a shepherd, to tend cattle; to guard.
βουκόλ-ος, ου, m., a cow-herd, herdsman.
βουλεύ-ω, σω, to take counsel, deliberate; to decide; to plan; to give counsel, advise.
βουλ-ή, ῆς, f., will, determination; purpose, plan, counsel; a council.
βούλομαι, F. βουλήσομαι, to will, be willing, wish. It sometimes takes η as augment; e.g., ἠβουλήθην, as well as ἐβουλήθην.
βοῦς, βοός, m. and f., an ox or cow; in pl. cattle (generally).
βραδύνω, F. βραδυνῶ, to make slow, delay; intrans. to loiter, be tardy.
βραδ-ύς, εῖα, ύ (tardus), slow, heavy; sluggish.
βραχ-ύς, εῖα, ύ (brevis), short, little, petty.
βρέφ-ος, εος, n., an infant, babe.
βρέχω, F. βρέξω, to wet (on the surface), moisten, soak.
βροντ-άω, ήσω, to thunder.
βρυχάομαι, βρυχήσομαι, to roar or bellow.
βρυχηθμ-ός, οῦ, m., a roar, bellow.
βρώσκω. (See βιβρώσκω.)
βωμ-ός, οῦ, a raised place; a stand, altar.

Γ

γαῖ-α, ας, f., the earth; a land, or country.
γάλα, γάλακτ-ος, n., milk.
γαλήν-η, ης, f., stillness of sea, a calm.
γάρ, conj., for, (introducing the reason why). It is sometimes used, like nam in Latin, to strengthen a question, as, τίς γάρ; why, who? (See ἀλλά.)
γαστήρ, γαστρός, f., the paunch, belly, womb.
γέ, a limiting particle, at least; used also to call special attention to something; even.
γείτων, γείτον-ος, m. and f., a neighbour, borderer.
γελάω, γελάσομαι, to laugh, to laugh at (one).
γενναίως, adv., nobly, magnanimously, generously; bravely.
γεννάω, ήσω, to beget (trans.); to bring forth; to grow.
γέν-ος, εος, n., race, descent; offspring, descendant; lineage; class, kind.
γέραν-ος, ου, m., a crane.
γέρων, γέροντ-ος, m., an old man.
γεύω, γεύσω, to give one to taste; mid. γεύομαι, to taste.
γέφυρ-α, ας, f., a bridge.
γεωργ-ός, οῦ, m., a husbandman, farmer, labourer.
γηραι-ός, ά, όν, or -ός, ός, όν, aged, old.
γῆρας, γήραος, n., contracted γήρως, old age.
γίγας, γίγαντ-ος, m., a giant: in pl., as proper name, The Giants.
γίγνομαι, or γίνομαι, F. γενήσομαι, 2 aor. ἐγενόμην, to come into being, to be born; to be, to arise, happen, occur.
γιγνώσκω, F. γνώσομαι, aor. ἔγνων, opt. γνοίην, imperat. γνῶθι, inf. γνῶναι, part. γνούς, P. ἔγνωκα, to begin or learn to know; to perceive, distinguish; to form or give an opinion, judge, decide.

γλαυκ-ός, ή, όν, gleaming, glancing, glaring; (with idea of colour), grey, pale blue, light blue.
γλαυκῶπις, γλαυκώπιδ-ος, epithet of Athena (Minerva), fierce-eyed; blue-eyed, azure-eyed; (γλαυκός, and ὤψ, the eye).
γλυκ-ύς, εῖα, ύ, sweet; delightful, dear (beloved).
γλῶττ-α, or γλῶσσ-α, ης, f., the tongue; a language.
γνάθ-ος, ου, f., a jaw; mouth.
γναφεῖ-ον, ου, or κναφεῖον, n., a fuller's shop, a fulling mill.
γον-εύς, έως, m., a father: in pl., parents, ancestors.
Γοργί-ας, a, m., Gorgias, an orator and philosopher of Leontini in Sicily.
γοῦν, adv., at least then, accordingly; at all events.
γράμμα, γράμματ-ος, n., a thing written, a character, i.e., letter of the alphabet: in pl., letters, the alphabet; a letter (epistle); documents, writings; learning.
γραῦς, γραός, f., an old woman.
γράφω, γράψω, to scratch, scrape; sketch, write, inscribe, engrave.
Γρύλλ-ος, ου, m., Gryllus, son of Xenophon.
γυμνάζω, F. γυμνάσω, to train in gymnastic exercises, to accustom (a person) to (a thing): mid. and pass., to practise one's self, to exercise.
γυμν-ός, ή, όν, naked, unclad, uncovered.
γυμν-όω, ώσω, to strip naked, to bare; to spoil, bereave.
γυνή, γυναικ-ός, voc. γύναι, a woman (Lat. femina): in voc. a term of respect, mistress, lady; wife, spouse.
γύψ, γῦπός, m., a vulture.

Δ

δ' for δέ.
δαίμων, δαίμον-ος, m. and f., a god, goddess; providence; lot, fortune, chance; genius.
δάκνω, F. δήξομαι, 2 aor. ἔδακον, to bite, champ (the bit); sting, prick; gall.
δάκρῠ-ον, ου, n. (poetic form, δάκρυ), a tear.
δακρύ-ω, σω, to weep, shed tears; lament.
δάκτυλ-ος, ου, m., a finger: μέγας δάκτυλος, the thumb.
δάμαλ-ις, εως, f., a young cow, heifer (juvenca).
Δανάη, ης, f., Dănăë, daughter of Acrisius, king of Argos.
δαπάνημα, δαπανήματ-ος, n., usually in pl., expense, outlay.
δαρεικ-ός, οῦ, m., a Daric, a Persian gold coin, equal to about a guinea, English money:—said to be called from king Darius. So the French have pieces called "Louis d'or" and "Napoleon."
Δαρεῖ-ος, ου, m., Darius, king of Persia.
δασ-ύς, εῖα, ύ, thick, shaggy, rough; of dense foliage.
δάφν-η, ης, f., a laurel, a bay-tree.
Δάφνις, Δάφνιδ-ος, m., Daphnis, a Sicilian hero. Also f., a nymph.
δέ, conj., in the second place, on the other hand; but, and: it usually responds to μέν.
δέησ-ις, εως, f. (δέομαι), an entreating, prayer, petition; want, need.
δεῖ, impers. verb, it is necessary, it behoves, there is need of (opus est), one ought: F. δεήσει, 1 aor. ἐδέησε, &c.
δεῖγμα, δείγματ-ος, n. (δείκνυμι), a sample, specimen, proof.
δείκνυμι (see Verbs in -μι), and δεικνύω, to show, point out; explain

δειλ-ός, ή, όν, cowardly; wretched; worthless; miserable.
Δεινί-ας, ου, m., Dinias, an Athenian.
δειν-ός, ή, όν, dreadful, terrible, calamitous; mighty, powerful; clever, skilful.
δεῖπν-ον, ου, n., a meal; the chief meal, dinner. (Lat. cœna.)
δέκα, indecl. numeral, ten.
δένδρ-ον, ου, n., a tree.
δεξι-ά, ᾶς, f., the right hand: ἐν δεξιᾷ, on the right.
δεξι-ός, ά, όν, on the right hand; hence, fortunate, lucky, favourable.
δέομαι, F. δεήσομαι, to need, be in want of; beg, ask.
δέρω, F. δερῶ, 1 aor. ἔδειρα, 2 aor. pass. ἐδάρην, with inf. δαρῆναι, to take off the skin, flay; to beat, cudgel (like our phrases, to tan, and to hide).
δεσπότ-ης, ου, m., a lord, master, autocrat; owner.
δεύτερ-ος, α, ον, the second, latter of two (as to time); inferior (as to rank and position): ἐκ δευτέρου, a second time.
δέω, F. δήσω, P. δέδεκα, P. pass. δέδεμαι, 1 aor. pass. ἐδέθην, to bind, tie; fetter, imprison.
δή (shortened from ἤδη), adv., now; already: in narrative, well now.
δηλονότι (δῆλον ὅτι), adv., clearly, evidently.
δηλ-ός, ή, όν, also ός, όν, clear, evident, conspicuous.
δηλ-όω, ώσω, to make clear, make evident, &c.; to declare.
Δημήτηρ, Δημητρός, f., Demeter (Ceres), goddess of corn and of agriculture.
δι' for διά.
δι.ά, prep. governing the gen. and accus. (1.) With the gen., through and through, quite through; (of time), through, during; (of cause), arising through, by means of. (2.) With the accus. (1 and 2 poetic), with the same meanings. διὰ παντός, always.

διαβαίνω (see βαίνω), to pass over or through, to cross.
διαγιγνώσκω (see γιγνώσκω), to distinguish; resolve, decide; give judgment.
διάδημα, διαδήματ-ος, n., a band or fillet (for the head), a diadem.
διαθήκ-η, ης, f. (διατίθημι), a disposition (of property), will, testament; a covenant.
διαιρ-έω, ήσω (see αἱρέω), to take one from another, separate; divide, cut in two, distribute; distinguish.
δίαιτ-α, ης, f., life, way of life; food; dress; maintenance.
διαιτητ-ής, οῦ, m., an arbitrator, umpire.
διακον-έω, ήσω, to be a διάκονος,— i.e., to wait on, serve; to supply, administer.
διακόσι-οι, αι, α, two hundred.
διαλανθάνω (see λανθάνω), to escape notice, lie hid.
διαλέγω (see λέγω), to pick out, choose, distinguish: mid. to converse with, to discourse; argue.
διαλύω (see λύω), to loose from one another, unravel; break up; dismiss; put an end to, destroy.
διαπαντός, i.e., διὰ παντός, throughout, always.
διαπορθμεύω, to ferry over, transport.
διασπ-άω, άσομαι, P. διέσπακα, to tear in pieces; to distract.
διαστρώννυμι, and -υω, F. διαστρώσω, to spread, lay out (as couches, or chairs).
διατελέω, to finish, accomplish.
διατέμνω, διατεμῶ, to cut through, to cut in twain, sever.
διατί (i.e., διὰ τί), wherefore. (Lat. quamobrem).
διατριβ-ή, ῆς, f., a wearing away; waste of time, delay.
διαφέρω (see φέρω), to carry across; bring to an end; carry different ways: intrans. to differ; excel.
διαφεύγω, to flee through, escape.
διαφθείρω, διαφθερῶ, διέφθαρκα, διέφθαρκα, to destroy utterly.
διδάσκαλ-ος, ου, m. and f., a teacher.

διδάσκω, F. διδάξω, to teach : mid. to have one taught for one's self ; e.g., to get one's children taught.
δίδυμ-ος, η, ον, also ος, ον, double, twofold, twin.
δίδωμι (see Verbs in -μι), to give, grant, offer.
διερευνάω, ήσω, to search through, examine minutely.
διήγημα, διηγήματος, n., a tale, narrative.
διίστημι (see Verbs in -μι), F. διαστήσω, to divide, cause disunion : in pass. to stand apart, to differ, disagree; to stand at intervals.
δικάζω, δικάσω, to judge, determine.
δίκαι-ος, a, ον, attentive to rules; upright; scrupulous, honest, just; well merited.
δικαστήρι-ον, ου, n., a court of justice ; judgment-seat.
Διογέν-ης, εος, m., Diogenes, the famous Cynic philosopher.
Διονύσι-ος, ου, m., Dionysius, tyrant of Syracuse.
διότι, conj., = διὰ [τοῦτο] ὅτι, because that, since; wherefore, (in indirect sentences.)
δίπους, δίποδος, two-footed; two feet long.
δίς, adv., twice.
διψάω (contracts αε, &c. into η, not a): inf. διψῆν, to thirst. to be parched.
διώκω, διώξω, διώξομαι, to pursue, hunt; drive away.
δμώς, δμωός, m., a slave taken in war; a slave, attendant, domestic.
δοκέω, F. δόξω, to think, expect, imagine : intrans. to seem, appear : impers. δοκεῖ, it seems good, it pleases.

δολιχόδειρος, ος, ον, long-necked, having long necks.
δόμ-ος, ου, m., (domus,) a building, house.
δόναξ, δόνακ-ος, m., a reed; dart; writing-reed (pen).
δόξ-α, ης, f., an opinion; estimation, good report ; honour, glory.
δορ-ά, ᾶς, f., a hide of a beast, (when taken off.)
δόρυ, gen. δόρατ-ος, a stem ; tree ; hence, the shaft of a spear; a spear.
δουλεύ-ω, σω, to act the slave ; be subject to; obey.
δοῦλ-ος, ου, m., a slave, bondman.
δραχμ-ή, ῆς, f., a drachma, a silver coin worth about 9¾d.
δράω, F. δράσω, to do, fulfil, perform.
δύναμαι, F. δυνήσομαι (see ἵσταμαι, Verbs in -μι), to be strong, to be able; to be equivalent to ; to signify (mean).
δύναμ-ις, εως, f., power, strength, ability.
δυνατ-ός, ή, όν, mighty, able, strong; (of things) possible.
δύο, gen. and dat. δυοῖν (see p. 53), two.
Δύσπαρ-ις, ιδος, unlucky Paris (Alexander).
δύστην-ος, ος, ον, wretched, unhappy ; unfortunate.
δύω, F. δύσω, 2 aor. ἔδυν, to put on, (as clothes, armour, &c.); to enter (a house, country).
δώδεκα, twelve.
δῶμα, δώματος, n., a house; chief room, hall.
δῶρ-ον, ου, n., a gift, present.

E

ἐάν, conj. (contracted into ἤν, and in Attic, ἄν, if, if perchance. In good writers it is always joined with the subjunctive mood.
ἑαυτ-οῦ, ῆς, οῦ, of himself, herself, itself : reflex. pron., for which see p. 56, (contracted into αὑτοῦ).
ἐάω, F. ἐάσω, P. εἴακα, to allow, permit; let alone, let pass.

ἐγγυ-άω, F. -ήσω, to give over as a pledge; to plight, betroth.
ἐγγύς, adv., near, at hand.
ἔγκαυμα, ἐγκαύματ-ος, n., a mark made by burning into (the flesh, &c.), a brand; a sore from burning.
ἐγκέφαλ-ος, ου, m., within the head (κεφαλή): hence, the brain.
ἐγχέω, F. ἐγχεῶ, aor. ἐνέχεα, to pour in, (as water, wine, &c.)
ἔγχ-ος, εος, n., a spear, lance, pike; sometimes even a sword.
ἐγώ, gen. ἐμοῦ, I (see p. 54). Lat. ego.
ἔγωγε (Lat. equidem), I at least, I for my part.
ἐθέλω (or θέλω), F. ἐθελήσω, to will, be willing; to wish, desire.
εἰ, conj., if; whether (in questions). Used with indicative and optative moods.
εἰδέναι. (See οἶδα in Vocabulary and in Irregular Verbs.)
εἶδον, used as 2 aor. of ὁράω (which see); subj. ἴδω, opt. ἴδοιμι, imperat. ἰδέ, part. ἰδών, inf. ἰδεῖν, to see, behold; to look at.
εἴθε (Lat. utinam), interjection, O that, would that.
εἰκάζω, F. εἰκάσω, P. pass. ᾔκασμαι, to make like, liken; compare; conjecture.
εἰκός, gen. εἰκότος, neuter of perf. particip. of εἴκα (ἔοικα), likely, probable, reasonable: as a subst. τὸ εἰκός, probability, likelihood.
εἴκοσι (indeclinable numeral), twenty. (See p. 54.)
εἰκότως, adv., in likelihood, naturally; reasonably, with good reason.
Εἰλήθυι-α, as, f., Ilethyia, goddess of birth.
εἰμί (see Irregular Verbs), to be.
εἶμι (see Irregular Verbs), to go; pres. used by Attics as fut. I shall go.
εἶπον, used as aor. of φημί. (See Irregular Verbs.)
εἰρήνη, ης, f., peace, time of peace.

εἷς, μία, ἕν, numeral adj. (see p. 53); one.
εἰς or ἐς, prep. governing accus. only, into, to, towards.
εἴσειμι, to go into. (See εἶμι.)
εἰσέρχομαι (see ἔρχομαι), to go into, enter.
εἴσομαι (from obsolete verb εἰδέω, or εἴδω), F. of οἶδα (which see, Irregular Verbs), I shall know. (See also εἶδον.)
εἰσοπτρίζομαι, to look into a mirror.
εἰσφέρω (see φέρω) εἰσοίσω, &c., to bring or carry into; to contribute; to introduce, propose.
εἶτα (deinde), adv., then, next, in the next place; then, therefore (ita.)
εἴτε (εἰ τέ), conj., whether.
ἐκ (before a vowel ἐξ), from out of, away from out of, forth from; from.
ἕκαστ-ος, η, ον, every, every one; each (quisque).
ἑκάτερ-ος, α, ον, each of two; each by himself.
Ἑκάτ-η, ης, f., Hecate, goddess of the lower world and of magic.
ἐκβάλλω (see βάλλω), to throw out, to throw away; banish, cast out or away; reject.
ἐκδιδάσκω (see διδάσκω), to teach thoroughly; inform accurately (edocere.)
ἐκδιώκω (see διώκω), to chase away; to banish.
ἐκεῖ, adv., there, in that place (illic).
ἐκεῖθεν, adv., from that place, thence (illinc).
ἐκεῖν-ος, η, ο, that person there; that well-known person (like Lat. ille.)
ἐκθερμ-αίνω, -ανῶ, to warm thoroughly.
ἐκθρώσκω, F. ἐκθοροῦμαι, aor. ἐξέθορον, to leap out of, or forth.
ἐκκαθ-αίρω, F. -αρῶ, to cleanse out, purify thoroughly.
ἐκκλησί-α, as, f., an assembly, or public meeting; also, the place of meeting, assembly hall.
ἐκκολά-πτω, -ψω, to scrape out, erase; peck out; hatch.

ἐκλανθάνω (see λανθάνω), to escape notice entirely : in mid. to forget utterly.
ἐκπέμπω (see πέμπω), to send forth, or out, or away.
ἐκπετάννυμι, F. ἐκπετάσω, to stretch forth; spread out, unfold, display.
ἐκρίπτω (see ῥίπτω), to throw out or away, cast forth.
ἐκτάδην (ἐκτείνω), adv., stretched out at full length.
ἐκτίθημι (see τίθημι), to set forth, put out ; expose, exhibit.
ἐκτυφλ-όω, F. -ώσω, to render entirely blind.
Ἕκτωρ, Ἕκτορ-ος, m., Hector, son of Priam, king of Troy.
ἐκφοβ-έω, ήσω, to frighten away, terrify : pass. to be afraid.
ἐλαττ-όω, ώσω (or ἐλασσόω, from ἐλάσσων, smaller), to make less, diminish : pass. to come worst off, be defeated ; be diminished.
ἐλαύνω, F. ἐλάσω, Attic ἐλῶ, to drive, set in motion ; ride ; advance, (as an army on march.)
ἔλαφ-ος, ου, m. and f., a deer, (stag or hind.)
ἐλε-έω, F. -ήσω, to pity, feel compassion for; show mercy to.
ἐλεημοσύν-η, ης, f., pity, mercy ; alms.
Ἑλέν-η, ης, f., Helen, wife of Menelaus, carried off by Paris.
ἔλε-ος, ου, m., pity, mercy, compassion.
ἐλεύθερ-ος, α, ον, free, free-spirited ; liberal, generous.
ἐλευθερ-όω, F. ώσω, to free, set free, release.
ἐλθεῖν, ἐλθών. &c., 2 aor. of ἔρχομαι, to come ; go.
Ἑλλάς, Ἑλλάδ-ος, f., Greece.
Ἕλλην, Ἕλλην-ος, m., a Greek : Ἕλληνες, the Greeks.
Ἑλληνικ-ός, ή, όν, Hellenic. Greek.
ἐλπίζω, F. ἐλπίσω, Attic ἐλπιῶ, to hope ; expect ; think, suppose.
ἐμαυτ-οῦ, ῆς, οῦ, myself. (See p. 56.)

ἐμβαίνω (see βαίνω), to go into, enter ; embark.
ἐμβάλλω (see βάλλω), to throw into ; put in ; to excite, inspire ; introduce ; to fall upon, attack.
ἐμβρόντητ-ος, ος, ον, thunderstruck (attonitus); as a subst. crazy (fool).
ἐμ-ός, ή, όν, my, or mine : possessive pronoun from (ἐγώ) ἐμοῦ.
ἐμπίπρημι, aor. ἐνέπρησα, to kindle, set on fire, burn. The pres. ought to be ἐμπίμπρημι, but the second μ is omitted to avoid the recurrence of the μ sound. So ἐμπίπλημι, and not ἐμπίμπλημι.
ἐμπίπτω (see πίπτω), to fall into ; to light upon ; fall in with ; happen.
ἐμπλέκω, F. ἐμπλέξω, to weave or plait in, to intertwine ; entangle.
ἔμπροσθεν, or ἔμπροσθε (before consonants), adv., before, in front of; earlier, sooner. Sometimes it is a prep. and governs gen.,—before. (Lat. ante.)
ἐμφαγεῖν, inf. of 2 aor. ind. ἐνέφαγον (the used pres. being ἐσθίω, which see), to take some food ; feed upon, eat, devour.
ἐν, prep., governing the dative only, in (i.e., being within); on; at or by, (near) : ἐν δείπνῳ, at dinner ; ἐν οἴνῳ (inter pocula), at wine.
ἐναλλάττω, or ἐναλλάσσω, F. -ξω, to give one thing in exchange for another, to barter, to change.
ἐνάλλομαι, F. ἐναλοῦμαι, aor. ἐνηλάμην, to leap on, (and so like insultare, in Lat.,) to leap on contemptuously ; to rush at.
ἐναντία, adv. (n. pl. of ἐναντίος, α, ον), over against, opposite ; to the face, in the presence of.
ἐναύω, to kindle, set fire to.
ἔνδον, adv., within, in; in the house, at home (domi).
ἔνδοξ-ος, ος, ον, of high fame ; honoured ; glorious.
ἐνδύω, and ἐνδύνω, F. ἐνδύσομαι (see δύω), to put on, clothe ; enter.
ἔνειμι (see εἰμί), to be in or at :

ἔνεστι (used impersonally), it is possible; it is in one's power.
ἕνεκα, prep. with gen., on account of; for the sake of (like causā and gratiā in Lat.); because of.
ἔνθα, adv., then; thereupon; just then: as relative, where.
ἐνθάδε, adv., thither; here; there; now.
ἐνθουσι-άζω, άσω (ἔνθεος), to be inspired, possessed by a god; to be in ecstasy.
ἐνιαυτ-ός, οῦ, m., a year.
ἔνι-οι, αι, α, pl., some.
ἐνίοτε, adv., sometimes.
ἐνοικ-έω, ήσω, to dwell in.
ἔνοπλ-ος, ος, ον, in armour, armed.
ἐνοχλ-έω, ήσω, imperf. ἠνώχλουν (with double augment), to give annoyance to; trouble, annoy, pester.
ἐνταῦθα, adv., here; there; at the very time; then.
ἐντέλλω (the active seldom used, the mid., ἐντέλλομαι, being almost always employed), to enjoin, command.
ἐντρυφ-άω, F. ήσω, to luxuriate or revel in; to make sport of, mock.
ἐξ, prep. with gen., used instead of ἐκ before vowels, out of; without, &c. (See ἐκ.)
ἐξαιρ-έω, ήσω, 2 aor. ἐξεῖλον, to take out or away, remove.
ἐξαιτ-έω, ήσω, to demand from another; to beg (a person) off; to obtain by asking.
ἐξανίστημι (see ἵστημι, in Vocabulary, and Irregular Verbs), to raise up, rouse; excite: mid. to change one's abode or residence.
ἔξειμι, to go out; come out.
ἔξειμι, impersonal forms only used; e.g., ἔξεστιν, it is allowed.
ἐξελαύνω, ἐξελάσω, to drive forth.
ἐξελέγ-χω, F. ξω, to search out; try; convict and confute.
ἐξεπίτηδ-ες, adv., on set purpose; hence, maliciously.
ἐξέρχομαι (see ἔρχομαι); to go or come forth.

ἐξέτασ-ις, εως, f., a drawing out in line; scrutiny; review.
ἐξευρίσκω, ἐξευρήσω, aor. ἐξεῦρον, to find out, discover; win.
ἐξοιδ-έω, F. ήσω, to be swollen up: ἐξῳδηκώς, perf. part.
ἐξονειδ-ίζω, F. ίσω, Attic ιῶ, to cast up to a person, taunt with, reproach.
ἐξουσί-α, ας, f. (ἔξεστι), power; permission, authority.
ἔξω, adv., on the outside, without; beyond.
ἔοικα, 2 perf. from old stem, εἴκω, to be like: particip. ἐοικώς, shortened into εἰκώς, εἰκυῖα, εἰκός, (see εἰκός, in Vocabulary,) to be, or to look like; to be probable, to seem.
ἐπ' for ἐπί.
ἐπᾴδω (see ᾄδω), to sing to or over; to harp upon; inculcate.
ἐπαιν-έω, F. ἔσω, mid. ἔσομαι, to approve; praise, commend.
ἔπαιν-ος, ου, m., approval, praise, panegyric.
ἐπαίρω, F. ἐπαρῶ, to lift up, raise, elevate, exalt; rouse.
Ἐπαμινώνδ-ας, ου, m., Epaminondas, a famous Theban general.
ἐπανέρχομαι (see ἔρχομαι), to come or go back; return.
ἐπαρκ-έω, F. ἔσω, to ward off, defend; hinder; be enough for.
ἐπαχθίζω, to load, burden with.
ἐπεί, conj., since; seeing that.
ἐπειδάν (ἐπειδὴ ἄν), conj., as soon as, whenever.
ἐπειδή (ἐπεὶ δή), conj., since; seeing that.
ἔπειτα (ἐπὶ εἶτα), thereupon; in the next place; then; therefore.
ἐπενδύνω, or -δύω, to put on (one part of dress or armour) over (another).
ἐπερείδω, F. ἐπερείσω, to press, or drive against: pass. to lean on, press against.
ἐπί, prep., governing accusative, genitive, and dative. (1.) With accus. it indicates motion towards or

against, — *to, towards, against.* (2.) With *gen.*, rest or motion,— *upon, at, near.* (3.) With *dat.*, nearness to,—*in* or *at* (a time or place), *for* (a purpose.)

ἐπιβαίνω (see βαίνω), to go upon, tread upon; arrive at; to mount upon; embark.

ἐπιβάλλω (see βάλλω), to throw upon; add to; attack.

ἐπιβάτ-ης, ου, *m.*, one who mounts; a rider; a passenger; a marine (soldier).

ἐπιβοάω, F. ἐπιβοήσομαι, to call upon, shout to; cry out against; invoke.

ἐπιβουλεύ-ω, F. -σω, to devise plans against one, to plot; lay snares for.

ἐπίβουλ-ος, ος, ον, plotting; treacherous, stealthy; designing.

ἐπιγελά-ω, -σομαι, to laugh at, deride; smile to.

ἐπιγίγνομαι (see γίγνομαι), to come after, happen after; accrue to.

ἐπιγράφω (see γράφω), to graze, scratch; write upon; mark; inscribe, engrave; write down, enroll.

ἐπιδείκνυμι (see *Irregular Verbs*), to exhibit, show off, display.

ἐπιδίδωμι (see *Irregular Verbs*), to give in addition; to give freely; to give one's self up to, devote to.

ἐπιεικῶς, fairly; tolerably; pretty well; pretty much.

ἐπιζητ-έω, ήσω, to seek after; wish for, desiderate.

ἐπίθεσ-ις, εως, *f.*, application.

ἐπικαθίζω, to set upon: *intrans.* to sit upon.

ἐπικαλ-έω, -σω, to call on or to; appeal to; invite; invoke; to call by a surname.

ἐπικλώθω, F. ἐπικλώσω, to spin to one, (as the Fates;) to allot, decree, destine.

ἐπιλαμβάνω (see λαμβάνω), to receive in addition; to attain: *in mid.* to hold on by; seize; to attack, (as of battle or disease.)

ἐπιλανθάνω (see λανθάνω), to make to forget: *mid.* to forget, lose thought of.

ἐπιλέγω (see λέγω), to say in addition; to choose, select.

ἐπιμελῶς, *adv.*, carefully.

ἐπιμηχανάομαι, to devise plans against, plot.

ἐπιπέμπω, to send after or again; send against; let loose.

ἐπιπλάττω (or πλάσσω), F. ἐπιπλάσω, to spread a plaster on.

ἐπισκέπτομαι (better ἐπισκοπέω), F. ἐπισκέψομαι, P. ἐπέσκεμμαι, to look upon, visit, examine.

ἐπισκώ-πτω, F. -ψω, to laugh at, jeer, make game of.

ἐπιστέλλω, F. ἐπιστελῶ, to send to; tell; enjoin, command; give in charge to.

ἐπιστολ-ή, ῆς, *f.*, a commission; a letter, epistle.

ἐπιστρέ-φω, F. ψω, to turn towards; turn : *mid. and pass.* to turn one's self towards; to turn round; to care for.

ἐπιταράττω (or -σσω), F. -ξω, to trouble yet more, give additional (extra) annoyance.

ἐπιτείνω, F. ἐπιτενῶ, to stretch out upon (as on a frame); to tighten; to increase; to urge on, excite; to strain after.

ἐπιτίθημι, to lay by or upon; to put to, add; suggest; attack.

ἐπίτομ-ος, ος, ον, cut off; shortened: ἡ ἐπίτομος (*scil.* ὁδός), the short road.

ἐπιτρέχω, F. ἐπιθρέξομαι, or ἐπιδραμοῦμαι, to run to or after; follow; attack.

ἐπιφων-έω, -ήσω, to mention by name; to add, subjoin.

ἐπιχειρ-έω, -ήσω, to put one's hand to; attempt, endeavour.

ἐπόμνυμι, and -υω, F. ἐπομοῦμαι, to swear to (do a thing); to swear in confirmation.

ἐράω, to love.

ἐργάζομαι, F. -άσομαι, P. εἴργασμαι, to work, labour; do, perform; effect.

ἔργ-ον, ου, n., a work; deed; thing; matter.
ἐρίζω, F. ἐρίσω, to strive; quarrel; vie with.
ἔρι-ον, ου, n., wool.
ἔρις, ἔριδος, f., (aceus. ἔριδα, or ἔριν,) strife, rivalry; quarrel. As a proper name, The Goddess of Contention.
ἐριφ-ος, ου, m. and f., a young goat, a kid.
Ἑρμῆς, οῦ, m., Hermes (Mercury), messenger of the gods.
(ἔρομαι), for which ἐρωτάω is used by the Attics as pres.; fut. ἐρήσομαι, aor. ἠρόμην, to ask, inquire. (See ἐρῶ.)
(ἑρπύζω), aor. εἵρπυσα, (the only part used by Attics, who preferred ἕρπω,) to creep, crawl.
ἕρπω, imperf. εἷρπον, to go slowly; creep, crawl.
ἔρχομαι, F. ἐλεύσομαι, Ρ. ἐλήλυθα, aor. ἦλθον (for ἤλυθον), to come; go, go away.
ἐρῶ (fut. of old pres. εἴρω), to be about to speak; proclaim; say; promise, &c.: the perf. is εἴρηκα, P. pass. εἴρημαι.
ἔρως, ἔρωτ-ος, m., love, affection. As a proper name, Eros (Cupid), god of love.
ἐρωτ-άω, -ήσω (see ἔρομαι), to ask, inquire.
ἐρωτικ-ός, ή, όν, of or belonging to love; amorous; amatory.
ἐς, or εἰς, prep. with aceus. only, into; unto, towards.
ἐσθίω, F. ἔδομαι, P. ἐδήδοκα, P. pass. ἐδήδεσμαι, 2 aor. ἔφαγον, to eat.
ἑταῖρ-ος, ου, m., a companion.
ἕτερ-ος, α, ον (alter), the other; one of two; the second; different.
ἔτι, adv., yet, still; henceforth.
ἑτοῖμ-ος, η, ον, or ος, ος, ον, ready, prepared; certain, sure.
ἔτ-ος, εος, n., a year.
εὖ, adv. (bene), well.
εὖγε (εὖ, γέ) adv., well; well done; bravo.

εὐγνώμ-ων, ων, ον, of good feeling; fair; charitable; reasonable.
εὐδοκιμ-έω, F. -ήσω, to be in good estimation; to be honoured, respected; famous.
εὐεργετ-έω, F. -ήσω, to be a benefactor; do well; do good to, show kindness to.
εὐεργέτ-ης, ου, m., one who does well to others, a benefactor.
εὐήθει-α, ας, f., goodness of heart; simplicity; honesty; also, folly.
εὐθαρσ-ής, ής, ές, of good courage; daring.
εὐθετ-έω, F. -ήσω, to set in order, arrange duly or well.
εὔθυμ-ος, ος, ον, cheerful; spirited, of good spirits.
εὐθυμότερ-ον, adv., n. of compar. of preceding, more cheerfully.
εὐθ-ύς, εῖα, ύ, straight, direct: as adv., εὐθύς, directly, straightway; straight towards. εὐθύς (adv.) properly refers to time, and εὐθύ (adv.) to place.
εὐμεγέθ-ης, ης, ες, of good size; large, great.
εὐμήκ-ης, ης, ες, of good length; tall, long.
εὔμορφ-ος, ος, ον, of good form, well made; comely.
εὔοσμ-ος, ος, ον, of good smell; fragrant.
εὔπορ-ος, ος, ον, easily passed through; easy; steady; ingenious; inventive.
εὐπράγι-α, ας, well-doing; welfare, success.
εὑρίσκω, F. εὑρήσω, aor. εὗρον, to find, discover; invent; obtain.
Εὐρυβιάδ-ης, ου, m., Eurybiades, commander of the Spartan fleet at Salamis.
Εὐρυδίκ-η, ης, f., Eurydice, wife of Orpheus.
εὐρ-ύς, εῖα, ύ, wide, broad; extensive.
εὐτέλει-α, ας, f., cheapness; economy; frugality; shabbiness.
εὐτυχέω, to be successful, have good luck, turn out well.

εὐφραίνω, F. εὐφρανῶ, to inspirit; gladden: pass. and mid. to make merry; enjoy one's self.
εὐφυῶς, ingeniously; cleverly.
εὔχομαι, F. εὔξομαι, to pray; vow; pay one's vows; boast, speak proudly; profess.
εὐώνυμ-ος, ος, ον, of good name; of good omen, lucky, fortunate; (in reference to omens), on the left hand.
εὐωχέω, to entertain sumptuously: in mid. and pass. to fare sumptuously, feast; relish, enjoy.
ἔφιππ-ος, ος, ον, on horseback; riding.
ἐφίστημι, F. ἐπιστήσω (see ἵστημι), to place upon; to set over, by, or near: intrans. to stand upon, by, or near; to impend; to stand still, halt.
ἐχθ-ρός, ρά, ρόν, hateful; hostile: as a subst., an enemy.
ἔχω, F. ἕξω, or σχήσω, P. ἔσχηκα, 2 aor. ἔσχον, with inf. σχεῖν, subj. σχῶ, opt. σχοίην, part. σχών, to have; hold; keep; know: mid. to cling to, with gen.
ἕωθεν, adv., from the morning; in the morning; at dawn.

Z

ζάω, contracted ζῶ, ζῇς, ζῇ: inf. ζῆν: imperf. ἔζων, F. ζήσω (rare), to live; to be strong, be fresh and vigorous.
Ζεύς, voc. Ζεῦ, gen. Διός, accus. Δία, Zeus (Jupiter, i.e., Ζεύς πατήρ).
ζηλοτυπέω, to be jealous of; to emulate; to envy.
ζηλ-όω, F. -ώσω, to envy; imitate; rival.
ζημι-όω, F. ώσω, to cause damage to one; to punish, fine.
Ζηνόφαντ-ος, ου, m., Zenophantus.
Ζήνων, Ζήνωνος, m., Zeno, founder of the Stoic school of philosophy.
ζητ-έω, F. ήσω, to seek, ask, search for.
ζωογονέω, to produce; propagate (animals).
ζῷ-ον, ου, n., a living creature, animal.
ζωρ-ός, ός, όν, pure; unadulterated, (of wine.)
ζωρότερ-ος, α, ον, compar. of foregoing.

H

ἤ, (1.) advers. conj. (aut), or: (2.) interrog. whether, (in indirect questions): (3.) compar. as, than, (like quam, in Lat.)
ἦ, adv., truly, verily, certainly: interrog. (like an and num), pray, is it really so?
ἡγέομαι, F. ἡγήσομαι, to lead the way, act as guide; take the command of (troops); to suppose, imagine, (like ducere.)
ᾔδειν, ᾔδεις, &c. (See οἶδα, and Irregular Verbs.)
ἡδέως (ἡδύς), gladly, with pleasure.
ἤδη, adv. (jam), already; before now; forthwith.
ᾔδη, ᾔδης, &c., Attic for ᾔδειν.
ἡδί-ων, ων, ον, compar. of ἡδύς.
ἡδον-ή, ῆς, f., pleasure, enjoyment.
ἡδ-ύς, εῖα, ύ, sweet; pleasant; (of men), kind, dear.
ἥκω, F. ἥξω, I am come; i.e., I have come, I am here, (used as a perf.)
ἡλίκ-ος, η, ον, of what size; how great; as great as. (Lat. quantus.)
ἧλος, ου, m., a nail; stud; wart; knot.

ἡμέρ-α, as, f., a day.
ἡμεροδρομέ-ω, to be a ἡμεροδρόμος, i.e.. a day runner, or courier ; to post.
ἥμερ-ος, ος, ον, or α, ον, tame, (of animals ;) cultivated, civilized.
ἡμέτερ-ος, α, ον, our (noster).
ἤμ-ην, imperf. mid. of εἰμί, to be.
ἡμιτελ-ής, ής, ές, half-finished, (applied to a house which has lost its head ; or, perhaps, which is childless.)
ἡμίφλεκτ-ος, ος, ον, half-burnt, scorched, singed.
ἤν, conj., with subj. (for ἐάν), if. in case that.
ἤνεγκε. See (φέρω.)

ἦπου, adv., of a truth ; beyond a doubt ; certainly.
"Ηρα, as, f., Hera (Juno), sister and wife of Zeus.
Ἡρακλ-ῆς, contracted for Ἡρακλέης: voc. Ἡράκλεις, (contracted for Ἡράκλεες,) and a shorter form,"Ηρακλες : gen. Ἡρακλέεος, contracted Ἡρακλέους, m.; Heracles (Hercules.)
ἥρω-ς, ἥρω-ος, m., a hero, demi-god; a free-man ; warrior.
ἥττ-ων, ων, ον, or ἥσσων, (irregular compar. of κακός,) less ; lower ; weaker ; inferior ; unequal to.
Ἥφαιστ-ος, ου, m., Hephaestus (Vulcan), god of fire.

Θ

θάλαμ-ος, ου, m., an inner room ; bed-room ; store-room.
θάλαττ-α (θάλασσα), ης, f., the sea.
θάνατ-ος, ου, m., death. As a proper name, Death.
θαρρέω, or θαρσέω, to be of good courage ; to be audacious ; to be daring, bold.
θαρρύνω, or θαρσύνω, or θρασύνω, to encourage, cheer on : intrans. take courage.
θαρσ-ύς, -εῖα, ύ. (See θρασύς.)
θαυμάζω (-άσω), θαυμάσομαι, to wonder, be astonished, marvel at, to admire ; esteem.
θαυμαστ-ός, ή, όν, wonderful, marvellous, strange.
θε-ά, as, f., a goddess; (but θεά, a sight.)
θεάομαι, θεάσομαι, to view, behold, look at ; contemplate.
θέλω, θελήσω, shortened form of ἐθέλω, to will, be willing.
θέμις, θέμιτος, or θέμιδος, accus. θέμιν, law (of usage, like jus and fas in Lat.), right.
Θεμιστοκλ-ῆς, έους, m., Themistocles, a famous Athenian.
θεός, οῦ, m., God ; a deity : and so f. ἡ θεός.

θεράπαιν-α, ης, f., a waiting-maid, maid-servant.
θεραπεύ-ω, -σω, to act as attendant; pay court to ; fawn on ; flatter ; " dance attendance to."
θερμ-αίνω, -ανῶ, to warm, heat : pass. be heated.
θερμ-ός, ή, όν, warm, hot ; hasty (in temper.)
θέρμ-ος, ου, m., a kind of lupine.
θέρ-ος, εος, n., summer.
Θέτις, Θέτιδος, f., Thetis, mother of Achilles.
Θετταλί-α, as, f., Thessaly a district of Greece.
θέω, F. θεύσομαι, to run ; move quickly.
Θηβαῖ-ος, α, ον, Theban, belonging to Thebes (in Boeotia).
θήγω, θήξω, to sharpen, whet ; provoke.
θήκ-η, ης, f., a case, box, chest.
θήρ, θηρ-ός, m., a wild beast, beast of prey ; a monster.
θήρ-α, as, f., the chase; eager pursuit.
θηρ-άω, θηράσω, mid. θηράσομαι, to take part in the chase, hunt ; to pursue eagerly.
θηρευτικ-ός, ή, όν, of or belonging to hunting ; fond of the chase.

θηρεύω, to hunt, chase; catch in hunting.
θηρί-ον, ου, from θήρ, (a diminutive in formation, but not in use,) beast, animal; wild beast.
θηριώδ-ης, ης, ες, full of wild beasts; brutal, savage, ferocious.
θησαυρ-ός, οῦ, m., a store, treasure; store-house; chest.
θνήσκω (from stem θαν-), F. θανοῦμαι, aor. ἔθανον, to die; perish.
θνητ-ός, ός, όν, or ή, όν, subject to death, mortal, human.
θόρυβ-ος, ου, m., noise, din, uproar, clamour.
θρασύνω (see θαρρύνω), to encourage, embolden: pass. to be bold; be confident in.
θρασ-ύς, εῖα, ύ, bold, spirited; foolhardy (audax); arrogant.
θρην-έω, -ήσω, to wail, lament.
θυγάτηρ, θυγατρός (for θυγατέρος), a daughter.
θῦμ-ός, οῦ, m., the soul; life; breath; spirit; courage; passion; heart, (of the kindly feelings;) mind, (intellectually.)
θύρ-α, ας, f., door, entrance, gate.
θυσί-α, ας, f., a sacrifice; victim.
θυσιάζ-ω, to sacrifice, offer a victim, or gift.
θύω, F. θύσω, P. τέθυκα, aor. pass. ἐτύθην, to make sacred offerings; sacrifice; celebrate.
θώς, θωός, m. or f., a jackal.

I

ἰάομαι, ἰάσομαι, to heal, cure.
ἰατρική (scil. τέχνη), properly the fem. of ἰατρικός, ἡ, όν, the medical art, surgery; medicine.
ἰατρ-ός, οῦ, m., a surgeon, physician, doctor.
Ἴδη, ης, f., Mount Ida, near Troy.
ἴδι-ος, α, ον (also -ος, -ος, -ον), one's own; private; peculiar.
ἰδών, ἰδεῖν, &c., 2 aor. part. and inf. of εἶδον. (See also ὁράω.)
ἱερ-εύς, έως, m., a priest; sacrificer.
ἱερ-ός, α, ον (also -ός, -ός, -όν), sacred, consecrated, holy: τὰ ἱερά, as pl. subst. the victims; the internal parts of the victims; and hence, the auspices.
Ἰθακήσι-ος, α, ον, of or belonging to Ithaca (e.g., Ulysses.)
ἱκαν-ός, ή, όν (ἵκω or ἱκάνω), becoming, suitable; sufficient for; satisfactory; (of time,) considerable, pretty long.
Ἴλι-ος, ου, f., and Ἴλι-ον, ου, n., Ilium, Troy.
ἵνα, conj., that; in order that: as an adv. (of place,) in what place, where; to what place, whither.
Ἴναχ-ος, ου, m., Inachus, a river of Argolis.
Ἰνδ-ός, οῦ, m., an Indian.
ἱππ-εύς, έως, m., a horseman, rider; knight.
ἱπποκόμ-ος, ου, m., a horse-tender, groom. It is properly an adjective of two terminations, -ος, -ος, -ον, horse-tending.
ἵππ.ρ-ος, ου, m., a horse: when f., it means either a mare, or a body of cavalry (equitatus).
Ἴσις, Ἴσιδος, f., Isis, an Egyptian goddess.
ἴσ-ος, η, ον, equal, fair, impartial; level, flat, (of ground.)
ἵστημι, (see Irregular Verbs,) to cause to stand, set up, or erect; to set in order, or arrange; to check, stop; rouse, excite; establish. The pres., imperf., fut., and 1 aor. active, are transitive; the other tenses intransitive: the pres., imperf., fut., and 1 aor. mid., are also sometimes transitive.
ἱστί-ον, ου, n., a web; cloth; sheet; sail.
ἰσχυρῶς, adv., strongly; very much; exceedingly.

ἴσως, adv., (from ἴσος,) equally, fairly; probably (the chances being equal), perhaps.
Ἰφικλ-ος, ου, or Ἰφικλ-ῆς, έους, m., Iphiclus, or Iphicles, father of Protesilaus.
ἰχθύ-s, ος, m., a fish.
ἴχν-ος, εος, n., a track, footstep; trace, mark.
Ἰώ, Ἰοῦς, f., Io, daughter of Inachus.

K

κἀγώ, for καὶ ἐγώ, and I.
Κάδμος, ου, m., Cadmus, a Phoenician, son of king Agenor, and brother of Europa.
καθ', for κατά, before an aspirated vowel.
καθαίρω, F. καθαρῶ, to make clean, purify, cleanse, purge.
κάθαρμα, καθάρματ-ος, n., that which is removed by cleaning, offscourings; a castaway, outcast, worthless fellow.
καθέζομαι, F. καθεδοῦμαι, to set one's self down, sit down; sit still; encamp.
καθεύδω, F. καθευδήσω, imperf. καθηῦδον, or ἐκάθευδον, to lie down to sleep; to sleep, rest, be still.
καθίζω, F. καθίσω, Att. καθιῶ, to cause to sit down, seat, set: intrans. to sit down, be seated.
καθίημι (κατά, ἵημι—see ἵημι, Irregular Verbs), καθήσω, P. καθεῖκα, to send or let down; to reach.
καθικνέομαι, F. καθίξομαι, to come down, reach to, touch; strike.
καθίπταμαι, and καταπέτομαι, F. καταπτήσομαι, aor. κατεπτάμην, to fly down.
καθίστημι (see ἵστημι, Irregular Verbs), to set down; set in order, arrange, (as soldiers;) station, appoint; establish, confirm: intrans. to settle.
καί, conj., and, also.
καιν-ός, ή, όν, fresh, new; newly discovered; strange.
καιρ-ός, οῦ, m., due proportion (of one thing to another); due measure (of time); and hence, right time, crisis, season, occasion, opportunity.
καίτοι, adverbial conj., and yet, yet.
καίω, or κάω, F. καύσω, and καύσομαι, to kindle; burn, scorch; (of cold,) pinch.
κἀκεῖνος, and he; for καὶ ἐκεῖνος.
κακοδαίμων, ων, ον, ill-fated; unhappy, wretched.
κακ-ός, ή, όν, bad; ugly; cowardly; base, wicked, &c.
κακῶς, adv., badly, ill; like a coward.
καλέω, F. καλέσω, (mid. καλέσομαι), Att. καλῶ, to call, invite, summon; call by name.
Καλλιδημίδ-ης, ου, m., Callidemides.
καλλί-ων, ων, ον, compar. of καλός, more beautiful, &c.
κάλλ-ος, εος, n., beauty, comeliness.
καλ-ός, ή, όν, beautiful; seemly; honourable; good.
καλώδι-ον, ου, n. (from κάλως), a small cord.
κάλ-ως, ω, m., a rope, sail-rope, cable.
καλῶς, adv., beautifully; well.
κἀμέ, for καὶ ἐμέ, and me.
καμμ-ύω, for καταμύω, F. -ύσω, to close the eyes; nod, doze.
κάμνω, F. καμοῦμαι, aor. ἔκαμον, intrans. to be weary, tired; to be sick; afflicted: trans. to labour, work.
κἄν, for καὶ ἐάν, and if.
κἀπειδή, for καὶ ἐπειδή, and when; and as soon as.
κἀπί, for καὶ ἐπί, and upon.

κάρα, n., used only in the nom. and accus. sing., the head, top, summit.

Καστωλ-ός, οῦ, m., Castolus, a city of Lydia.

κατ', for κατά.

κατά, prep. governing gen. and accus., down, or downwards. (1.) With gen., down from; down over; towards; against; concerning. (2.) With accus., down to, or along (opposed to ἀνά); throughout; in; over; at; according to.

καταβαίνω (see βαίνω), to go down, descend.

καταβάλλω (see βάλλω), to throw down, strike down; lay down, pay down.

καταγελάω, F. καταγελάσομαι, to laugh down or at, deride, mock, jeer.

κατάγ-νυμι, F. κατάξω, aor. κατέαξα, to break down or in pieces, shatter; weaken.

καταγωνίζομαι, καταγωνίσομαι, καταγωνιοῦμαι, to struggle against; overpower, conquer.

καταδιώ-κω, F. -ξω, or -ξομαι, to hunt down; pursue hard; overtake; capture.

κατ-ᾴδω, F. -ᾴσω, and -ᾴσομαι, to sing to; to deafen by singing; to sing in derision of one.

κατακλίνω, F. κατακλινῶ, to lay down; cause to lie down: in pass. to recline at table.

καταλαμβάνω, καταλήψομαι, to seize upon; hold down; check; overtake, catch.

καταλείπω, F. -ψω, to leave behind, forsake, abandon; allow.

καταμύ-ω, -σω, to close the eyes; drop asleep; nod, doze.

καταπέμ-πω, F. -ψω, to send down.

καταπηδάω, to leap down from.

καταπλή-ττω (or -πλήσσω), F. -ξω, to strike down; astound; terrify.

καταπλουτ-ίζω, F. -ίσω, Att. -ιῶ, to make very rich, enrich.

κατάρατ-ος, ος, ον, accursed; abominable.

κατασκευ-άζω, F. -άσω, to prepare; furnish; finish; adorn.

κατασοφίζομαι, to overpower by fallacies; outwit, wheedle.

κατασπ-άω, F. -άσω, to draw or drag down.

κατασύρω, to pull down; ravage, plunder.

κατατίθημι (see Irregular Verbs), to put or lay down; lay by, deposit; lay aside: mid. pay down.

καταφέρω, F. κατοίσω, to carry or bring down; overthrow, destroy.

καταφεύ-γω, F. -ξομαι, to flee for refuge, take refuge; escape.

καταφλέ-γω, F. -ξω, to burn down, consume.

καταφρον-έω, F. -ήσω, to think down upon; i.e., to think little of, despise.

καταφρόνησ-ις, εως, f., contempt; overweening self-conceit.

κατεσθίω (see ἐσθίω), to eat up, (literally, eat down,) devour.

κατέχω (see ἔχω), to hold down or back, restrain; possess, occupy; seize, arrest.

κάτω (κατά), adv., underneath, (opposed to ἄνω,) below; (of time,) afterwards.

κάτωθε, or, before a vowel, κάτωθεν, from below; below, beneath.

καυχ-άομαι, F. -ήσομαι, to speak loud; vaunt, boast, brag.

κεῖμαι, 2d sing. κεῖσαι, 3d, κεῖται, F. κείσομαι, to be laid; to lie, be inactive.

κείρω, F. κερῶ, to cut short, crop, clip, shave.

κελεύ-ω, F. -σω, to drive on, urge, impel; order, command.

κεν-ός, ή, όν, empty; fruitless, vain; bereft of.

κεράννυμι, and -ύω, F. κεράσω, Att. κερῶ, to mix, mingle.

κέρας, κέρατος (κέρως), n., a horn; bow; wing of an army.

κεραυν-όω, F. -ώσω, to strike with a thunderbolt, to blast.

κερδῷ-ος, α, ον, bringing gain; wily, crafty.

κέρκ-ος, ου, f., the tail of a beast, (οὐρά is the more general term, applicable to birds also.)
κεφαλ-ή, ῆς, f., the head.
κῆπ-ος, ου, m., a garden.
κηρ-ός, οῦ, m., bee's wax; wax.
κηρύ-ττω, or -σσω, F. κηρύξω, to act as herald; make proclamation, announce.
κιθαρ-ίζω, F. -ίσω, to play on the cithara or harp.
κινδυνεύ-ω, -σω, to incur danger, run a risk.
κίνδυν-ος, ου, m., danger, risk, hazard.
κιν-έω, F. -ήσω, to move, excite, stir.
κίων, κίον-ος, m., a pillar; sometimes, like στήλη, a grave-stone.
κλαίω, Att. κλάω, F. κλαύσομαι, to weep, lament, wail; to weep for, deplore.
Κλέαρχος, ου, m., Clearchus, a Greek general.
κλειν-ός, ή, όν, glorious, famous, illustrious.
κλέπτ-ης, ου, m., a thief.
κλέπτ-ω, F. κλέψ-ω, or -ομαι, to steal; cheat, beguile; conceal; do (a thing) in an underhand way.
κλῆρ-ος, ου, m., a lot; drawing of lots; the thing allotted.
κλίν-ω, F. κλινῶ, to incline,—i.e., make to bend; lay down, to recline, lean; draw to a close.
κλισί-α, ας, f., a tent, hut; a reclining place, couch.
κλοπ-ή, -ῆς, f., theft, fraud.
κοῖλος, η, ον, hollow, hollowed, concave.
κοιμ-άω, -ήσω, to lull to rest or sleep: in pass. to fall asleep; lie a-bed, rest; die.
κοιν-ός, ή, όν, common, public, general.
κοινωνί-α, ας, f., communion, intercourse, fellowship.
κολάζω, F. κολάσομαι, to check; chastise, punish.
κόλαξ, κόλακ-ος, m., a flatterer, fawner, parasite.

κολοι-ός, οῦ, m., a jackdaw (graculus).
κόλπ-ος, ου, m. (sinus), the bosom; the fold or lap of a robe; a bay.
κολυμβ-άω, -ήσω, to dive; to jump in and swim.
κόμ-η, ης, f., the hair; foliage of trees.
κομίζω, F. κομίσω, Att. κομιῶ, to take care of, tend, provide for; to carry, bear; bring.
κονίζω, F. κονίσω, to render dusty; cover with dust.
κοπρί-α, ας, f., a dunghill.
κόπτ-ω, κόψω, to strike, smite; chop off; hammer, forge.
κόραξ, κόρακ-ος, m., a raven, or crow.
κόρ-η, ης, f., a maiden, girl (puella); a daughter; a doll; a pupil of the eye.
κόρυς, κόρυθ-ος, f., a helmet: accus. κόρυθα, and κόρυν.
κορυφή, ῆς, f., the head, top, summit.
κοσμ-έω, -ήσω (κόσμος), to arrange, set in order; adorn; set off.
κόσμ-ος, ου, m., order, decency; ornament, honour; the world.
κοτύλ-η, ης, f., a hollow vessel, cup; the socket of a joint; an Athenian liquid measure = half a pint.
κοὐδείς, for καὶ οὐδείς, and no one.
κουρ-εύς, έως, m., a barber, hairdresser; gossip.
κοχλί-ας, ου, m., a snail with a spiral shell.
κράζω, F. κεκράξομαι, aor. ἔκραγον, to croak; scream; clamour.
κρανί-ον, ου, the skull.
κρατ-έω, ήσω, to be strong, powerful; to rule; conquer.
κρέας, κρέατος, Att. κρέως, flesh, a carcass.
κρείττων, ων, ον, irregular compar. of ἀγαθός, stronger; braver; better; too great for.
κρέμαμαι, pres. pass. and mid. of following.
κρεμάννυμι, κρεμάσω, Att. κρεμῶ, ᾷς, ᾷ, to hang up, suspend.
κριθή, ῆς, f., barley; generally used in pl. κριθαί.

κρίνω, f. κρινῶ, aor. ἔκρινα, to separate, divide; select; judge, decide.
κρι-ός, οῦ, m., a ram; battering-ram.
κριτ-ής, οῦ, m., a judge, umpire.
κροτ-έω, -ήσω, to make to rattle; to strike together, clap (hands.)
κρύ-ος, εος, n., cold, chilling cold; frost.
κρύ-πτω, f. -ψω, to hide, cover, conceal.
κτεν-ίζω, -ίσω, to comb, curry.
κτῆμα, κτήματος, n., a possession, property : pl. wealth, goods.
κυβερνήτ-ης. ου, m., a steersman, pilot; guide.
Κύκλωψ, Κύκλωπ-ος, m., a Cyclops, or one-eyed monster.
κυλινδ-έω, f. -ήσω, for κυλίνδω, to roll, roll along.
κύλιξ, κύλικ-ος, f., a cup, drinking-vessel.
κῦμα, κύματ-ος, n., the swell of the sea, wave, billow.
κυνηγ-ός, οῦ, dog-leading; a hunter.
κύπελλ-ον, ου, n., a beaker, cup; a bellied drinking-vessel.
κύρι-ος, ου, m., a lord, master, ruler; guardian.
Κῦρος, ου, m., Cyrus.
κύων, κυνός, m. or f., a dog or bitch.
κώμ-η, ης, f., a village, country town.
κών-ωψ, -ωπος, m., a gnat, or mosquito.
κώπ-η, ης, f., a handle.
κωφ-ός, ή, όν, blunt, obtuse; dumb; deaf.

Λ

Λάγ-ος, ου, m., Lagus, a Macedonian, father of Ptolemy, king of Egypt.
λαγ-ώς, λαγώ, m., a hare.
λάθρᾶ, adv., secretly, stealthily, unknown to, treacherously.
λαι-ά, ᾶς, f., the left hand. It is properly the fem. of λαιός (laevus), and is almost entirely confined to poetry.
λαιμ-ός, οῦ, m., the throat, gullet.
Λακεδαιμόνι-ος, ου, m., a Lacedaemonian, a Spartan.
λακτίζ-ω, f. λακτίσω, to kick with the heel; trample on; knock, beat.
λαλ-έω, f. ήσω, to talk, babble, chatter; to indulge in incessant trifling talk.
λάλ-ος, ος, ον, talkative, babbling.
λαμβάνω, f. λήψομαι, p. εἴληφα, aor. ἔλαβον, to take; receive; catch, overtake, get; apprehend.
λαμπ-άς, λαμπάδ-ος, f., a torch, lamp.
λαμπρ-ός, ά, ον, bright, brilliant, gleaming, glancing.
λανθ-άνω, f. λήσω, aor. ἔλαθον (Lat. lutere). r. λέληθα, to escape notice, to be unseen, unknown, be concealed.
λα-ός, ου, m. (Att. λεώς, λεώ), the people at large; a people, tribe, or nation.
λέαιν-α, ης, f., a lioness.
λέβης, λέβητος, m., a caldron, or kettle; urn; vase.
λέγω, f. λέξω, to lay; lay in order, arrange; choose, pick out; count, tell; say, speak : λέγεται, impers., it is said.
λειμών, λειμῶν-ος, m., a meadow; holm.
λεῖ-ος, α, ον, also -ος, -ος, -ον, smooth (Lat. laevis, or levis), level.
λείπω, f. λείψω, aor. ἔλιπον, p. λέλοιπα, to leave; fail; be deficient.
Λεοντῖν-ος, ου, m., a native of Leontium, in Sicily.
λεπτ-ός, ή, όν (λέπω, to peel), peeled off; hence, fine, thin, lean.
λευκ-ός, ή, όν, light, bright, clear, white.
λέων, λέοντ-ος, m., a lion.
λεώς, λεώ, Attic form of λαός, the people.

λιιψόρ-ος, ος, ον, bearing people; crowded : as *subst.* a highway, a thoroughfare.
Λήδ-α, -ας, (or -ης,) *f.*, Leda, mother of Helen, Castor, and Pollux.
Λήθ-η, ης, *f.*, Lethe, the river of oblivion in the lower world. *As a common noun*, forgetfulness, oblivion.
ληστ-ής, οῦ, *m.*, a robber, pirate.
λίαν, *adv.*, very, very much, excessively.
λίθ-ος, ου, *m.*, a stone ; gem.
λιμήν, λιμέν-ος, *m.*, a harbour, haven, place of refuge.
λίμν-η, ης, *f.*, a lake, pool ; marsh.
λιμ-ός, οῦ, *m.*, hunger ; famine.
λιμώττω, or λιμώσσω, to be hungry; to be starved, to famish.
λογίζομαι, F. λογίσομαι, or λογιοῦμαι, to calculate ; consider ; conclude.
λογισμ-ός, οῦ, *m.*, a calculation, reckoning, account.
λόγ-ος, ου, *m.*, a word ; speech ; reason ; account ; praise.

λοιδορ-έω, ήσω, to rail at, revile, reproach.
λοιμ-ός, οῦ, *m.*, a plague, pestilence.
λοιπ-ός, ή, όν, remaining, the rest.
λού-ω, -σω, to wash, cleanse ; bathe.
Λυδί-α, ας, *f.*, Lydia, a district of Asia Minor.
Λυδ-ός, οῦ, *m.*, a Lydian.
λύκ-ος, ου, *m.*, a wolf.
Λυκοῦργ-ος, ου, *m.*, Lycurgus.
λυμαίνομαι, *v. pass.* λελύμασμαι, to cleanse one's self: *also*, to outrage, maltreat, injure.
λυπ-έω, -ήσω, to cause pain, grieve, distress.
λύπ-η, ης, *f.*, pain, grief.
λυπηρ-ός, ά, όν, painful ; grievous ; troublesome.
λυσιτελ-έω, ήσω, to benefit, profit.
λύ-ω, F. λύσω, P. λέλῠκα, to loose, unbind, set free, release, dismiss.
λῷστ-ος, η, ον (λώιστος), *super.* of ἀγαθός, (λωίων, λῷστος,) more desirable, better.

M

μάζ-α, or μᾶζ-α, ης, *f.*, a cake (of barley meal.) (See ἄρτος.)
μαθητ-ής, οῦ, *m.*, a learner, pupil, disciple.
Μαῖ-α, ας, *f.* (*Μαία*), daughter of Atlas, and mother of Hermes.
μαίνομαι, F. μανοῦμαι, P. μέμηνα (*as pres.*), to rage, be angry.
μαι-όομαι, F. ώσομαι, to act as a midwife, deliver.
μαιώτρ-α, -ων, *n. pl.*, midwife's wages or fee.
μακαρίζω, to pronounce happy ; to bless, congratulate.
μακρ-ός, α, ον, long; deep; broad ; extensive, large.
μάλα, *adv.*, very, very much.
μαλακ-ός, ή, όν, soft, gentle, light ; tender, delicate.
μάλιστα, *adv.*, most of all, especially, (*superl.* of μάλα.)

μᾶλλον, *adv.*, more, more especially, (*compar.* of μάλα.)
μανθάνω, F. μαθήσομαι, *aor.* ἔμαθον, to learn, understand ; notice, perceive.
Μαντίνει-α, ας, *f.*, Mantinea, a town in Arcadia.
μάντ-ις, μάντ-εως, *m.*, a diviner, seer, prophet.
μαστίγ-όω, F. ώσω, to whip, flog.
μάται-ος, α, ον, also -ος, -ος, -ον, foolish ; idle ; trifling.
μάτην, *adv.* (*frustra*), in vain, fruitlessly ; at random.
μάχαιρ-α, ας, *f.*, a large knife ; a short sword ; dagger.
μάχ-η, ης, *f.*, battle, fight, combat.
μάχομαι, μαχήσομαι, engage in battle, to fight ; quarrel.
μέγα, *adv.*, greatly ; *neuter* of μέγας.
μεγάλως, *adv.*, greatly, exceedingly.

μέγας, μεγάλη, μέγα (see p. 46), great, large.
μεθίστημι, to change the position of; to remove (from one place to another), to flit.
μεθύσκω, F. μεθύσω, to make drunk, intoxicate.
μεῖζ-ων, ων, ον, compar. of μέγας, greater, larger.
μειράκι-ον, ου, n., dimin. from μεῖραξ, a boy, lad, stripling.
μειρακίσκ-ος, ου, m., a lad, boy, youth.
μείρομαι, aor. ἔμμορον, P. ἔμμορα, to receive as one's due; be allotted. In perf. and pluperf. pass. εἵμαρται, and εἵμαρτο, it is allotted, destined, fated.
μελαγχολάω, to be melancholy-mad.
μέλᾱς, μέλαινα, μέλαν, black, dark, obscure.
μέλει, impers., it is for a care; it concerns (est curæ mihi.)
μέλι, μέλιτ-ος, n., honey.
μέλιττ-α, (or -σσα,) ης, f., a bee (apis.)
Μελιταῖ-ος, α, ον, Maltese: from Μελίτη, Malta.
μέλλω, F. μελλήσω, aor. with double augment, ἠμέλλησα, to be about to do, purpose; to delay, loiter.
μέλ-ος, εος, n., a limb, member; also a song, strain, music.
μέμνημαι, P. pass. of μιμνήσκω, to remember, (which see.)
μέμφομαι, F. μέμψομαι, to blame, find fault with, complain of.
μέν, conj. adv., (responded to by δέ,) in the first place, on the one hand: ὁ μέν, the one; ὁ δέ, the other: οἱ μέν, some; οἱ δέ, others.
Μενέλᾱ-ος, ου, m., Menelaus, husband of Helen, and king of Lacedæmon.
Μένιππ-ος, ου, m., Menippus, a Cynic philosopher.
μέντοι, adv., certainly, indeed, assuredly for that matter.
μένω, F. μενῶ, aor. ἔμεινα (Lat. maneo), to stand fast, remain, abide.

Μένων, Μένωνος, m., Menon, a Thessalian, one of the leaders of the Greeks in the expedition of Cyrus the younger.
μέρ-ος, εος, n., a part, share, portion, division.
μερ-ίζω, F. ίσω, Att. -ιῶ, to divide, share, distribute, apportion.
μέσ-ος, η, ον (medius), middle; in the middle; middling, moderate.
μεστ-ός, ή, όν, full, filled with, sated; wearied.
μετά, prep., governing accus., gen., and dat., in the midst of, among, between; into the midst of; after. It governs the dat. in poetry only.
μεταβάλλω, to throw round; change, alter; turn back.
μεταλαμβάνω (see λαμβάνω), to receive a share of, partake; assume.
μεταξύ, adv. (μετά), in the midst of, between; meanwhile, whilst.
μεταπέμπω, to send one after another: mid. to send for one, summon.
μετοικέω, to change one's residence, remove.
μετριότης, μετριότητ-ος, f., moderation, the middle course, temperance.
μετρίως, adv., moderately, temperately; enough.
μή, adv., not (in dependent clauses, and in independent clauses giving a command; hence, with imperat. and subjunct.:) also a conj.—lest, that not, whether.
μηδέ (neque), nor, neither; not even.
μηδείς, μηδεμία, μηδέν (μηδέ, εἷς), not even one, no one, none.
μηδέπω, adv., nor as yet; not as yet; by no means.
μήκιστ-ος, η, ον (μῆκος, length), superl. of μακρός, longest. tallest: as an adv., in the highest degree.
μῆλ-ον, ου, n. (mālum), an apple; a fruit-tree. τὰ μῆλα (mālæ), the cheeks.
μήν, adv. (vero), indeed, truly, in sooth, verily.
μήν, μην-ός, m., a month; the moon.

μῆνιγξ, μήνιγγ-ος, f., a membrane; the membrane of the brain.
μήτηρ, μητρός, f. (see p. 28), a mother.
μιάρ-ός, ά, όν, stained, defiled, polluted, filthy: as a subst., worthless wretch.
Μίδ-ας, ου, m., Midas, a king of Phrygia.
μικρ-ός, ά, όν, small, little, tiny. παρὰ μικρόν, nearly, almost.
μιμνήσκω, F. μνήσω, to remind, recall to one's memory: mid. more usual: P. pass. as pres., μέμνημαι, I remember: subjunct. μέμνωμαι: opt. μεμνήμην, or μεμνώμην.
μῖσ-έω, F. ήσω (μῖσος, hatred), to hate, abhor.
μισθ-ός, οῦ, wages, pay, hire, reward.
μνημονεύω, to remember, call to mind; to remind one.
μοῖρ-α, ας, f., properly a part or portion; hence, one's lot, fate, destiny.

μόν-ος, η, ον, alone, only, solitary.
μορμολυκεῖ-ον, ου, n., a hobgoblin, bugbear.
μόσχ-ος, ου, m. or f., a young shoot: hence, offspring; a calf, a young bull, a heifer.
Μοῦσ-α, ης, f., The Muse, goddess of music, poetry, &c. There were nine Muses.
μουσικῶς, adv., musically; elegantly.
μοχθηρ-ός, ά, όν, subject to hardship, distressed, afflicted, wretched; troublesome.
μοχλ-ός, οῦ, m., a lever, crow-bar, bar, or bolt.
μυῖ-α, ας, f., a fly.
μυκτήρ, μυκτῆρος, m., the nose: pl. the nostrils.
μυλών, μυλῶν-ος, m., a place for a mill, a mill-house, a mill.
μύρι-οι, αι, α, ten thousand.
μύρμηξ, μύρμηκ-ος, m., an ant.
μῦς, μυ-ός, m. (see p. 26), a mouse.
μωραίνω, to be silly, foolish; to play the fool.

N

ναί, adv., yea, verily, yes, ay.
νά-ός, οῦ, m., (Att. νεώς—see p. 21,) a dwelling; especially, a temple.
ναυαγέ-ω, ήσω, to be shipwrecked; to go to ruin.
ναῦς, νεώς, f., a ship.
ναύτ-ης, ου (nauta), m., a seaman, sailor; a voyager by sea.
νεανί-ας, ου, m., a young man, youth.
νεανίσκ-ος, ου, m., a youth, a young man (under forty).
Νεῖλ-ος, ου, m., the Nile.
νεκρικ-ός, ή, όν, belonging to the dead.
νεκροπομπ-ός, ός, όν, conducting the dead; ghost-conductor.
νεκρ-ός, οῦ, m., a dead body, corpse.
νέκταρ, νέκτάρ-ος, n., nectar, the drink of the gods.
Νεμέ-ᾱ, ας, f., Nemea, a town and forest in Argolis. τὰ Νέμεᾰ, n. pl., the Nemean games.
νέμω, F. νεμῶ, aor. ἔνειμα, to distribute, apportion, assign: mid. to possess; inhabit; enjoy; to feed or tend cattle.
νεόγαμ-ος, ος, ον, newly married.
νέ-ος, α, ον, also -ος, -ος, -ον, young, new, fresh.
νεωλκέω, to haul up a ship on land.
νεώνητ-ος, ος, ον, newly bought.
νεώς, νεώ, m. (see p. 21, art. 9), Attic form of ναός, a temple.
νεώτερ-ος, α, ον, compar. of νέος, younger, more fresh, more recent.
νή, affirmative adv., used in asseverations; as, νὴ Δία, "by Zeus."
νήπι-ος, α, ον, also -ος, -ος, -ον, not speaking (infant); i.e., very young: hence, childish, silly.
Νηρηΐς, Νηρηΐδ-ος, f., a Nereid, sea nymph.
νῆσ-ος, ου, f., an island.
νικ-άω, ήσω, to conquer, prevail, gain, win.

νίκ-η, ης. f., victory, conquest, superiority.
Νῖν-ος, ου, f., Nineveh.
νομ-εύς, έως, m., a shepherd, herdsman.
νομ-ή, ῆς, f., pasture, food, (like νομός.)
νομίζω, F. νομίσω, Att. νομιῶ, to regard as a custom; to believe, think, suppose, consider; acknowledge.
νόμ-ος, ου, m., a usage, custom, law; but νομός, pasture.
νό-ος, ου, m. (contr. νοῦς), the mind, head, intellect, reason.
νοσέ-ω, ήσω, to be sick, to ail, suffer from disease (νόσος).
νοῦς, gen. νοῦ, m., (contr. for νόος,) the mind.
νύμφ-η, ης, f., a bride; a nymph.
νυμφί-ος, α, ον, marriageable: as a subst., a bridegroom, husband.
νῦν, adv., now, at this very time (nunc).
νύν, now; well now, (the now of sequence;) then, thereupon.
νύξ, νυκτ-ός, f. (nox), night, darkness.
νωχελ-ής, ής, ές, moving slowly; sluggish, dull.

Ξ

ξαίνω, F. ξανῶ, to scratch; comb, card.
Ξανθίππ-η, ης, f., Xantippe, wife of Socrates.
ξανθ-ός, ή, όν, yellow, auburn, fair, blonde (as applied to hair).
ξενί-α, ας, f., hospitality; the right of hospitium, as between states or individuals.
Ξενοκράτ-ης, εος (ους), Xenocrates, a philosopher.
ξέν-ος, ου, m., a guest-friend, stranger; also a host, entertainer.
Ξενοφῶν (see p. 30), Xenophon, a distinguished Athenian, famed as a philosopher, writer, and military commander.
ξηρ-ός, ά, όν, dry, dried up, withered, parched.
ξίφ-ος, εος, n., a sword.
ξύλον, ου, n., wood, timber; a piece of wood.
ξυνουσί-α, or συνουσία, ας, f., a friendly meeting; intercourse; society.
ξυρ-όν, οῦ, n., a razor.

Ο

ὁ, ἡ, τό, the article this, the. (See p. 21.)
ὀβολ-ός, οῦ, m., an obol, a coin worth about three-halfpence.
ὀγκ-άομαι, ήσομαι, to bray (like an ass). Compare d-onk-ey.
ὁδ-ός, οῦ, f., a way, path, road; expedition; way or means.
ὀδούς, ὀδόντ-ος, m., a tooth.
ὀδύρομαι, to wail, mourn, lament.
Ὀδυσσ-εύς, έως, Ulysses, king of Ithaca (hodie, Theaki).
ὅθεν (unde), adv., whence, from whence; from whom, &c.
οἶδα, I know; a perf. with pres. signification. (See εἶδον, εἰδέναι, and Irregular Verbs.)
οἰκέτ-ης, ου, m., an inmate of one's house; a house-servant, domestic, menial, slave.
οἰκί-α, ας, f., a house, abode; household, &c.
οἰκίδι-ον, ου, n., dimin. from οἶκος, a little house.
οἴκοι, adv., at home (domi).
οἶκ-ος, ου, m., a house, dwelling.
οἶμαι, contr. for οἴομαι.
οἰμωγ-ή, ῆς, f., weeping and wailing.

οἰμώζω, f. οἰμώξομαι, to wail, lament, pity.
οἶνος, ου, m., wine.
οἰνοχό-ος, ου, m., pouring out wine; cup-bearer.
οἴομαι, F. οἰήσομαι, aor. ᾠήθην, to suppose, consider, judge.
οἶ-ος, α, ον, such as (qualis); of what sort.
οἶ-ος, η, ον, alone, only.
Οἴτ-η, ης, f., Œta, a mountain in Thessaly.
οἴχομαι, f. οἰχήσομαι, imperf. ᾠχόμην, to be gone; to have gone; to die.
ὀλέθρι-ος, ος, ον, destructive, deadly, fatal.
ὀλίγ-ος, η, ον, few, little, small.
ὁλκάς, ὁλκάδ-ος, f., a ship of burthen, a merchantman.
ὅλ-ος, η, ον, whole, perfect, complete.
ὅλως, adv., wholly, altogether; in short.
Ὀλυμπιάς, Ὀλυμπιάδ-ος, f., an inhabitant of Olympus; a goddess: in pl. the contests at the Olympic games.
Ὅμηρ-ος, ου, m., Homer.
ὁμιλ-έω, ήσω, to be together; associate with, mix with.
ὄμνυμι, F. ὀμοῦμαι, P. ὀμώμοκα, to swear, affirm by oath.
ὁμογεν-ής, ής, ές, of the same family, akin.
ὅμοι-ος, α, ον, like, resembling, similar; common.
ὁμοίως, adv., in like manner, similarly.
ὁμόνεκρ-ος, ος, ον, companion in death, fellow-ghost.
ὁμότεχν-ος, ος, ον, of the same art or craft, fellow-workman.
ὁμόψηφ-ος, ος, ον, voting with; siding with; being a party to.
Ὀμφάλ-η, ης, f., Omphale, queen of Lydia.
ὄμφαξ, ὀμφακ-ος, f., an unripe grape.
ὄναρ, n., used in nom. and accus. sing. only, a dream: the other cases are supplied by ὄνειρος, with irreg. pl. ὀνείρατα.

ὀνειδ-ίζω, F. ίσω, to cast reproaches on one; revile, reproach, upbraid.
ὀνίνημι, F. ὀνήσω, 2 aor. mid. ὠνήμην, or ὠνάμην, opt. ὀναίμην, to profit, benefit: mid. to have the advantage of, be a gainer.
ὄνομα, ὀνόματ-ος, n., name; fame, reputation.
ὀνομ-άζω, F. -άσω, to name; address by name.
ὄνος, ου, m. and f., an ass.
ὀξύθῡμ-ος, ος, ον, quick-tempered, passionate, irascible.
ὀξ-ύς, εῖα, ύ, sharp, pointed; acute, (of pain;) pungent, (in taste;) hasty, passionate; swift.
ὀξύχολ-ος, ος, ον, quick to anger, passionate.
ὀπίσω, adv., behind, backwards, (of place;) hereafter, (of time;) again.
ὁποῖ-ος, α, ον, of what kind or quality (qualis).
ὁπόσ-ος, η, ον (quot), how many; as many as.
ὀπτ-άω, ήσω, to roast, broil; fry; bake.
(ὄπτομαι), F. ὄψομαι, I shall see. (See ὁράω.)
ὅπως, conj., how, in what way; so that; when, as soon as.
ὁράω, imperf. ἑώρων, F. ὄψομαι, P. ἑώρᾱκα and ἑόρᾱκα, pass. aor. ὤφθην, P. pass. ἑώρᾱμαι and ὦμμαι, to see, look at, observe; think; understand.
ὀργ-ίζω, F. ίσω, Att. -ιῶ, to make angry, irritate, provoke: mid. be angry.
ὀρθῶς, adv., right; safe, well; truly, really.
ὀρ-ίζω, -ίσω, Att. -ιῶ (ὅρος, a boundary), to set a limit, separate from; to bound, determine, define.
ὁρμ-άω, ήσω, to set in motion; urge on, excite: intrans. to hurry, rush; set out; make an effort.
ὄρνε-ον, ου, n., = ὄρνις, a bird.
ὄρνις, ὀρνῑθ-ος, m. or f. (see p. 32), a bird, fowl; hen; omen.
ὄρ-ος, εος, n., a mountain; hill; chain of hills.

ὄροφ-ος, ου, m., a roof.
ὄρτυξ, ὄρτυγ-ος, m., a quail.
Ὀρφ-εύς, έως, m., Orpheus.
ὀρχ-έομαι, F. -ήσομαι, to dance; leap, bound.
ὅς, ἥ, ὅ, *relative pron.*, who, which, that (*qui*): ὅς, ἥ, ὅν, *possessive*, his, her's, its.
ὁσάκις, and ὁσάκι, *adv.*, as often as.
ὅσ-ος, η, ον, how many, how much (*quantus*); as many as, as much as.
ὅσπερ, ἥπερ, ὅπερ, which very one (*qui quidem*); which indeed; who (you must know).
ὀστέ-ον, ου, contr. ὀστοῦν, *pl.* ὀστέα, contr. ὀστᾶ, a bone.
ὅστις, ἥτις, ὅτι (written sometimes ὅ, τι), *gen.* οὕτινος, ἧστινος, &c., Att. *gen.* ὅτου, *dat.* ὅτῳ, whosoever, whichsoever: *interrog.* who, what.
ὅταν, *adv.* (for ὅτ' ἄν, *i.e.*, ὅτε ἄν), whenever, as soon as.
ὅτε, *adv.*, when; since; seeing that.
ὅτι, *conj.*, that, because.
οὐ, *adv.*, not. οὐ is used before consonants, οὐκ before unaspirated vowels, and οὐχ before aspirated vowels; as, οὐ λέγω, οὐκ ἐάω, οὐχ ὁράω.
οὐδαμῶς, *adv.*, by no means, in no wise.
οὐδέ (οὐ δέ), but not; and not; not even.
οὐδείς, οὐδεμία, οὐδέν (οὐδέ εἷς), not even one, no one, none.
οὐδέποτε, *adv.*, and not ever, never.
οὐδέπω, *adv.*, and not yet, not as yet.
οὐκ, not. (See οὐ.)
οὐκέτι, *adv.*, no more, no further, no longer.

οὔκουν, *adv.*, not therefore; so not; not then? *But* οὐκοῦν, therefore, then, accordingly, (*losing the negative force.*)
οὖν, *adv.*, then, therefore, accordingly, consequently.
οὐρ-ά, ᾶς, *f.*, the tail of beasts, birds, &c.; (a more general term than κέρκος, which see.)
οὐραν-ός, οῦ, *m.*, heaven, the firmament of heaven.
οὖς, ὠτός, *n.*, the ear; a handle or ear of a jar, &c.
οὔτε (οὐ τέ), and not; neither, nor.
οὔτις, οὔτινος (οὐ τίς), not any one, no one. *As proper name*, Οὖτις, *accus.* οὖτιν, Nobody, Noman.
οὗτος, αὕτη τοῦτο (see p. 57), this (*hic*), this well known (person.)
οὑτοσί, αὑτηί, τουτί (*hicce*), this man here, this identical individual.
οὕτω, or οὕτως (before a vowel), *adv.*, in this manner, thus.
οὐχ, *adv.*, not. (See οὐ.)
ὀφείλω, F. ὀφειλήσω, to owe, be in debt for (something), to be under an obligation; to be bound; doomed, destined.
ὀφθαλμ-ός, οῦ, *m.*, the eye.
ὄφ-ις, εως, *m.*, a serpent, snake.
ὄφλημα, ὀφλήματ-ος, *n.*, a fine, a debt.
ὄχλ-ος, ου, *m.*, a crowd of people, the populace, mob.
ὄψ-ις, εως, *f.*, a sight, appearance, vision; face; eye-sight.
ὄψ-ον, ου, *n.*, boiled meat; flesh (generally); anything taken with bread or flesh, as vegetables, fish, &c.

Π

πάγκἄλ-ος, η, ον, or -ος, -ον, all beautiful; all good.
παιδεύ-ω, -σω, to bring up a child; train, teach, educate.
παιδί-ον, ου, *n.*, a young child, little child, infant.

Παιήων, Παιήονος, or Παιάν, or Παιών, Pæon, the physician of the gods.
παῖς, παιδ-ός, *m.* or *f.*, a child (boy or girl); boy, youth; *f.* a girl, a slave.

παίω, F. παίσω (παιήσω), to strike, smite, knock.
παλαι-ός, ά, όν, old, aged, ancient, antique; venerable.
παλαίστρ-α, ας, f., a palæstra, wrestling school, gymnasium.
πάλιν, adv., back, backwards; again, afresh.
πάλλω, to wield, brandish, swing.
παμμεγέθ-ης, ης, ες, very great.
Πανόπ-η, ης, f., Panopé.
πανοῦργ-ος, ος, ον, ready for anything; knavish, roguish, villanous, crafty; up to everything.
πάνυ, adv., altogether, entirely.
παρ' for παρά.
παρά, prep., governing accus., gen., and dat. (see p. 34), beside. With accus., along, beside, to; with gen., from beside, from, by means of; with dat., beside, near, at, among.
παραβάλλω (see βάλλω), to throw beside, or to; give; put side by side. compare; deliver.
παραγίγνομαι (see γίγνομαι), to be near; to be present; stand by one, support.
παράδεισ-ος, ου, m., a park; pleasure grounds; paradise.
παραδίδωμι, to hand over, give up, deliver; grant, bestow.
παράδοξ-ος, ος, ον, contrary to expectation; strange, incredible.
παρακαλ-έω, έσω, to call to one; send for, invite; entreat; exhort; encourage.
παραλαμβάνω, to receive from another; receive; undertake.
παραλογίζομαι, to calculate wrong; cheat.
παραμένω, to stay with, remain, abide.
παραμυθέομαι, to encourage, exhort; console, soothe.
παράπαν (παρὰ πᾶν), adv., altogether, entirely.
παραπέμπω, to send past; escort, conduct, convoy; despatch.
παράσῖτ-ος, ος, ον, eating at another's table; hence, a flatterer, parasite.
παρατείνω, to stretch beside; protract; extend; defer.
παρατίθημι, to place beside; hold forth; propose; intrust.
παρει-ά, ᾶς, f., the cheek.
πάρειμι (see Irregular Verbs), to be beside, present, at hand.
πάρειμι (see Irregular Verbs), to go by, or past; pass over; come forward.
παρέχω (see ἔχω), to hold in readiness; afford, furnish, supply.
παρθέν-ος, ου, f., a maid, maiden.
παρίημι (see Irregular Verbs), to let fall beside; let pass; omit, neglect.
Πάρις, Πάριδ-ος, and Πάριος, m., Paris, son of Priam.
παρίστημι (see Irregular Verbs), to place near; present: pass. to stand near or by; assist.
Παρμενίων, Παρμενίων-ος, m., Parmenio, one of the generals of Alexander.
παροδίτ-ης, ου, m., a passer-by, traveller, wayfarer.
πάροδ-ος, ου, f., a way past or through, passage: ἐν παρόδῳ, by the way, in passing.
παροικ-έω, ήσω, to dwell beside, live near.
πᾶς, πᾶσα, πᾶν (see p. 45), all, the whole, any, every.
παστ-ός, οῦ, m., a bed-chamber.
πάσχω, F. πείσομαι, aor. ἔπαθον (pāti, from patior), P. πέπονθα, to suffer, endure; to be treated.
πατάσσω, πατάξω, to beat, knock, strike, wound.
πατ-έω, ήσω, to tread, walk; traverse; trample on.
πᾰτήρ, πατρός, (see p. 28), m., a father: in pl. parents, forefathers.
πατρίς, πατρίδ-ος, f. (patria), one's native country, fatherland.
παύω, F. παύσω, to put an end to, stop, allay: intrans. and mid. to cease, give over, desist.
πέδ-η, ης, f. (pedica), fetters.

πεδί-ον, ου, n., a plain, a flat country.
πείθω, F. πείσω, 2 aor. ἔπιθον, to persuade, prevail on, (governs accus.): in mid. to persuade one's self, believe, trust to; obey, listen to, (governs dat.)
πεῖρ-α, ας, f., a trial, attempt, experiment.
πειρ-άω, F. -άσω (but mid. πειράομαι more used), to try, attempt, strive.
πέλαγ-ος, εος, n. (pelagus), the open sea, the ocean.
πέλεκ-υς, εως, m., an axe, hatchet.
πέμπω, F. πέμψω, P. πέπομφα, to send; let go, dismiss.
πένης, πένητ-ος, m., a day-labourer; a poor man.
πέντε, indecl., five.
πέπειρ-ος, ος, ον, ripe, mellow, mature.
περ-άω, -άσω, to force (a passage) through; pass through or over; cross; penetrate; reach: but περάω, F. περάσω, to carry over sea for sale; to sell.
περί, prep., governing accus., gen. and dat., all round, about, near; concerning.
περιβάλλω, to throw around, surround; put on, (of clothes, &c.)
περιγίγνομαι, to overcome, surpass, be over and above; remain; escape; survive.
περιδ-έω, ήσω, to bind round, bandage.
περιέχω, to hold all round, embrace, surround, encompass; hold on by; surpass.
Περικλῆς, Περικλέους (see 'Ηρακλῆς), m., Pericles, a celebrated Athenian.
περιμένω, to wait for one, await, expect.
περιπλέκω, to fold around, cling to, embrace.
περιπόθητ-ος, ος, ον, much longed for, much loved or desired.
περιφέρω, to carry round or about, revolve.

περιχέω, F. περιχεῶ, to pour round or over; to spread out.
Περσεφόν-η, ης, f., Persephonê (Proserpine), wife of Hades, and queen of lower world.
Πέρσης, ου, m., Perses. (See p. 14, 5 (2), and p. 16, note.)
Πέρσης, ου, m., a Persian. (See p. 16, note.)
πέτρ-α, ας, f., a rock, a ledge of rock; while πέτρος means a piece of rock, a (small) stone.
πή, indef., somehow; some place, somewhere: interrog. πῆ, how, what way; whither, where.
πηγ-ή, ῆς, f., a fountain, spring, well; source.
πήγνυμι and πηγνύω, F. πήξω, P. πέπηγα, to make fast, fix, fasten; stiffen.
πηδ-άω, ήσω, or -ήσομαι, to spring, bound, leap; throb.
Πηλεύς, Πηλέως, m., Peleus, father of Achilles.
πηλίκ-ος, η, ον, how great, how large, of what size.
πήρ-α, ας, f., a leather pocket, wallet, scrip.
πήρωσ-ις, εως, f., maiming of the limbs or senses; blindness.
πιάζω, to lay hold of, catch.
πίθ-ος, ου, m., a wine-jar, flagon, jar.
πικρῶς, adv., from πικρός, bitterly, severely; sadly; harshly.
πῖμελ-ής, ής, ές, fat.
πινακίς, πινακίδ-ος, f., a little tablet, memorandum-book.
πίνω, F. πίομαι and πιοῦμαι, P. πέπωκα, to drink.
πιπράσκω, F. περάσω, P. πέπρακα, to sell. (See περάω, περάσω.)
πίπτω, F. πεσοῦμαι, 2 aor. ἔπεσον, P. πέπτωκα, to fall, fall down.
πιστεύ-ω, σω, to trust to, have confidence in, believe; obey.
πιστ-ός, ή, όν, trustworthy, faithful, true.
πιστ-όω, -ώσω, to make trustworthy, confirm faith: mid. give mutual pledges: give security.

Πιττακ-ός, οῦ, m., Pittacus, one of seven wise men of Greece.
Πλάτων, Πλάτων-ος, m., Plato.
πλεῖστ-ος, η, ον, superl. of πολύς, most, very much.
πλεί-ων, ων, ον, compar. of πολύς, more, greater.
πλέκ-ω, F. πλέξω, to twine, twist, plait, weave ; devise.
πλέ-ω, F. πλεύσομαι, to sail, travel by sea.
πλέ-ων, ων, ον, for πλείων, (which see.)
πληγ-ή, ῆς, f., a blow, stroke ; calamity, plague. (Lat. plāga.)
πλῆθ-ος, εος, n., a great number, crowd, multitude.
πλήν, adv. or prep., besides, except, save ; more than, over, beyond.
πλήττ-ω, or πλήσσ-ω, F. πλήξω, P. πέπληγα, to strike ; wound.
πλοῖ-ον, ου, n., a ship, merchantman, transport ; boat.
πλό-ος, contr. πλοῦς, gen. πλοῦ, and later πλόος (of 3d Declension), a sailing, voyage.
πλούσι-ος, α, ον, wealthy, rich.
πλουτ-έω, ήσω, to be rich.
πλουτ-ίζω, ίσω, Att. -ιῶ, to make rich, enrich.
Πλούτων, Πλούτων-ος, m., Pluto, god of nether world.
πνέ-ω, F. πνεύσω, or πνεύσομαι, to blow, breathe.
πνίγ-ω, F. πνίξω, to choke, suffocate, stifle, drown.
πόθεν, adv., whence ? by what means ? how ?
ποῖ, adv., whither (= quo : but πῇ = qua.) ποῖ χθονός, to what part of earth, (like ubi terrarum.)
ποι-έω, F. ήσω, to make, produce, cause, effect, bring to pass.
ποιητ-ής, οῦ, m., (literally, a maker), a poet, writer.
ποιμήν, ποιμέν-ος, m., a herdsman, shepherd.
ποίμνι-ον, ου, n., a herd of cattle, flock of sheep.
ποῖ-ος, α, ον, (qualis), of what kind, of what nature.

πολέμι-ος, α, ον (also -ος, -ος, -ον), belonging to war, hostile : οἱ πολέμιοι, the enemy.
πόλεμ-ος, ου, m., a battle, fight, war.
πόλ-ις, εως, f., a city ; state, republic.
πολίτ-ης, ου, m., a member of the body politic, citizen ; freeman.
πολλάκις, adv., many times, often, frequently.
πολυόμματ-ος, ος, ον, many-eyed.
πολύς, πολλή, πολύ (see p. 46), many, (opposed to ὀλίγος;) much; great. The neut. sing. and pl. are often used as adverbs.
Πολύφημ-ος, ου, m., Polyphemus, one of the Cyclopes, and son of Neptune.
πον-έω, ήσω, to toil, labour ; be afflicted, distressed.
πονηρ-ός, ά, όν, (literally, causing pain), painful, hurtful ; worthless, bad, wicked.
πορεύ-ω, σω, to cause to go, bring, carry : mid. to go, travel, journey ; sail.
πορθμεῖ-ον, ου, n., a passage over, ferry, ferry-boat ; fare for crossing a ferry.
πορθμ-εύς, έως, m., a ferryman, boatman, sailor.
πόρθμι-ον, ου, n. (Same as πορθμεῖον.)
πορφυρίς, πορφυρίδ-ος, f., a purple robe.
Ποσειδῶν, Ποσειδῶνος, m., Poseidon (Neptune), god of the sea.
πόσ-ος, η, ον, (quantus,) of what number ? of what kind ? how much ? how great ?
ποταμ-ός, οῦ, m., a river, stream.
πότε, interrog. when ? at what time ? indef. at some time, once upon a time.
πότερον, interrog. adv. (utrum), whether or no ?
πότερ-ος, α, ον, whether of the two ? (uter.)
πότ-ος, ου, m., a drinking, drinking-bout, carousal. παρὰ πότον, while

drinking (inter pocula). ποτόν φάρμακον, a potion.
ποῦ, interrog. adv., where? how? As indef. πού (enclitic), somewhere, somehow.
πούς, ποδ-ός, m., a foot, leg.
πρᾶγμα, πράγματ-ος, n., a thing done, deed ; matter, affair.
πράττ-ω, or πράσσω, F. πράξω, to do, work, effect, accomplish.
πρέπει, impers. (decet), it is suitable, it becomes, it is seemly.
πρέπ-ω, to be distinguished (among a number), to be manifest; be like; become, beseem.
πρέσβυς, πρέσβυ-ος, and πρέσβεως, an old man, elder ; ambassador.
Πρίαμ-ος, ου, m., Priam.
πρίασθαι, to buy, (2 aor. of ὠνέομαι.)
πρίν, adv., before, formerly, before that (priusquam.)
πρό, prep., governing gen., before (of place), in front of ; before (of time) ; by reason of, for, through.
πρόβατ-ον, ου, n., used mostly in pl. πρόβατα, cattle, (especially) sheep.
προδίδωμι, to give up, betray, abandon.
προῖκα, adv. (really the accus. of προίξ, a gift), freely, gratuitously (gratis.)
προκάλυμμα, προκαλύμματ-ος, n., a veil, curtain, screen ; cloak.
προκατακλίν-ω, to set one down before others (at meals): mid. to recline (at meals) in a more honourable place.
προνο-έω, to perceive beforehand, provide, anticipate.
προπηδ-άω, to spring (forward) before others.
πρός, prep., governing accus., gen., and dat., in front of ; from before ; near, at, to, towards, against.
προσαγορεύ-ω, to address, salute, accost.
προσάπτω, προσάψω, to fasten to, attach to, append : mid. to touch, lay hold on, reach.
πρόσειμι (εἶμι, to go), to go towards, advance, approach.

προσέρχομαι, to go to ; come forward ; approach.
προσέτι, adv., moreover, besides.
προσέχω, to hold to ; bring near ; give attention to (π. τὸν νοῦν) : mid. to cling to, remain with.
προσθήκ-η, ης, f., an addition, supplement, a douceur, into the bargain.
προσκαλ-έω, F. έσω, to call to, summon, invite ; call to one's help.
προσκυν-έω, F. -ήσομαι, to kiss the hand to ; hence, do homage, worship, adore.
προσλαμβάνω, receive in addition ; take to one as partner ; acquire.
(προσόπτομαι), προσοράω, προσόψομαι, to look to, behold, see, regard.
προσπαίζω, F. προσπαίξομαι, to make sport with, joke with, make game.
προσπίπτω (see πίπτω), to fall upon or against; attack ; prostrate one's self before.
προστάττ-ω, or προστάσσω, F. προστάξω, to place in a position, arrange ; appoint, enjoin, intrust.
προστίθημι, to put to, add : mid. associate one's self with; assign.
προσφέρω (see φέρω), to bring to, to add, contribute ; to attach ; approach ; agree with.
προτάττ-ω, or προτάσσω, F. προτάξω, to post in front, appoint before : mid. to take the lead.
πρότερον, adv., before, sooner, earlier, (neut. of following.)
πρότερ-ος, α, ον (πρό), before others ; in front of ; sooner, earlier.
προτιμάω, to honour specially ; prefer ; esteem highly.
προτρέχω (see τρέχω), to run forward ; outrun.
προὔργου, contr. for πρὸ ἔργου, (literally, for a work or object, i.e., of service,) useful ; profitable.
προφέρω, to carry forward, advance ; allege ; propose ; display.
προχωρ-έω, -ήσω, to go forward, advance ; succeed.
πρώην, adv., lately ; just now ; day before yesterday ; the other day.

πρῴρα, or πρῷρα, ας, f., the prow; fore part of the ship, ship's head, bow.
Πρωτεσίλα-ος, ου, m., Protesilaus, the first Greek killed at the siege of Troy.
πρῶτον, and πρῶτα, adv. (neut. sing. and pl. of following), first; in the first place (primum).
πρῶτ-ος, η, ον (πρό), first, foremost; earliest.
πτέρυξ, πτέρυγ-ος, f., a wing.
Πτοιόδωρ-ος, ου, m., Ptœodorus.
Πτολεμαῖ-ος, ου, m., Ptolemy.
Πυθαγόρας, gen. Πυθαγόρου, m., Pythagoras the philosopher.
πύλ-η, ης, f., a valve or wing (of folding-doors): usually in pl. the gates (of a city, as opposed to θύρα, a house door).
πυνθάνομαι, F. πεύσομαι, P. pass. πέπυσμαι, to ask, inquire; hear, learn.
πῦρ, πυρ-ός, n. (in pl. τὰ πυρά, and dat. πυροῖς), fire; watch-fires.
πυρ-ός, οῦ, m., wheat.
πυρ-όω, F. ώσω, to set on fire; burn with fire; to fire, (harden by fire.)
πυρριχ-ίζω, F. -ίσω, to dance the war-dance, or Pyrric dance.
πώγων, πώγων-ος, m., the beard.
πωλ-έω, F. -ήσω, to exchange, barter; sell.
πῶμα, πώματ-ος, n., a lid, cover.
πώποτε, adv., at any time :—usually joined with a negative.
πῶς, interrog. adv., how? in what way? indef., in any way; in some way, somehow or other.

Ρ

ῥάβδ-ος, ου, f., a rod, wand, stick.
ῥᾴδι-ος, α, ον, (also -ος, -ος, -ον,) easy; ready; obliging.
ῥᾳδίως, adv., easily; readily.
ῥάκ-ος, εος, n., a rag; ragged garment.
ῥᾴων, ων, n., ῥᾷον, compar. of ῥᾴδιος, more easy.
ῥεῦμα, ῥεύματ-ος, n., a stream, river; flood.
ῥέω, F. ῥεύσομαι, to flow, run, gush.
ῥήτωρ, ῥήτορ-ος, m. (rhetor), a public speaker, orator; pleader.
ῥιζοτόμ-ος, -ος, -ον, cutting roots (for medical purposes); herb doctor; quack.
ῥίπτω, F. ῥίψω, to throw, cast, hurl.
ῥίς, ῥιν-ός, f., the nose: in pl. the nostrils.
ῥόπαλ-ον, ου, n., a club, cudgel; stick.

Σ

σαίρ-ω, F. σαρῶ, to grin (ringi); to sweep; clean.
σάκ-ος, εος, n., a shield.
σάνδαλ-ον, ου, n., a wooden sole, sandal; woman's shoe; slipper.
σαπρ-ός, ά, όν, n., rotten, putrid; old; filthy.
Σαρδανάπᾰλ-ος, ου, m., Sardanapālus, last king of Assyrian empire of Nineveh.
σατράπ-ης, ου, m., a satrap; i.e., governor of a (Persian) province.
σαυτοῦ, contr. for σεαυτοῦ.
σεαυτ-οῦ, ῆς, of thyself: a reflex. pron., on which see p. 56.
σείω, F. σείσω, to shake; disturb; move to and fro.
σελήν-η, ης, f., the moon.
Σεμέλ-η, ης, f., Semele, mother of Bacchus.
σεμν-ός, ή, όν, revered; august; holy; stately, majestic; dignified; proud, haughty.
Σερίφι-ος, ου, m., an inhabitant or native of Serīphus, one of the Cyclades islands.

σήμαντρ-ον, ου, n., a seal, a stamp.
Σιδών, Σιδῶν-ος, f., Sidon, a city of Phœnicia.
Σινωπ-εύς, έως, m., an inhabitant or native of Sinope, a town in Asia Minor, on south shore of Black Sea.
σῖτί-ον, ου, n., usually in pl. τὰ σῖτία, food made of corn, bread; victuals, provisions.
σῖτ-ος, ου, m., but in pl. τὰ σῖτα, corn; meal, flour; bread; food, provisions.
σιωπ-άω, F. -ήσομαι, to be silent, keep silence; not to speak of, keep secret.
σκαφίδι-ον, ου, n., a small vessel or tub; a little skiff or boat.
σκέλ-ος, εος, n., the leg.
σκεῦ-ος, εος, n., a vessel or implement: in pl. utensils; gear, tackle; baggage (of an army); stores, &c.
σκην-ή, ῆς, f., a covered place; tent; hut; house.
σκι-ά, ᾶς, f., a shadow, shade.
σκιρτ-άω, -ήσω, to spring, leap, bound; frolic about.
σκληρ-ός, ά, όν, dry; hard; harsh, rough, stern.
σκοπ-έω, F. σκέψομαι, F. ἔσκεμμαι (from σκέπτομαι), to look at; inspect, examine; contemplate.
Σκύθ-ης, ου, m., a Scythian.
σκύλαξ, σκύλακ-ος, m. and f., a young dog, whelp, puppy.
σκώπτω, F. σκώψομαι, to ape, mimic; scoff at, jeer, mock; cut jokes on.
σοβ-έω, ήσω, to say σοῦ, σοῦ (shoo, shoo) to a bird; to drive away; to shake; to bustle along, go hastily: σόβει ἐς Ἄργος, off with you to Argos.
Σόλων, Σόλων-ος, m., Solon.
σοφιστ-ής, οῦ, m., a skilled person; clever man; a teacher; a sophist.
σοφ-ός, ή, όν, skilled; clever; wise; prudent; shrewd.
σπήλαι-ον, ου, n., a cave, grotto, cavern.

σπουδ-άζω, -άσω, or -άσομαι, to make haste; be eager, in earnest; busy.
σπουδ-ή, ῆς, f., haste, speed; zeal; anxiety.
σταθμός, οῦ, m., pl. often, τὰ σταθμά, a shelter; dwelling; quarters, halting-place, or stage.
στασι-άζω, F. -άσω, to make a rising; rebel, revolt; quarrel; be at variance with.
στέλλω, F. στελῶ, P. ἔσταλκα, to set, place; get ready; send; dispatch; start.
στεναγμ-ός, οῦ, m., groaning; sighing; wailing.
στένω (used in pres. and imperf. only), to groan; lament; bewail.
στερ-έω, F. -ήσω, pass. usually στέρομαι, to deprive of; bereave of.
στέφαν-ος, ου, m., a wreath, garland; fillet; crown.
στέφω, F. στέψω, to surround; wreathe; crown.
στῆθ-ος, εος, n., the breast; the heart, (as seat of feeling.)
στήλ-η, ης, f., an upright stone, a pillar, post; gravestone.
στολ-ή, ῆς, f., equipment; clothing, dress; a garment, robe.
στόμα, στόματ-ος, n., the mouth, an opening; passage, &c.
στρατεύομαι, and στρατεύω, to take the field; be in active service; act as a soldier.
στρατηγ-έω, F. -ήσω, to act as a στρατηγός, or general; to command.
στρατηγ-ός, οῦ, m., the leader of an army; a general.
στρατι-ά, ᾶς, f., an army; squadron; (military) expedition.
στρατιώτ-ης, ου, m., a soldier.
στρατόπεδ-ον, ου, n., a camp, encampment; squadron.
στρουθί-ον, ου, n., dimin. of στρουθός, a young or little bird; especially a sparrow.
σύ, σοῦ, 2d pers. pron. (see p. 54), thou.
συγγιγνώσκω, F. συγγνώσομαι, to

think with, agree with ; yield to, allow ; confess ; pardon.

συγγνώμ-η, ης, f., fellow-feeling with ; allowance ; pardon.

συγκαλ-έω, F. -έσω, to call together, invite.

συγχαίρω, to rejoice with, congratulate.

συγχωρ-έω, F. -ήσω and -ήσομαι, to unite; make concessions to ; agree ; pardon.

συλλαμβάνω (see λαμβάνω), to take along with ; seize, apprehend ; comprehend ; assist.

συμπλέω, F. συμπλεύσομαι, to sail along with.

συμπόσι-ον, ου, n., a drinking-party ; feast, banquet.

συμφέρω (see φέρω), to collect ; contribute ; to agree together ; to conduce to, profit. τὸ σύμφερον.

συμφορ-ά, ᾶς, f., an event, chance ; misfortune, calamity.

σύν, prep. with dat., together with, with. (See p. 15.)

συνάγω, F. συνάξω, to lead or bring together, collect, assemble.

συναντ-άω, F. -ήσω, to fall in with, meet.

συναρπά-ζω, -σω, (corripere), to seize and carry off ; to carry off.

συνδιαπράττ-ω, συνδιαπράξω, to assist in performing.

συνδόκει (placet), impers., it pleases; it seems good.

συνεῖδον, 2 aor. of συνοράω, to see plainly ; understand.

συνεῖδον, 2 aor. of σύνοιδα (see οἶδα, Irregular Verbs), to be conscious, convinced of.

σύνειμι, συνέσομαι (see εἰμί), to have intercourse with, associate with.

συνείρω, to string together, connect; continue in discourse.

συνεπιλαμβάνω, to lay hold of along with (some one) ; to take a hand at, assist.

συνέρχομαι (see ἔρχομαι), to come together, meet; live with

συνεστι-άω, F. -άσω, to entertain in one's house ; feast along with.

συνεχῶς, adv. (from adj. συνεχής, holding together), continuously, incessantly.

συνίημι, or ξυνίημι (see ἵημι), to throw together, i.e., conjecture ; perceive, understand.

συνομολογ-έω, F. -ήσω, to confess, acknowledge ; promise.

(συνόπτομαι), συνοράω, F. συνόψομαι, to see at a glance; survey; behold.

συνουσί-α, ας, f., friendly intercourse ; sociality ; geniality.

συντρίβ-ω, F. συντρίψω, (con-tundere), to bruise, crush, smash, shatter.

συρρέω, F. συρρεύσομαι, F. συνερρύηκα, to flow together. meet, combine.

σῦ-s, συ-ός, m. or f. (see μῦς, p. 26), a swine. pig, hog, boar, sow.

συστρατιώτ-ης, ου, m., a fellow-soldier.

σφαῖρ-α, ας, f., a ball, sphere, globe.

σφάλλω, F. σφαλῶ, 1 aor. ἔσφηλα, to cause to stumble or fall ; to foil : pass. to be foiled ; to make a mistake, to blunder.

σφενδόν-η, ης, f. (funda), a sling.

σφραγ-ίζω, F. -ίσω, Att. -ιῶ, to seal, stamp, mark.

σχολ-άζω, F. -άσω, to be at leisure, to have time to do a thing.

σχολαστικ-ός, ή, όν, one having leisure ; an idler ; a simpleton.

σχολ-ή, ῆς, f., leisure ; rest, case; idleness.

σώζω, F. σώσω, to save, rescue, preserve.

Σωκράτ-ης, -εος (-ους), m., Socrates.

σῶμα, σώματ-ος, n., a body, a corpse ; carcass.

σῶ-ος, α, ον, contr. σῶς, a defective adj., safe, sure, certain.

σωτηρί-α, ας, f., safety, deliverance.

σώφρ-ων, ων, ον, of sound mind ; self-controlling, moderate ; prudent, wise.

T

τἀληθές, for τὸ ἀληθές, the truth, the real thing.
ταραχώδ-ης, ης, ες, perplexing, confusing.
τάττω, or τασσω, F. τάξω, to arrange, put in order; draw up; appoint.
ταῦρ-ος, ου, m., a bull.
τάχιστ-ος, η, ον, superl. of ταχύς, quickest, swiftest, speediest.
ταχύ, adv., neut. of following, quickly.
ταχ-ύς, εῖα, ύ, swift, quick, fast, speedy.
ταῶς, ταῶ, m., a peacock.
τέ, enclitic conj., and. (Lat. que.)
τεῖχ-ος, εος, n., a wall, (especially that of a city.)
τέκν-ον, ου, n., a child; offspring.
τελευτ-άω, ήσω, to bring to an end; to end one's life; to die.
τέλ-ος, εος, n., an end, limit: as adv., in fine.
τέμνω, F. τεμῶ, aor. ἔτεμον (or ἔταμον), to cut, hew, &c.
τένων, τένοντ-ος, m., a sinew, muscle.
τεράστιος, ος, ον, strange, monstrous.
τέσσαρες, or τέτταρες, four.
τετραίνω, or τιτράω, F. τρήσω, to bore through.
τέττιξ, τέττιγ-ος, m., (cicāda,) a grasshopper.
τηλικ-οῦτος, -αύτη, -οῦτο, of such a size or age; so young.
τήμερον, or σήμερον, adv., this same day, to-day.
τηνικαῦτα, at this or that time of day; then, at that time.
τί, adv., neut. of τίς, what? why?
τίθημι (see Irregular Verbs), to place, set, fix, settle; make.
Τιθων-ός, οῦ, m., Tithonus, brother of Priam.
τίκτω, F. τέξω, aor. ἔτεκον, to bring forth, beget, procure.
τίλλω, F. τιλῶ, aor. ἔτιλα, (Lat. vellico), to pluck, pull, pluck out.
τιμ-άω, ήσω, to honour, reverence, worship; value.

τίμ-ή, ῆς, f., worth; honour, esteem; worship; regard.
τιμωρ-έω, ήσω, to punish, take vengeance on.
τιμωρί-α, ας, f., revenge, vengeance, punishment.
τινάσσω, F. τινάξω, to brandish, shake; cause to quiver.
τίς, indef., some one, any one; a certain person. (See p. 33.)
τίς, interrog., who? which? what? (See p. 33.)
Τισσαφέρν-ης, -εος, (-ους), Tissaphernes, a Persian satrap and general.
τίτραω and τιτραίνω, late forms of τετραίνω, to bore through, pierce.
τλήμ-ων, -ων, -ον, patient; bold, wretched.
τοί (old dat. for τῷ), adv., therefore, accordingly; in truth, truly.
τοιγαροῦν, adv., so then; assuredly, certainly; wherefore.
τοίνυν, adv., therefore, then; moreover, furthermore.
τοι-οῦτος, -αύτη, -οῦτο, or -οῦτον, of such kind, of such nature.
τοῖχ-ος, ου, m., a wall (of a house or court.)
τολμά-ω, F. ήσω, to have the courage to (do), to dare; undertake; venture.
τολμηρί-α, ας, f., boldness.
τολοιπόν, adv., for the future; for the rest; accordingly.
τόπ-ος, ου, m., a place, spot (locus); a passage in a book.
τοσαυτάκις, adv., so many times, so often.
τοσ-οῦτος, -αύτη, -οῦτο, or -οῦτον, so much; so great; so numerous.
τότε, adv., at that time, then.
τοὔνομα, contr. for τὸ ὄνομα, the name.
τράπεζ-α, ης, f., a table; dining-table.
τραυματί-ας, ου, m., a wounded man.
τράχηλ-ος, ου, m., the throat, neck.

GREEK VOCABULARY. 211

τράχ-ύς, εῖα, ύ, rough, rugged; harsh; savage.
τρεῖς, τρεῖς, τρία, three. (See p. 53.)
τρέπω, F. τρέψω, 2 aor. ἔτραπον, P. τέτροφα, to turn, alter; rout: *mid.* and *pass.* turn one's self to.
τρέφω, F. θρέψω, P. τέτροφα, to make solid, *i.e.*, to thicken; *hence*, to fatten, nourish, feed.
τρέχω, F. θρέξομαι, or δραμοῦμαι, 2 aor. ἔδραμον, to run, hasten, hurry.
τρίβω, F. τρίψω, to rub, thrash, grind; wear down; spend.
τρίβων, τρίβων-ος, *m.*, a worn garment, a threadbare cloak or robe.
τριήρ-ης, ης, ες (τρίς, and ἄρω), triply equipped; *hence*, as a *fem. subst.* ἡ τριήρης (*scil.* ναῦς), a trireme, or ship with three banks of oars.
τρίς, *adv.* (τρεῖς), three times.
τρίτ-ος, η, ον, third.
Τροί-α, ας, *f.*, Troy, The Troad.
τρόπαι-ον, ου, *n.*, (*tropæum*,) a trophy.
τρόπ-ος, ου, *m.*, (τρέπω,) a turn, way, means; direction; turn of mind, disposition.

τροπωτήρ, τροπωτῆρ-ος, *m.*, a thole-strap; an oar-loop, or twisted leathern thong, which fastened the oars to the thole.
τροφ-ή, ῆς, *f.*, food, nutriment; rearing.
τροφ-ός, οῦ, *m.* and *f.*, a rearer, feeder, nurse.
τρύβλι-ον, ου, *n.*, a cup, bowl.
τρύζω, (used only in *pres.* and *imperf.*,) to make a low murmuring noise, to murmur, buzz; sing.
τρυφ-ή, ῆς, *f.*, softness; luxury; effeminacy; conceit.
Τρωάς, Τρωάδ-ος, *f.*, the district around Troy; The Troad.
τρώγω, F. τρώξομαι, aor. ἔτραγον, to chew, gnaw (as herbivorous animals.)
τυγχάνω, F. τεύξομαι, aor. ἔτυχον, to hit, hit upon; happen upon; meet by chance; gain.
τυφλ-ός, ή, όν, blind; dark; obscure.
τυφλ-όω, F. ώσω, to make blind, deprive of sight.

Υ

ὑβρ-ίζω, F. -ιῶ, and ὑβριοῦμαι, to act insolently towards; to outrage, insult.
ὕβρ-ις, εως, *f.*, violence; insolence; outrage.
ὑβριστ-ής, οῦ, *m.*, an overbearing person, an insolent man.
ὑγίει-α, ας, *f.*, health, soundness of body or of mind.
ὑγι-ής, ής, ές, healthy, sound, strong, hearty.
ὕδρ-ος, ου, *m.*, a water-serpent.
ὕδωρ, ὕδατ-ος, *n.*, water.
υἱ-ός, οῦ, *m.*, a son. There is a form, υἱέος in the *gen.*, υἱεῖ in the *dat.*, &c., as if from a *nom.*, υἱεύς.
ὕλ-η, ης, *f.*, a wood, forest; timber.
ὑπάρχω, F. ὑπάρξω, to begin; to begin to exist,—*i.e.*, arise, be; to belong to.

ὑπεισέρχομαι, to come in by stealth, to come in unawares.
ὑπεναντίον, *adv.*, *neut.* of *adj.* ὑπεναντίος, in opposition to, on the contrary.
ὑπέρ, *prep.*, with *accus.* and *gen.*, over, above; beyond, across; for the sake of.
ὑπέρ-α, ας, *f.*, (ὑπέρ,) usually in *pl.*, the uppermost ropes; the mainsail brace.
ὑπερεκ-τίνω, F. -τίσω, P. -τέτικα, to pay on behalf of another; to pay for.
ὑπερέρχομαι, to pass over, go beyond; exceed.
(ὑπερόπτομαι), ὑπεροράω, F. ὑπερόψομαι, to overlook, let pass; despise, slight.
ὑπέρογκ-ος, ος, ον, exceedingly swol-

ἰen; large, very great; very important.
ὑπερχαίρω, to rejoice exceedingly.
ὑπηρεσί-α, ας, f., a ship's crew; hard service; assistance, attendance; obedience.
ὑπηρετ-έω, F. -ήσω, to do service for, work for; aid, serve, assist.
ὑπηρέτ-ης, ου, m., a rower, seaman; labourer; servant, attendant.
ὑπισχνέομαι, F. ὑποσχήσομαι, to undertake, promise, engage.
ὕπν-ος, ου, m., sleep.
ὑπό, prep., with accus., towards and under, beneath: gen. from under, by: dat. under, beneath.
ὑποβολιμαῖ-ος, α, ον, substituted by stealth; supposititious, counterfeit.
ὑποδέχομαι, ὑποδέξομαι, to receive kindly; give ear to, listen to; promise.
ὑποζύγι-ον, ου, n., a beast of burden or draught.
ὑποκριτ-ής, οῦ, m., an actor; a dissembler, hypocrite.
ὑπολαμβάνω, to take up; answer, reply; engage; suppose.
ὑπομένω, to remain behind; endure, bear; hold out, persevere.
ὑπομιμνήσκω, F. ὑπομνήσω, to remind, recollect, remember.
ὑποπνίγω, to choke, suffocate; drown.
ὑποταράττω, or -σσω, F. ὑποταράξω, to stir up an under-current of trouble; to trouble a little, disturb: pass. to be somewhat troubled.
ὑποφέρω, F. ὑποίσω, to bear up; undergo, sustain; endure, suffer.
ὕστερον, adv. (neut. of adj. ὕστερος), afterwards, at length; after, too late.
ὑφ', for ὑπό, under.
ὑφαπλ-όω, F. -ώσω, to spread out beneath; unfold.
ὑψηλ-ός, ή, όν, lofty, high.

Φ

φαγών, 2 aor. part. of ἐσθίω, to eat.
φαίνω, F. φανῶ, aor. ἔφηνα, to bring to light, show, exhibit: mid. and pass. to appear, seem.
φακ-ῆ, ῆς, f., a dish of lentils; pulse; porridge.
φανερ-ός, ά, όν, open, clear, visible, manifest, evident.
φαρμακ-εύς, έως, m., a medicine vendor; sorcerer; poisoner.
φάρμακ-ον, ου, n., a drug, medicine, poison.
φάσκω, strengthened form of φημί, to say, assert; affirm.
φέρω, F. οἴσω, 1 aor. ἤνεγκα, 2 aor. ἤνεγκον, P. ἐνήνοχα, to bear, carry; bring.
φεύγω, F. φεύξομαι, 2 aor. ἔφυγον, to flee away, run.
φήμ-η, ης, f., (fama,) a rumour, saying, voice, report; speech.
φημί, F. φήσω (see Irregular Verbs), to say, speak, declare.
φιλ-έω, F. -ήσω, to love, regard.
φιλί-α, ας, f., love, affection, friendship.
Φίλιππ-ος, ου, m., Philip.
φιλόκαλ-ος, ος, ον, loving the beautiful; an admirer of the fair.
φιλοκινδύνως, adv., in a foolhardy way, in a venturesome way.
φίλ-ος, η, ον, loved, dear; friendly: as subst. a friend.
φιλοσοφί-α, ας, f., love of learning; study, philosophy.
φίλτατ-ος, superl. of φίλος, most beloved, dearest.
φλέψ, φλεβ-ός, f. (sometimes m.), a vein.
φλυαρέω, to talk nonsense, play the fool, trifle: τὸ φλυαροῦν, for φλυαρέον, neut. of pres. part.
φοβ-έω, F. ήσω, to frighten, scare, terrify.
φορ-έω, F. ήσω, to bear, carry, wear.
φόρτ-ος, ου, m., a load, cargo, burden.

φρέαρ, φρέατ-ος, n., a well, cistern; pit.
φρον-έω, f. -ήσω, to think, consider, reflect.
Φρύξ, Φρυγ-ός, nom. pl. Φρύγες, m. or f., a Phrygian.
φυγάς, φυγάδ-ος, m. or. f., a fugitive, exile.
φυγ-ή, ῆς, f., flight, banishment, exile.
φυλακ-ή, ῆς, f., watching, guarding; a garrison; a prison.
Φυλάκι-ος, α, ον, of or belonging to Phylace.
φυλάττω, or -σσω, f. φυλάξω, to guard, watch, protect.
φύλλ-ον, ου, n., a leaf; in pl. leaves, foliage.
φύσ-ις, εως, f., nature, essence; shape; constitution.
φων-ή, ῆς, f., sound, voice, report.
φωνητικ-ός, ή, όν, suited for speaking; able to speak.
φώρ, φωρ-ός, m. (fur), a thief, smuggler.
φῶς, contr. for φάος, n., light; deliverance; joy.

X

Χαιρώνει-α, ας, f., Chæronea, a town in Bœotia.
χαίρω, f. χαιρήσω, to rejoice, be glad.
χαίτ-η, ης, f., long hair; a horse's or lion's mane; foliage (of trees).
χαλῖν-ός, οῦ, m. (pl. sometimes, τὰ χαλινά, n.), a bridle, bit, reins.
χαρί-εις, -εσσα, -εν (see p. 44), graceful, beautiful, elegant.
χαριέντως, adv. (χαρίεις), becomingly, decorously; gracefully.
χαρίζομαι. f. χαριοῦμαι, to gratify.
χάρις, χάριτ-ος, f., grace, favour, kindness; service; delight.
Χάρων, Χάρων-ος, m., Charon, ferryman of the Styx.
χαυν-όω, f. -ώσω, to make loose; render proud, puff up.
χεῖλ-ος, εος, n., the lip.
χειμών, χειμῶν-ος, m., a storm; winter.
χείρ, χειρ-ός, f., the hand.
χειροτον-έω, -ήσω, to stretch out the hand (in voting), to vote.
χελιδών, χελιδόν-ος, f., a swallow.
χηλ-ή, ῆς, f., a horse's hoof; a claw, a talon.
χήν, χην-ός, m. or f., a goose, gander.
χήρ-α, ας, f., a widow.
χθές, adv., yesterday.
χίλι-οι, αι, α, one thousand.
χιτών, χιτῶν-ος, m., an upper robe, frock, mantle; coat of mail.
χιών, χιόν-ος, f., snow.
χλαμύς, χλαμύδ-ος, f., a cloak, mantle, or cape; military cloak.
χόρτ-ος, ου, m., an enclosed place (hortus); feeding-ground; fodder, grass, hay.
χράομαι, inf. χρῆσθαι, to use, put in force; experience.
χρή, impers., it is fated, it is necessary; it behoves; one must.
χρῆμα, χρήματ-ος, n. (χράομαι), a thing that one needs; a thing, matter, affair: in pl. goods; money; property.
χρήσιμ-ος, η, ον, (also ος, ος, ον,) useful, serviceable; fit, proper.
χρόν-ος, ου, m., time; a period, season.
χρύσε-ος, α, ον, contr. χρυσ-οῦς, ᾶ, οῦν, made of gold, golden; gold-coloured.
χρυσί-ον, ου, n., dimin. from following, a piece of gold, gold; a gold coin; money.
χρυσ-ός, οῦ, m., gold; gold coin; money.
χύτρ-α, ας, f., an earthen pot, jar.
χωρίς, (1.) adv., separately; apart: (2.) As a prep. with gen., without; far from.

Ψ

ψαύ-ω, F. ψαύ-σω, to touch, graze, handle; reach; gain.
ψόφ-ος, ου, m., an inarticulate sound; noise, crash, din.
ψυχαγωγ-έω, F. -ήσω, to conduct the spirits of the dead to the lower world.
ψυχ-ή, ῆς, f., breath, life; soul, spirit.
ψύχ-ω, F. ψύξω, to blow; to cool, refresh, revive; to chill, dry up.

Ω

ὦ, interj., (of address), O! (of surprise or pain), ah! woe's (me.)
ὠδίς, ὠδῖν-ος, f., pain of child-birth, pang, throe.
ὠκ-ύς, εῖα, ύ, swift, fleet, rapid; keen.
ὠμόλιν-ον, ου, n., raw flax; coarse linen; a barber's towel or shoulder-cloth.
ὦμ-ος, ου, m., the shoulder (and upper arm, = humerus.) Also the shoulder of a beast, = armus.
ὠν-έομαι, F. -ήσομαι, to buy, purchase.
ὠ-όν, οῦ, n. (ovum), an egg.
ὥρ-α, ας, f. (hora), a season; time of day, hour; nick of time; time of life; age.
ὡς, conj., as (ut); that (quod.)
ὧς, adv., thus (sic.)
ὥσπερ, adv., as, even as, just as.
ὥστε, adv., like as, just as, so that wherefore.
ὠχρ-ός, ά, όν, pale, wan, bloodless.

ENGLISH VOCABULARY.

A

A (a certain), τίς.
About (around), περί (accus., gen., and dat.) : about (on both sides), ἀμφί, (accus., gen., and dat.)
Action, ἔργ-ον, n.: before we take action, πρὸ ἔργου.
Admire, θαυμάζ-ω, ἄγαμαι.
Advise, βουλεύ-ω, βουλεύ-ομαι.
Against, εἰς (accus.) ; ἐπί and πρός, (accus.)
Air, ἀήρ, ἀέρ-ος, m. (the lower air, properly) ; αἰθήρ, αἰθέρ-ος, (the upper air.)
All, every, πᾶς, πᾶσα, πᾶν ; ἅπας, ἅπασα, ἅπαν.
Along (parallel to), παρά, (accus.)
Along with, σύν (dat.) ; μετά (gen.)
Altar, βωμ-ός, οῦ, m.

Ambassador, πρεσβ-ύς, έως, m.
Among, ἐν, with dat.
Anchor, ἄγκυρ-α, as, f.
And, καί (τέ, δέ.)
Apple, μῆλ-ον, ου, n.
Aristippus, 'Αρίστιππ-ος, ου, m.
Army, στράτευμα, τος, n.; στρατί-α as, f.
Arrange, τάττω, or τάσσω ; F. τάξω
Artaxerxes, 'Αρταξέρξ-ης, ου, m.
Ass, ὄν-ος, ου, m. or f.
At, ἐπί (dat.) ; ἐν (dat.)
Athena (Minerva), 'Αθην-ᾶ, ᾶς, f.
Athens, 'Αθῆν-αι, ῶν, f. pl.
Athenian, 'Αθηναῖ-ος, ου, m. ; pl. οἱ 'Αθηναῖοι, the Athenians.
Away (from), ἀπό (gen.)

B

Bad, κακ-ός, ή, όν.
Ball, σφαῖρ-α, ας, f.
Barber, κουρ-εύς, έως, m.
Barley, κριθ-ή, ῆς, f.
Battle, μάχ-η, ης, f.
Be, εἰμί ; γίγνομαι.
Bear, ἄρκτ-ος, ου, m. or f.
Beard, πώγων, πώγων-ος, m. ; γένει-ον, ου, n.
Beast (wild), θήρ, θηρ-ός, m.; θηρί-ον, ου, n.: beast of burden, ὑποζύγι-ον.
Beautiful, καλ-ός, ή, όν ; χαρί-εις, εσσα, εν.
Because of, ἕνεκα (gen.) ; διά (gen.)
Becomingly, εὖ ; πρεπόντως.

Before, (i.e., previous to, or in front of,) πρό (gen.)
Beg off (for one's own satisfaction), ἐξαιτέ-ομαι.
Believe, πιστεύ-ω (dat.) ; πείθ-ομαι, (dat. or accus., and inf.)
Beside, παρά (dat.)
Bite, δάκνω ; F. δήξομαι ; 2 aor. ἔδακον.
Black, μέλ-ας, αινα, αν. (See p. 45)
Blessings, ἀγαθ-ά, ῶν, n.
Boar, σῦς, σὺ ός, m. ; κάπρ-ος, ου, m.
Boat, (floating vessel, generally,) πλοῖ-ον, ου, n. ; σκαφ-ίς, ίδος, f. ; σκάφι-ον, ου, n. ; σκάφ-η, ης, f.

Body, σῶμα, σώματ-ος, n.
Book, βιβλί-ον, ου, n.; βίβλ-ος, ου, f.
Both, conj., τέ; both—and, καί—καί; καί—τέ; τέ—τέ.
Boy, παῖς, παιδ-ός, m.
Bread (wheaten), ἄρτ-ος, ου, m.; (barley), μάζ-α, or μᾶζ-α, ης, f.
Bridge, γέφυρ-α, ας, f.
Bright, λαμπρ-ός, ά, όν.
Broad, εὐρ-ύς, εῖα, ύ.
Brother, ἀδελφ-ός, οῦ, m.
Bull, ταῦρ-ος, ου, m.; βοῦς, βο-ός, m.
Burn, καίω; F. καύσω.
Bushy (shaggy), δασ-ύς, εῖα, ύ; also, thickly wooded.
But, ἀλλά, δέ.

C

Cable, κάλ-ως, κάλ-ω, m. (See p. 21.)
Cake, μάζ-α, or μᾶζ-α, ης, f.; πλακοῦς, πλακοῦντ-ος, m.; πόπανον, n.
Call on (invoke), καλ-έω, ἔσω.
Carefully, ἐπιμελῶς, adv.; σπουδαίως, adv.
Carry, φέρω, κομίζω.
Cast, ῥίπτω, βάλλω.
Catch, αἱρέω; 2 aor. εἷλον:—λαμβάνω; 2 aor. ἔλαβον.
Cauldron, λέβης, λέβητ-ος, m.
Cavalry, ἡ ἵππος, οἱ ἱππεῖς.
Certain (a), τίς; (sure, firm), βέβαι-ος, α, ον.
Chamber. (See Room.)
Chase (in hunting), θήρ-α, ας, f.
Chase (to), διώκω.
Cheek, παρει-ά, ᾶς, f.
Chest (breast), στῆθ-ος, εος, n.
Chest (i.e., box), θήκ-η, ης, f.; κιβωτ-ός, οῦ, f.; λάρναξ, λάρνᾰκ-ος, f.
Child (son or daughter), παῖς; (infant), παιδί-ον, ου, n.; βρέφ-ος, εος, n.
Citizen, πολίτ-ης, ου, m.
City, πόλ-ις, πόλ-εως, f.; ἄστ-υ, ἄστ-εος, n.
Cloak, χλαμύς, χλαμύδ-ος, f.; τρίβων, τρίβων-ος, m., a thread-bare cloak.
Company (i.e., in company with), σύν: companionship, συνουσία.
Consult (i.e., take counsel with anybody), βουλεύω; more frequently, mid., βουλεύομαι (περί), or συμβουλεύομαί τινι περί τινος.
Cottage, σκην-ή, ῆς, f.; καλύβ-η, ης, f.
Counsel (take counsel). (See Consult, above.)
Court-yard, αὐλ-ή, ῆς, f.: the king's court or palace, αἱ βασιλέως θύραι.
Crane, γέραν-ος, ου, m.
Crop (to), κείρω.
Cup, φιάλ-η, ης, f.; κύλιξ, κύλικ-ος, f.; κύπελλ-ον, ου, n.
Cut, κείρ-ω, τέμνω.
Cutlass, μάχαιρ-α, ας, f.; ξίφ-ος, εος, n.
Cyrus, Κῦρ-ος, ου, m.

D

Daughter, θυγάτηρ, θυγατρ-ός, f; κόρ-η, ης, f.
Day, ἡμέρ-α, ας, f.; ὥρ-α, ας, f.
Deaf, κωφ-ός, ή, όν.
Dear, φίλ-ος, η, ον; φίλι-ος, a. ον, or ος, ος, ον.
Death, θάνατ-ος, ου, m.
Deep, βαθ-ύς, εῖα, ύ.
Deliberate, βουλεύ-ω, βουλεύ-ομαι.
Dense (of a wood, &c.), δασ-ύς, εῖα, ύ.
Descend, καταβαίν-ω.
Desire (wish), ἐθέλ-ω, or θέλ-ω.
Desire (order), κελεύ-ω.
Dinner, δεῖπν-ον, ου, n.
Doctor (physician), ἰατρ-ός, οῦ, m.
Door, θύρ-α, ας, f.
Down (from), κατά, with gen.
Dry, ξηρ-ός, ά, όν.

E

Each, ἕκαστ-ος, η, ον.
Eagle, ἀετ-ός, οῦ, m.
Eat, ἐσθίω; of herbivorous animals, τρώγω, usually.
Educate, παιδεύ-ω.
Egg, ὠ-όν, οῦ, n.
Empty, κεν-ός, ή, όν.

Enemy, πολέμι-ος, ου, m.; ἐχθρ-ός, οῦ, m.
Every, πᾶς, πᾶσα, πᾶν.
Expose, ἐκτίθημι.
Eye, ὀφθαλμ-ός, οῦ, m.; ὅμμα, ὅμματ-ος, n.

F

Faithful, πιστ-ός, ή, όν; ἀληθ-ής, ής, ές; βέβαι-ος, α, ον, or ος, ον.
Fall-into position, καθίσταμαι.
Farmer, γεωργ-ός, οῦ, m.
Father, πατήρ, πατρ-ός, m.
Ferocious, ἄγρι-ος, α, ον, and ος, ος, ον; ὠμ-ός, ή, όν.
Field, ἀγρ-ός, οῦ, m.
Fierce, ἄγρι-ος, α, ον.
Find, εὑρίσκ-ω.
Five, πέντε.
Floor (thrashing), ἅλως, ἅλω, f. (See p. 21.)
Flow, ῥέω, ῥεύσομαι.
Fly, μυῖ-α, ας, f.
Foolish, νήπι-ος, α, ον; μωρ-ός, ά, όν; or μῶρ-ος, α, ον.

For my, thy, his, her, our, &c., part, μέν in the first clause, followed by δέ in the second (and succeeding ones, if necessary).
For, (motion towards,) εἰς, with accus.; e.g., he sets out for Greece, i.e., to Greece.
Force, δύναμ-ις, εως, f.
Forest, ὕλ-η, ης, f.
Fore-part (of ship), πρώρ-α, ας, f.
Fox, ἀλώπηξ, ἀλώπεκ-ος, f.
Friend, φίλ-ος, ου, m.
Friendly, φίλ-ος, η, ον; φίλι-ος, α, ον, or ος, ος, ον.
From (beside), ἀπό, or παρά.
From (out of), ἐκ, or ἐξ.

G

Garden, κῆπ-ος, ου, m.; χόρτ-ος, ου, m.
Garment (of poverty), ῥάκ-ος, εος, n.
Gate, πύλ-η, ης, f.
Gazelle, δορκάς, δορκάδ-ος, f.
General, στρατηγ-ός, οῦ, m.
Giant, γίγας, γίγαντ-ος, m.
Girl, κόρ-η, ης, f.
Give, δίδωμι.
Give back, ἀποδίδωμι.
Glory, δόξ-α, ης, f.
God, θε-ός, οῦ, m.
Goddess, θε-ά, ᾶς, f.

Good, ἀγαθ-ός, ή, όν.
Goods, τὰ ἀγαθά.
Goose, χήν, χην-ός, m. or f.
Government, ἀρχ-ή, ῆς, f.
Grant, δίδωμι.
Great haste—in or with great haste, σὺν πολλῇ σπουδῇ.
Great, μέγας, μεγάλη, μέγα.
Greece, Ἑλλάς, Ἑλλάδ-ος, f.
Greek, Ἕλλην, Ἕλλην-ος, m.
Groom, ἱπποκόμ-ος, ου, m.
Guard, φυλάττ-ω, or σσω: F. φυλάξω

H

Habit, ἔθ-ος, εος, n.
Hair, κόμ-η, ης, f.; θρίξ, τρίχ-ός, f.
Hand, χείρ, χειρ-ός, f.
Harbour, λιμήν, λιμέν-ος, m.
Hare, λαγ-ώς, λαγ-ώ, m.
Haste, σπουδ-ή, ῆς, f.
He, αὐτ-ός, gen. οῦ, m., (but in this sense only in the *oblique cases*); ἐκεῖν-ος, ὅδε, (when *he* is emphatic, like *ille*); and the article ὁ. (See p. 56.)
Head, κεφαλ-ή, ῆς, f.
Hear, ἀκούω, (with *accus.* of *thing heard*, and gen. of *person from whom*.)
Here, ἐνθάδε, ἐνταῦθα.
Herself, ἑαυτῆς.
High, ὑψηλ-ός, ή, όν.

Himself, ἑαυτοῦ, contr. αὑτοῦ. (See p. 56.)
His, her, its, their, &c., expressed by *gen.* of αὐτ-ός, ἐκεῖν-ος, ἑαυτ-οῦ (when referring to the subject). The article often serves as a *possessive pronoun*.
Hit, τύπτ-ω; βάλλ-ω (to hit with something thrown).
Honey, μέλι, μέλιτ-ος, n.
Horse, ἵππ-ος, ου, m. and f.
Horseman, ἱππ-εύς, έως, m.; οἱ ἱππεῖς, cavalry.
House, οἰκ-ος, ου, m.; οἰκί-α, ας, f.; δόμ-ος, ου, n. (*domus*).
Hunt, διώκω, θηρεύω, θηράω.
Husbandman, γεωργ-ός, οῦ, m.; ἀρότ-ης, ου, m.
Hut, σκην-ή, ῆς, f.; καλύβ-η, ης, f.

I & J

I, ἐγώ. (See p. 54.)
Ignorant (unlearned), ἀμαθ-ής, ής, ές: (inexperienced), ἄπειρ-ος, ος, ον; νήπι-ος, ος, ον, or ος, α, ον.
In, ἐν, with *dat.*
Indeed, (I, indeed; *i.e.*, I, for my part,) ἐγὼ μέν: μήν; δή.
Infant, παιδί-ον, ου, n.; βρέφ-ος, εος, n.; νήπι-ος.

Infantry, πεζ-οί, ῶν, m.; τὸ πεζικόν.
Inscription, γράμματ-α, ων, n.; pl. of γράμμα, a letter.
Into, εἰς, with *accus.*
Island, νῆσ-ος, ου, f.
Itself, ἑαυτ-οῦ, αὐτ-οῦ, n.
Jackal, θώς, θω-ός, m.
Javelin, βέλ-ος, εος, n.; παλτ-όν, οῦ, n.
Judge, κριτ-ής, οῦ, m.

K

Key, κλείς, κλειδ-ός, f., (*clavis*.)
King, βασιλεύς; ἄναξ.

L

Lacedæmonian, Λακεδαιμόνι-ος, ου, m.
Land, γῆ, γῆς, f.; ἀγρ-ός, οῦ, m. (a piece of land for tillage).
Land (*verb*), *trans.* ἐκβιβάζω, ἐξάγω, ἀποβιβάζω: *intrans.* to go on shore, ἐκβαίνειν, ἀποβαίνειν, with τῆς νεώς sometimes added, and sometimes εἰς τὴν γῆν.

Large, μέγας. (See p. 46.)
Law, νόμ-ος, ου, m.
Learning, σοφί-α, ας, f.
Leave, λείπω.
Let go, λύω; let alone, ἐάω.
Letter (of the alphabet), γράμμα, τος, n.; στοιχεῖ-ον, ου, n.: epistle, ἐπιστολ-ή, ῆς, f.

ENGLISH VOCABULARY. 219

Liberty, ἐλευθερί-α, ας, f.
Light, (not heavy,) κοῦφ-ος, η, ον.
Line (of troops), τάξ-ις, εως, f.
Lion, λέων, λέοντ-ος, m.
Lioness, λέαιν-α, ης, f.
Lip, χεῖλ-ος, εος, n.
Live-long, πᾶς, πᾶσα, πᾶν, or ὅλος, η, ον, in the accus. in expressions of time; as, ὅλην τὴν νύκτα, the live-long night.
Loaf, ἄρτος, ου, m.
Long, μακρ-ός, ά, όν.
Lycurgus, Λυκοῦργ-ος, ου, m.

M

Maiden, κόρ-η, ης, f.
Majority (the), οἱ πολλοί.
Make laws, τίθημι νόμους.
Man, ἄνθρωπ-ος, ου, m.; ἀνήρ, ἀνδρ-ός, m.
Mane, χαίτ-η, ης, f.
Many, πολλ-οί, αί, ά.
Master, δεσπότ-ης, ου, m.
Meadow, λειμών, λειμῶν-ος, m.
Merchantman (ship), ὁλκάς, ὁλκάδ-ος, f.
Midnight: about midnight, περὶ μέσας νύκτας.
Month, μήν, μην-ός, m.
Moon, σελήν-η, ης, f.
Mother, μήτηρ, μητρ-ός, f.
Mountain, ὄρ-ος, εος, n.
Mouse, μῦς, μυ-ός, m.
Much, πολύς, πολλή, πολύ. (See p. 46.)
Muse, Μοῦσ-α, ης, f.
My, my own, ἐμ-ός, ή, όν; or gen. μοῦ, ἐμοῦ, ἐμαυτ-οῦ, ῆς, οῦ.

N

Narrow, στεν-ός, ή, όν.
Near, ἐγγύς, adv.; πλησίον, adv.; also παρά, with dat. or accus.
Neck, αὐχήν, αὐχέν-ος, m.; τράχηλ-ος, ου, m.
Night, νύξ, νυκτ-ός, f.: by night, νυκτός.
Nightingale, ἀηδών, ἀηδόν-ος, f.
Nine, ἐννέα.
Not, οὐ (οὐκ, οὐχ), in definite clauses, and those stating facts. With imperatives, with indefinite clauses, and with clauses expressing doubt, μή is used.

O

Of, (about,) περί: of, (out of,) ἐκ: of, (made of,) ἐκ. Of is generally expressed by the gen. of a subst., without any prep.
Old, παλαι-ός, ά, όν: old-man, γέρων, γέροντ-ος, m.
Old-woman, γραῦς, γρα-ός, f.
On, (of place,) ἐν, with dat.; ἐπί, with gen.: on, (signifying time), ἐν, or simply dative case; as, ἐν τῇ τρίτῃ ἡμέρᾳ, on the third day.
One, εἷς, μία, ἕν.
Only (adj., agreeing with noun), μόν-ος, η, ον: only (adv.), μόνον.
Order, bid, command, κελεύ-ω.
Our, ἡμέτερ-ος, α, ον, or gen. of pers. pron., ἡμῶν. Often not expressed at all, when it is very evident to whom "our, my, his," &c., refer. The article shows sufficiently the meaning, and becomes equal to a possessive. (See His.)
Out of, ἐκ, or ἐξ.

P

Palace, αὐλ-ή, ῆς, f.; βασίλει-α, ων, n. pl.
Pale, ὠχρ-ός, ά, όν; λευκ-ός, ή, όν.
Parched, ξηρ-ός, ά, όν.
Parent, γον-εύς, έως, m. or f.
Part, μέρ-ος, εος, n.
Pay, μισθ-ός, οῦ, m.
Peacock, τα-ῶς, τα-ῶ, m.
Perses, Πέρσ-ης, ου; voc. Πέρση.
Persian, Πέρσ-ης, ου; voc. Πέρσα.
Persuade, πείθ-ω.
Pillar, κίων, κίον-ος, m.: a tombstone, στήλ-η, ης, f.
Plain, πεδί-ον, ου, n.
Plait, πλέκ-ω.
Plato, Πλάτων, Πλάτων-ος, m.
Ploughman, ἀρότ-ης, ου, m.
Poet, ποιητ-ής, οῦ, m.
Poor, πτωχ-ός, ή, όν.
Poplar, αἴγειρ-ος, ου, f.

Port, λιμήν, λιμέν-ος, m.
Portion, μέρ-ος, εος, n.
Position,—to fall into position, καθίσταμαι.
Post one's self, καθίσταμαι.
Priest, ἱερ-εύς, έως, m.
Prison, φυλακ-ή, ῆς, f.; δεσμ-οί, ῶν, m. pl.
Prophet, μάντ-ις, εως, m.
Province, ἀρχ-ή, ῆς, f.
Prow, πρῷρ-α, ας, f.
Prudence, σοφί-α, ας, f.; φρόνησ-ις, εως, f.; σωφροσύν-η, ης, f.
Purse, πήρ-α, ας, f.; βαλάντι-ον (or βαλλάντιον), ου, n.
Pursue, διώκω.
Put-in-prison, βάλλω, or δίδωμι, εἰς φυλακήν.
Put-in-position, (of troops), καθίστημι.

Q

Queen, βασίλει-α, ας, f.; but βασιλεία means sovereign power.
Quickly, ταχύ, ταχέως, adv.; διὰ τάχους; ἀπὸ τάχους.

R

Razor, ξυρ-όν, οῦ, n.
Remain, μένω.
Return, (give back,) ἀποδίδωμι.
Review, ἐξέτασ-ις, εως, f.
Review, i.e., hold a review, ποιεῖσθαι ἐξέτασιν.
Revolt, ἀφίστημι.
Rich, πλούσι-ος, α, ον; ὄλβι-ος, α, ον.
Ride, ἱππεύω.
River, ποταμ-ός, οῦ, m.
Road, way, journey, ὁδ-ός, οῦ, f.

Robe (of wealth), cloak, χλαμύς, χλαμύδ-ος, f.: (of poverty), τρίβων. (See Cloak.)
Rod, ῥάβδ-ος, ου, f.
Room (upper), ἀνώγ-εων, ἀνώγ-εω, n.; ὑπερῷ-ον, ου, n.
Rope (cable), κάλ-ως, κάλ-ω, m.
Rule, βασιλεύω; ἄρχω (in active); κρατέω, (the last two governing gen. or dat.)
Run, θέω; τρέχω, F. δραμοῦμαι.

S

Safety, σωτηρί-α, ας, f.
Sail, πλέω; F. πλεύσομαι, (or πλεύσω.)

Sailor, ναύτ-ης, ου, m.
Same (the), ὁ αὐτ-ός, ή, ό, contr. αὑτός, αὑτή, ταὐτό, or ταὐτόν.

ENGLISH VOCABULARY. 221

Savage, ἄγρι-ος, α, ον.
Say, λέγω.
Scut (tail of hare), κέρκ-ος, ου, f.
Scythian, Σκύθ-ης, ου, m.
Sea, sea-shore, θάλαττ-α, or -σσα, gen. ης, f. : by land and sea, καὶ κατὰ γῆν καὶ κατὰ θάλατταν.
See, βλέπω, ὁράω.
Sell, πωλέω.
Send, στέλλω, ἀποστέλλω, πέμπω.
Send for (to one's self), μεταπέμπομαι.
Serpent, ὄφ-ις, ὄφ-εως, m.
Servant, ὑπηρέτ-ης, ου, m.; οἰκέτ-ης, ου, m.; θεράπων, θεράποντ-ος, m.; δμώς, δμω-ός, m. (rare in prose.)
Set free, λύω.
Seven, ἑπτά.
Shaggy, δασ-ύς, εῖα, ύ; λάσι-ος, α, ον; and λάσι-ος, ος, ον.
Sharp, ὀξ-ύς, εῖα, ύ (of anything—instrument, pain, person, &c.)
Shave, κείρω, ἀποκείρω, ξυράω, or ξυρέω.
Shear, ἀποκείρω, κείρω.
Sheep (a), οἶς, οἰ-ός, m. or f.
Shepherd, ποιμήν, ποιμέν-ος, m.
Shield, ἀσπίς, ἀσπίδ-ος, f.
Ship, ναῦς, νεώς, f. ; πλοῖ-ον, ου, n.
Silver, ἄργυρ-ος, ου, m. : made of silver, ἀργύρε-ος, α, ον, contr. ἀργυροῦς, ᾶ, οῦν.
Six, ἕξ.
Slave, δοῦλ-ος, ου, m.

Slay, κτείνω, ἀποκτείνω.
Sling, σφενδόν-η, ης, f. : to sling, σφενδονά-ω.
Small, μικρ-ός, ά, ον.
Smooth, λεῖ-ος, α, ον.
Snow, χιών, χιόν-ος, f.
Socrates, Σωκράτ-ης, εος, contr. ους, m.
Soldier, στρατιώτ-ης, ου, m. : heavy-armed soldier, ὁπλῖτ-ης, ου.
Some, τὶς, τὶς, τί.
Some (kind), τίς, τίς, τί.
Somewhere, ποῦ (enclitic.)
Son, υἱ-ός, οῦ, m.
Speak, (speak of,) λέγω.
Staff, βακτηρί-α, ας, f.; ῥάβδ-ος, ου, f. (a wand, small staff.)
Stalk, (to walk in a stately manner,) βαδίζω, F. βαδιοῦμαι; σοβέω.
Stand, (cause to stand,) ἵστημι; perf., ἕστηκα, as pres. "I stand."
Stay, μένω.
Steep, ὄρθι-ος, α, ον; or ὀρθι-ος, ος, ον.
Step, βῆμα, βήματ-ος, n. (steps of stairs, &c.) ; ἴχν-ος, εος, n.
Stick, ῥάβδ-ος, ου, f.; βακτηρί-α, ας, f.
Stone, λίθ-ος, ου, m.
Strike, τύπτω, βάλλω.
Swallow, χελιδών, χελιδόν-ος, f.
Sweet, γλυκ-ύς, εῖα, ύ.
Swift, ὠκ-ύς, εῖα, ύ; ταχ-ύς, εῖα, ύ.
Sword, ξίφ-ος, εος, n.; μάχαιρ-α, ας, f.

T

Table, τράπεζ-α, ης, f.
Tail, οὐρ-ά, ᾶς, f. ; κέρκ-ος, ου, f.
Take, λαμβάνω, αἱρέω.
Take counsel (deliberate), βουλεύομαι.
Take the field, στρατεύομαι.
Taste, γεύομαι, with gen.
Teach, διδάσκω, παιδεύω.
Temple, να-ός, οῦ, m.; νεώς, νεώ, m.
Ten, δέκα.
Tent, σκην-ή, ῆς, f.
Tenth, δέκατ-ος, η, ον.
The, ὁ, ἡ, τό.

Their. (See His.)
Thick, παχ-ύς, εῖα, ύ ; δασ-ύς, εῖα, ύ, (shaggy.)
Thief, κλέπτ-ης, ου, m. ; κλώψ, κλωπ-ός, m. ; φώρ, φωρ-ός, m.
Third, τρίτ-ος, η, ον.
Thirty, τριάκοντα.
This, these, οὗτος, αὕτη, τοῦτο (For pl. see p. 57.)
Thorn, ἄκανθ-α, ης, f.
Thou, σύ. (See p. 54.)
Thousand, χίλι-οι, χίλι-αι, χίλι-α.
Thrashing-floor, ἅλως, ἅλω, f.

Through, διά, with gen.
Throw, ῥίπτω, βάλλω, ἵημι.
Tissaphernes, Τισσαφέρν-ης, εος,
contr. ους.
To, (towards,) εἰς, with accus. : to
the side of, up to, παρά, or πρός,
with accus.
Tongue, γλῶττ-α, or γλῶσσα, ης, f.

Tooth, ὀδούς, ὀδόντ-ος, m.
Torch, λαμπάς, λαμπάδ-ος, f.
Towards, εἰς, with accus.
Town, πόλ-ις, εως, f.; ἄστυ, ἄστεος,
n.
Trireme, τριήρ-ης, εος, contr. ους, f.
Twenty, εἴκοσι.
Two, δύο.

U & V

Unyoke, λύω.
Up, ἀνά, with accus.
Upper (room). (See Room.)
Used-to, expressed by imperf. ind. of
verb; e.g., ἔλεγε, "used to say."
Venerable, σεμν-ός, ή, όν; αἰδέσιμ-ος,
ος, ον.

Very, superl. of adj.; e.g., very
great, μέγιστος.
Very much, μάλιστα, or πλεῖστον.
Visible, δῆλ-ος, η, ον; φανερ-ός, ά,
όν.
Voice, φων-ή, ῆς, f.
Vulture, γύψ, γῦπ-ός, m.

W

Waggon, ἅμαξ-α, ης, f.
Wallet, πήρ-α, ας, f.
War, πόλεμ-ος, ου, m.
Warrior, ἥρως, ἥρω-ος, m.; στρα-
τιώτ-ης, ου, m.
Wave, κῦμα, κύματ-ος, n.
Weapon, βέλ-ος, εος, contr. βέλους,
n.; ὅπλ-ον, ου, n.
Wear, φορέω.
What? τί.
Where? ποῦ, πῇ.
Which, relative, ὅς, ἥ, ὅ.
Which, interrog., τίς, τίς, τί.
White, λευκ-ός, ή, όν.
Who, relative, ὅς, ἥ, ; interrog. τίς,
τίς.
Why? τί, διά τι.
Wicked, κακ-ός, ή, όν; πονηρ-ός, ά,
όν.
Wild (beast), θήρ, θηρ-ός, m.; θηρί-ον,
ου, n.
Wine, οἶν-ος, ου, m.

Wing, πτέρυξ, πτέρυγ-ος, f.
Wise, σοφ-ός, ή, όν; σώφρων, m. and
f.; n. σῶφρον; gen. σώφρον-ος.
Wish, ἐθέλω, θέλω, βούλομαι.
With, (along with,) σύν, with dat.:
with, (in the midst of,) μετά, with
gen. With, sign of dat. of the
instrument, to be expressed by
dat. only.
Without, prep., ἄνευ, χωρίς, with
gen. When meaning outside, ἔξω.
Wolf, λύκ-ος, ου, m.
Woman, γυνή, γυναικ-ός, f.
Wonder at, θαυμάζω, ἄγαμαι.
Wood, ὕλ-η, ης, f.
Word, μῦθ-ος, ου, m.; λόγ-ος, ου,
m.; ἔπ-ος, εος, n.
Worthless, κακ-ός, ή, όν; φαῦλ-ος,
η, ον; οὐδενὸς ἄξιος.
Wound, τιτρώσκω, βάλλω.
Wreath, στέφαν-ος, ου, m.
Write, γράφω.

X

Xenophon, Ξενοφῶν, τος, m. (See
p. 30.)

Xerxes, Ξέρξ-ης, ου, m.

THE DECLENSIONS, &c.,

WITH THE CASES IN AN ALTERED ORDER.

FIRST DECLENSION.

	SINGULAR.	DUAL.	PLURAL.
(1.) N.	αὐλ-ή,	αὐλ-ά,	αὐλ-αί,
	a court.	two courts.	courts.
V.	αὐλ-ή,	αὐλ-ά,	αὐλ-αί,
	O court.	O two courts.	O courts.
A.	αὐλ-ήν,	αὐλ-ά,	αὐλ-άς,
	a court.	two courts.	courts.
G.	αὐλ-ῆς,	αὐλ-αῖν,	αὐλ-ῶν,
	of a court.	of two courts.	of courts.
D.	αὐλ-ῇ,	αὐλ-αῖν,	αὐλ-αῖς,
	to or for a court.	to or for two courts.	to or for courts.

	SINGULAR.	DUAL.	PLURAL.
(2.) N. & V.	σκι-ά,	σκι-ά,	σκι-αί,
	a shadow.	two shadows.	shadows.
A.	σκι-άν,	σκι-ά,	σκι-άς,
	a shadow.	two shadows.	shadows.
G.	σκι-ᾶς,	σκι-αῖν,	σκι-ῶν,
	of a shadow.	of two shadows.	of shadows.
D.	σκι-ᾷ,	σκι-αῖν,	σκι-αῖς,
	to or for a shadow.	to or for two shadows.	to or for shadows.

	SINGULAR.	DUAL.	PLURAL.
(3.) N. & V.	γλῶττ-α (or γλῶσσ-α), a tongue.	γλώττ-α, two tongues.	γλῶττ-αι, tongues.
A.	γλῶττ-αν, a tongue.	γλώττ-α, two tongues.	γλώττ-ας, tongues.
G.	γλώττ-ης, of a tongue.	γλώττ-αιν, of two tongues.	γλωττ-ῶν, tongues.
D.	γλώττ-ῃ, to or for a tongue.	γλώττ-αιν, to or for two tongues.	γλώττ-αις, to or for tongues.

	SINGULAR.	DUAL.	PLURAL.
(4.) N.	τελών-ης, a toll collector.	τελών-α, two toll collectors.	τελῶν-αι, toll collectors.
V.	τελών-η	τελών-α	τελῶν-αι
A.	τελών-ην	τελών-α	τελών-ας
G.	τελών-ου	τελών-αιν	τελων-ῶν
D.	τελών-ῃ	τελών-αιν	τελών-αις

SECOND DECLENSION.

	SINGULAR.	DUAL.	PLURAL.
(1.) N.	δοῦλ-ος, masc., a slave.	δούλ-ω, two slaves.	δοῦλ-οι, slaves.
V.	δοῦλ-ε	δούλ-ω	δοῦλ-οι
A.	δοῦλ-ον	δούλ-ω	δούλ-ους
G.	δούλ-ου	δούλ-οιν	δούλ-ων
D.	δούλ-ῳ	δούλ-οιν	δούλ-οις

	SINGULAR.	DUAL.	PLURAL.
(2.) N. V. & A.	μῆλ-ον, neut., an apple.	μήλ-ω, two apples.	μῆλ-α, apples.
G.	μήλ-ου	μήλ-οιν	μήλ-ων
D.	μήλ-ῳ	μήλ-οιν	μήλ-οις

THE ARTICLE, ὁ, ἡ, τό, the.

	SINGULAR.			DUAL.			PLURAL.		
	Masc.	Fem.	Neut.	Masc.	Fem.	Neut.	Masc.	Fem.	Neut
N.	ὁ	ἡ	τό	τώ	τώ (τά)	τώ	οἱ	αἱ	τά
A.	τόν	τήν	τό	τώ	τώ (τά)	τώ	τούς	τάς	τά
G.	τοῦ	τῆς	τοῦ	τοῖν	ταῖν	τοῖν	τῶν	τῶν	τῶν
D.	τῷ	τῇ	τῷ	τοῖν	ταῖν	τοῖν	τοῖς	ταῖς	τοῖς

ATTIC SECOND DECLENSION.

	SINGULAR.	DUAL.	PLURAL.
N. & V.	λαγ-ώς, masc., a hare.	λαγ-ώ, two hares.	λαγ-ῴ, hares.
A.	λαγ-ών	λαγ-ώ	λαγ-ώς
G.	λαγ-ώ	λαγ-ῴν	λαγ-ῶν
D.	λαγ-ῷ	λαγ-ῴν	λαγ-ῷς
N. V. & A.	ἀνώγε-ων, neut., an upper chamber.	ἀνώγε-ω, two upper chambers.	ἀνώγε-ω, upper chambers
G.	ἀνώγε-ω	ἀνώγε-ῳν	ἀνώγε-ων
D.	ἀνώγε-ῳ	ἀνώγε-ῳν	ἀνώγε-ῳς

THIRD DECLENSION.

	SINGULAR.	DUAL.	PLURAL.
N. & V.	λειμών, masc., a meadow.	λειμῶν-ε, two meadows.	λειμῶν-ες, meadows.
A.	λειμῶν-α	λειμῶν-ε	λειμῶν-ας
G.	λειμῶν-ος	λειμών-οιν	λειμών-ων
D.	λειμῶν-ι	λειμών-οιν	λειμῶ-σι

	SINGULAR.	DUAL.	PLURAL.
N. & V.	ἥρω-ς, a hero.	ἥρω-ε, two heroes.	ἥρω-ες, heroes.
A.	ἥρω-α = ἥρω	ἥρω-ε	ἥρω-ας
G.	ἥρω-ος	ἡρώ-οιν	ἡρώ-ων
D.	ἥρω-ι	ἡρώ-οιν	ἥρω-σι

	SINGULAR.	DUAL.	PLURAL.
N.	ἰχθύ-ς, masc., *a fish.*	ἰχθύ-ε, *two fishes.*	ἰχθύ-ες = ἰχθῦς, *fishes.*
V.	ἰχθύ	ἰχθύ-ε	ἰχθύ-ες = ἰχθῦς
A.	ἰχθύ-ν	ἰχθύ-ε	ἰχθύ-ας = ἰχθῦς
G.	ἰχθύ-ος	ἰχθύ-οιν	ἰχθύ-ων
D.	ἰχθύ-ι	ἰχθύ-οιν	ἰχθύ-σι

	SINGULAR.	DUAL.	PLURAL.
N. & V.	ποιμήν, masc., *a shepherd.*	ποιμέν-ε, *two shepherds.*	ποιμέν-ες, *shepherds.*
A.	ποιμέν-α	ποιμέν-ε	ποιμέν-ας
G.	ποιμέν-ος	ποιμέν-οιν	ποιμέν-ων
D.	ποιμέν-ι	ποιμέν-οιν	ποιμέ-σι

	SINGULAR	DUAL	PLURAL
N.	ἀνήρ, masc., *a man = Latin, vir.*	ἄνδρε, *two men.*	ἄνδρ-ες, *men.*
V.	ἄνερ	ἄνδρ-ε	ἄνδρ-ες
A.	ἄν-δ-ρα (for ἀνέρα)	ἄνδρ-ε	ἄνδρ-ας
G.	ἀν-δ-ρός	ἀνδρ-οῖν	ἀνδρ-ῶν
D.	ἀν-δ-ρί	ἀνδρ-οῖν	ἀνδρά-σι

	SINGULAR.	DUAL.	PLURAL.
N. & V.	Ξενοφῶν, masc., *Xenophon.*		
A.	Ξενοφῶντ-α		
G.	Ξενοφῶντ-ος		
D.	Ξενοφῶντ-ι		

	SINGULAR	DUAL	PLURAL
N. V. & A.	σῶμα, neut., *a body.*	σώματ-ε, *two bodies.*	σώματ-α, *bodies.*
G.	σώματ-ος	σωμάτ-οιν	σωμάτ-ων
D.	σώματ-ι	σωμάτ-οιν	σώμα-σι

	SINGULAR.	DUAL.	PLURAL.
N. & V.	ὄρνις, m. or f., a bird or fowl.	ὄρνιθ-ε two birds.	ὄρνιθ-ες, birds.
A.	ὄρνιθ-α, or ὄρνιν	ὄρνιθ-ε	ὄρνιθ-ας
G.	ὄρνῑθ-ος	ὀρνίθ-οιν	ὀρνίθ-ων
D.	ὄρνιθ-ι	ὀρνίθ-οιν	ὄρνι-σι

	SINGULAR.	DUAL.	PLURAL.
N.	μάντι-ς, masc., a prophet or seer.	μάντε-ε, two prophets.	μάντε-ες = μάντεις, prophets.
V.	μάντι	μάντε-ε	μάντε-ες = μάντεις
A.	μάντι-ν	μάντε-ε	μάντε-ας = μάντεις
G.	μάντε-ως	μαντέ-οιν	μάντε-ων
D.	μάντε-ϊ = μάντει	μαντέ-οιν	μάντε-σι

	SINGULAR.	DUAL.
N. V. & A.	τεῖχο-ς, neut., a wall.	τείχε-ε = τείχη, two walls.
G.	τείχε-ος = τείχους	τειχέ-οιν = τειχοῖν
D.	τείχε-ϊ = τείχει	τειχέ-οιν = τειχοῖν

PLURAL.

N. V. & A. τείχε-α = τείχη
walls.

G. τειχέ-ων = τειχῶν

D. τείχε-σι

	SINGULAR.	DUAL.	PLURAL.
N.	βασιλ-εύς, masc., a king.	βασιλέ-ε, two kings.	βασιλέ-ες, -εῖς, kings.
V.	βασιλ-εῦ	βασιλέ-ε	βασιλέ-ες, -εῖς
A.	βασιλέ-ᾱ	βασιλέ-ε	βασιλέ-ᾱς, -εῖς
G.	βασιλέ-ως	βασιλέ-οιν	βασιλέ-ων
D.	βασιλέ-ϊ, βασιλεῖ	βασιλέ-οιν	βασιλεῦσι

ADJECTIVES.

SINGULAR.

	Masc.	Fem.	Neut.
N.	σεμν-ός, venerable.	σεμν-ή	σεμν-όν
V.	σεμν-έ	σεμν-ή	σεμν-όν
A.	σεμν-όν	σεμν-ήν	σεμν-όν
G.	σεμν-οῦ	σεμν-ῆς	σεμν-οῦ
D.	σεμν-ῷ	σεμν-ῇ	σεμν-ῷ

DUAL.

N. V. & A.	σεμν-ώ	σεμν-ά	σεμν-ώ
G. & D.	σεμν-οῖν	σεμν-αῖν	σεμν-οῖν

PLURAL.

N. & V.	σεμν-οί	σεμν-αί	σεμν-ά
A.	σεμν-ούς	σεμν-άς	σεμν-ά
G.	σεμν-ῶν	σεμν-ῶν	σεμν-ῶν
D.	σεμν-οῖς	σεμν-αῖς	σεμν-οῖς

SINGULAR.

	Masc.	Fem.	Neut.
N.	βαρ-ύς, heavy.	βαρ-εῖα	βαρ-ύ
V.	βαρ-ύ	βαρ-εῖα	βαρ-ύ
A.	βαρ-ύν	βαρ-εῖαν	βαρ-ύ
G.	βαρ-έος	βαρ-είας	βαρ-έος
D.	βαρ-έϊ, -εῖ	βαρ-είᾳ	βαρ-έϊ, -εῖ

DUAL.

N. V. & A.	βαρ-έε	βαρ-εία	βαρ-έε
G. & D.	βαρ-έοιν	βαρ-είαιν	βαρ-έοιν

PLURAL.

	Masc.	Fem.	Neut.
N. & V.	βαρ-έες, -εῖς	βαρ-εῖαι	βαρ-έα
A.	βαρ-έας, -εῖς	βαρ-είας	βαρ-έα
G.	βαρ-έων	βαρ-ειῶν	βαρ-έων
D.	βαρ-έσι	βαρ-είαις	βαρ-έσι

	SINGULAR.	
N. πολ-ύς, much, many.	πολλ-ή	πολ-ύ
V. πολ-ύ	πολλ-ή	πολ-ύ
A. πολ-ύν	πολλ-ήν	πολ-ύ
G. πολλ-οῦ	πολλ-ῆς	πολλ-οῦ
D. πολλ-ῷ	πολλ-ῇ	πολλ-ῷ
	PLURAL.	
N. & V. πολλ-οί	πολλ-αί	πολλ-ά
A. πολλ-ούς	πολλ-άς	πολλ-ά
G. πολλ-ῶν	πολλ-ῶν	πολλ-ῶν
D. πολλ-οῖς	πολλ-αῖς	πολλ-οῖς
	SINGULAR.	
N. μέγ-ας, great, large.	μεγάλ-η	μέγ-α
V. μέγ-α	μεγάλ-η	μέγ-α
A. μέγ-αν	μεγάλ-ην	μέγ-α
G. μεγάλ-ου	μεγάλ-ης	μεγάλ-ου
D. μεγάλ-ῳ	μεγάλ-ῃ	μεγάλ-ῳ
	PLURAL.	
N. & V. μεγάλ-οι	μεγάλ-αι	μεγάλ-α
A. μεγάλ-ους	μεγάλ-ας	μεγάλ-α
G. μεγάλ-ων	μεγάλ-ων	μεγάλ-ων
D. μεγάλ-οις	μεγάλ-αις	μεγάλ-οις

THE RELATIVE PRONOUN, *Who, Which, That.*

	SINGULAR.			DUAL.			PLURAL.		
	Masc.	Fem.	Neut.	Masc.	Fem.	Neut.	Masc.	Fem.	Neut.
N.	ὅς	ἥ	ὅ	ὥ	ἅ	ὥ	οἵ	αἵ	ἅ
A.	ὅν	ἥν	ὅ	ὥ	ἅ	ὥ	οὕς	ἅς	ἅ
G.	οὗ	ἧς	οὗ	οἷν	αἷν	οἷν	ὧν	ὧν	ὧν
D.	ᾧ	ᾗ	ᾧ	οἷν	αἷν	οἷν	οἷς	αἷς	οἷς

THE THREE PERSONAL PRONOUNS.

	SINGULAR.	DUAL.	PLURAL.
N.	ἐγώ, I [ego].	νώ, we two.	ἡμεῖς, we.
A.	ἐμέ, or μέ, me.	νώ, us two.	ἡμᾶς, us.
G.	ἐμοῦ, or μοῦ, of me.	νῷν, of us two.	ἡμῶν, of us.
D.	ἐμοί, or μοί, to or for me.	νῷν, to or for us two.	ἡμῖν, to or for us.

	SINGULAR.	DUAL.	PLURAL.
N.	σύ, thou [tu].	σφώ, you two.	ὑμεῖς, you.
A.	σέ	σφώ	ὑμᾶς
G.	σοῦ	σφῷν	ὑμῶν
D.	σοί	σφῷν	ὑμῖν

	SINGULAR.	PLURAL.
N.	—	σφεῖς, they
A.	ἕ [se], him.	σφᾶς
G.	οὗ [sui]	σφῶν
D.	οἷ [sibi]	σφίσι

	SINGULAR.			DUAL.		
	Masc.	Fem.	Neut.	Masc.	Fem.	Neut.
N.	οὗτος, this.	αὕτη	τοῦτο	τούτω	(ταύτᾱ)	τούτω
A.	τοῦτον	ταύτην	τοῦτο	τούτω	(ταύτᾱ)	τούτω
G.	τούτου	ταύτης	τούτου	τούτοιν	ταύταιν	τούτοιν
D.	τούτῳ	ταύτῃ	τούτῳ	τούτοιν	ταύταιν	τούτοιν

	PLURAL.		
	Masc.	Fem.	Neut
N.	οὗτοι	αὗται	ταῦτα
A.	τούτους	ταύτας	ταῦτα
G.	τούτων	τούτων	τούτων
D.	τούτοις	ταύταις	τούτοις

FORMATION OF THE

TENSES OF GREEK VERBS.

The following Rules attempt to account for the formation of all the Tenses of Regular Verbs. But analogy is so often departed from in conjugation, and dialectic peculiarities so often occur, that it is impossible to provide for every irregularity. As many verbs are defective, the student cannot be too earnestly urged to consult a good List of Irregular Greek Verbs, in regard to each.

THE principal parts of a Greek verb are :—

ACTIVE.

Present, λύω
Future, λύσω
Perfect, λέλυκα

PASSIVE.

Future, λυθήσομαι
Perfect, λέλυμαι

I.—ACTIVE VOICE.

I.—IMPERFECT TENSE.

RULE.—The imperfect active is formed from the present by prefixing the augment, and changing the termination -ω into -ον; as,—

λύω   ἔλυον
τύπτω   ἔτυπτον

II.—FUTURE TENSE.

1. RULE I.—In verbs not liquid, the future active is formed from the present by inserting σ before -ω; as,

FORMATION OF TENSES.

λύω   λύσω
γράφω   γράψω
λέγω   λέξω

2. RULE II.—Liquid verbs do not insert σ; they only shorten the penult * if it is long, and are declined as contracted forms; † as,—

μένω   μενῶ, εῖς, εῖ, &c.
σπείρω   σπερῶ, εῖς, εῖ, &c.
φαίνω   φανῶ, &c.
κρίνω   κρῐνῶ, &c.

SPECIAL RULES.

A. MUTE VERBS.

3. (1.) Before -σω reject τ, δ, θ, σ, and ν;‡ as,—

ἀνύτω   ἀνύσω
ᾄδω   ᾄσω
πλήθω   πλήσω
πλάσσω, or πλάττω πλάσω
σπένδω   σπείσω ‖
τύπτω   τύψω
νομίζω   νομίσω (Att. νομιῶ)

4. (2.) Many verbs in -σσω and -ζω make -ξω § in the future; as,—

---

* The long penult is shortened by rejecting the latter of two vowels or consonants; as, σπείρω, σπερῶ; τέμνω, τεμῶ. The variable vowels are short in the future.

† In the future, -ῶ, -εῖς, &c., are contracted for -έω, -έεις, &c.; hence the circumflex.

‡ See Appendix, page 153, ii. 10.

‖ See note, p. 31.

§ Most of these verbs have stems ending in a guttural; thus, πράσσω has its stem πραγ-, and κράζω, κραγ-. Hence -ξω in the future.

ACTIVE VOICE.

πράσσω, or πράττω   πράξω
κράζω   κράξω

5. (3.) And some have both -σω and -ξω *

B. PURE VERBS.

6. (1.) Verbs in -άω, -έω, -όω, change the short vowel into its corresponding long before -σω; as,—

τιμάω   τιμήσω
φιλέω   φιλήσω
δηλόω   δηλώσω

7. (2.) *Exc.*—But some verbs retain the vowel of the present; as,—

ἐάω   ἐάσω
γελάω   (γελάσω) γελάσομαι
τελέω   τελέσω
ἀρόω   · ἀρόσω

8. (3.) And some in -έω have both forms; as,—

αἰνέω   αἰν-έσω, or -ήσω (Epic, &c.)
πονέω   πον-έσω, or -ήσω

9. (4.) Some in -έω make their future in -εύσω; as,

πνέω   πνεύσω
ῥέω (to flow) ῥεύσω

III.—FIRST AORIST.

1. RULE.—The first aorist active is formed from the future by prefixing the augment, and changing -ω into -α; as,—

---

* It must be observed that the different forms generally belong to different dialects. Hence the student must be careful to consult a good Lexicon, or List of Irregular Greek Verbs.

λύσω   ἔλυσα
τύψω   ἔτυψα
τιμήσω   ἐτίμησα
λέξω   ἔλεξα

2. But in liquid verbs the penult is lengthened by changing ε of the future into ει, and a short variable vowel into its own long; as,—

μένω   μενῶ   ἔμεινα
σπείρω   σπερῶ   ἔσπειρα
στέλλω   στελῶ   ἔστειλα
φαίνω   φανῶ   ἔφηνα
πιαίνω   πιᾰνῶ   ἐπίᾱνα
κρίνω   κρῐνῶ   ἔκρῑνα
ἀμύνω   ἀμυνῶ   ἤμῡνα

3. There are a few first aorists which do not retain the characteristic of the future; as,—

δίδωμι   δώσω   ἔδωκα
τίθημι   θήσω   ἔθηκα
ἵημι   ἥσω   ἧκα

Also εἶπα (φημὶ) ἤνεγκα (φέρω) ἔχεα (χέω)

IV.—FIRST PERFECT.

1. RULE.—The first perfect active is formed from the future by prefixing the augment (with reduplication),* and changing -ω or -σω into -κα or -ἀ (*i.e.*, making -κα from -ω or -σω, -χα from -ξω, and -φα from -ψω); as,

---

* See p. 62, 11. But it must be remembered that those verbs have no reduplication which begin (a) with a vowel, (b) with a double consonant, (c) with two consonants, except certain combinations made up of a mute followed by a liquid.

ACTIVE VOICE.

ψάλλω	ψαλῶ	ἔψαλκα
ἀγγέλλω	ἀγγελῶ	ἤγγελκα
φαίνω	φανῶ	πέφαγκα *
λύω	λύσω	λέλυκα
πλέκω	πλέξω	πέπλεχα
τύπτω	τύψω	τέτυφα

2. In some verbs the radical vowel † is changed; as

στέλλω	στελῶ	ἔσταλκα
τείνω	τενῶ	τέτακα ‡
σπείρω	σπερῶ	ἔσπαρκα

3. βάλλω makes βέβληκα, and μένω, μεμένηκα.

V.—FIRST PLUPERFECT.

RULE.—The first pluperfect active is formed from the perfect by changing -α into -ειν, and prefixing the syllabic augment (when possible); as,—

λέλυκα	ἐλελύκειν
τέτυφα	ἐτετύφειν
ἤγγελκα	ἠγγέλκειν

VI.—SECOND AORIST. ∥

1. RULE.—The second aorist active is formed from the simple stem of the verb by prefixing the augment, and adding the termination -ον; as,—

---

* See p. 154, 12, Appendix.

† This phrase is used merely for convenience, and to agree with general usage. The simple stem of the verb is found in the second aorist (when it exists); as, ἔ-λιπ-ον: but this is usually strengthened in the present by the insertion of a vowel or consonant. The radical vowel is often changed. See vi., below.

‡ Some verbs reject ν before κ; as τείνω: so also κρίνω, κέκρικα.

∥ The form called the second aorist is found chiefly in those verbs

Pres.	Simple Stem.	2 Aor.
τύπτω	τυπ-	ἔτυπον
βάλλω	βαλ-	ἔβαλον
λείπω	λιπ-	ἔλιπον
λαμβάνω	λαβ-	ἔλαβον
λανθάνω	λαθ-	ἔλαθον

2. Some verbs seem to have had two stems; thus, τέμνω has 2 aor. ἔτεμον and ἔταμον; and many verbs have α, ε, ι, υ, in the aorist, while the present has η, ω, ε, ει, αι, ι, or ευ. See vii. 2, below, with examples.

VII.—THE SECOND PERFECT.

1. RULE.—The second perfect active is formed from the simple stem of the verb by prefixing the augment (with reduplication), and adding the termination -α; as,—

Pres.	Simple Stem.	2 Perf.
τύπτω	τυπ-	τέτυπα

2. But the radical vowel is often changed; viz.,

α, from presents in ε or ει, into ο;
α, from presents in η or αι, into η;
ε, from presents in ε, or ει, or ι, into ο;
ι, from presents in ει, into οι.

As,—

δέρκομαι	ἔδρακον	δέδορκα
κτείνω	ἔκτανον	ἔκτονα
λανθάνω (λήθω)	ἔλαθον	λέληθα

---

which have no first aorist; for very few verbs have both tenses. Pure verbs, as a general rule, have no second aorist; also those verbs whose stem in the second aorist would be the same as in the present—*e.g.*, λέγω.

φαίνω   ἐφάνην (2 aor. pass.)   πέφηνα
τίκτω   ἔτεκον   τέτοκα
λείπω   ἔλιπον   λέλοιπα

VIII.—SECOND PLUPERFECT.

RULE.—The second pluperfect is formed from the second perfect by prefixing the augment, and changing -α into -ειν ; as, τέτυπα, ἐτετύπειν.

II.—PASSIVE VOICE.

I.—PRESENT.

RULE.—The present passive (and middle) is formed from the present active by changing -ω into -ομαι; as,

τύπτω   τύπτομαι

II.—IMPERFECT.

RULE.—The imperfect passive (and middle) is formed from the present by prefixing the augment, and changing -μαι into -μην ; as,—

τύπτομαι   ἐτυπτόμην
δύναμαι   ἐδυνάμην

III.—FIRST FUTURE.

1. RULE.—The first future passive is formed from the future active by changing -ω or -σω into -θησομαι; as,—

ἀγγελῶ   ἀγγελθήσομαι
λύσω   λυθήσομαι
τύψω   τυφθήσομαι *

2. Many verbs insert σ before -θήσομαι:—
    (a) Certain pure verbs; as,—
    κλείω   κλεισθήσομαι
    κλαίω   κλαυσθήσομαι
    τελέω   τελεσθήσομαι

    (b) Verbs which reject a consonant (τ, δ, θ, σ, ζ) in the future active; † as,—
    πείθω   πείσω   πεισθήσομαι

3. Some verbs shorten the last vowel of the future stem; as,—
    αἱρήσω   αἱρεθήσομαι
    δώσω   δοθήσομαι

IV.—FIRST AORIST.

RULE.—The first aorist passive is formed from the first future passive, by prefixing the augment, and changing -θήσομαι into -θην; as,—
    λυθήσομαι   ἐλύθην
    τυφθήσομαι   ἐτύφθην
    τελεσθήσομαι   ἐτελέσθην
    δοθήσομαι   ἐδόθην
    τεθήσομαι   ἐτέθην

V.—PERFECT.

1. RULE.—The perfect passive is formed from the

---

* The rules of euphony, p. 153, must be attended to.
† See Appendix, Euphony, p. 153, i. 3.

PASSIVE VOICE.

first future passive, by prefixing the augment (with reduplication), and rejecting -θησο- before -μαι;* as,—

βουλευθήσομαι   βεβούλευμαι
λειφθήσομαι   λέλειμμαι

2. *Exc.*—But σ before -θησομαι does not always remain before -μαι; and some verbs which have not σ in the future assume it before -μαι (see p. 153, 7); as,

μνησθήσομαι   μέμνημαι
σωθήσομαι   σέσωσμαι

3. A few verbs lengthen the last vowel of the future stem ; as,—

αἱρεθήσομαι   ᾕρημαι

4. In the Attic dialect, ν before μ (see p. 154, 13) is sometimes changed into σ ; thus, πέφανμαι should become πέφαμμαι, but is made πέφασμαι.

5. The three verbs, τρέπω, τρέφω, and στρέφω, change the vowel of the future stem, making τέτραμμαι, τέθραμμαι, ἔστραμμαι.

VI.—THE PLUPERFECT.

RULE.—The pluperfect passive is formed from the perfect passive, by prefixing the augment, and changing -μαι into -μην ; as,—

τέτυμμαι   ἐτετύμμην
λέλυμαι   ἐλελύμην

---

* In declining the perfect passive, the rules of euphony must be carefully attended to,—viz., p. 153, 1, 2, 3, 5, 6, 7, 8, 9; and p. 154, 11, 12, 13. It must further be remarked that, in the terminations -σθον, -σθε, -σθαι, -σθω, -σθων, the σ is rejected when another consonant precedes; as, τέτυφθον, for τέτυπσθον.

VII.—SECOND AORIST.

Rule.—The second aorist passive is formed from the simple stem of the verb, by prefixing the augment, and adding the termination -ην; as,—

Pres.	Simple Stem.	2 Aor.
λείπω	λιπ-	ἐλίπην

VIII.—SECOND FUTURE.*

Rule.—The second future passive is formed from the simple stem, by adding -ήσομαι; as,—

Pres.	Simple Stem.	2 Fut.
τύπτω	τυπ-	τυπήσομαι

IX.—THIRD FUTURE, OR PAULO-POST FUTURE.

Rule.—The third future passive is formed from the simple stem, by prefixing the reduplication, and adding -σομαι; as,—

λύω   λελύσομαι

III.—MIDDLE VOICE.

I.—PRESENT AND IMPERFECT.

[See corresponding tenses of Passive, p. 237.]

II.—FUTURE.

Rule.—The future middle is formed from the future active, by changing -ω into -ομαι, and in liquid verbs into -οῦμαι; as,—

---

* The second future is of rare occurrence. See note ‖, p. 235.

λύσω   λύσομαι
μενῶ   μενοῦμαι

III.—FIRST AORIST.

RULE.—The first aorist middle is formed from the future middle, by prefixing the augment, and changing -ομαι into -αμην; as,—

τύψομαι   ἐτυψάμην
λέξομαι   ἐλεξάμην

N.B.—In liquid verbs the penult is lengthened, as in the first aorist active, which see, p. 234, 2

IV.—SECOND AORIST.

RULE.—The second aorist middle is formed from the simple stem, by prefixing the augment, and adding -όμην; as,—

Pres.	Stem.	2 Aor
λείπω	λιπ-	ἐλιπόμην

[See the Second Aorist Active.]

GENERAL VIEW.

ACTIVE VOICE.

PRESENT.—Either simple or strengthened stem.

Imperfect.—From present; prefix augment, and change -ω into -ον.

FUTURE.—From present; insert σ before ω in pure and mute verbs; in liquid verbs shorten the penult (if long) without insertion of σ.

Aorist I.—From future; prefix augment, and change -ω into -α.

PERFECT I.—From future; augment (with reduplication), and change -ω or -σω into -κα or -ά.

Pluperfect I.—From perfect; augment, and change -α into -ειν.

Aorist II.—Simple stem, with augment, and termination -ον.

Perfect II.—From simple stem; augment (with reduplication), and add the termination -α.

Pluperfect II.—From second perfect; augment, and change -α into -ειν.

PASSIVE VOICE.

Present.—From present active; change -ω into -ομαι.

Imperfect.—From present; augment, and change -μαι into -μην.

FUTURE.—From the future active; change -ω or -σω into -θησομαι.

Aorist I.—From future; augment, and change -θησομαι into -θην.

PERFECT.—From future; augment (with reduplication), and reject -θησο- before -μαι.

Pluperfect.—From perfect; augment, and change -μαι into -μην.

Aorist II.—From simple stem; augment, and add -ην.

MIDDLE VOICE.

Present.—From present active; change -ω into -ομαι.

Imperfect.—From present; augment, and change -μαι into -μην.

Future.—From future active; change -ω into -ομαι.

Aorist I.—From future; augment, and change -ομαι into -αμην [or, add -μην to first aorist active].
Aorist II.—From simple stem; augment, and add -ομην.

TABLE

SHOWING THE FORMATIONS ACCORDING TO THE PRECEDING SCHEME.

Note, that those forms which become principal parts, are also given, in bolder type, and with a waved line underneath, in the column to which each properly belongs, as being themselves derived.

PRINCIPAL PARTS.	ACTIVE.	PASSIVE.	MIDDLE.
τύπτω	ἔυπτον	τύπτομαι ἐτυπτόμην	τύπτομαι ἐτυπτόμην
	τύψω		
τύψω	ἔτυψα τέτυφα	τυφθήσομαι	τύψομαι ἐτυψάμην
τέτυφα	ἐτετύφειν		
τυφθήσομαι		ἐτύφθην τέτυμμαι	
τέτυμμαι		ἐτετύμμην	
Simple Stem. τυπ-	ἔτυπον τέτυπα ἐτετύπειν	τυπήσομαι τετύψομαι ἐτύπην	ἐτυπόμην

PURE VERBS—

		INDICATIVE.	SUBJUNCTIVE.
ACTIVE.	Pres.	λύω	λύω
	Imperf.	ἔλυον	—
	Fut.	λύσω	—
	Aor.	ἔλυσα	λύσω
	Perf.	λέλυκα	λελύκω
	Pluperf.	ἐλελύκειν	—
PASSIVE.	Pres.	λύομαι	λύωμαι
	Imperf.	ἐλυόμην	—
	Fut. I.	λυθήσομαι	—
	Aor.	ἐλύθην	λυθῶ
	Perf.	λέλυμαι	λελυμένος ὦ
	Pluperf.	ἐλελύμην	—
	Fut. III.	λελύσομαι	—
MIDDLE.	Pres.	λύομαι	λύωμαι
	Imperf.	ἐλυόμην	—
	Fut.	λύσομαι	—
	Aor.	ἐλυσάμην	λύσωμαι

PURE VERBS.

λύω, *I loose.*

OPTATIVE.	IMPERATIVE.	INFINITIVE.	PARTICIPLE.
λύοιμι	λῦε	λύειν	λύων
λύσοιμι	—	λύσειν	λύσων
λύσαιμι	λῦσον	λῦσαι	λύσας
λελύκοιμι	λέλυκε	λελυκέναι	λελυκώς
λυοίμην	λύου	λύεσθαι	λυόμενος
λυθησοίμην	—	λυθήσεσθαι	λυθησόμενος
λυθείην	λύθητι	λυθῆναι	λυθείς
λελυμένος εἴην	λέλυσο	λελύσθαι	λελυμένος
λελυσοίμην	—	λελύσεσθαι	λελυσόμενος
λυοίμην	λύου	λύεσθαι	λυόμενος
λυσοίμην	—	λύσεσθαι	λυσόμενος
λυσαίμην	λῦσαι	λύσασθαι	λυσάμενος

MUTE VERBS—

		INDICATIVE.	SUBJUNCTIVE.
ACTIVE.	Pres.	τύπτω	τύπτω
	Imperf.	ἔτυπτον	—
	Fut.	*τύψω [τυπτήσω]	—
	Aor. I.	ἔτυψα [ἐτύπτησα]	τύψω
	Perf. I.	*τέτυφα [τετύπτηκα]	τετύφω
	Pluperf. I.	*ἐτετύφειν	—
	Aor. II.	ἔτυπον	τύπω
	Perf. II.	*τέτυπα	τετύπω
	Pluperf. II.	*ἐτετύπειν	—
PASSIVE.	Pres.	τύπτομαι	τύπτωμαι
	Imperf.	ἐτυπτόμην	—
	Fut.	*τυφθήσομαι	—
	Aor. I.	ἐτύφθην [ἐτυπτήθην]	τυφθῶ
	Perf.	τέτυμμαι [and τετύπτημαι]	τετυμμένος ὦ
	Pluperf.	ἐτετύμμην	—
	Aor. II.	ἐτύπην	τυπῶ
	Fut. II.	τυπήσομαι	—
	Fut. III.	*τετύψομαι	—
MIDDLE.	Pres.	τύπτομαι	τύπτωμαι
	Imperf.	ἐτυπτόμην	—
	Fut.	τύψομαι [τυπτήσομαι]	—
	Aor. I.	ἐτυψάμην	τύψωμαι
	Aor. II.	*ἐτυπόμην	τύπωμαι

NOTE.—Those parts which are not found, or which are used only in brackets exist, and some of them are more Attic than those of the

MUTE VERBS.

τύπτω, I strike.

OPTATIVE.	IMPERATIVE.	INFINITIVE.	PARTICIPLE.
τύπτοιμι	τύπτου	τύπτειν	τύπτων
τύψοιμι	—	τύψειν	τύψων
τύψαιμι	τύψον	τύψαι	τύψας
τετύφοιμι	τέτυφε	τετυφέναι	τετυφώς
τύποιμι	τύπε	τυπεῖν	τυπών
τετύποιμι	τέτυπε	τετυπέναι	τετυπώς
τυπτοίμην	τύπτου	τύπτεσθαι	τυπτόμενος
τυφθησοίμην	—	τυφθήσεσθαι	τυφθησόμενος
τυφθείην	τύφθητι	τυφθῆναι	τυφθείς
τετυμμένος εἴην	τέτυψο	τετύφθαι	τετυμμένος
τυπείην	τύπηθι	τυπῆναι	τυπείς
τυπησοίμην	—	τυπήσεσθαι	τυπησόμενος
τετυψοίμην	—	τετύψεσθαι	τετυψόμενος
τυπτοίμην	τύπτου	τύπτεσθαι	τυπτόμενος
τυψοίμην	—	τύψεσθαι	τυψόμενος
τυψαίμην	τύψαι	τύψασθαι	τυψάμενος
τυποίμην	τυποῦ	τυπέσθαι	τυπόμενος

post-classical times, are marked with an asterisk. The forms in regular formation.

MUTE VERBS—

		INDICATIVE.	SUBJUNCTIVE.
ACTIVE.	Pres.	πλέκω	πλέκω
	Imperf.	ἔπλεκον	—
	Fut.	πλέξω	—
	Aor. I.	ἔπλεξα	πλέξω
	Perf.	πέπλεχα	πεπλέχω
	Pluperf.	ἐπεπλέχειν	—
	Aor. II.	* ἔπλακον	πλάκω
	Perf. II.	* πέπλακα	πεπλάκω
	Pluperf. II.	* ἐπεπλάκειν	—
PASSIVE.	Pres.	πλέκομαι	πλέκωμαι
	Imperf.	ἐπλεκόμην	—
	Fut.	πλεχθήσομαι	—
	Aor. I.	ἐπλέχθην	πλεχθῶ
	Perf.	πέπλεγμαι	πεπλεγμένος ὦ
	Pluperf.	ἐπεπλέγμην	—
	Aor. II.	ἐπλάκην	πλακῶ
	Fut. II.	πλακήσομαι	—
	Fut. III.	πεπλέξομαι	—
MIDDLE.	Pres.	πλέκομαι	πλέκωμαι
	Imperf.	ἐπλεκόμην	—
	Fut.	πλέξομαι	—
	Aor. I.	ἐπλεξάμην	πλέξωμαι
	Aor. II.	* ἐπλακόμην	πλάκωμαι

πλέκω, I plait.

OPTATIVE.	IMPERATIVE.	INFINITIVE.	PARTICIPLE.
πλέκοιμι	πλέκε	πλέκειν	πλέκων
πλέξοιμι	—	πλέξειν	πλέξων
πλέξαιμι	πλέξον	πλέξαι	πλέξας
πεπλέχοιμι	πέπλεχε	πεπλεχέναι	πεπλεχώς
πλάκοιμι	πλάκε	πλακεῖν	πλακών
πεπλάκοιμι	πέπλακε	πεπλακέναι	πεπλακώς
πλεκοίμην	πλέκου	πλέκεσθαι	πλεκόμενος
πλεχθησοίμην	—	πλεχθήσεσθαι	πλεχθησόμενος
πλεχθείην	πλέχθητι	πλεχθῆναι	πλεχθείς
πεπλεγμένος εἴην	πέπλεξο	πεπλέχθαι	πεπλεγμένος
πλακείην	πλάκηθι	πλακῆναι	πλακείς
πλακησοίμην	—	πλακήσεσθαι	πλακησόμενος
πεπλεξοίμην	—	πεπλέξεσθαι	πεπλεξόμενος
πλεκοίμην	πλέκου	πλέκεσθαι	πλεκόμενος
πλεξοίμην	—	πλέξεσθαι	πλεξόμενος
πλεξαίμην	πλέξαι	πλέξασθαι	πλεξάμενος
πλακοίμην	πλακοῦ	πλακέσθαι	πλακόμενος

MUTE VERBS—

		INDICATIVE.	SUBJUNCTIVE.
ACTIVE.	Pres.	τρέπω	τρέπω
	Imperf.	έτρεπον	—
	Fut.	τρέψω	—
	Aor. I.	έτρεψα	τρέψω
	Perf. I.	τέτροφα [and τέτραφα]	τετρόφω
	Pluperf. I.	ἐτετρόφειν [or ἐτετράφειν]	—
	Aor. II.	έτραπον	τράπω
	Perf. II.	* τέτροπα	τετρόπω
	Pluperf. II.	* ἐτετρόπειν	—
PASSIVE.	Pres.	τρέπομαι	τρέπωμαι
	Imperf.	ἐτρεπόμην	—
	Fut.	* τρεφθήσομαι	—
	Aor. I.	ἐτρέφθην	τρεφθῶ
	Perf.	τέτραμμαι	τετραμμένος ὦ
	Pluperf.	ἐτετράμμην	—
	Aor. II.	ἐτράπην	τραπῶ
	Fut. II.	τραπήσομαι	—
	Fut. III.	τετρέψομαι [or τετρά-]	—
MIDDLE.	Pres.	τρέπομαι	τρέπωμαι
	Imperf.	ἐτρεπόμην	—
	Fut.	τρέψομαι	—
	Aor. I.	ἐτρεψάμην	τρέψωμαι
	Aor. II.	ἐτραπόμην	τράπωμαι

τρέπω, I turn.

OPTATIVE.	IMPERATIVE.	INFINITIVE.	PARTICIPLE.
τρέποιμι	τρέπε	τρέπειν	τρέπων
τρέψοιμι		τρέψειν	τρέψων
τρέψαιμι	τρέψον	τρέψαι	τρέψας
τετρόφοιμι	τέτροφε	τετροφέναι	τετροφώς [or τετραφώς]
τράποιμι	τράπε	τραπεῖν	τραπών
τετρόποιμι	τέτροπε	τετροπέναι	τετροπώς
τρεποίμην	τρέπου	τρέπεσθαι	τρεπόμενος
τρεφθησοίμην		τρεφθήσεσθαι	τρεφθησόμενος
τρεφθείην	τρέφθητι	τρεφθῆναι	τρεφθείς
τετραμμένος εἴην	τέτραψο	τετράφθαι	τετραμμένος
τραπείην	τράπηθι	τραπῆναι	τραπείς
τραπησοίμην		τραπήσεσθαι	τραπησόμενος
τετρεψοίμην		τετρέψεσθαι	τετρεψόμενος
τρεποίμην	τρέπου	τρέπεσθαι	τρεπόμενος
τρεψοίμην		τρέψεσθαι	τρεψόμενος
τρεψαίμην	τρέψαι	τρέψασθαι	τρεψάμενος
τραποίμην	τραποῦ	τραπέσθαι	τραπόμενος

MUTE VERBS—

		INDICATIVE.	SUBJUNCTIVE.
ACTIVE	Pres.	πείθω	πείθω
	Imperf.	ἔπειθον	—
	Fut.	πείσω	—
	Aor. I.	ἔπεισα	πείσω
	Perf.	πέπεικα	πεπείκω
	Pluperf.	ἐπεπείκειν	—
	Aor. II.	ἔπιθον	πίθω
	Perf. II.	πέποιθα	πεποίθω
	Pluperf. II.	ἐπεποίθειν	—
PASSIVE	Pres.	πείθομαι	πείθωμαι
	Imperf.	ἐπειθόμην	—
	Fut. I.	πεισθήσομαι	—
	Aor. I.	ἐπείσθην	πεισθῶ
	Perf.	πέπεισμαι	πεπεισμένος ὦ
	Pluperf.	ἐπεπείσμην	—
	Aor. II.	* ἐπίθην	πιθῶ
	Fut. II.	* πιθήσομαι	—
	Fut. III.	* πεπείσομαι	—
MIDDLE	Pres.	πείθομαι	πείθωμαι
	Imperf.	ἐπειθόμην	—
	Fut.	πείσομαι	—
	Aor. I.	ἐπεισάμην	πείσωμαι
	Aor. II.	ἐπιθόμην	πίθωμαι

πείθω, I persuade.

OPTATIVE.	IMPERATIVE.	INFINITIVE.	PARTICIPLE.
πείθοιμι	πεῖθε	πείθειν	πείθων
πείσοιμι		πείσειν	πείσων
πείσαιμι	πεῖσον	πεῖσαι	πείσας
πεπείκοιμι	πέπεικε	πεπεικέναι	πεπεικώς
πίθοιμι	πίθε	πιθεῖν	πιθών
πεποίθοιμι	πέποιθε	πεποιθέναι	πεποιθώς
πειθοίμην	πείθου	πείθεσθαι	πειθόμενος
πεισθησοίμην		πεισθήσεσθαι	πεισθησόμενος
πεισθείην	πείσθητι	πεισθῆναι	πεισθείς
πεπεισμένος εἴην	πέπεισο	πεπεῖσθαι	πεπεισμένος
πιθείην	πίθητι	πιθῆναι	πιθείς
πιθησοίμην		πιθήσεσθαι	πιθησόμενος
πεπεισοίμην		πεπείσεσθαι	πεπεισόμενος
πειθοίμην	πείθου	πείθεσθαι	πειθόμενος
πεισοίμην		πείσεσθαι	πεισόμενος
πεισαίμην	πεῖσαι	πείσασθαι	πεισάμενος
πιθοίμην	πιθοῦ	πιθέσθαι	πιθόμενος

LIQUID VERBS—

		INDICATIVE.	SUBJUNCTIVE.
ACTIVE	Pres.	ἀγγέλλω	ἀγγέλλω
	Imperf.	ἤγγελλον	—
	Fut.	ἀγγελῶ	—
	Aor. I.	ἤγγειλα	ἀγγείλω
	Perf.	ἤγγελκα	ἠγγέλκω
	Pluperf.	ἠγγέλκειν	—
	Aor. II.	ἤγγελον	ἀγγέλω
PASSIVE	Pres.	ἀγγέλλομαι	ἀγγέλλωμαι
	Imperf.	ἠγγελλόμην	—
	Fut. I.	ἀγγελθήσομαι	—
	Aor. I.	ἠγγέλθην	ἀγγελθῶ
	Perf.	ἤγγελμαι	ἠγγελμένος ὦ
	Pluperf.	ἠγγέλμην	—
	Aor. II.	ἠγγέλην	ἀγγελῶ
	Fut. II.	ἀγγελήσομαι	—
	Fut. III.	—	—
MIDDLE	Pres.	ἀγγέλλομαι	ἀγγέλλωμαι
	Imperf.	ἠγγελλόμην	—
	Fut.	ἀγγελοῦμαι	—
	Aor. I.	ἠγγειλάμην	ἀγγείλωμαι
	Aor. II.	ἠγγελόμην	ἀγγέλωμαι

LIQUID VERBS.

ἀγγέλλω, I report.

OPTATIVE.	IMPERATIVE.	INFINITIVE.	PARTICIPLE.
ἀγγέλλοιμι	ἄγγελλε	ἀγγέλλειν	ἀγγέλλων
ἀγγελοίμι		ἀγγελεῖν	ἀγγελῶν
ἀγγείλαιμι	ἄγγειλον	ἀγγεῖλαι	ἀγγείλας
ἠγγέλκοιμι		ἠγγελκέναι	ἠγγελκώς
ἀγγέλοιμι	ἄγγελε	ἀγγελεῖν	ἀγγελών
ἀγγελλοίμην	ἀγγέλλου	ἀγγέλλεσθαι	ἀγγελλόμενος
ἀγγελθησοίμην		ἀγγελθήσεσθαι	ἀγγελθησόμενος
ἀγγελθείην	ἀγγέλθητι	ἀγγελθῆναι	ἀγγελθείς
ἠγγελμένος εἴην	ἤγγελσο	ἠγγέλθαι	ἠγγελμένος
ἀγγελείην	ἀγγέληθι	ἀγγελῆναι	ἀγγελείς
ἀγγελησοίμην		ἀγγελήσεσθαι	ἀγγελησόμενος
ἀγγελλοίμην	ἀγγέλλου	ἀγγέλλεσθαι	ἀγγελλόμενος
ἀγγελοίμην		ἀγγελεῖσθαι	ἀγγελούμενος
ἀγγειλαίμην	ἄγγειλαι	ἀγγείλασθαι	ἀγγειλάμενος
ἀγγελοίμην	ἀγγελοῦ	ἀγγελέσθαι	ἀγγελόμενος

GENEALOGICAL CHART OF THE GREEK VERB.

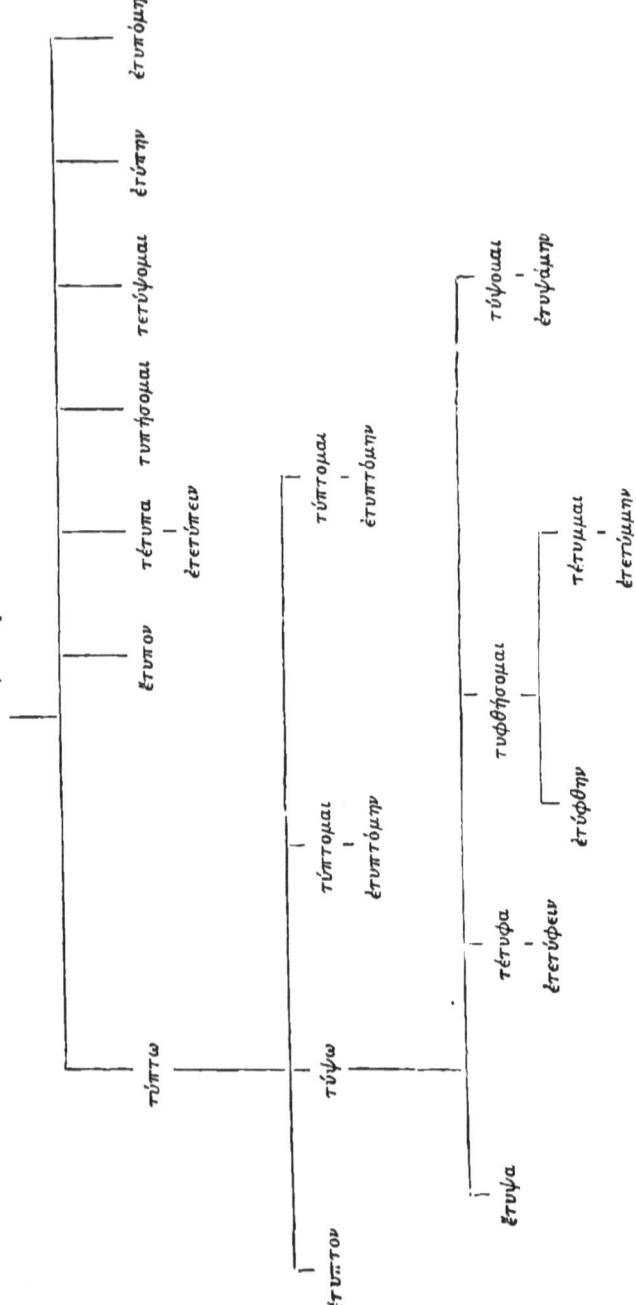

www.ingramcontent.com/pod-product-compliance
Lightning Source LLC
Chambersburg PA
CBHW031351230426
43670CB00006B/503